D1105277

HOW LATIN AMERICA
FELL BEHIND

HOW LATIN AMERICA
FELL BEHIND

*Essays on the Economic Histories
of Brazil and Mexico,
1800–1914*

EDITED BY STEPHEN HABER

STANFORD UNIVERSITY PRESS

Stanford, California   1997

Stanford University Press
Stanford, California
© 1997 by the Board of Trustees of the
Leland Stanford Junior University
Printed in the United States of America

CIP data appear at the end of the book

Stanford University Press publications are distributed exclusively by Stanford University Press within the United States,
Canada, Mexico, and Central America; they are distributed
exclusively by Cambridge University Press throughout the
rest of the world.

Acknowledgments

This volume of essays emerged out of a conference held at Stanford University in January 1992. That conference brought together economic historians of Latin America, development economists, historians of technology, political scientists, and economic historians of Europe and the United States. The purpose of the meeting was twofold: to develop an understanding of the causes of Latin America's laggard economic performance in the nineteenth century, and to find common methodological ground between Latin American historians and economic historians of the United States and Western Europe. The chapters found herein are not the papers presented at the conference, but represent the results of those three days of discussion and debate. Indeed, some participants chose to rethink their work completely, while other essays were written later.

I and the other contributors to this volume are indebted to all of the conference participants for their insights, suggestions, and questions. The conference participants included Frederick Bowser, Enrique Cárdenas, Margaret Chowning, John H. Coatsworth, James Conklin, Paul David, Lance E. Davis, Stanley L. Engerman, Albert Fishlow, Avner Greif, Stephen Haber, Anne G. Hanley, Terry Lynn Karl, Nathaniel Leff, Douglas Cole Libby, Carlos Marichal, Kathleen Morrison, Robert A. Packenham, Leandro Prados de la Escosura, Nathan Rosenberg, Jean-Laurent Rosenthal, Richard Salvucci, Julie Schaffner, Kenneth L. Sokoloff, William Summerhill, John D. Wirth, Gavin Wright, and Mary A. Yeager.

Major financial support for the conference and this volume was provided by a research innovation grant from Stanford University's Center for Latin American Studies. We are much in debt to Terry Lynn Karl, Director of the center, and Kathleen Morrison, Associate Director, for their generous support. Additional support was provided by the Stanford University Departments of Economics and History, the Hewlett Fund of Stanford's Institute for International Studies, and Stanford's Program in Science, Technology, and Society. We thank the chairs and directors of these departments and institutes in 1992: Gavin Wright (Economics), David Kennedy (History), Walter Falcon (International Studies), and Timothy Lenoir (Science, Technology, and Society).

We are also indebted to the editorial staff of the Stanford University Press, and its director, Norris Pope. In particular, we would like to thank Charles Allen and John Feneron for their editorial guidance, efficiency, and good-natured professionalism in the production of this volume. Moramay López Alonso and Armando Razo provided able assisstance with the preparation of the manuscript. Thanks are also due to John Coatsworth, who read and commented on this volume in its entirety.

S.H.

27615495

BUSINESS/SCIENCE/TECHNOLOGY DIVISION
CHICAGO PUBLIC LIBRARY
400 SOUTH STATE STREET
CHICAGO, IL 60605

Contents

Tables and Figures

Tables

Figures

Contributors

ENRIQUE CÁRDENAS is Professor of Economics and Rector, Universidad de las Américas—Puebla.

MARGARET CHOWNING is Assistant Professor of History, University of California, Berkeley.

STANLEY L. ENGERMAN is John H. Munro Professor of Economics and Professor of History, University of Rochester, and Research Associate, the National Bureau of Economic Research.

STEPHEN HABER is Professor of History and Associate Dean for the Social Sciences, Stanford University.

HERBERT S. KLEIN is Professor of History, Columbia University.

NATHANIEL H. LEFF is Professor of Economics, Graduate School of Business, Columbia University.

CARLOS MARICHAL is Professor of History, Centro de Estudios Históricos, El Colegio de México.

RICHARD J. SALVUCCI is Professor of Economics, Trinity University.

KENNETH L. SOKOLOFF is Professor of Economics, University of California, Los Angeles, and Research Associate, the National Bureau of Economic Research.

WILLIAM SUMMERHILL is Assistant Professor of History, University of California, Los Angeles.

HOW LATIN AMERICA
FELL BEHIND

CHAPTER I

Introduction: Economic Growth and Latin American Economic Historiography

STEPHEN HABER

The tremendous gap in per capita incomes between the major economies of Latin America and the economies of the North Atlantic is not a product of the twentieth century. The ratio of Latin American per capita incomes to Organization for Economic Cooperation and Development per capita incomes has been remarkably stable over the past 90 years.[1] Rather, the income gap is the product of the eighteenth and nineteenth centuries. During this earlier period the economies of the North Atlantic underwent a process of structural transformation that produced sustained economic growth. The economies of Latin America did not follow this growth path, stagnating for most of the period. According to one estimate, from 1800 to 1913 per capita gross domestic product (GDP) grew one and one-half-fold in Mexico and not at all in Brazil. United States GDP per capita grew six-fold during the same period. In 1800 per capita income in the United States was slightly less than twice that in Mexico and roughly the same as in Brazil. By 1913 U.S. GDP was four times that of Mexico and seven times that of Brazil.

The consequences of this lag in Latin America's economic development have dominated scholarship in Latin American history since its inception as a scholarly discipline in the 1940's. To an overwhelming degree the field of modern Latin American history is fundamentally about the social movements and political conflicts engendered by widespread poverty and inequality. Perhaps in no other field of history have scholars dedicated themselves to the study of the social, political, and cultural ramifications of economic change the way Latin Americanists have. Indeed, the focus of the Latin American historiography on the material world has been one of its greatest strengths.

This volume seeks to shed light on the causes of the nineteenth century lag in Latin America's economic development. The essays are linked by three common features. The first is their focus on both understanding the obstacles to growth in the early nineteenth century and the process by which those obstacles were overcome at the end of the century, when the Latin American economies began to grow rapidly. The second is their focus on the two largest economies of Latin America, which have the longest traditions of empirical research on the nineteenth century, Brazil and Mexico. The third and perhaps most important feature is that all of the essays are influenced by the growth-economics tradition. They therefore constitute a break with the long-standing dependency tradition in Latin American social and economic historiography.

The growth-economics tradition traces its origins to an extraordinary group of scholars who during the 1950's pioneered the use of quantitative techniques to study the process of economic growth. The growth economists, the most notable of whom were Moses Abramowitz and Simon Kuznets, developed and refined a wide arsenal of analytic tools and quantitative techniques, including national-income accounting and the measurement of productivity, and set out to measure systematically the long-term factors in economic growth around the world. The result was a convincing demonstration of the power of harnessing these new quantitative techniques to large bodies of empirical data in order to test hypotheses about the sources and patterns of economic change.[3]

The growth-economics research method became the model for research in U.S. economic history. Fundamental to this approach were four notions. First, the questions subject to examination should be stated in precise language. Second, the hypotheses under consideration should be explicitly specified, logically consistent, and falsifiable. Third, the relevant variables should be explicitly specified, and the data should be systematically gathered and analyzed. Fourth, the hypotheses should be evaluated in light of the quantitative and qualitative evidence, with care given to biasing the tests *against* the hypotheses under consideration in order to insure that the results are not driven by statistical artifact.[4] As a result, U.S. economic history has made important substantive advances over the past three decades and has developed into a cohesive discipline characterized by methodological debate, shared research agendas, and continual disciplinary self-examination.

This has not been the case for the field of Latin American economic history. Instead, Latin Americanists pursued a very different research program, which not only eschewed the basic theoretical assumptions of growth economics but also avoided the systematic use of quantitative data to test explicitly framed hypotheses. In order to understand how and why that happened, and in order to understand the long-term intellectual consequences of that divergence, this essay examines the development of the fields of Latin American and U.S. economic history since the 1960's.

The early growth economists directed most, though not all, of their research to the advanced industrial economies. In particular, they focused their attentions on the United States, using its economic history as a laboratory in which to study the growth process in general, thereby deriving lessons that could be applied to other countries. Their application of new quantitative methods to the study of U.S. economic growth set off a revolution in American economic history, giving rise to an approach that came to be called alternately cliometrics, econometric history, or the New Economic History. In fact, many of the pioneers of the New Economic History, including Richard Easterlin, Stanley Engerman, Robert Fogel, and Robert Gallman, had been students of Kuznets.[5]

By the early 1970's the New Economic History had swept aside the other, business history–oriented approaches to the study of American economic history. In so doing, it rewrote much of the economic historiography of the United States, overturning the standard interpretations of the Colonial indenture system, slavery, the course of industrial development, the impact of railroads, movements in the distribution of income and wealth, and a host of other issues.[6]

These accomplishments were the product of three interrelated research programs. The first of these was the measurement of the long-term factors in American economic growth. This research had a strong national-accounts orientation, owing to its intellectual origins in the work of Simon Kuznets, but it soon grew to encompass a broad range of issues affecting American productivity growth over the past two centuries, including changes in America's capital stock, labor force, wages, nutritional standards, educational levels, and mortality and fertility rates. This work also sought to go beyond the measurement of growth at the national level through the systematic examination of productivity growth in individual economic sectors, such as transportation, agriculture, or manufacturing.[7]

The second research program was the systematic study of the technological and institutional sources of economic growth. Scholars had long recognized that underneath the shift in savings rates, labor force allocation, and capital formation were important organizational and technical innovations. American economic historians therefore turned their powerful analytic tools to the study of the impact of those changes on the development of the U.S. economy. In its early years, this work was dominated by two key issues: the impact of the institution of slavery on the economic development of the U.S. South and the impact of the peculiar character of the American financial system on the structure and growth of the U.S. economy. This focus on the sources of growth soon grew to encompass a broad range of issues, including the causes and consequences of inventive activity, the diffusion of technical innovations, the proliferation of consumer credit, the economics of racial and sexual discrimination, the dynamics of migration, and the structure of land tenure.[8]

The third research program involved the formal application of economic theory to the understanding of institutional change. If the character of American economic and political institutions played a role in American economic development, scholars began to wonder how those institutions developed and changed over time. They were also curious as to why some societies developed institutional environments conducive to economic growth while others did not. Beginning with the work of Lance Davis and Douglass North, economic historians began to theorize systematically about how institutional change makes economic activity possible by reducing transactions costs and increasing certainty. Central to this approach was the study of how the specification of property rights created incentives (or disincentives) for productivity-enhancing investments in new technologies and techniques.[9] This formal theorizing about institutions and economic development was soon linked to the empirical tradition of cliometrics. This approach has concentrated in particular on the financial history of the United States, analyzing the relationship between regulation, the development of financial institutions and financial markets, and economic performance.[10]

These advances have not been made without considerable controversy and debate.[11] As is the case with all scientific research programs, the intellectual frontiers of the discipline have always been strongly contested. Indeed, there has been, at times, considerable acrimony and personal enmity. Unlike in some fields of scholarly inquiry, however, controversies in American economic history have focused on the quality of evidence, the proper application of methods, and the logical consistency of models. Thus, while there are ongoing debates about a number of crucial issues (such as the current debates over the history of sexual and racial discrimination in American labor markets), there are well-defined rules of evidence and argumentation that structures those debates. In short, American economic historians have agreed on *how* they will disagree, and this has been crucial to the development of the field as a cohesive and coherent discipline.

The revolution in approaches and methods that took place in American economic history did not occur in the Latin American context. This is not to argue that there were no scholars who followed in the traditions pioneered by Abramowitz and Kuznets. But it is to argue that the approaches and methods of the New Economic History were eclipsed by a competing research program that did not stress the systematic specification and testing of hypotheses. The result was that Latin American economic history developed a much weaker factual and methodological corpus.

Of the three research programs that have dominated the field of U.S. economic history, perhaps the one that has had the greatest resonance among Latin American economic historians has been the study of long-term factors in economic growth. Even here, however, the amount of work that has been done is only a small part of what has been accomplished in the U.S. context. This work has consisted primarily in the estimation of Latin American national incomes back to the late nineteenth century. Some of this research was sponsored by Latin American governments, through their central banks or statistical agencies, but much has also been done by Latin American graduate students at U.S. universities, particularly the University of Chicago.[12] Some economic historians of Latin America, Carlos Díaz Alejandro, David Denslow, Clark Reynolds, Markos Mamalakis, Nathaniel Leff, and William McGreevey being the most notable examples, also framed their work in the tradition of the measurement of long-term factors in growth.[13] But the pace of this work slowed by the 1970's. The kind of ongoing research on structural change, the sources of growth, capital accumulation, long-term trends in the distribution of income and the distribution of the labor force that took place in the United States did not occur in the Latin American field.

The other major research program of the New Economic History, the study of the technological and institutional sources of growth, found even fewer followers among Latin Americanists. From the late 1950's to the late 1960's, a number of scholars worked in the Kuznetsian tradition of studying the process of modern economic growth through the detailed analysis of individual economic sectors. Pioneering this approach was Stanley Stein, who in the late 1950's wrote what is still the classic work on Brazil's industrialization. In fact, one of Stein's first essays, on the history of the Brazilian textile industry, was published in a volume edited by none other than Kuznets himself.[14] Throughout the 1960's and early 1970's work in this vein continued, much of it sponsored by the Yale Economic Growth Center.[15] By the mid-1970's, however, this research program began to fall out of favor among younger scholars. This is not to argue that this research tradition completely disappeared.[16] It is to say, however, that it became a minor current within a field pursuing a very different research program.

The use of formal theory to understand how institutions structure economic growth found even less resonance among Latin Americanists. There was, of course, an old institutionalist tradition among Latin American economic historians, going back to William Glade's *Latin American Economies*.[17] But the property-rights/transaction-costs approach to the study of economic activity, associated with Douglass North, found few takers among Latin American historians. Until the late 1980's, the only attempt to introduce the Northian property-rights approach to understand how Latin America's institutional environment impeded growth was John Coatsworth's now classic article on nineteenth-century Mexico. Two of Coatsworth's students, Robert Holden and David Walker, subsequently adapted some of the property-rights concepts to their work on land survey companies and merchant enterprise, respectively. In addition, a recent book by Jeremy Adelman employs property-rights theory in order to understand the divergent paths taken by Argentine and Canadian agriculture.[18]

In short, the self-reinforcing advance of scholarship that took place in the U.S. context, characterized by disciplinary self-examination, debate over method, and shared research agendas, did not occur among Latin Americanists. In fact, some of the Latin American field's most prominent scholars, whose early work was strongly influenced by the growth-economics tradition, openly abandoned this approach by the 1970's.

The reason for this divergence in the Latin American and U.S. historiographies is three-fold. First, while many first-rate Ph.D. dissertations in economic history were done by Latin American graduate students studying in Great Britain and the United States, those students generally did not continue to work as economic historians when they returned home. Low academic salaries in Latin America coupled with attractive offers of senior government positions served as powerful incentives to leave the university. This served to slow the growth of the New Economic History in most Latin American countries, because the scholars who could train the next generation of economic historians were to be found in economic ministries, not classrooms.

Second, the spread of the New Economic History to Latin American countries was further slowed because of the high cost of processing large bodies of quantitative data. Because the United States led the world in computer technology and had relatively affluent universities, it should not be surprising that it was the first place to see the widespread application of quantitative techniques to historical questions. In the Latin American context, the high cost of computers served as a major obstacle until recent years, when the personal computer revolution dramatically lowered the cost of data processing.

The third factor impeding the spread of the New Economic History to the Latin American context was that it was eclipsed by a rival research program. Instead of pursuing questions about the rate and structure of Latin American economic growth through the application of the methods and approaches of cliometrics, the Latin American field in the United States adopted a model of research that fundamentally rejected neoclassical economic logic, the dispassionate analysis of systematically gathered quantitative data, and the specification of testable hypotheses.

In part, the rejection of the growth economics tradition grew out of a view sober critique of neoclassical economics. Beginning in the late 1940's and gaining ground through the 1960's, Latin American economists began to assess critically the fundamental tenets of neoclassical thought as applied to Latin America. In particular, they called into question two of the central notions of growth economics: that the economic laws that govern developed economies apply equally well to underdeveloped economies, and that economic relations between developed and underdeveloped economies always yield economic gains for both.[19] In regard to the first claim, development economists such as Ragnar Nurkse and W. Arthur Lewis argued that developing economies were unlike developed economies in that the former possessed "unlimited supplies of labor," which meant that the laws of motion of underdeveloped economies were fundamentally different from those governing the developed world.[20] In addition, development economists also argued that the process of "late industrialization" was markedly different from the industrialization of the advanced economies and required sets of policies that addressed those differences. This view was buttressed not only by the seeming success of import substituting models of development during the 1940's and 1950's but was also supported by the influential work of Alexander Gerschenkron on the industrial history of the European "follower" countries.[21] In regard to the second claim of growth economics (that trade between the developed and underdeveloped economies was always mutually beneficial), Hans Singer and

Raul Prebisch had independently demonstrated that, at least as far as the limited evidence they amassed indicated, the terms of trade of Latin American countries had deteriorated in a secular manner from the late nineteenth century through the 1940's. Trade was therefore not necessarily an engine of growth.[22]

In the short run, this critique of growth economics resulted in the appearance of a number of economic histories of Latin America written from a structuralist (as the Prebisch school was called) point of view. These works, such as Celso Furtado's study of Brazil and Aldo Ferrer's study of Argentina, sought to explain the divergent growth paths of Latin America and the United States. Their intellectual origins in the critique of neoclassical economics resulted, unfortunately, in their rejection of the powerful analytic and quantitative methods of growth economics. Indeed, Ferrer managed to write an economic history of Argentina without including a single statistical table.[23] As Ferrer explained the approach,

> The method followed in this book is to analyze the formation of the Argentine economy by differentiating between the historical stages within which the economic system has developed according to a certain pattern. . . . The work of Celso Furtado on the Brazilian economy underlines the value of this type of approach to the formation of an economy. Dispensing with the traditional economic historian's mass of data, the economic system can be defined in its different historical circumstances.[24]

In defense of the structuralist historians and other critics of growth economics, one might argue that their ideas about the *sui generis* nature of the Latin American economies were meant to be taken as hypotheses to be tested. Unfortunately, they were taken by a large part of the Latin American studies field, historians included, to be necessary truths. As Albert Hirschman put it so well,

> A strange thing happened once it had been pointed out that interaction between the rich and poor countries could in certain circumstances be in the nature of an antagonistic, zero-sum game: very soon it proved intellectually and politically attractive to assert that such was the essence of the relationship and that it held as an iron law through all phases of contacts between the capitalist center and the periphery.[25]

In short, many Latin Americanists came to believe—largely as an article of faith—that Latin American underdevelopment was a product of capitalism itself. They therefore rejected the neoclassical tradition of economic analysis. Most scholars operating in this vein unfortunately conflated the powerful analytic and quantitative tools of growth analysis with a particular set of policy prescriptions and thus abandoned the theoretically informed, systematic analysis of relevant data as a model for conducting research on Latin America's economic past. The result was the rapid rise and preeminence of a body of thought that came to be known as dependency theory.

Dependency theory wed Marxist notions of class analysis to a structuralist critique of international trade theory, though dependency was neither structuralism nor Marxism.[26] At the center of the theory was the notion that the terms of trade of Latin American countries deteriorated over time: the price of the region's primary product exports declined secularly relative to the price of its industrial imports from the North Atlantic economies. Economic exploitation thus occurred through "unequal exchange." In and of itself, this was not a new argument: the notion of a secular deterioration in Latin America's terms of trade had been made by Prebisch and Singer in the late 1940's. *Dependentistas* (as practitioners of dependency theory came to be called) went farther in their critique, however, arguing that the protection and subsidization of domestic industry suggested by the structuralists was not a sufficient solution. They argued that the dependence of Latin America's domestic elites on foreign capital and foreign political support, coupled with the substantial private gains domestic elites earned from the maintenance of unequal exchange, meant that the region's comprador bourgeoisie could not and would not advance a developmentalist economic project. They further argued that this model of growth gave rise to economies characterized by highly skewed distributions of income. The fundamentally undemocratic nature of economic growth in Latin America, in turn, gave rise to authoritarian political systems, because Latin America's antinationalist bourgeoisie could not, by definition, obtain hegemony. What was therefore needed, according to dependency theory, was a popular revolution that would eliminate this weak and dependent bourgeoisie as a political force, institute socialism, free the region from neocolonialism, and undo the trade mechanisms that kept Latin America in poverty.[27]

Dependency theory quickly came to be the dominant framework within historical, political, and sociological writing about Latin America. Stanley Stein, in a noted shift from his earlier, growth economics–influenced work, articulated the attractiveness of the theory:

The new school of economic historians [referring to the *dependentistas*] has focused not only upon the weaknesses of the national economy, but, unlike its predecessors, has traced them to the apparent structural constraints of the international capitalist system which, it is argued, inherently limits the development of the economies of Latin America and the benefits to be derived therefrom. In some instances, the argument of this group has been shredded by subsequent critical review of their thesis and statistical manipulation; yet as time provides perspective, one is left with the judgment that *the* critical issue has been located.[28]

Dependency theory quickly elbowed aside, though it did not annihilate, the traditional institutional and annales-school approaches that had been prevalent in Latin American economic historiography since the 1940's. In the few areas where there were already established research programs with well-defined rules of evidence and argumentation—Mexican colonial history being a case in point—dependency theory had a minimal impact.[29] But these were the exceptions. Indeed, the acceptance of the dependency model and its research program went far beyond the confines of economic history. With an amazing rapidity, the dependency framework came to be viewed as the most appropriate model to study Latin American politics, society, and economics. No other single viewpoint pervaded the field of Latin American history, nor historicized Latin American studies, as did dependency theory.[30] In fact, dependency became—and continues to be— the dominant organizing theme of the most widely used textbooks on Latin American history.[31]

Given the political climate of the late 1960's and early 1970's, the rapid rise to hegemony of the dependency view is perhaps understandable. Dependency theory was merely one reflection of a larger political and philosophical questioning of America's economic and political power around the world. In the Latin American context, the extension of this power took the form of the support of the U.S. government for the military dictators who had come to power throughout much of the region. There really was a confluence of interests between Latin American bourgeoisies, foreign capital, the U.S. government, and Latin American militaries. It is therefore easy to understand how many scholars then read this alliance back into the historical record and posited that it was responsible for the persistence of Latin American underdevelopment.

There were, unfortunately, three problems with the dependency model. The first was that it employed ad hoc economic reasoning. Typical of the kind of economic thinking employed by *dependentistas* was their view of how foreign direct investment (FDI) causes underdevelopment. They posited that FDI "decapitalizes" Latin America because the profits repatriated by foreign companies exceed the value of the original investment of those companies.[32] This view contains a rather extraordinary set of economic assumptions, which hold that the private returns to foreign investors always exceed the social returns of FDI to a receiving country. First, it assumes that FDI does not generate demand for domestically produced inputs, meaning it does not give rise to new domestic industries. Second, it assumes that FDI does not increase the incomes of the workers in foreign-owned enterprises, meaning it has no effects on the depth of the domestic market. Third, it assumes that FDI does not bring about technology transfer, meaning it plays no role in the spread of new types of industries using new processes. Fourth, it assumes that there are no "forward linkages" from FDI. In this view a foreign-owned railroad, for example, does not connect and integrate regional markets, thereby allowing domestic firms to capture scale economies that permit them either to adopt more efficient technologies in established industries or to enter into industries that previously did not exist. Finally, it assumes that foreign enterprises do not contribute to the tax base through the payment of export, income, and excise taxes. These are strong assumptions indeed. According to this line of reasoning, the only foreign investments that yield positive gains for development are those that lose money for their shareholders. In fact, the economic logic of this view would hold that British investors in American railroads underdeveloped the United States.

The second problem with the dependency model was that it rejected the notion that ideas should be subjected to scientific evaluation. Instead of framing carefully specified hypotheses and then testing them against systematically gathered evidence, *dependentistas* all too often made sweeping generalizations that were not supported by the evidence at hand. It is in this sense that dependency theory had its most negative—and most enduring— impact on the field of Latin American economic history. The research tradition that developed did not concentrate on the careful retrieval of data and the clear specification of testable hypotheses.[33] It was not that this would have been theoretically impossible, as Rosemary Thorp and Geoffrey Bertram's treatment of the Peruvian case makes clear. Rather, the problem was that *dependentistas*, for political and ideological reasons, were all too often intent on proving the theory to be correct. Thus, the dependency tradition gave rise to loose rules of evidence and argumentation that permitted the implicit and incomplete specification of hypotheses, tautological reasoning, and selective presentation of data.[34] The result was that there could be no meaningful debates over method, which limited the field's ability to advance in terms of technique and approach.[35] The lack of a tradition of careful data analysis and presentation, in turn, meant that there was no agreed-upon body of knowledge that could then serve as the basis to test new hypotheses, further limiting the advance of the discipline.

The third problem with the dependency model was that its central tenets were largely inconsistent with the empirical facts. When scholars took dependency ideas, expressed them as falsifiable hypotheses, and tested those hypotheses in the light of the historical record of the region's larger economies, they found that the theory had little explanatory power. Most of this critique came from non-*dependentistas* of both neoclassical and orthodox Marxist orientations.[36] Some of it inadvertently came from within the dependency school itself: scholars working within the dependency approach were often surprised to find that their results did not match the predictions of the theory.[37] Let us take a brief look at how well the theory matched with the actual empirical record.

At the heart of dependency theory was the notion that the terms of trade of Latin America deteriorated in a secular fashion. Thus, foreign trade underdeveloped Latin America. The basis for this claim was the terms-of-trade estimates that Prebisch and Singer had independently constructed. Yet when other scholars examined the terms-of-trade argument closely, by pushing estimates back into the nineteenth century and by subjecting the data to more careful analysis, they found that for long periods the terms of trade actually improved, even during the so-called era of export liberalism. The weight of the evidence points to the conclusion that there has been no secular deterioration in Latin America's terms of trade, but rather there have been cyclical swings with no discernable long-term trend.[38]

The other major tenet of dependency theory was the existence of a comprador bourgeoisie controlling a weak state that would not and could not act in the national interest. This tenet collapsed on a number of counts. In the first place, scholars working on the region's early industrial history found national bourgeoisies of considerable political power and developmentalist will in the nineteenth century. In fact, these national industrial elites were able to persuade their governments to erect high tariff barriers against foreign manufactures and to establish subsidy programs to support Latin America's infant industries.[39]

The dependency image of a weak and dependent bourgeoisie also did not square with research on the regulation of foreign enterprise. Latin American states were not prostrate in the face of foreign capital. Even during the period of export liberalism, Latin American governments were willing to regulate the activities of foreign capitalists for developmentalist ends.[40] In retrospect, dependency thinking about foreign capital and national sovereignty might have had a good deal of accuracy in regard to the smaller countries of Latin America, such as Honduras, Guatemala, or Cuba, but held limited explanatory power for the larger countries of the region such as Mexico, Brazil, or Argentina.

The final major tenet of dependency theory was that during times of international crisis, when the advanced industrial countries were too busy fighting wars or were too mired in depression to exert their control, the ties of dependency were loosened. During such periods, according to the dependency view, Latin American countries were therefore able to develop autonomously and rapidly. This tenet of the theory was based on the experience of Latin American economies during World War II, a period that saw a dramatic rise in industrial output in most countries.

This view fell on three counts. First, most of the region's industrial expansion of the Second World War turned out to have been the product of running existing plant and equipment around the clock. The major part of the installed capacity of Latin American manufacturing actually predated the war, indicating that industrial development had occurred prior to the disruption of international trade.[41] Second, on close examination, the Great Depression turned out not to have been the boon to Latin American industrialization that dependency theorists thought it was. While the latter part of the 1930's did witness impressive increases in domestic industrial investment and industrial output in many countries, the late 1920's and early 1930's turned out to have been periods of industrial contraction.[42] Third, the onset of modern Latin American industrialization coincided not with a period of international crisis but with the era of export liberalism. Contrary to what dependency theory would suggest, the expansion of incomes created by the late–nineteenth-century "export boom" coupled with the integration of markets made possible by the construction of foreign-owned railroads and the protection of activist states gave rise to a sustained period of industrial growth. In fact, the very areas that were most affected by the foreign investment boom of the late nineteenth century were the same areas that saw the most rapid industrial development. Moreover, this industry was domestically financed and owned.

Scholars working within the dependency framework were well aware of the increasingly obvious inconsistencies between the theory and empirical reality. Their response was two-fold. First, they created a more complicated variety of the theory, which came to be called associated dependent development.[43] Associated dependent development simply asserted that "development" could occur in the context of "dependency," implicitly conceding that dependency theory could not explain Latin American underdevelopment. Yet its proponents simultaneously asserted that underdevelopment was a product of dependency. In order to reconcile these mutually exclusive claims, associated dependent development engaged in a kind of circular reasoning that might best be thought of as a heads-I-

win-tails-you-lose model of argumentation. As Robert Packenham characterized it,

> If foreigners invest in agriculture, this promotes primary product dependency via
> the argument of declining terms of trade. If they invest in industry, this is "the new
> structure of dependency." If the national bourgeoisie is small, that is because for-
> eigners "debilitate" it; if the national bourgeoisie is large, it responds to external
> interests anyway as the internal agent of neo-colonialism. If the economy of a Latin
> American country is labor intensive, this is exploitation and maintains dependency;
> if it is capital intensive, this is the newer form of dependency which fosters unem-
> ployment, marginalization, and increasing inequalities. And so on.[44]

In short, hypotheses could not be tested because any variation in the independent variables, including successful domestic industrialization, was
taken as prima facie evidence of the existence of dependency.[45]

The second response to the collapse of dependency theory was an attempt to reform it from within. Many dependency-influenced scholars
were concerned that dependency theory had simultaneously historicized
the study of development and at the same time made history irrelevant. As
one dependency revisionist put it, "What exists is made eternal; today's
social relations are projected back into the past as if they have always existed; and what really happened in history disappears. . . . It is no longer
necessary (or even possible within the confines of the theory) to ask how
[an] exploitive export or peripheral relationship was itself constructed historically."[46] The revisionists therefore sought to resuscitate dependency
theory by applying it to concrete historical situations. Unfortunately, the
wide variance between the fundamental tenets of the theory and the empirical record of Latin America's economic history meant that this revisionist current had to sidestep questions about economic growth and focus
instead on sociological[47] and political[48] issues. Indeed, in order to avoid
discarding dependency theory in its entirety, this revisionist approach un-
critically accepted the economics of "dependent development."[49]

While the work that has come out of this research program has been
important and worthwhile in many respects, it has little to say about
the origins of Latin American underdevelopment. The social-relations emphasis of the sociological variant of dependency theory has meant that its
practitioners have ignored the issues that have long been of concern to
economic historians of Europe and the United States (not to mention
Mexican colonial historians) and that are the key to understanding per
capita income growth in predominantly agrarian societies, such as the
specification of property rights, the transformation of agricultural techniques, and the record of agricultural productivity growth.[50] This school of

dependency theory has even less to say about the development of modern industry, banking, transportation, and other economic sectors. The emphasis on ideology of the political variant of dependency theory has meant that its practitioners have focused almost purely on the history of economic policy debates. There is, of course, a significant difference between the study of the history of economic ideas and the study of the real-world performance of economies.[51]

Influenced both by the progressive debilitation of dependency theory as a research program and by the methodological and empirical accomplishments of U.S. economic history, economic historians of modern Latin America have begun in recent years to adopt the methods and approaches of the New Economic History. In early 1992, a group of Latin American economic historians working in the New Economic History tradition came together at a conference at Stanford University. The conference was unusual not only because of the type of work that was presented, but also because it departed from the usual tradition of Latin American history conferences: the discussants were not other Latin American historians but were either development economists or practitioners of the New Economic History of the United States and Europe. This volume emerged out of the three days of discussion and debate at that conference, though the essays found herein are not, strictly speaking, the papers presented at the conference. Indeed, some participants chose to rethink their work completely as a result of those three days of debate. Other essays were commissioned later, in order to provide balance or to address issues that were not taken up by the original participants at the 1992 meeting.

The essays presented here represent a broad range of work by historians of Brazil and Mexico, and they employ the methods of New Economic History in varying degrees and with varying focuses. Some of the work presented here has a strong national-accounts orientation, Richard Salvucci's contribution to this volume being perhaps the clearest case in point. Other contributors borrow heavily from the counterfactual methods of cliometrics, William Summerhill's essay being perhaps the archetype. A few of the contributors have drawn more heavily from the new institutional economics pioneered by Davis and North. They focus on the systematic study of the regulatory environment in order to understand the way that inefficient institutions impeded the smooth functioning of the market, thereby slowing the region's rate of economic growth, and use quantitative data to describe the evolution of these institutions. Carlos Marichal's article in this volume provides the clearest example of this type of work.

What all the contributors have in common, however, is that they combine neoclassical economic reasoning, tempered by institutional-analysis and transaction-costs approaches, with quantitative data and the careful specification of refutable hypotheses in order to understand how government regulatory policies, legal systems, institutional environments, and changes of political regime affected the course of Latin American economic growth.

The first two essays in this volume, by Nathaniel Leff and Enrique Cárdenas, provide general overviews of the nineteenth-century development of Brazil and Mexico, respectively. The Leff essay, "Economic Development in Brazil, 1822–1913," focuses on understanding the interplay among factor immobilities, a lagging domestic agricultural sector, high transport costs (produced by an unfavorable natural topography), Brazil's political institutions, and limited public finance in the country's woefully slow economic growth from independence to the 1890's. These issues are taken up again in the Cárdenas essay, "A Macroeconomic Interpretation of Nineteenth-Century Mexico." Cárdenas focuses in particular on the interaction between political stability and the performance of the mining sector, arguing that the destruction of physical capital during the wars for independence produced a long-term decline in mining output. The collapse of mining, in turn, had serious effects on foreign trade, government revenues, and the nontradable sector of the economy. It was not until the last decades of the century that a revival of mining, accompanied by a program of railroad construction, produced a sustained recovery of the Mexican economy.

These two essays suggest a series of testable hypotheses that are taken up in detail in the ensuing chapters. Both Leff and Cárdenas indicate that high transportation costs served as constraints on economic activity throughout much of the nineteenth century and argue that the arrival of the railroad in the last decades of the century therefore played a crucial role in igniting economic growth. This hypothesis is tested by William Summerhill in his essay "Transport Improvements and Economic Growth in Brazil and Mexico." Summerhill estimates the social savings of railroads (the percentage of GDP saved by the lower cost of shipping goods by railroad) for the Brazilian economy and compares these to Coatsworth's estimates for Mexico. By 1913, depending on what assumptions are built into the model, social savings resulting from the advent of the railroad may have been as high as 38.5 percent of GDP for Mexico and 22 percent of GDP for Brazil. The implication is clear: high transportation costs in the prerailroad era were a crucial obstacle to growth. Summerhill then goes on to examine the backward linkage effects of railroads in both countries, showing that direct links to the development of iron, steel, and engineering industries were weak. His analysis does indicate, however, that at least in the Brazilian case "the railways, and freight regulation, contributed to the emergence of an especially vibrant internal sector of the economy. . . . In contrast to what is asserted in much of the economic historiography of Latin America, railways in Brazil diminished the relative importance of the export sector, if anything reducing the degree of foreign economic 'dependence.'"[52]

The late arrival of the railroad in Brazil and Mexico was in large part a function of the inability of either the domestic capital markets or the public sector to finance railroad investment, a subject that Leff, Cárdenas, and Summerhill discuss in some detail. Why the domestic capital markets were slow to develop, and what the relationship was between financial market development and public finance is a subject addressed by Carlos Marichal in his article "Obstacles to the Development of Capital Markets in Nineteenth-Century Mexico." Marichal argues that "it was the state's fiscal and credit policies that were most directly responsible for the instability of Mexican financial markets and, therefore, for many of the difficulties in the development of modern capital markets during the greater part of the nineteenth century."[53] He then goes on to demonstrate how the Mexican government's repudiations and rollovers of its debts through much of the nineteenth century discouraged the development of securities markets, because individuals only come to recognize that holding a piece of paper (such as a stock or bond from a private corporation) can be a secure investment once they have had a favorable experience with government bonds. Even after these problems were overcome in the last decades of the nineteenth century, however, repressive bank regulatory policies served to slow the growth of Mexico's financial markets. The Mexican government, for reasons having to do with its own financing, remained committed to policies that did not favor the growth of small banks and discouraged the formation of broadly based securities markets.

What, then, were the real-world economic costs of such policies, and what were the exact contours of the differences in financial-market development between Mexico and Brazil? I take up this subject at length in my article "Financial Markets and Industrial Development: A Comparative Study of Government Regulation, Financial Innovation, and Industrial Structure in Brazil and Mexico, 1840–1930." I argue that the kinds of repressive regulatory policies discussed by Marichal in regard to Mexico were absent in Brazil in the years after 1889, which gave rise to a larger and more active securities market in Brazil. This larger and less concentrated securities market gave rise, in turn, to a faster growing and less concentrated textile industry, which I employ as a test case. In short, Mexican government legislation that restrained the development of financial institutions had the unintended effect of slowing the growth of industry and limiting competition among manufacturers. My work also suggests that there may have been significant productivity consequences of Mexico's more highly concentrated industrial structure. The results strongly indicate that domestic political considerations played a decisive role in shaping the course of economic growth in nineteenth-century Latin America.

Leff and Cárdenas both discuss the relatively poor performance of the domestic agricultural sector, suggesting that in large part it was a function of the high cost of transportation in the prerailroad era. As Leff puts it, "High transportation costs . . . [limited] the access of many agricultural producers to markets beyond their immediate locale. . . . Low-cost transportation facilities were therefore crucial for developing a high-productivity agriculture. Unfortunately, the country's geographical and topographical conditions made for relatively high transport costs from the production areas to the market centers."[54] In the Mexican case, Cárdenas suggests that in addition to transportation costs, the independence wars and the limited demand produced by a sluggish mining sector were contributing factors to an agricultural sector characterized by slow productivity growth.

The performance of the domestic agricultural sector is, as Leff notes, perhaps the most understudied area of Latin American economic history. Testing the hypotheses advanced by Leff and Cárdenas will therefore require us to build up a stock of knowledge far larger than is available at present. Margaret Chowning, in her article "Reassessing the Prospects for Profit in Nineteenth-Century Mexican Agriculture from a Regional Perspective: Michoacán, 1810–60," indicates how we might build up that stock of knowledge: through the careful analysis of notarial records in order to examine the economic performance of landed estates at the regional level. Her results for the state of Michoacán fly in the face of much of the conventional wisdom about the supposed consequences of the wars for Mexican independence and indicate that the presumed agrarian depression of the early nineteenth century may not in fact have taken place. Indeed, her work indicates that hacendados rather quickly found ways to restore hacienda profitability, including increased investments in productivity-enhancing reproducible capital.

A major theme of the articles by Cárdenas and Chowning is the impact of political independence on the course of Mexican economic growth. Chowning's work on Michoacán suggests that the destruction of physical capital during the wars for independence did not have a long-term impact on the performance of Mexican agriculture. Cárdenas, looking primarily at the mining economy, investment, and foreign trade, argues that output fell drastically during the first two decades after Mexico's independence and suggests that the economy might not have recovered until the last decades of the nineteenth century.

Richard Salvucci's article, "Mexican National Income in the Era of Independence, 1800–40," seeks to resolve this long-standing debate. Salvucci takes a national-accounts approach to the problem, first considering the available estimates for Mexico's national product and then constructing estimates based on the methods of Raymond Goldsmith. He argues that "there were sharp, localized reductions in production during the insurgency," but the "vision of generalized, catastrophic, sustained depression is unwarranted."[55] His research does agree, however, with Cárdenas's argument that the insurgency had lingering costs in terms of the collapse of silver mining, which reduced the means of payment, generated monetary astringency, and decreased the volume of domestic and international trade. Salvucci goes on to argue, however, that economic growth had already slowed in the last decades of the eighteenth century, because of Bourbon policies designed to drain Mexico of specie: "The economic costs of independence were imposed on what was already a weakening economy."[56]

The notion that the independence wars had significant, long-term costs contains the implicit hypothesis that the Mexican economy would have grown quickly in the absence of armed conflict. One way to assess this proposition is through a simple, counterfactual exercise: look at the record of economic growth of a similar Latin American country that obtained independence coterminously but did not go through a sustained period of armed conflict. Herbert S. Klein and I undertake this task in our article "Economic Consequences of Brazilian Independence." Through an analysis of Brazilian foreign trade, commercial policy, and industrial development, we argue that independence did not bring about a structural transformation of the Brazilian economy. Brazil was an agricultural economy prior to independence and continued to be so afterwards. As was also the case in Mexico, the transition to modern economic growth in Brazil, in which industry began to replace traditional economic activities, did not occur until the late nineteenth century. We further argue that this delayed transition to modern economic growth was not a function of Brazil's "dependency," which was allegedly made more extensive and profound because of British informal colonialism than it had been before under formal Portuguese colonialism. Our analysis of foreign-trade data, the history of commercial policy, and the record of industrialization leads us to conclude that "the dependency model, while explaining some features of the Brazilian economy at a superficial level, does not hold a great deal of explanatory power when one takes a detailed look at the empirical record."[57] Our short answer, then, to the question of the effect of independence on the Brazilian economy is that it had virtually no effect. "That Brazil had a nineteenth-century economy characterized by low rates of economic growth, free trade, and limited structural transformation is indisputable. It is difficult, however, to explain any of these features as a consequence of independence."[58]

One of the principal arguments of the Leff essay is that, given the intrinsic logic of Brazil's political economy, it is difficult to imagine a historically plausible alternative course of development. As Leff put it, "The pattern of economic change there appears to have been very much governed by existing structural parameters, with little scope for an alternative course."[59] In short, to posit a model of development for Brazil that parallels that of countries like the United States is to construct a historically impossible counterfactual.

Why did Brazil's and, more generally, Latin America's institutional environments develop in ways that dampened growth through the eighteenth and nineteenth centuries? What was it about the initial conditions of Latin America's economies at the time of conquest that gave rise to legal and political traditions that were not conducive to structural transformation and the broad-based sharing of the gains from growth? The issue of the endogeneity of institutional environments in Latin America and their relationship to the preexisting factor endowments at the time of European conquest is taken up in detail in the concluding article, "Factor Endowments, Institutions, and Differential Paths of Growth Among New World Economies," by Stanley L. Engerman and Kenneth L. Sokoloff. Engerman and Sokoloff argue that the endowment of the factors of production— broadly defined to include the nature and density of settlement of the indigenous population as well as more traditional factors such as the type and quantity of land and mineral wealth—played a key role in structuring the institutions that governed economic activity in the Americas. In particular, they argue that northern British colonies were unusual in that the climatic conditions there favored a regime of mixed farming, centered on grains, that exhibited no economies of scale in production, as opposed to agriculture in areas such as Brazil and the Caribbean where the soils and climate combined to favor the growing of crops like sugar, coffee, and cotton, which were of high value on the market and were more efficiently produced on large production units employing slave labor. In the case of areas like

Mexico and Peru, they argue that the large numbers of sedentary Indians in these countries coupled with their mineral resources gave rise to similar extremes in the distribution of political and economic power. The end result of these initial conditions was that the United States developed more democratic political institutions, more extensive domestic markets, and economic policies more conducive to self-reinforcing economic growth. In short, they argue against interpretations that have focused on a presumed "Iberian *mentalité*" (they note, for example, that the British sugar islands did not develop very differently from those of Spain) and on external constraints on economic development, such as the dependency school. They suggest, instead, that historians would do well to examine in greater detail the relationship between factor endowments, institutions, and economic growth, and suggest a practical model for doing so.

Clearly, the essays in this volume only begin to answer the range of questions that might be posed about Latin America's nineteenth-century economic climacteric. There is much empirical work yet to be done. It may also ultimately turn out to be the case that the growth-economics approach yields partial explanations for the region's economic stagnation, and that in time the field will need to assess hypotheses that borrow from other intellectual traditions. If there is a lesson to be learned from U.S. and European economic historiography, however, it is that the growth-economics tradition provides a set of easily falsifiable hypotheses that quickly yields returns to its practitioners and provides a well-defined and theoretically informed basis for further research.

Notes

The author would like to thank Jeremy Adelman, Edward Beatty, Jeffrey L. Bortz, Marsy A. Haber, Anne G. Hanley, Rebecca Horn, Herbert S. Klein, Mark Kleinman, Anne Krueger, Douglas Cole Libby, Noel Maurer, Robert Packenham, Mario Pastore, Jean-Laurent Rosenthal, Richard Salvucci, Kenneth L. Sokoloff, William Summerhill, Mauricio Tenorio, Eric Van Young, and the referee from Stanford Press for their comments on an earlier draft of this article. Any errors of interpretation are solely the responsibility of the author.

   1. Maddison 1989: 15.
   2. Calculated from Table 10.5, p. 270, this volume.
   3. The interest of economists in the causes of economic growth was itself a product of World War II. The Second World War was the first war that was fundamentally won by GNP: the United States simply outproduced the Axis powers, allowing it to put more troops and weaponry on the battlefield than its enemies. In addition, the problems of Europe's reconstruction and the sizable differences in per capita in-

come between Europe and the United States immediately after the war also played a role in encouraging economists to focus on growth. I am indebted to Moses Abramowitz for making this point clear to me. For an introduction to the growth-economics literature, see Kuznets 1953; Kuznets 1966.

4. For an excellent discussion of what was new about the New Economic History, see Davis 1966.

5. This is not to suggest, of course, that it was Kuznets and his students alone who created the New Economic History. The New Economic History was built on a broad scholarly base. In some respects, Alexander Gerschenkron (whose students included such major figures in cliometrics as Paul David, Albert Fishlow, Peter Temin, and Diedre McCloskey), William Parker (whose students included Gavin Wright), Douglass North, and Lance Davis were equally influential. But it is to say that these scholars all emphasized the clear specification of hypotheses and their testing in the light of systematically assembled data sets, and that these traditions of argumentation came out of the growth-economics research program of which Kuznets was one of the major progenitors. Perhaps in no area was this concern with method and evidence as clearly demonstrated as in the debates over the role played by railroads in American economic development, in which both Kuznets's and Gerschenkron's students were the major participants. It was no historiographic accident that the first major issue that the New Economic Historians addressed was the impact of railroads on the antebellum U.S. economy. Simon Kuznets and W. W. Rostow had long debated the importance of "leading sectors" in the growth process. According to the Rostovian view, there was perhaps no more important sector than railroads. The examination of the impact of the railroads on the U.S. economy therefore provided a historical test of the Rostovian view and resolved the leading-sectors debate in favor of Kuznets, who argued that the growth process was characterized by change across a broad front of interlinked sectors, not by rapid growth in any one "leading sector." See Fogel 1964; Fishlow 1966; David 1969.

6. For an excellent overview of the empirical accomplishments of the New Economic History, see Atack and Passell 1994.

7. The best introduction to the literature is Engerman and Gallman 1986. Also see Goldin and Rockoff 1992.

8. The best introduction to the literature is Fogel and Engerman 1971.

9. Davis and North 1971. Also see North 1990.

10. At the center of this field was Lance E. Davis, who had already pioneered the modern study of capital markets when he turned his attentions to the theory of institutional change. For some examples of how this field has evolved over the past two decades, see Davis 1963; Davis 1965; Lamoreaux 1986; Lamoreaux 1994.

11. Perhaps the most heated of these debates occurred over the economics of slavery. For an introduction to the debate, see Fogel and Engerman 1974; David et al. 1976; Fogel 1989.

12. Perhaps the best known example of this work is Contador and Haddad on Brazil. See Contador and Haddad 1975; Haddad 1978.

13. Denslow 1974; Díaz Alejandro 1970; Leff 1982a; Leff 1982b; Mamalakis 1976; McGreevey 1971; Reynolds 1970.

14. Stein 1955; Stein 1957.

15. For examples, see Baer 1965; Baer 1969; Leff 1968a; Leff 1968b; Mamalakis and Reynolds 1965.

16. A number of scholars, Nathaniel Leff and John Coatsworth being the most notable, continued to work in this vein. See Leff 1982a; Leff 1982b; Coatsworth 1981. In addition, through the 1970's and 1980's research on the sources of economic growth and stagnation continued among a number of young Latin American scholars, particularly in Brazil. For examples of this work, see Suzigan 1986; Peláez and Suzigan 1976; Villanova Villela and Suzigan 1975; Versiani and Mendonça de Barros 1977; Cárdenas 1988.

17. Glade 1969.

18. Coatsworth, it should also be noted, was also the only economic historian operating in a history department to adopt the methods of cliometrics. See Coatsworth 1978; Coatsworth 1981; Holden 1994; Walker 1986; Adelman 1994.

19. Hirschman 1981: chap. 1.

20. For an excellent discussion of this issue, see Hirschman 1981: 7–10.

21. Gerschenkron 1962.

22. The first articulation of this view can be found in United Nations 1950. For an overview of the perspective and a discussion of its implications, see Hirschman 1981: chap. 1. For a critique of this view, see Lal 1985.

23. I refer here to the first Spanish edition of 1963. The English translation included a statistical appendix of seven tables, but these referred to variables that were not at issue in the structuralist critique of neoclassical economics, such as population size, the extent of the railroad grid, and the ratio of agricultural exports to agricultural production. Much the same criticism could be leveled against Celso Furtado's structuralist interpretation of the economic history of Brazil. While Furtado presented quantitative data in tabular form, he did so for purposes of description, not in order to test hypotheses in the way that New Economic Historians were beginning to do. See Furtado 1968; Furtado 1970; Ferrer 1963; Ferrer 1967.

24. How the "pattern" of historical stages was determined in this and other structuralist works of economic history was something of a mystery, given the fact that Ferrer explicitly rejected the systematic presentation and analysis of quantitative data. Ferrer 1967: 1.

25. Hirschman 1981: 17.

26. The term *theory* was somewhat of a misnomer, because *dependentistas* did not specify and test hypotheses. As Robert Packenham has pointed out, the theory was not set up in a manner that would allow its implications to be tested in the light of empirical evidence. In fact, the epistemological holism of the theory made it difficult, if not impossible, to assess the validity of the model on empirical grounds. See Packenham 1992. For an excellent intellectual history of the development of dependency theory and its differentiation from earlier theories of development, see Klarén 1986. Marxist economics developed its own tradition of studying underdevelopment. See, for example, Mandel 1975.

27. Classic works spelling out the theory include Amin 1976; Frank 1967; Frank 1972; Cardoso and Faletto 1969; Sunkel and Paz 1970.

28. Stein and Cortés Conde, 1977: 5. Emphasis in the original.

29. In large part the dominance of annales-school approaches in Mexican colonial history can be explained by the long-term influence of titans like Woodrow Borah and Charles Gibson, who laid down the research questions and approaches of the field long before the advent of dependency theory. For examples of the annales approach, see Florescano 1971; Gibson 1964; Taylor 1972; Van Young 1981.

30. This is not to argue that all scholars who employed dependency theory did so uniformly. Indeed, the theory was so amorphous that many of its consumers invoked the theory in an implicit manner without even using the word *dependency*. There were also numerous variants of the model, some of which combined dependency with other intellectual traditions. The "Campinas School" of economic history, which became dominant in Brazil, for example, combined elements of dependency, Gerschenkron's notion of late industrialization, and orthodox Marxism. For an excellent discussion of the consumption of dependency ideas in Latin America and the United States, see Packenham 1992: chaps. 8 and 10. A complete bibliography would run to hundreds of titles. Some examples of book-length, historically focused works in the dependency tradition that might be of interest to readers of this essay would include the following: Abel and Lewis 1985; Batou 1990; Batou 1991; Becker 1983; Bendana 1988; Bergquist 1986; Bonilla 1974; Bonilla 1977; Burns 1970; Burns 1980; Cardoso and Faletto 1969; Cardoso de Mello 1982; Chilcote and Edelstein 1974; Cockcroft 1983; Cortés Conde and Hunt, 1985; Eakin 1989; Evans 1979; Frank 1967; Friedman 1984; Gentlemen 1984; Gootenberg 1989; Gootenberg 1993; Halperín Donghi 1969; Hamilton 1982; Hart 1987; Joseph 1982; Kofas 1986; LaFeber 1983; Langer 1989; Love and Jacobsen 1988; Monteón 1982; O'Brien 1982; Palacios 1983; Rock 1985; Ruiz 1988; Sanderson 1981; Spalding 1977; Stein and Stein 1970; Thorp and Bertram 1978; Weaver 1980; Wells 1985; White 1978; Zeitlan 1984.

31. For an excellent discussion of textbooks and dependency theory, see Eakin 1988.

32. The origins of this view can be traced to Baran and Sweezy's concept of monopoly capitalism: Baran and Sweezy 1966. For examples of its application, see Barnet and Müller 1974: chap. 7; Bennett and Sharpe 1985: 7, 75–76; Bergquist 1986: 88; Burns 1970: 362; Thorp and Bertram 1978: 12, 323. For an excellent critique of the view on theoretical grounds, see Weeks 1985: 24–27.

33. The lack of clear specification was noted even by scholars who were somewhat sympathetic to the intuitive appeal of dependency theory but who were concerned about the vague way that the theory was specified and its concepts operationalized. As Thorp and Bertram put it, "For all the intuitive appeal of the dependency analysis, it embodies several areas of difficulty and imprecision. . . . This imprecision stems from a further and fundamental weakness: the lack of a developed economic model underlying the notion of 'relatively greater autonomy.'" Thorp and Bertram 1978: 13–14.

34. These loose rules of evidence and argumentation were even noted by some dependency-influenced historians as cause for concern because they permitted the writing of a kind of positivistic, Whig history *al revés*. As Paul Gootenberg put it, "The old villains of history—the conservatives and erstwhile 'barbarians' who

obstructed liberal Progress, including free trade—have suddenly become its new heroes. . . . The dependency rehabilitation of such freakish characters as Dr. Francia of Paraguay—who are now held to offer nineteenth-century Latin America at its most vibrant and progressive path to development—should alert us that revisionism has gone astray." Gootenberg 1989: 10.

35. This is not to suggest that there were no debates within the dependency tradition, but it is to suggest that those debates tended to focus on conceptual approaches, not on issues of evidence, technique, and method. Thus, *dependentistas* debated whether the approach should be totalizing versus partial, dialectical versus nondialectical, historical versus ahistorical. They tended not, however, to debate more elementary, and ultimately more important, issues about what constitutes evidence and proof. For example, there were virtually no debates among *dependentistas* about how to determine whether movements in the terms of trade indicated a secular trend or a cyclical variation or even, at a more basic level, about how to properly estimate the terms of trade (the issue involves index number problems of a nontrivial nature). Similarly, there were no debates among *dependentistas* about the proper accounting methods to prove that FDI "decapitalized" an underdeveloped country. For that matter, *dependentistas* did not engage in discussion about how to estimate properly the magnitude of FDI or the proper methods to determine the returns on those investments. These are not simply "technical" issues. Methods influence results. Results drive interpretations.

36. Among the very best assessments of dependency theory in light of the empirical record written from the neoclassical perspective are Leff 1982a; Leff 1982b; Peláez 1976. Among the best assessments of the theory from an orthodox Marxist perspective is Weeks 1985.

37. See, for example, Eakin 1989: chap. 8.

38. On Brazil, see Leff 1982b: 74; Peláez 1976: 284–86. On Mexico, see Reynolds 1970: 43n–44n; Salvucci 1993; Beatty 1994. On Argentina, see Díaz Alejandro 1970: 3n, 85–89. The classic study on the terms of trade using European data is Kindleberger 1956. Also see Spraos 1983; Schneider 1981; Diakosavvas and Scandizzo 1991; Atallah 1958; and Díaz 1973.

39. Mexico began to make the move to high tariffs in the 1890's, Brazil by 1900, Argentina by 1905. During the Porfiriato, in fact, Mexico had tariff levels that were among the highest in the world. In addition to high tariffs, Latin American governments also directly subsidized their national industries. Examples of these subsidy programs in Mexico go back to the 1830's, with the establishment of the Banco de Avío, and extend through the Industrias Nuevas program of the Porfirio Díaz government. Similarly, the Brazilian government directly subsidized its nascent cotton textile industry during the 1890's through its Aid to Industry Bonds, which provided guaranteed loans to Brazilian manufacturers. On Mexican tariffs, see Haber 1989: 38. On Brazil, see Leff 1982a: 209–11; Topik 1987: 144–45; Stein 1957: chap. 7; Villanova Villela and Suzigan 1975: 109–15. For a sophisticated discussion of the countervailing effects of exchange rate fluctuations and changes in nominal tariff rates in Brazil, see Suzigan 1986: 38–45. On Argentina, see Díaz Alejandro 1970: chap. 5. On the Banco de Avío, see Potash 1983. On the Industrias Nuevas Program in Mexico, see Haber 1989: 38; 91–93. A forthcoming disserta-

tion by Edward Beatty examines the program in detail. For a discussion of similar programs in Colombia, see Safford 1988: 51–52. On the Aid to Industry program in Brazil, see Topik 1987: 135–38; Stein 1957: chap. 7; Suzigan 1986: 41.

40. As studies by William Summerhill and Noel Maurer make clear, the governments of Brazil and Mexico were so adept at regulating foreign-owned businesses that these investments did not return to their owners profits higher than those they could have earned in the London capital market. In the important transportation sector, for example, the Mexican and Brazilian governments set freight rates on the foreign-owned railroads. In the Brazilian case, the government actually created a rate structure that favored freight bound for the domestic market over freight bound for foreign markets, which meant that most of the gains from the railroads were captured by Brazilian agriculturalists and industrialists producing for the domestic market, not foreign railroad stockholders or the elites that dominated the export sector. See Summerhill, 1993; Maurer 1993. For an excellent case study of one of the largest British enterprises in Brazil, which highlights its inability to influence domestic politics, see Eakin 1989: chap. 8.

41. For an excellent discussion of the Mexican case, see Reynolds 1970: 167. On Brazil, see Fishlow 1972; Stein 1957. Much the same pattern holds for Latin America's industrial experience during World War I. See Dean 1969: chap. 6.

42. On Mexico, see Haber 1989; Cárdenas 1988. On Brazil, see Haber 1992.

43. Classic works would include Evans 1979; Cardoso and Faletto 1969.

44. Packenham 1992: 43.

45. The classic example of this type of work is Evans 1979. Evans himself noted the lack of "systematic, precise evidence that would constitute proof of the model," though he did not concede that such proof was impossible to obtain, given the way the theory was constructed. Evans 1979: 275.

46. Zeitlan 1984: 16–17. Also see Mallon 1988: 179; Gootenberg 1989: 10.

47. The sociological variant of this school of dependency sought to chronicle the resistance of traditional peoples to market relations. Its fundamental analytic framework typically ran in the following terms. Dependency theory is a useful body of thought, but it is limited in the sense that it does not address how export-led development transformed local economic and political systems not directly tied to the export economy. The result is that it does not address how subaltern classes resisted the arrival of "inorganic capitalism" and thereby limited the degree to which capitalist relations of production could become hegemonic. As Mallon put it, "Articulation [theory] could therefore provide a context in which it was possible to explain the penetration of capitalism, while at the same time understanding the multiple, long-lasting, and stubborn resistance of noncapitalist cultural, economic, political, and social forms of its dominance." Mallon 1983: 6. Also see Langer 1989.

48. The political variant of this school of dependency sought to understand the processes by which free-trade liberalism became hegemonic in nineteenth-century Latin America. It was fundamentally a minor revision of dependency theory that argued that the mechanisms by which countries became politically and ideologically subordinated were not automatic and inflexible. See, for example, Love and Jacobsen 1988; Gootenberg 1989; Gootenberg 1993.

49. One of the clearest articulations of this view can be found in the conclusion to Love and Jacobsen 1988. As the author of that essay put it, "The authors [of the essays in the volume] uniformly accept the broad contributions of dependency theory—whether the nineteenth century was a central period or the integration of countries into the newly capitalist international market the common parameter [sic] are no longer at issue. Instead, most essays are case studies of specific instances in which liberal policies and ideals were implemented in different Latin American countries." Mallon 1988: 179. Also see Gootenberg 1993: vii.

50. These are issues that have been addressed by historians of colonial Latin America operating in the annales-school tradition laid down by Borah and Gibson but have been largely ignored in the literature on the nineteenth and twentieth centuries. For examples of the colonial literature on property rights and agricultural techniques, see Brading 1978; Gibson 1964; Konrad 1980; Taylor 1972; Van Young 1981.

51. The Love and Jacobsen volume provides a good example of this emphasis on discourse and ideology. Of the seven contributors to the volume, only one, Steven Topik, attempts to link his discussion of political ideology and economic policy making to the performance of real economies. See Love and Jacobsen 1988. Also see Gootenberg 1989; Gootenberg 1993.

52. Summerhill, chap. 4, this volume.

53. Marichal, chap. 5, this volume.

54. Leff, chap. 2, this volume.

55. Salvucci, chap. 8, this volume.

56. Ibid.

57. Haber and Klein, chap. 9, this volume.

58. Ibid.

59. Leff, chap. 2, this volume.

References

Abel, Christopher, and Colin M. Lewis, eds. 1985. *Latin America, Economic Imperialism and the State: The Political Economy of the External Connection from Independence to the Present.* London.

Adelman, Jeremy. 1994. *Frontier Development: Land, Labour, and Capital on the Wheatlands of Argentina and Canada, 1890–1914.* Oxford.

Amin, Samir. 1976. *Unequal Development: An Essay on the Social Formation of Peripheral Capitalism.* New York.

Atack, Jeremy, and Peter Passell. 1994. *A New Economic View of American History from Colonial Times to 1940.* Second Edition. New York.

Atallah, M. K. 1958. *The Long-Term Movement of the Terms of Trade Between Agricultural and Industrial Products.* Rotterdam.

Baer, Werner. 1965. *Industrialization and Economic Development in Brazil.* Homewood, Ill.

———. 1969. *The Development of the Brazilian Steel Industry.* Nashville.

Baran, Paul, and Paul Sweezy. 1966. *Monopoly Capital.* New York.

Barnet, Richard J., and Ronald E. Müller. 1974. *Global Reach: The Power of the Multinational Corporations.* New York.

Batou, Jean. 1990. *One Hundred Years of Resistance to Underdevelopment: Latin American and Middle Eastern Industrialization and the European Challenge.*

———. 1991. *Between Developmental and Underdevelopment: The Precocious Attempts at Industrialization of the Periphery, 1800–1870.* Geneva.

Beatty, Edward. 1994. "Trends in U.S.–Mexican Trade, 1880–1923." Mimeo. Stanford.

Becker, David G. 1983. *The New Bourgeoisie and the Limits of Dependency: Mining, Class, and Power in "Revolutionary" Peru.* Princeton.

Bendana, Alejandro. 1988. *British Capital and Argentine Dependence, 1816–1914.* New York.

Bennett, Douglas C., and Kenneth E. Sharpe. 1985. *Transnational Corporations Versus the State: The Political Economy of the Mexican Automobile Industry.* Princeton.

Bergquist, Charles. 1986. *Labor in Latin America: Comparative Essays on Chile, Argentina, Venezuela, and Colombia.* Stanford.

Bonilla, Heraclio. 1974. *Guano y burguesía en el Perú.* Lima.

———. 1975. *Gran Bretaña y el Perú: 1826–1919.* Lima.

Brading, David A. 1978. *Haciendas and Ranchos in the Mexican Bajío: León, 1700–1860.* Cambridge, Eng.

Burns, E. Bradford. 1970. *A History of Brazil.* New York.

———. 1980. *The Poverty of Progress: Latin America in the Nineteenth Century.* Berkeley.

Cárdenas, Enrique. 1987. *La industrialización mexicana durante la gran depresión.* Mexico City.

Cardoso, Fernando Henrique, and Enzo Faletto. 1969. *Dependencia y desarrollo en América Latina: ensayo de interpretación sociológica.* Mexico City.

Cardoso de Mello, João Manuel. 1982. *O capitalismo tardio: uma contribuição ao revisão da formação e do descenvolvimento da economia brasileria.* São Paulo.

Chilcote, Ronald H., and Joel C. Edelstein, eds. 1974. *Latin America: The Struggle with Dependency and Beyond.* Cambridge, Mass.

Coatsworth, John H. 1978. "Obstacles to Economic Development in Nineteenth Century Mexico." *American Historical Review* 83, no. 1: 80–100.

———. 1981. *Growth Against Development: The Economic Impact of Railroads in Porfirian Mexico.* De Kalb, Ill.

Cockcroft, James. 1983. *Mexico: Class Formation, Capital Accumulation, and the State.* New York.

Contador, Cláudio, and Cláudio L. S. Haddad. 1975. "Produção real, moeda e preços: a experiência brasileira no periodo 1861–1970." *Revista brasileira de estatística* 36: 407–40.

Cortés Conde, Roberto, and Shane J. Hunt, eds. 1985. *The Latin American Economies: Growth and the Export Sector, 1880–1930.* New York.

David, Paul A. 1969. "Transport Innovation and Economic Growth: Professor Fogel on and off the Rails." *Economic History Review* 22: 506–25.

David, Paul A., et al. 1976. *Reckoning with Slavery: A Critical Study in the Quantitative History of American Negro Slavery.* New York.

Davis, Lance E. 1963. "Capital Immobilities and Finance Capitalism: A Study of Economic Evolution in the United States, 1820–1920." *Explorations in Economic History* 1: 88–105.

———. 1965. "The Investment Market, 1870–1914: The Evolution of a National Market." *The Journal of Economic History* 25: 355–99.

———. 1966. "Professor Fogel and the New Economic History." *The Economic History Review* 19(3): 657–63.

Davis, Lance E., and Douglass C. North. 1971. *Institutional Change and American Economic Growth.* Cambridge, Eng.

Dean, Warren, 1969. *The Industrialization of São Paulo, 1880–1945.* Austin, Tex.

Denslow, David A. 1974. "Sugar Production in Northeastern Brazil and Cuba, 1858–1908." Ph.D. diss., Yale University.

Diakosavvas, Dimitris, and Pasquale L. Scandizzo. 1991. "Trends in the Terms of Trade of Primary Commodities, 1900–1982: The Controversy and Its Origins." *Economic Development and Cultural Change* 39(2): 231–64.

Díaz, Ramon P. 1973. *The Long-Run Terms of Trade of Primary Producing Countries: A Study of Trend Forecasts and Their Policy Implications.* London.

Díaz Alejandro, Carlos F. 1970. *Essays on the Economic History of the Argentine Republic.* New Haven, Conn.

Eakin, Marshall C. 1988. "Surveying the Past: Latin American History Textbooks and Readers." *Latin American Research Review* 23, no. 3: 248–57.

———. 1989. *British Enterprise in Brazil: The St. John d'el Rey Mining Company and the Morro Velho Gold Mine, 1830–1960.* Durham, N.C.

Engerman, Stanley L., and Robert E. Gallman, eds. 1986. *Long Term Factors in American Economic Growth.* Chicago.

Evans, Peter. 1979. *Dependent Development: The Alliance of Multinational, State, and Local Capital in Brazil.* Princeton.

Ferrer, Aldo. 1963. *La economia Argentina: las etapas de su desarrollo y problemas actuales.* Mexico City.

———. 1967. *The Argentine Economy.* Berkeley.

Fishlow, Albert. 1966. *American Railroads and the Transformation of the Antebellum Economy.* Cambridge, Mass.

———. 1972. "Origins and Consequences of Import Substitution in Brazil." In Luis Eugenio Di Marco, ed. *International Economics and Development: Essays in Honor of Raul Prebisch.* New York.

Florescano, Enrique. 1971. *Origen y desarrollo de los problemas agrarios en México, 1500–1821.* Mexico City.

Fogel, Robert W. 1964. *Railroads and American Economic Growth: Essays in Econometric History.* Baltimore.

———. 1989. *Without Consent or Contract: The Rise and Fall of American Slavery.* New York.

Fogel, Robert W., and Stanley L. Engerman, eds. 1971. *The Reinterpretation of American Economic History.* New York.

————. 1974. *Time on the Cross: The Economics of American Negro Slavery.* Boston.

Frank, Andre Gunder. 1967. *Capitalism and Underdevelopment in Latin America: Historical Studies of Chile and Brazil.* New York.

————. 1972. *Lumpenbourgeoisie, Lumpendevelopment: Dependence, Class, and Politics in Latin America.* New York.

Friedman, Douglas. 1984. *The State and Underdevelopment in Spanish America: The Political Roots of Dependency in Peru and Argentina.* Boulder, Colo.

Furtado, Celso. 1968. *The Economic Growth of Brazil: A Survey from Colonial to Modern Times.* Berkeley.

————. 1970. *Economic Development of Latin America: Historical Background and Contemporary Problems.* Cambridge, Eng.

Gentlemen, Judith. 1984. *Mexican Oil and Dependent Development.* New York.

Gerschenkron, Alexander. 1962. *Economic Backwardness in Historical Perspective: A Book of Essays.* Cambridge, Mass.

Gibson, Charles. 1964. *The Aztecs Under Spanish Rule: A History of the Indians of the Valley of Mexico.* Stanford.

Glade, William. 1969. *The Latin American Economies: A Study of Their Institutional Evolution.* New York.

Goldin, Claudia, and Hugh Rockoff, eds. 1992. *Strategic Factors in Nineteenth Century American Economic History: A Volume to Honor Robert W. Fogel.* Chicago.

Gootenberg, Paul. 1989. *Between Silver and Guano: Commercial Policy and the State in Postindependence Peru.* Princeton.

————. 1993. *Imagining Development: Economic Ideas in Peru's "Fictitious Prosperity" of Guano, 1840–1880.* Berkeley.

Haber, Stephen H. 1989. *Industry and Underdevelopment: The Industrialization of Mexico, 1890–1940.* Stanford.

————. 1992. "Business Enterprise and the Great Depression in Brazil: A Study of Profits and Losses in Textile Manufacturing." *Business History Review* 66: 335–63.

Haddad, Cláudio L. S. 1978. *Crescimento do produto real no Brasil, 1900–1947.* Rio de Janeiro.

Halperín Donghi, Tulio. 1969. *Historia contemporánea de América Latina.* Madrid.

Hamilton, Nora. 1982. *The Limits of State Autonomy: Post-Revolutionary Mexico.* Princeton.

Hart, John M. 1987. *Revolutionary Mexico: The Coming and Process of the Mexican Revolution.* Berkeley.

Hirschman, Albert O. 1981. *Essays in Trespassing: Economics to Politics and Beyond.* Cambridge, Eng.

Holden, Robert H. 1994. *Mexico and the Survey of Public Lands: The Management of Modernization, 1876–1911.* De Kalb, Ill.

Joseph, Gilbert M. 1982. *Revolution from Without: Yucatán, Mexico, and the United States, 1880–1924.* Cambridge, Eng.

Kindleberger, Charles P. 1956. *The Terms of Trade: A European Case Study.* New York.

Klarén, Peter F. 1986. "Lost Promise: Explaining Latin American Underdevelopment." In Peter F. Klarén and Thomas J. Bossert, eds., *Promise of Development: Theories of Change in Latin America*, pp. 3–33. Boulder, Colo.

Kofas, Jon V. 1986. *Dependence and Underdevelopment in Colombia*. Tempe, Ariz.

Konrad, Herman W. 1980. *A Jesuit Hacienda in Colonial Mexico: Santa Lucía, 1576–1767*. Stanford.

Kuznets, Simon. 1953. *Economic Change: Selected Essays in Business Cycles, National Income, and Economic Growth*. New York.

———. 1966. *Modern Economic Growth: Rate, Structure, and Spread*. New Haven, Conn.

LaFeber, Walter. 1983. *Inevitable Revolutions: The United States in Central America*. New York.

Lal, Deepak. 1985. *The Poverty of "Development Economics."* Cambridge, Mass.

Lamoreaux, Naomi. 1986. "Banks, Kinship, and Economic Development: The New England Case." *The Journal of Economic History* 46, no. 2: 647–68.

———. 1994. *Insider Lending: Banks, Personal Connections, and Economic Development in Industrial New England*. New York.

Langer, Erik. 1989. *Economic Change and Rural Resistance in Southern Bolivia, 1880–1930*. Stanford.

Leff, Nathaniel H. 1968a. *The Brazilian Capital Goods Industry, 1929–1964*. Cambridge, Mass.

———. 1968b. *Economic Policy-Making and Development in Brazil, 1947–1964*. New York.

———. 1982a. *Underdevelopment and Development in Brazil*, Vol. 1, *Economic Structure and Change, 1822–1947*. London.

———. 1982b. *Underdevelopment and Development in Brazil*. Vol. 2, *Reassessing the Obstacles to Economic Development*. London.

Love, Joseph, and Nils Jacobsen, eds. 1988. *Guiding the Invisible Hand: Economic Liberalism and the State in Latin American History*. New York.

Maddison, Angus. 1989. *The World Economy in the 20th Century*. Paris.

Mallon, Florencia E. 1983. *The Defense of Community in Peru's Central Highlands: Peasant Struggle and Capitalist Transition, 1860–1940*. Princeton.

———. 1988. "Economic Liberalism: Where We Are and Where We Need to Go." In Joseph L. Love and Nils Jacobsen, eds., *Guiding the Visible Hand: Economic Liberalism and the State in Latin American History*, pp. 177–86. New York.

Mamalakis, Markos J. 1976. *The Growth and Structure of the Chilean Economy from Independence to Allende*. New Haven, Conn.

Mamalakis, Markos J., and Clark W. Reynolds. 1965. *Essays on the Chilean Economy*. Homewood, Ill.

Mandel, Ernest. 1975. *Late Capitalism*. London.

Maurer, Noel. 1993. "Profits and Power in the Porfiriato: The Rate of Return on Business Enterprise, 1900–1910." Mimeo. Stanford.

McGreevey, William P. 1971. *An Economic History of Colombia, 1845–1930*. Cambridge, Eng.

Monteón, Michael. 1982. *Chile in the Nitrate Era: The Evolution of Economic Dependence, 1880–1930*. Madison, Wisc.

North, Douglass C. 1990. *Institutions, Institutional Change, and Economic Performance*. Cambridge, Eng.

O'Brien, Thomas F. 1982. *The Nitrate Industry and Chile's Crucial Transition: 1870–1891*. New York.

Packenham, Robert A. 1992. *The Dependency Movement: Scholarship and Politics in Development Studies*. Cambridge, Mass.

Palacios, Marco. 1983. *El café en Colombia, 1850–1970: una historia económica, social y política*. Mexico City.

Peláez, Carlos Manuel. 1976. "The Theory and Reality of Imperialism in the Coffee Economy of Nineteenth Century Brazil." *Economic History Review* 39, no. 2: 276–90.

Peláez, Carlos Manuel, and Wilson Suzigan. 1976. *História monetária do Brasil: análise da política, comportamento e instituiçoes monetárias*. Brasília.

Potash, Robert A. 1983. *The Mexican Government and Industrial Development in the Early Republic: The Banco de Avío*. Amherst, Mass.

Reynolds, Clark W. 1970. *The Mexican Economy: Twentieth Century Structure and Growth*. New Haven, Conn.

Rock, David. 1985. *Argentina 1516–1982: From Spanish Colonization to the Falklands War*. Berkeley.

Ruiz, Ramón Eduardo. 1988. *The People of Sonora and Yankee Capitalists*. Tucson, Ariz.

Safford, Frank. 1988. "The Emergence of Economic Liberalism in Colombia." In Joseph L. Love and Nils Jacobsen, eds. *Guiding the Invisible Hand: Economic Liberalism and the State in Latin American History*, pp. 35–62. New York.

Salvucci, Richard. 1993. "The Mexican Terms of Trade, 1825–1883: Calculations and Consequences." Mimeo. Trinity University.

Sanderson, Steven E. 1981. *Agrarian Populism and the Mexican State: The Struggle for Land in Sonora*. Berkeley.

Schneider, Jurgen. 1981. "Terms of Trade Between France and Latin America, 1826–1856: Causes of Increasing Economic Disparities?" In Paul Bairoch and Maurice Lévy-Leboyer, eds., *Disparities in Economic Development Since the Industrial Revolution*. New York.

Spalding, Hobart A., Jr. 1977. *Organized Labor in Latin America: Historical Case Studies of Workers in Dependent Societies*. New York.

Spraos, John. 1983. *Inequalising Trade? A Study of Traditional North/South Specialization in the Context of Terms of Trade Concepts*. Oxford.

Stein, Stanley J. 1955. "Brazilian Cotton Textile Industry, 1850–1950." In Simon Kuznets, Wilbert E. Moore, and Joseph J. Spengler, eds., *Economic Growth: Brazil, India, Japan*. Durham, N.C.

———. 1957. *The Brazilian Cotton Manufacture: Textile Enterprise in an Underdeveloped Area*. Cambridge, Mass.

Stein, Stanley J., and Roberto Cortés Conde. 1977. "Editors' Introduction: The Economic Historiography of Latin America." In Roberto Cortés Conde and Stanley J. Stein, eds., *Latin America: A Guide to Economic History, 1830–1930*, pp. 3–28. Berkeley.

Stein, Stanley J., and Shane J. Hunt. 1971. "Principal Currents in the Economic Historiography of Latin America." *The Journal of Economic History* 31, no. 1: 222–53.

Stein, Stanley J., and Barbara H. Stein. 1970. *The Colonial Heritage of Latin America: Essays on Economic Dependence in Perspective.* New York.

Summerhill, William. 1993. "Profits and British-Owned Railways in Brazil, 1862– 1913." Paper presented at the Meeting of the American Historical Association, San Francisco, Jan. 6.

Sunkel, Osvaldo, and Pedro Paz. 1975. *El subdesarrollo latinoamericano y la teoría del desarrollo.* Mexico City.

Suzigan, Wilson. 1986. *Indústria brasileira: origem e desenvolvimento.* São Paulo.

Taylor, William B. 1972. *Landlord and Peasant in Colonial Oaxaca.* Stanford.

Thorp, Rosemary, and Geoffrey Bertram. 1978. *Peru 1890–1977: Growth and Policy in an Open Economy.* New York.

Topik, Steven. 1987. *The Political Economy of the Brazilian State, 1889–1930.* Austin, Tex.

United Nations, Economic Commission for Latin America. 1950. *The Economic Development of Latin America and Its Principal Problems.* New York.

Van Young, Eric. 1981. *Hacienda and Market in Eighteenth Century Mexico: The Rural Economy of the Guadalajara Region, 1675–1820.* Berkeley.

Versiani, Flavio Rabelo, and José Roberto Mendonça de Barros. 1977. *Formação econômica do Brasil: a experiência da industrialização.* São Paulo.

Villanova Villela, Annibal, and Wilson Suzigan. 1975. *Política do governo e crescimento da economia brasileira, 1889–1945.* Rio de Janeiro.

Walker, David W. 1986. *Kinship, Business, and Politics: The Martinez del Rio Family in Mexico, 1824–1867.* Austin, Tex.

Weaver, Frederick S. 1980. *Class, State, and Industrial Structure: The Historical Process of South American Industrial Growth.* Westport, Conn.

Weeks, John. 1985. *Limits to Capitalist Development: The Industrialization of Peru, 1950–1970.* Boulder, Colo.

Wells, Allen. 1985. *Yucatán's Gilded Age: Haciendas, Henequen, and International Harvester, 1860–1915.* Albuquerque.

White, Richard A. 1978. *Paraguay's Autonomous Revolution, 1810–1840.* Albuquerque.

Zeitlan, Maurice. 1984. *The Civil Wars in Chile (or the Bourgeois Revolutions that Never Were).* Princeton.

CHAPTER 2

Economic Development in Brazil, 1822-1913

NATHANIEL H. LEFF

This chapter focuses on two features of Brazil's economic history: the virtual stagnation of real per capita income in the country as a whole from independence in 1822 through most of the nineteenth century; and the shift, circa 1900, to several decades of sustained, rapid economic development.[1] Few observers would expect a simple explanation for such large economic phenomena. In fact, the story is complex and involves many causes.

An Aggregate View and the Special Experience of the Northeast

In the United States, real per capita income grew at a long-term rate of approximately 1.5 percent per year in the nineteenth century. Long-term growth at that annual rate for a period of 91 years (the time interval between 1822 and 1913) implies a cumulative increase of per capita income from an initial level of 100 to an index of 388 at the end of the period. By contrast, the data available for Brazil suggest a very different economic experience in the nineteenth century. Although real output was able to keep pace with Brazil's rapid population growth (1.8 percent per year), real per capita income seems to have grown very little between 1822 and 1913.[2] Further, most of the per capita income growth that took place in Brazil between 1822 and 1913 seems to have occurred in the period 1900–13. Those years were indeed a period of rapid economic progress. By the same token, the years 1822–99 seem to have been a long period of disappointing economic achievement in Brazil.

Disaggregation of these figures in terms of geographic regions is also helpful in understanding Brazil's economic experience during the nineteenth century. The country's overall performance masks a significant differential in the pace of development between regions. In part, the poor aggregate experience of the Brazilian economy during the nineteenth century reflects the especially dismal performance of the country's large northeast region, where almost half of Brazil's population resided.[3] A rough estimate suggests that real per capita income in the northeast *fell*, by approximately 30 percent between 1822 and 1913. Our first task, then, is to try to understand why the large northeast region did so poorly. We then proceed to a more general analysis, encompassing the rest of the country as well.

Exports were the main source of productivity growth in nineteenth-century Brazil. International trade was important both for permitting higher income from available resources and for stimulating capital formation, including public-sector and foreign investment, in economic infrastructure. The northeast's negative economic experience during the nineteenth century stemmed largely from the poor export performance of the two products in which the region had an international comparative advantage: sugar and cotton. In 1822, sugar and cotton accounted for 49 percent of Brazil's aggregate export revenues, while coffee (produced in the southeast) accounted for 19 percent. In the course of the nineteenth century, Brazil's export receipts from sugar and cotton showed little long-term growth and actually declined in terms of receipts per capita. In 1913, sugar and cotton provided only 3 percent of Brazil's total export revenues. By contrast, real income from coffee exports increased at a long-term annual rate of approximately 5 percent. By 1913, coffee accounted for 60 percent of Brazil's aggregate export revenues.

The decline of the northeast's sugar and cotton exports reflected the fact that nineteenth-century Brazil had a stronger comparative advantage in coffee than in sugar or cotton. That is, a unit of foreign exchange could be earned with fewer domestic resources in coffee than in sugar or cotton. Because the domestic-resource cost of foreign exchange was much lower in coffee than in sugar or cotton, the northeast experienced a nasty case of the "Dutch disease." As the foreign currency provided by coffee exports grew as a source of supply in Brazil's foreign-exchange market, the country's overall exchange rate increasingly reflected the importance of coffee and its pressures for real-currency appreciation. Revenues of the producers of Brazil's various export commodities and the volume of output that they supplied varied in function of changes in the mil-réis (the Brazilian currency) price that producers received. Mil-réis prices for individual commodities, in turn, varied both with changes in the specific commodity's international price and with changes in Brazil's overall exchange rate. In fact, much of the variance in the mil-réis prices for Brazilian cotton and sugar resulted from changes in the mil-réis sterling exchange rate. Therefore, the coffee-dominated exchange rate squeezed factor returns and priced ever-larger quantities of the northeast's sugar and cotton out of the world market.

In introductory economics textbooks, when a new export activity emerges with a stronger comparative advantage than that of the country's traditional export activity, factors are reallocated to earn the higher returns available in the new activity, and income rises. By contrast, in the Brazilian historical context, the northeast's adjustment was constrained by some rigidities imposed by geography. The northeast's specific types of land (and climate) were not well-suited to coffee production and were therefore not reallocated to coffee. Consequently, transfer of other productive factors from sugar and cotton to coffee required interregional migration. The large distances between Brazil's regions, however, meant high transportation costs, such that migration involved an investment. Brazil's slave market financed the transfer of slaves, and most of the northeast's stock of slaves was indeed bid away to the southeast. But much of the northeast's labor force was free, and large-scale transfer of free labor was precluded by the absence of a capital-market institution to finance free workers' investment in interregional migration.

Economic theory points to a key condition that must be satisfied if the integration of multiple geographical regions in a single political unit is to constitute an economically optimal currency area. That condition is intersectoral factor mobility.[4] As we have seen, nineteenth-century Brazil did not satisfy that condition. Under these circumstances, one may wonder whether the northeast might not have been better off economically as a separate political entity, with its own exchange rate. The northeast's trade and development would then have been governed by its own (rather than by Brazilian) comparative advantage. In fact, the northeast's political elite did attempt to secede from Brazil during the nineteenth century, but maintenance of the country's territorial integrity was a key priority for Brazil's political leadership, which used military force to repress secession. The northeast therefore remained within Brazil, and the region's monetary and trade conditions were greatly aggravated by its being part of a political entity that did not meet the conditions for an optimum currency area. The northeast's dismal economic experience was an important part of Brazil's overall poor record in the nineteenth century.

The Elastic Supply of Labor

In the southeast, coffee exports grew rapidly, with major linkage effects on the regional economy. But long-term increase in real wages, and hence in income for much of the population, was constrained by two labor-market institutions that provided an elastic supply of labor to Brazil's "advanced" sector throughout the nineteenth century.[5] Accordingly, output and the demand for workers in the Southeast coffee region could increase rapidly without generating an increase in real wages.

First, importation of slaves from Africa enabled Brazil's plantation owners to satisfy their growing demand for labor with relatively little utilization of workers from the country's domestic agricultural sector. Consequently, the export activities could expand their output substantially without bidding up wages within the Brazilian economy. In the first half of the nineteenth century, the British government attempted to stop the importation of slaves from Africa. The economic advantages that importation afforded Brazil's planter class were so great that the Brazilian state resisted British interventionism for half a century. Between 1800 and 1852 (when the British navy finally forced suspension of slave imports), approximately 1.3 million slaves were imported to Brazil. This amounted to more than one-fifth of the growth of the country's total population and an ever larger share of the increase in the Southeast's labor force.

The increase in the supply of slave labor to the coffee sector seems to have been sufficiently great that the real cost of labor did not rise over the century. Pedro Carvalho de Mello has collected data on nominal slave purchase prices and rental rates between 1835 and 1888 (the year of abolition) in Rio de Janeiro.[6] Regression equations estimated with Mello's undeflated data show an annual trend rate of increase of 2 percent for the slave-purchase time series and an annual rate of increase of 1.8 percent for the slave-rental series between 1835 and 1888. Deflated with observations for the price of coffee, Mello's time series can be regressed against a time trend to ascertain the rate of change of real labor costs in nineteenth-century Brazil's "advanced" sector. Over the years 1835–88, the regressions show an annual trend rate of change of −0.1 percent (with a *t*-ratio of 0.39) for the deflated purchase-price series, and an annual trend rate of change of −0.3 percent (with a *t*-ratio of 1.43) for the deflated rental-rate series.

These regressions, in which coffee prices are used as the deflator, indicate that real labor costs for Brazil's coffee producers did not increase in the half century between 1835 and 1888. We lack an annual index of consumer prices that could be used to deflate the nominal slave price and rental series in order to assess rigorously the time trend in real consumption wages for coffee workers. As discussed elsewhere, however, data on the medium-term rate of increase of consumer prices in Rio de Janeiro suggest that consumer prices rose at least as rapidly as the current-price series for coffee labor.[7] Thus despite the great growth of coffee production and the rapid expansion of the southeast's economy, the supply of labor apparently kept pace with the demand for labor, obviating upward pressure on labor costs or worker incomes.

The second labor-market institution involved immigration. As noted, in 1852 the British government stopped Brazil's importation of slaves from Africa. Following a long-term interaction between domestic economics and politics, slavery was abolished within Brazil in 1888. From the viewpoint of maximizing coffee-planter returns, the mounting pressures for abolition posed a potential problem. Unless accompanied by other changes in the labor market, abolition would bring a sharp rise in labor costs. Accordingly, some of the coffee sector's political leadership sought a monopsonistic, class solution to protect planter interests. Their approach to the impending problem was, in effect, to shift downward the supply schedule of labor in anticipation of the planters' growing demand for workers. To achieve this objective, they developed a new labor-market institution that would maintain an elastic supply of low-cost labor from overseas.

To endogenize the supply of labor, the coffee planters pressed Brazil's central government and the government of São Paulo province to pay the transportation costs of immigrants from southern Europe. Such subsidies had two important consequences for potential European immigrants. First, without raising Brazilian wages, transportation subsidies increased the net private returns from immigrating to Brazil. In addition, the subsidies overcame the capital-market imperfection that might otherwise have prevented destitute Europeans from immigrating at all. By paying transportation costs, Brazil could attract immigrants who, if they could have financed their own immigration, might have gone to the United States or to Argentina, where wages were higher.

The Brazilian policy intervention to attract European immigration achieved its objective. Immigration, mostly from Southern Europe, accelerated sharply. The increase was most dramatic in the case of the province where coffee production was expanding most rapidly, São Paulo. Between 1880 and 1885, an average of 4,300 immigrants entered São Paulo annually. In 1886, the figure was 9,500, and in 1887, the year before abolition, the figure was 33,000. Overall, between 1885 and 1909 some 2.8 million European immigrants entered Brazil. Almost all of these people went to the southeast. Between 1890 and 1913, the stock of coffee trees in São Paulo province (a proxy for the demand for labor) increased at a rate of approximately 6.5 percent per year. In addition, the demand for workers also rose in manufacturing as well as in other activities in the booming southeast. Despite these pressures on the demand side of the labor market, however, real wages apparently did not increase.[8]

One may wonder why the supply of labor to the advanced sector in the southeast came from overseas rather than from within Brazil. In principle, workers from within Brazil might have come either from the domestic agricultural sector (see below) in the southeast or from the declining northeast. The inability to attract many workers from the domestic agricultural sector in the southeast is not surprising. Incomes earned in that sector made for an opportunity cost that was apparently well above the labor costs offered by subsidized immigration.

The failure to draw on labor supply from the northeast is more puzzling. It seems unlikely that transportation costs for would-be immigrants from the northeast to the southeast exceeded the cost of transporting workers from Southern Europe to Brazil. Another possibility is that supply constraints (perhaps reflecting sociocultural rigidities or political restrictions) limited labor mobility in the northeast. In fact, supply constraints do not seem to have been a problem. There is evidence of considerable labor mobility in the northeast.[9] And as regards extraregional labor mobility, between 1872 and 1910 hundreds of thousands of northeasterners emigrated to the booming Amazon region. Migration to the southeast, however, involved greater distances, higher costs, and a larger investment. As noted earlier, the absence of a capital-market institution to finance those investments seems to have been important in limiting migration from the northeast to the southeast during the nineteenth century. Hence, our question reduces to, Why were the coffee planters in the southeast more willing to finance immigration from Europe than from the northeast? Part of the answer may have been then-prevalent racial attitudes on the part of the coffee planters, which led them to prefer European to mulatto workers.[10]

The consequences of large-scale subsidized immigration from overseas are clear. The program continued through the beginning of the twentieth century the economic structure that importation of slaves from Africa had provided earlier. The highly elastic supply of labor from overseas meant that output could expand at a rapid pace in Brazil's advanced sector without raising the wages of workers in the rest of the economy. The similarities between Brazil's historical experience in the nineteenth century and W. A.

Lewis's celebrated model, "Economic Development with Unlimited Supplies of Labour," are evident.[11] There were, however, two important differences between Brazil's historical experience and the Lewis model. In the Brazilian case, the elastic supply of labor came from overseas. Also, in Brazil the elastic supply of labor continued "forever"—with ensuing long-term consequences for capital-labor ratios, wages, and technical progress. Continuing importation of labor from abroad enabled Brazil's planters to maintain their returns but had adverse effects on the rest of the population. This experience suggests that conclusions concerning the welfare effects of population growth in nineteenth-century Brazil may be a function of the observer's class perspective. Explicitly or implicitly, historians often discuss welfare effects over time, and their unit of study is usually "the nation." In the Brazilian case, class interests were so obviously disparate that it raises questions concerning the validity of using the nation as the unit of analysis.

The Domestic Agricultural Sector

Like most studies of Brazil's economic history before the twentieth century, we have focused thus far on conditions in the country's export activities. The greater availability of data for those activities should not lead us to exaggerate their quantitative importance. In fact, most of Brazil's labor force was engaged in the domestic agricultural sector: the production of food for local consumption and the internal market.[12] Brazil's domestic agricultural sector in the nineteenth century has been little studied. In the words of two scholars, the sector usually appears only "between the lines" of the country's historiography.[13] Consequently, detailed information on this sector is scanty. Nevertheless, the domestic agricultural sector was too important a feature of Brazil's economy during the nineteenth century to be ignored. As a first approximation, the following statements can be advanced concerning the sector's size and composition.

Socially, this sector comprised many of the people in Brazil's population who, in the words of one historian, "were not slaves, but could not afford to be masters."[14] This observation suggests one way of forming an impression of the quantitative importance of the domestic agricultural sector in the Brazilian economy: an examination of the proportions of free people and of slaves in Brazil's total population. This procedure obviously provides only a very approximate picture. All of Brazil's slaves were not engaged in exports or in urban-based activities; many free people did work in those activities and in roles other than plantation owners. Bearing this caveat in mind, let us see what analysis of the population in terms of its slave and free portions suggests.

Brazil's social structure has often been conceptualized in terms of a master/slave dichotomy. That approach ignores the presence of a very large intermediate stratum of squatters, sharecroppers, and small farmers. At the very beginning of the nineteenth century, at least one-half and perhaps as much as two-thirds of Brazil's population was free.[15] Relatively few of these people—poor whites, mulattoes, freedmen, and *caboclos* (peasants of mixed Indian and white ancestry)—were large slaveowners engaged in production for the export market. Lacking alternative opportunities in a predominantly agrarian economy, many people in this intermediate social stratum were engaged in production of food for domestic consumption.

In 1820, some 70 percent of Brazil's population was free.[16] Until 1852 (when importation of slaves from Africa was stopped), only a small percentage of these people was employed in export activities, which relied heavily on slaves for most occupations. With the decline of slavery, free people were increasingly employed in export activities, but by that time the free population had grown rapidly as a result of high rates of natural increase.[17] Consequently, the number of people in the domestic agricultural sector remained large relative the country's total labor force.

The impression that much of Brazil's labor force was not engaged in export production is corroborated if we consider disaggregated population surveys for specific locales during the nineteenth century.[18] Further, the limited information available on the sectoral composition of Brazilian output also suggests that a large fraction of the labor force was engaged in the domestic agricultural sector. In 1911–13, exports accounted for approximately 16 percent of gross domestic product (GDP) in Brazil. During the nineteenth century, exports had grown at a higher rate than output in the rest of the economy. Consequently, earlier in the century, the share of exports in aggregate economic activity had been even lower than 16 percent. Further, labor productivity was generally higher in exports than in other activities of the Brazilian economy. Hence, the export sector's share in the total labor force was even smaller than its share in GDP. There were of course other activities in this economy besides exports and the domestic agricultural sector. In absolute terms, many people were employed in transportation, commerce, crafts, manufacturing, and government. Those activities were located to a great extent in the cities, however, and as late as 1890 only 11 percent of Brazil's population resided in urban centers of 10,000 or more inhabitants. These considerations suggest that a large fraction of Brazil's labor force was engaged in the domestic agricultural sector during the nineteenth century.

This sector seems to have consisted of two parts. First, there were people who lived as sharecroppers, smallholders, or squatters in or near the areas of export production. Because of factor-market imperfections, these people rarely engaged in production of the principal export crops. Their main products were such foodstuffs as manioc, beans, and maize. In addition, the observations of contemporaries suggest that these people took much of their total income in the form of leisure. Second, part of the labor force in the domestic agricultural sector was engaged in farming on the abundant lands in Brazil's interior, relatively far from the areas of export production. Output consisted mainly of cattle ranching and of semisubsistence agricultural cultivation. In the latter case, production was mainly in the form of small-scale family farming under the overlordship of a large local landowner. With labor scarce relative to land, cultivation was land-extensive. Population in this sector was increasing rapidly, while abundant lands existed further in the interior. Consequently, the production frontier shifted ever farther from the markets and centers of consumption. As marginal physical productivity fell with soil depletion on the intensive margin, incremental production shifted, with rising transport costs, to the extensive margin. Until the end of the nineteenth century, it is hard to believe that the value of output per worker in the domestic agricultural sector was more than, at best, constant over time.

Transportation Costs and the Slow Pace of Economic Development

Because a large portion of Brazil's labor force was employed in the domestic agricultural sector, the modest rate of per capita output growth in that sector weighed heavily on the pace of aggregate development. We noted earlier that exports were the main avenue to economic development in nineteenth-century Brazil. The central importance of the export activities reflects a default, the poor performance of the rest of the economy.

High transportation costs affected both the level and the growth of productivity in Brazil's domestic agricultural sector, limiting the access of many agricultural producers to markets beyond their immediate locale. As a result, the volume of intraregional, interregional, and international trade was curtailed. Because of the high ratio of land to labor, cultivation was land-extensive, and distances to the markets were large. Low-cost transportation facilities were therefore crucial for developing a high-productivity agriculture. Unfortunately, the country's geographical and topographical conditions made for relatively high transport costs from the production areas to the market centers.

Rivers and coastal shipping were used for transportation, but some of the country's rivers (the Amazon, for example) were poorly located from the viewpoint of promoting economic development. Other rivers flowed in a direction that was not advantageous from the perspective of production for markets. Geographical conditions also imposed another problem that hampered low-cost shipments of bulky commodities from deep in the interior. Unlike the United States with its Mississippi and Great Lake systems, Brazil did not have an extensive *network* of navigable, interconnecting waterways. Further, road conditions were also poor, to the extent that at the beginning of the period wheeled vehicles could seldom be used in the interior. Transport costs were so high that they absorbed a third of the value of coffee shipments during the prerailroad era. Similar conditions prevailed in the northeast. Thus the cost of shipping cotton from the São Francisco Valley to Bahia in the 1850's amounted to some 50 percent of the prices received. Under these conditions of high-cost transportation and poor access to markets, abundant land was not associated with a high value of output per worker in agriculture.

The combination of high transportation costs and a large domestic agricultural sector also had other consequences for the Brazilian economy. Because of Brazil's poor internal transportation facilities, food produced on more distant land involved higher supply prices. Inelasticity in the supply of foodstuffs meant that when income and demand in the economy's advanced sector increased, prices rose. Unlike many other countries, Brazil experienced a long-term inflation during the nineteenth century. Price inflation was a feature of the Brazilian economy that had its own welfare costs, both direct (higher uncertainty) and indirect (presumably, lower cash balances and lower investment). In addition, conditions in the domestic agricultural sector constrained Brazil's industrial development. Low income levels and high costs for transporting goods to the hinterland limited the size of the market for manufactured goods in Brazil. The Brazilian government imposed protective tariffs on many industrial products during the nineteenth century, but protection against imports could not assure would-be Brazilian industrialists access to a market that did not yet exist. Industrialization based on the internal market clearly required the prior emergence of a domestic market.

More generally, high transport costs diminished the net receipts that producers obtained from shipment of bulky, low-value foodstuffs to the market. As a result, income in the domestic agricultural sector was reduced—both because of the low value received for output and because of the disincentive effect that unfavorable relative prices had on the quantities produced. Low prices in the domestic agricultural sector were reflected in a small marginal value product for labor and, as a consequence, in widespread substitution of leisure for monetary income. Finally, high transport costs for foodstuffs also had an important intersectoral effect. The country's steep price-distance gradients in regional markets meant rising incremental costs for food, the economy's wage good, in the face of buoyant demand conditions. Expanding aggregate demand therefore reduced the returns to capital and the rate of expansion in the advanced sector, with little impact on higher real output levels in the economy's backward sector.

Efforts at modifying geographical conditions and lowering costs by construction of transportation infrastructure were slow to materialize in nineteenth-century Brazil. In contrast with the United States, there was virtually no canal construction. The country's rivers also remained largely without improvements.[19] Consequently, the boats used for internal transportation were small and entailed high unit costs. The country's first railroad legislation was promulgated in 1835, but actual railway construction was late in coming to Brazil. The country's earliest railway, extending some 15 kilometers, was built in 1854. Ten years later, approximately 424 kilometers of track were in operation. As late as 1890, however, the country had only 9,973 kilometers of operating trackage. This did not amount to much in terms of Brazil's overall expanse of some 8.1 million square kilometers.[20] Furthermore, the country's road network was extremely limited. As late as 1923, São Paulo state, one of the largest and most developed in the country, had only 1,025 kilometers of highways (of which 55 kilometers were macadamized) suitable for automobile use.

Railroads might have helped this situation by lowering transportation costs. This would have provided a necessary condition for linking part of the domestic agricultural sector with the rest of the economy and permitting it to shift from subsistence to market-oriented production (for the domestic market or for exports), whether in the family farms or in large-scale agriculture. Lower transportation costs would also have provided producers with the stimulus of market demand and might thereby have induced higher output levels. On the supply side, producers would have been able to reap the gains from specialization and local comparative advantage. Hence even with unchanged physical productivity, lower transport costs

TABLE 2.1
Length of Railway Track in Brazil, 1854–1914

Year	Kilometers	Year	Kilometers
1854	14	1894	11,260
1864	470	1900	15,320
1874	1,280	1904	16,320
1876	2,080	1914	26,060
1884	6,240		

SOURCE: IBGE 1939:218.

might have raised the value of production in the domestic agricultural sector, both by increasing the quantities produced and, with new relative prices, by altering the composition of output.[21]

Notwithstanding these potential benefits, nineteenth-century Brazil was late in initiating large-scale railroad construction. Table 2.1 presents data on the late start and the slow pace of railroad construction. Thus despite Brazil's vast territorial expanse, as late as 1884 the country had only 6,240 kilometers of track. This amounted to approximately 0.7 kilometers of track per 1,000 square kilometers of territory. Further, in terms of timing, the great increase in railway construction toward the interior began only in the 1890's. Indeed, the largest absolute rise in railway track occurred only in the twenty years before 1914. To gain some comparative perspective, note that in 1900, railway trackage in the United States was almost 20 times as great as in Brazil. Even after the large post-1900 increase in Brazil's railway construction, in 1914 the country had only 26,060 kilometers of track. This was a figure that the United States had surpassed by the 1850's.

Why were the railways built so late in Brazil? The difficult terrain often led to high construction costs, but these would have been no obstacle if the railroads had also generated substantial benefits. Capital immobilies were also a problem. Although some of the first railroads in the coffee region were built with local capital participation, construction of Brazil's railways in general depended heavily on foreign investment. In the nineteenth century, this was largely British, and British investment was directed away from Brazil by such non-market considerations as imperial policy. In addition, private rates of return on Brazilian railway investments were apparently not high enough to attract substantial British capital from its alternative opportunities during most of the nineteenth century.

Brazil's limited attractiveness to foreign investors, however, is not a sufficient explanation of the long delay before large-scale railway construction began. If private returns were low but investment in low-cost transportation facilities were justified in terms of external economies and high social returns, another approach might have been followed. In principle, the task of providing Brazil with an adequate transportation system might have been undertaken by government—central, provincial, or local. That was the course followed with many of the "public improvements" that were supplied in the nineteenth-century United States. In fact, Brazil did not follow that approach until the end of the period. For reasons discussed below, during most of the century Brazilian governments failed to provide on a sufficient scale the infrastructure investment needed for the country's economic development.

Railroads and the Acceleration of Economic Development

Once the railways were extended, economic development seems to have proceeded along the lines outlined above. Even with unchanged output levels, the higher ex-farm prices made possible by low-cost transportation would have raised producer incomes.[22] In addition, producers in the domestic agricultural sector responded to the new market opportunities opened by lower transport costs. Producers increased the volume of their output for the market, while the fall in transportation costs also led to new patterns of intraregional specialization. Another feature was a rise in the price elasticity of the food supply.[23]

Some numerical information on these developments is available for Minas Gerais. This large state had approximately 21 percent of Brazil's population in 1900. Despite its geographical proximity to São Paulo and that province's large regional market, Minas Gerais was not economically well-developed. In the 1890's, however, the province "caught railroad fever": half of Minas Gerais's pre-1899 trackage was laid in that decade.[24] Table 2.2 presents data on the subsequent increase in food shipments from Minas Gerais. As the high growth rates for the decade 1900–10 indicate, a domestic market existed for the products of the domestic agricultural sector, and supply responded effectively once low-cost transportation was made available. Import substitution in food was an important part of this development pattern.[25]

The process through which railroads promoted economic growth in the domestic agricultural sector had some special features. The railways helped domestic agricultural producers not only by reaching the distant interior, but also by existing in the zones of export production. Part of the country's food supply was produced in and around the plantation areas.

TABLE 2.2

*Growth of Food Shipments
from Minas Gerais, 1900–10*

Product	Annual geometric growth rate (%)
Corn	10.5
Beans	17.4
Rice	40.0
Livestock [a]	10.4

SOURCE: Computed from data presented in Wirth 1977: 44, 46.
[a] 1895–1905

Food producers in those areas benefited directly from the new availability of low-cost transportation to the regional market. In addition, the lines opened in the export zones lowered the cost of shipments that originated in the far interior and proceeded, via the railroad, to the markets. Under these conditions, even railways that had been built primarily to carry export commodities came to transport large volumes of products from the domestic agricultural sector.

Table 2.3 presents data on this phenomenon in the province of São Paulo. The data relate to three major railroads that were built mainly to transport coffee. As the table indicates, even on those railways, products other than coffee came to account for a sizable share of total shipments.

TABLE 2.3

*Total Freight and Non-Coffee Freight
on Three of Brazil's "Coffee" Railways, 1876–1915*

(annual averages)

	Paulista Railway		Mogiana Railway		Sorocabana Railway	
Period	Share of non-coffee shipments (%)	All freight shipped (tons)	Share of non-coffee shipments (%)	All freight shipped (tons)	Share of non-coffee shipments (%)	All freight shipped (tons)
1876–80	n.a.	n.a.	50	29,200	98	16,200
1881–85	37	132,000	36	57,300	n.a.	n.a.
1886–90	50	209,400	57	111,100	85	61,100
1891–95	63	520,100	63	215,900	85	139,700
1896–1900	57	728,400	58	395,700	82	248,100
1901–05	48	785,600	51	531,300	73	269,500
1906–10	48	1,018,800	56	720,600	76	412,600
1911–15	63	1,356,000	70	1,097,300	86	588,000

SOURCE: Computed from data in Saes 1976: 79.
NOTE: n.a. indicates data are not available.

Much of the tonnage consisted of foodstuffs and industrial raw materials transported from the hinterland to the expanding regional market.

Table 2.3 shows that, on the Sorocabana Railway, the proportion of goods other than coffee was very high at the outset. On the other two railways, the share of noncoffee products rose steadily to dominate total shipments. Overall, the volume of domestic agricultural products shipped on these lines increased at a pace similar to that of coffee shipments—and this in the heyday of the São Paulo coffee boom! Between 1886–90 and 1911–15, the amount of noncoffee products in Table 2.3 rose at an annual geometric rate of 9.5 percent. This compares with a long-term growth at an annual rate of 7.2 percent for coffee shipments on these lines.

The growth in shipments of domestic agricultural products was facilitated by the Brazilian government's tariff and rate-setting policies.[26] Brazil experienced considerable price inflation in the decades before 1913. As a consequence both of normal regulatory lag and of hostility to the foreign railway companies, however, the government's rate-setting authorities resisted efforts to raise transportation charges to keep pace with the country's inflation. Thus, not only did shipping costs fall when the railways were opened but, in addition, the price of railway transportation declined thereafter relative to the general price level. This rate-setting policy led to government subsidies for the railways and, eventually, to nationalization. What is important in the present context is that government regulation further lowered real freight charges for producers in the domestic agricultural sector.

The structure of railway rates also discriminated in favor of the domestic agricultural sector. Between 1874 and 1900, the rates charged for shipments of foodstuffs on the railways listed in Table 2.3 ranged between 26 and 49 percent of the rates charged for coffee. For livestock and timber the rates were even lower. Moreover, in 1899 the government implemented a general policy that obliged the railway companies to lower their charges on domestically produced foodstuffs. As a consequence, the domestic agricultural sector drew special and disproportionate advantage from the fall in transport costs that the railroads made possible. For this reason, it is difficult to make meaningful comparisons with shipping costs in the prerailroad era, which might serve as a basis for comparative welfare analysis. In the earlier period, freight charges for the domestic agricultural sector's high-weight/low-value commodities had often been so high in many areas that these products had not been shipped at all.

The government's policy with respect to import duties also promoted economic growth in the domestic agricultural sector. At the turn of the century, the government imposed protective tariffs on many foodstuffs produced in Brazil.[27] The fact that politicians from Minas Gerais took a prominent role in this policy initiative suggests that the new measures should not be viewed as determined randomly or by a process that was completely exogenous. The advent of low-cost transportation had greatly increased the potential economic returns that protective tariffs offered to domestic food producers. Political returns rose correspondingly for the political entrepreneurs who would implement the necessary policy measures. From this perspective, provision of the import tariffs can be regarded almost as endogenous to the process.

The economic consequences of the new import duties were clear-cut: reduced uncertainty and a larger market for the domestic agricultural sector. Moreover, the fact that part of the sector's market growth came at the expense of imports helped avoid a potential pitfall. That would have been a situation in which large increases in domestic food supply pressed on stationary, price-inelastic demand and thus reduced aggregate revenues for producers. The policy initiative also had broader economic effects. As noted, the new tariffs were implemented in conjunction with the heightened domestic supply response that low-cost transportation made possible. Under those conditions, the import tariffs led to import substitution in many food products and intensified intersectoral linkages within the Brazilian economy.

The northeast also benefited to some extent from a decline in transport costs. In areas where railways were built, internal freight charges for sugar and cotton appear to have fallen some 50 percent from their level in the prerailroad era. Railways could promote economic development only when they were built, however, and because of the poor economic prospects of the northeast's export activities, little railway construction took place in the region. In the southeast, however, extension of the railways seems to have opened a new period of generalized economic development.

Prior to the extension of the railways, a rising value of output per capita in Brazil had been limited mainly to the export sector. By lowering transport costs in a vast, land-rich country, railways permitted more rapid growth of income in the large domestic agriculture sector. The downward shift in internal freight charges also led to other structural shifts and new intersectoral linkages within the Brazilian economy. Thus the internal market for manufactured products also expanded. Supported by ample tariff protection, Brazil's cotton textile industry increased its output at an annual geometric rate of 11 percent between 1885 and 1915.[28] As noted earlier, Brazil's economic development proceeded much more rapidly after 1900 than in the preceding century. For the reasons discussed, the extension of the railways seems to have played a key role in the shift to the new development trajectory. This experience is also consistent with interpreting Brazil's slow economic development during the earlier period as stemming largely from an absence of the external economies that railways would have provided. Because of the country's factor endowment and geographical features, the availability of low-cost transportation was of special importance for economic development in nineteenth-century Brazil.

The Brazilian State and the Public-Finance Constraint on Public Investment

The preceding discussion raises an obvious question. We can well understand the failure of private entrepreneurs to invest in railways in the Brazilian interior. Much of the economic benefits of that investment came in the form of external economies, such that the railroads' social returns exceeded their private returns. But why did the Brazilian state not provide the resources—either through direct investment or through subsidies—to equip the country with railways earlier, so that Brazil could have been launched on its path of long-term economic development much sooner in the nineteenth century?

One possibility is that the vision of implementing a rational public-investment policy was distorted by the lens of Brazilian politics. The large landowners had considerable influence in Brazilian politics during the nineteenth century, and they are generally not considered to have been a very "progressive" or "development-oriented" group. In fact, what was needed in this context was not an interest in development but an interest in wealth maximization. Brazil's landowners displayed ample evidence of such an interest.[29] Thus, responding to the prospect of favorable returns, Brazilian planters allocated sufficient resources—even to products with a long gestation period, for example, cocoa in Bahia and coffee in São Paulo—to make possible sharp increases in output. Further, far from explaining the failure of Brazil's governments to provide large infrastructure investments, an interpretation that emphasizes the role of the large landowners in Brazilian politics only sharpens the question. For, following Joseph Schumpeter's insight concerning the convergence of monopoly and socialism, one would expect large landowners to be especially energetic in pressing for public investment.[30] This is because landowners with extensive holdings and market power can internalize and appropriate most of the social benefits of infrastructure investment. Therefore Brazil's internal political conditions should have led to *large* government investment in economic infrastructure.

Another possibility is that ideology inhibited a rational public-investment policy. In principle, Brazil's political leadership may have been constrained by nineteenth-century doctrines of laissez-faire. Voices of economic liberalism were heard in nineteenth-century Brazil, but, in practice, Brazilian governments did intervene in the economy, imposing protective tariffs as well as providing subsidies—for example, for European immigration and for technological modernization of the northeast's sugar industry—when these did not require a large financial input. Likewise, the Brazilian state was so little bound by the canons of nineteenth-century economic orthodoxy that it ran frequent fiscal deficits and maintained economic policies that led to chronic inflation and long-term exchange-rate depreciation.

Another possible explanation for the government's lack of support for new railroads suggests that it would be naive to expect the Brazilian state in the nineteenth century to demonstrate an interest in promoting economic development. The country's political and administrative elites are generally considered to have been more interested in self-aggrandizement and bureaucratic expansion than in economic development. Such concerns, however, are perfectly consistent with a large promotional role for the public sector. Expanded state investment and subsidy programs would have meant more government jobs and greater control over society's economic resources. Thus the existence of self-seeking motives is hardly an adequate explanation of the Brazilian state's failure to pursue a more active public-investment policy.

One set of conditions does seem to have constrained the Brazilian state's developmental activity: public finance. Through most of the nineteenth century, the fiscal resources the Brazilian state had at its disposal to pay for infrastructure investment and subsidy programs were small relative to the country's development needs. Table 2.4 presents data on the Brazilian central government's expenditure in successive decades of the nineteenth century. Because of Brazil's long-term price inflation, figures in nominal mil-réis would not tell much about the state's fiscal capacity in real terms. Accordingly, using Brazil's exchange rate as a rough proxy for a price deflator, we express the fiscal data in terms of foreign currency, the pound sterling. Further, the relative price of exports in Great Britain (Brazil's principal foreign supplier) changed during the nineteenth century. Consequently, to get an idea of the import capacity of the central government's

TABLE 2.4

Sterling Value of Central Government Expenditure in Nineteenth-Century Brazil

(current and constant Sterling prices)

Period	Average annual expenditure in current Sterling prices (000£)	Expenditure per capita in current prices (£)	Average annual expenditure in constant (1880) prices (000£)	Expenditure per capita in constant (1880) prices (£)
1823–31	1,747	0.344	999	0.196
1832–41	2,377	0.401	1,703	0.286
1842–51	3,170	0.460	2,918	0.423
1852–61	4,919	0.614	4,534	0.566
1862–71	10,051	1.075	7,923	0.846
1872–81	13,769	1.252	12,483	1.128
1882–91	14,873	1.113	18,146	1.097
1891–1901	14,679	0.887	18,146	1.097
1902–11	29,609	1.409	33,519	1.598

SOURCES: Computed from data on the mil-réis value of central government expenditure presented in Onody 1960: 195–98 and from data on the sterling/mil-réis exchange rate. The series in constant sterling prices was computed using the index of export prices of the United Kingdom, Brazil's major foreign supplier, which is available in Imlah 1958: 94–98.

fiscal resources in real terms, we also present the data in constant sterling prices.

During most of the century, Brazil's fiscal system was highly central- ized. Table 2.4 therefore tells much about the total spending of Brazil's public sector (including the provincial and local governments). Thus, until the 1880's, the tax revenues of the central government were approximately 4.5 times larger than those of the provincial governments. The central government's share in total public-sector *expenditure* was even larger, for the central government had much greater access to foreign and domestic borrowing. Likewise, the tax revenues collected by local governments in nineteenth-century Brazil were a small fraction of total public-sector reve- nues. Table 2.4 thus provides important information concerning the level and growth of total public-sector expenditure.[31]

As the data indicate, for the first four decades after independence, the central government's expenditures per capita were well below £1. It was only with the Paraguayan War (1864–70) that per capita expenditure ex- ceeded £1. And it was not until the first decade of the twentieth century that central-government expenditure in current prices approached £1.5 per capita. Different measuring rods may be used to assess these expenditure levels. In the present context, the most pertinent comparison is with the magnitude of the development task that Brazil faced in the nineteenth century. As noted earlier, the country's initial conditions with respect to social overhead capital were poor. In addition, difficult geographical conditions meant that the costs of providing the country with a low-cost transportation system were high. Viewed in terms of providing infrastructure investment adequate for the country's development needs, the fiscal resources available to the Brazilian state until the end of the nineteenth century seem to have been relatively small.

The central government's low expenditure levels reflected basic features of the fiscal situation that confronted the Brazilian state in its efforts to raise tax revenues. Public finance was constrained by the paucity of tax bases that would yield revenues commensurate with the costs of tax collection. Consequently, government expenditure levels did not reach the scale that would have been socially optimal if such transaction costs did not have to be considered. As noted earlier, the Brazilian state had major incentives (if only for its own self-aggrandizement) to enlarge the volume of economic resources at its disposal. The country's landowners, who would have appropriated most of the benefits of expanded public investment, also stood to gain. But a large increase in fiscal penetration (increase in the size of the tax base) within the broader society also involved significant economic costs. The net marginal social benefits of public-finance expansion were thus low. As a result, such fiscal expansion understandably (and rationally) encountered resistance on the part of Brazil's socioeconomic elites.

Because of the great distances, poor communications, and low literacy rates present in nineteenth-century Brazil, the costs involved in tapping most potential tax bases were high. By contrast, the administrative costs of collecting taxes on imports and exports were relatively low. Accordingly, the Brazilian state's revenues and expenditures depended heavily on foreign-trade duties. Between 1830 and 1885, some 70 percent of the government's revenues came from taxes on imports and exports. As this number indicates, generalized taxes on agricultural land were not an important source of government revenue in nineteenth-century Brazil. In this respect, Brazil contrasted notably with countries otherwise as diverse as India and Japan in the nineteenth century.[32] Not only would the administrative costs (including a cadastral survey) of generalized land taxation have been high, but the revenue prospects of such an effort were meager. An important difference with India and Japan was Brazil's abundance of land and the ensuing low ratios of labor to land in the domestic agricultural sector. With little pressure of population on land, Ricardian rent, the basis for land taxation, was small. These conditions, which made for high transactions costs and a low economic surplus in the domestic agricultural sector, meant that the net fiscal yield of generalized land taxation would have been small.

Fiscal prospects in Brazil's foreign-trade sector were more attractive. There, transactions costs were not so large relative to the size of the economic surplus as to lower sharply the net social gains of taxation. Because of these differences between the foreign-trade sector and the domestic agricultural sector, government revenues and expenditures depended heavily on the value of Brazil's foreign-trade receipts. The tax rates imposed on this base, however, could not be set at arbitrarily high levels lest exports and imports diminish to the point where tax revenues would fall. Unfortunately, through most of the nineteenth century, Brazil's foreign trade volume was too small to provide the fiscal resources needed to finance infrastructure development.[33] A comparative perspective from the United States is useful in this context. The central government in the United States also relied heavily on foreign-trade duties as a source of tax revenue in the nineteenth century, but foreign trade provided a much larger tax base in the United States. From the 1820's through the 1850's, U.S. export receipts were approximately five times larger than those of Brazil. In the subsequent four decades, the ratio was even higher, 6.8 to 1. As these numbers indicate, the central government in the United States could draw on a much larger tax base to support its expenditure programs.

The Brazilian state attempted to supplement its revenues by borrowing, both at home and abroad. In 1864, before the sharp rise in government expenditure that came with the Paraguayan War, government debt (including money issued by the government) amounted to £5.5 per capita. Moreover, the Brazilian state's borrowing was not limited to foreign sources. Between 1841 and 1889, the share of domestically held obligations in the government's total debt-service payments ranged from 42 to 62 percent. Although borrowing afforded the Brazilian state a welcome short-term addition to its fiscal resources, it did not solve the country's public-finance problem. The scope for borrowing was set ultimately by debt-service capacity and hence by tax revenues. Until the end of the nineteenth century, the volume and growth of Brazil's foreign trade were too small to permit a high level of government expenditure.

Constitutional Structure and the Public-Finance Constraint

As noted earlier, nineteenth-century Brazil was a country of large distances and poor communications. Brazil's political elite wanted, nevertheless, to hold the country together as a single political entity. The constitutional structure implemented in the face of these tensions further limited the state's capacity to mobilize tax revenues.

Between 1834 and 1840, Brazil experimented with a decentralized ("federal") fiscal system. Serious centrifugal pressures emerged, however, and a tightly centralized constitutional structure was reinstituted. Throughout most of the nineteenth century, then, control over economic policy and public finance in Brazil was concentrated in the central government. The centralized constitutional structure affected public finance (and thus the pace of infrastructure investment and economic development) in two ways. First, Brazil's provincial governments and municipalities were not able to play the large public-investment role that the state and local governments filled in the United States. Brazil's provincial and local governments were legally empowered to make promotional investments, but under the prevailing constitutional structure they lacked the fiscal resources to fulfill developmental responsibilities that required large expenditures.

Second, the centralized constitutional structure may also have limited the volume of public-finance resources that Brazil's socioeconomic elites were willing to accord to the *central* government. Public-finance theory has emphasized that even under relatively favorable conditions, the supply of public goods is likely to be socially suboptimal; individual political participants are unlikely to reveal their true preferences concerning the supply of public goods. That standard problem was exacerbated in nineteenth-century Brazil by the centralized political structure. Because of their geographical dispersion, political participants in Brazil had very different preferences concerning the net benefits of potential public-investment projects that would be located in diverse provinces. Such location-specific preferences can be accommodated within a political system having decentralized fiscal functions, but with a unitary political structure and multiple regional participants—the situation that prevailed in Brazil during most of the century—the supply of public goods is likely to be especially suboptimal.[34]

Brazil's experience in the Paraguayan War supports the interpretation that the public-choice conditions we have discussed limited the size of government revenue and expenditure during the nineteenth century. The war confronted Brazil's elites with the need for a classic public good—national defense—which appeared to benefit all political participants. In response, central-government expenditures and tax revenues increased sharply. Thus the war offered a generalized public good, which, for a while, relaxed the constraint on the supply of public finance.

The absence of representative democracy—another feature of nineteenth-century Brazil's political constitution—also limited the system's capacity to implement social preferences in a rational manner. In a representative democracy, the ruling party is likely to be more responsive to the wishes of other political participants.[35] By contrast, in a hereditary monarchy such as existed in nineteenth-century Brazil, where the chief executive is not chosen by or responsible to broader socioeconomic elites, the state can achieve greater autonomy vis-à-vis other political actors. But since participants in a less-representative system can exert less control over the allocation of fiscal resources, they have less assurance that they (rather than other participants) will benefit from the way in which their taxes are used. Because of this uncertainty, political actors in a less democratic political system will rationally accede to a lower level of taxation than will participants in a more representative system. In the latter case, taxpayers have more control over allocational decisions and, consequently, greater assurance that their taxes will be spent in accordance with their own preferences.

Some of Brazil's political leaders recognized how the government's constitutional structure limited its public-finance ability and the country's economic development. In 1889, they introduced a new constitution, which transformed Brazil from a centralized imperial regime (the system that we have discussed) to a federal republic. This shift involved more than a superficial change, for it included some changes that were significant in the present context. The new constitutional structure decentralized power and functions and gave Brazil's states far more autonomy in fiscal affairs and overseas borrowing. Some state (and local) governments responded energetically to the opportunities that the new arrangements offered. A number of states raised their taxes and their spending on economic infrastructure. Also, recognizing that their credit rating was better than that of the country as a whole, some states and municipalities took advantage of the new structure to borrow aggressively overseas, largely for infrastructure investment. Between 1888 and 1915, the external debt of Brazil's overall public sector rose from £33 million to £172 million. State and local borrowing accounted for fully 42 percent of this large increment. Similarly, the 1906 program for coffee valorization was largely the effort of the major coffee-producing states and might not have been feasible under the earlier, centralized structure.

Also important were the new constitution's "republican" aspects. These, too, facilitated greater responsiveness on the part of the central government to private-sector economic interests. The new structure featured election of the chief of state by Brazil's socioeconomic elites—a change from the previous system of hereditary succession. In addition, the chief executive no longer had lifetime incumbency. Private-sector elites gained on both grounds. Not only could they exert more power in the initial selection of the chief executive, but they also had the enhanced influence on the central government's decision making that came with recurring elections.

The Onset of Long-Term Economic Development

Between 1898 and 1913, the Brazilian central government's spending, valued at constant pound sterling prices, rose at a trend rate of 10 percent per year. This rate of growth contrasts with the much slower expansion, at a trend rate of 2.1 percent per year, during the previous period, 1878–97. To some extent, the extraordinary fiscal expansion that began in 1898 reflects recovery from a cyclical trough. More important, the acceleration of government spending was driven by an export boom that increased tax receipts. Thus the decade 1902–11 saw a 52 percent rise in the constant pound sterling value of Brazil's exports as compared with the previous decade. Government spending, however, rose by much more than would be expected, in light of the historic relation between Brazil's exports and its public finance (a long-term elasticity of unity). The additional growth in government spending is consistent with the constitutional changes that we have noted.

The sharp, sustained increase in government spending was important for its effects both on the economy's supply side and on demand conditions. Some of the increased public-sector expenditure added to Brazil's infrastructure. Also, coming in conjunction with the sharp rise in export demand, higher government spending constituted an upward demand shock on the economy. Brazil had experienced export booms before. The country had also had periods—for example, the Paraguayan War—when government spending had risen rapidly. This time, however, the spurt in demand encountered the more elastic food-supply conditions and the intensified intersectoral linkages that came with extension of the railways. As a result, the growth in demand now generated a sharp rise in real output. Not only did output growth accelerate in the first decade of the twentieth century, but that decade was also a period in which price inflation was below Brazil's long-term trend.[36]

Decadal growth rates show real agricultural output growing at an annual rate of 3.5 percent between 1900 and 1909, industrial output growing at an annual rate of 5.6 percent, and aggregate real output (an index whose movements approximate those of real GDP), at an annual rate of

4.2 percent.[37] Brazil was now launched on a path of long-term economic growth. Between 1900 and 1947, aggregate real output rose at a trend rate of 4.4 percent per year, and per capita real output at 2.3 percent per year. That pace of economic progress exceeds the rate at which per capita GDP increased in the United States and in the countries of Western Europe at the onset of their modern economic development.

We can now recapitulate the main lines of Brazil's economic experience in the nineteenth century. Declining per capita income in Brazil's large northeast region, the result of poor performance of the region's exports, is one feature of the story. The elastic supply of labor to the economy's advanced sector is another. Finally, one key reason for Brazil's limited economic progress during the nineteenth century is a feature to which historians have traditionally given little attention: conditions in the domestic agricultural sector. As Brazil's subsequent experience was to demonstrate, the availability of low-cost transportation was crucial for productivity growth in that sector. Unfortunately, nature did not endow Brazil's interior with low-cost transport facilities. Until the end of the century, neither did the market or the political process.

Because the nineteenth century was a long period of meager economic progress for Brazil—and one of falling behind other countries in the world economy—it would be easy to end this chapter with a sense of missed opportunities. But an opportunity cannot be missed unless it was in fact available. We are therefore led to a basic question: *could* Brazil's long-term economic course have been very different from the path it actually followed? One can easily imagine alternative scenarios that would have led to higher rates of economic development in nineteenth-century Brazil. One alternative would have involved expansion based on rising productivity within the domestic sector rather than the orientation toward exports and the international economy. We can also imagine ways in which Brazil's development might have been happier even within the framework of export-led growth. For example, if Brazilian governments had invested earlier and on a larger scale in social overhead capital (as happened in the United States), or if Brazil had restricted the flow of labor from overseas (as occurred in Australia), Brazil's economic development would have been very different.

To be meaningful for historical analysis, counterfactuals should be empirically relevant and truly conceivable for the historical period under consideration.[38] In fact, those alternative scenarios were not historically available for nineteenth-century Brazil. In a country where a central thrust of governmental policy was to increase the supply of labor from overseas, it is idle fantasy to speculate on a development pattern based on restricting the importation of workers. Furthermore, in view of the relatively low return on investment available in nineteenth-century Brazil (not least to the state itself, in terms of tax revenues), it is not surprising that the economy's expansion path inclined toward export growth. Finally, given the economic and political conditions that we have discussed, it would not be realistic to expect public-investment programs very different from what in fact occurred. Likewise, with Brazil's low level of social overhead capital, an alternative development scenario based on the economy's domestic sector was not possible.

Historical research can elucidate the limits of what was possible. Such analysis can clarify the extent to which events followed the course they did not because of accidents or random shocks but rather because of initial conditions and their intrinsic logic over time. As such, the study of history can spare later observers depressing reflections that have no basis in the realm of the possible. Brazil's economic history in the nineteenth century seems to have been a relatively extreme case in this genre. The pattern of economic change there appears to have been very much governed by existing structural parameters, with little scope for an alternative course.

This chapter also sheds light on some basic questions that have long intrigued students of Brazil's economic history. For example, one may wonder whether Brazil's economic development was driven primarily by political or by market forces. As our discussion of railroads, import tariffs, and subsidized immigration suggests, posing the question in such "either/or" terms is not helpful. Entrepreneurs—both economic and political—responded to the opportunity set that Brazil offered. In turn, political intervention shifted the country's economic constraints and incentives; economic change altered the results of diverse political initiatives. Brazil's economic experience—both the initial period of slow long-term growth and the country's subsequent breakthrough to sustained development—clearly reflects the interplay of economic and political forces.

This chapter also has some general lessons for understanding long-term economic development. I mention four obvious points. First, economic theory works in the real world. For example, economists have elaborated theoretical conditions necessary for an optimum currency area. The northeast's miserable experience in the nineteenth century can be read as a morality tale that illustrates what happens when people violate these conditions. Second, geography matters. We saw examples when we considered the importance of low-cost transportation for the domestic agricultural sector and when we discussed the rigidities that constrained factor reallocation from sugar and cotton to coffee. A third lesson is that public finance matters. As we have seen, the supply of fiscal resources can be crucial for economic development. Finally, political institutions can play a relatively autonomous role in the development process. Constitutional structure had independent effects in transmitting (and in some ways distorting) the policy preferences of Brazil's socioeconomic elites. Brazil's experience, first with a centralized and subsequently with a decentralized political structure, suggests that institutions can be more than an epiphenomenon of socio-political conditions.

I also note some implications for the research agenda in Brazilian historiography. A refocusing on topics whose importance is now evident, and about which we know far too little, would be helpful. Thus I suggest a shift in research attention from the colonial period to the nineteenth century. In terms of economic subject matter, I suggest a shift from study of the export and urban-based activities to study of the large and as yet little known domestic agricultural sector. In terms of social history, researchers might give less attention to the masters and the slaves and more attention to the people who comprised the intermediate social strata, the free poor. Recognizing the importance of geography, we might give less emphasis to research on the cities and the coastal provinces and more to the interior, particularly Minas Gerais. Regarding specific topics, it would be enlightening to know more about Brazil's demographic history and especially about the conditions associated with the high rate of natural increase of Brazil's free population; about the revenue and spending patterns of Brazil's provincial and *municipio* governments during the nineteenth century; and about the social and cultural conditions related to the relative absence in nineteenth-century Brazil of the "spirit of association" that Alexis de Tocqueville found so prominent a feature in the supply of public goods in the United States during the nineteenth century.

Notes

I am grateful to the Faculty Research Program of the Columbia Business School for financial support and to the conference participants, particularly Stanley Engerman, Stephen Haber, and Nathan Rosenberg, for helpful comments. I bear sole responsibility for this chapter's deficiencies.

    1. I draw on earlier research in Leff 1982a; Leff 1982b. Those studies provide the sources for data not otherwise cited in this paper.

    2. Leff 1982a: chap. 2, appen. 2.

    3. This section draws on material presented in Leff 1982b: chap. 2.

    4. Mundell 1961.

5. This section draws on data and analysis presented in Leff 1982a: chap. 4.

6. Carvalho de Mello 1977: 50, 66.

7. During this period, consumer prices in Rio de Janeiro seem to have risen at an annual rate of at least 2 percent. See Leff 1982a: chap. 6.

8. Leff 1982a: chap. 4 appen.

9. Cowell 1977.

10. Levine 1971.

11. Lewis 1954.

12. The domestic agricultural sector is sometimes referred to as the "subsistence" sector. That term is misleading inasmuch as it also connotes minimal income levels, a condition that may not have applied to people in the interior of nineteenth-century Brazil. I therefore prefer the term *domestic agricultural sector*, which more clearly indicates the nature of the goods produced and their economic destination.

13. The phrase is from Reigelhaupt and Forman 1970: 103.

14. Prado 1963: 419. This work provides numerous observations on the people and activities of the domestic agricultural sector. See, e.g., pp. 183–86, 214–19, 302, 328–39, 400–2. But those observations are presented in a conceptual framework that ignores their importance.

15. See the population estimates presented in Simonsen 1962: 271; Prado 1963: 117.

16. This statement is based on population estimates that are presented in Simonsen 1962: 271; Stein 1957: 294; Manchester 1933: 183.

17. Leff and Klein 1974.

18. Leff 1982a: 21.

19. On the importance of canals and improved internal waterways in the economic development of the United States during the nineteenth century, see Goodrich 1961.

20. The ratio of Brazil's railway trackage to its territorial size in 1890 would remain very small even if large, relatively uninhabited areas like the Amazon region were excluded from the calculation. Note, moreover, that the extent to which an area is inhabited or not also depends on the availability of low-cost transportation facilities.

21. A formal model analyzing the impact of lower transportation costs on agricultural development is presented in Katzman 1974, esp. pp. 683–86. In addition to raising the ex-farm prices of all agricultural products, lower-cost transportation changes the relative prices that producers face at different locations. This differential price impact of freight charges on diverse products provides a basis for intraregional specialization even under homogenous production conditions. Producers who are more distant from the major consumption center will find that their comparative advantage lies in crops that are cheaper to transport, while producers closer to the market will specialize in products on which transportation costs weigh more heavily. The gains due to relative-price effects and compositional change are additional to those that stem from increase in market production per se.

22. On the magnitude of this output-valuation effect in less-developed economies, see Usher 1968, esp. part 2.

23. Leff 1982a: 117–20, 146–61.

24. Wirth 1977: 58. A map showing the timing of railway construction in the Minas region is presented on p. 417 of Webb 1959.

25. The data of Table 2.2 show exceptionally high growth for shipments of rice. This occurred in the context of import substitution in rice. Information on that process is presented in Mandell 1971: 167–68, 201–4, 217–19.

26. On what follows here, see Saes 1976: 80–81; Wirth 1977: 44, 50, 180; 1978: 40–41.

27. Luz 1961; Levine 1978: 119, 126, 130; Wirth 1977: 47, 180; Mandell 1971: 167–68, 201–4, 217–19.

28. Computed from data in Stein 1957: 191. The data there also show similar rates of growth for employment and looms installed in the cotton textile industry.

29. Concerning the general question of sociocultural conditions as a constraint on economic development in nineteenth-century Brazil, see Leff 1982b: chap. 3.

30. Schumpeter 1942.

31. Brazil's fiscal heterodoxy often led to budget deficits; hence, government expenditures were not constrained to equal revenues. Nevertheless, expenditures could not be totally unrelated to revenues because of the inflationary and balance-of-payments consequences of complete decoupling.

32. Bird 1974: chap. 5.

33. Information on the size and growth of Brazil's international trade in the nineteenth century is provided in Leff 1982a: chap. 5.

34. Public-finance behavior in contemporary less-developed countries supports these analytical perspectives. With other conditions held constant, the share of total government taxation in GDP is higher in less-developed countries that have a decentralized fiscal system. See Lotz and Morss 1970: 334–38.

35. Breton 1974: 44–48, 113–16, 156.

36. Leff 1982a: 101–2.

37. Haddad 1974: table 1.

38. See the thoughtful discussion on the use of counterfactuals in economic history in Engerman 1980. Engerman also quotes with approval Jon Elster's statement concerning "the need for a dynamic criterion of legitimacy, the requirement that the alternative state be capable of insertion into the real past."

References

Bird, Richard. 1974. *Taxing Agricultural Land in Developing Countries.* Cambridge, Mass.

Breton, Albert. 1974. *The Economic Theory of Representative Democracy.* Chicago.

Carvalho de Mello, Pedro. 1977. "The Economics of Labor on Brazilian Coffee Plantations, 1835–1888." Ph.D. diss., University of Chicago.

Cowell, Bainbridge, Jr. 1975. "Cityward Migration in the Nineteenth Century: The Case of Recife, Brazil," *Journal of InterAmerican Studies and World Affairs* 7 (Feb.): 43–63.

Engerman, Stanley L. 1980. "Counterfactuals and The New Economic History." *Inquiry* 23 (June): 157–72.

Goodrich, Carter, ed. 1961. *Canals and American Economic Development*. New York.

Haddad, Cláudio. 1974. "Growth of Real Output in Brazil, 1900–47." Ph.D. diss., University of Chicago.

IBGE [Instituto Braziliero de Geografia e Estatística]. 1939. *Brazil—1938*. Rio de Janeiro.

Imlah, Albert H. 1958. *Economic Elements in the Pax Britannica*. Cambridge, Mass.

Katzman, Martin T. 1974. "The Von Thunen Paradigm, The Industrial-Urban Hypothesis, and the Spatial Structure of Agriculture." *American Journal of Agricultural Economics* 56 (Nov.): 683–96.

Leff, Nathaniel H. 1982a. *Underdevelopment and Development in Brazil*. Vol. 1, *Economic Structure and Change, 1822–1947*. London.

———. 1982b. *Underdevelopment and Development in Brazil*. Vol. 2, *Reassessing the Obstacles to Economic Development*. London.

Leff, Nathaniel H., and Herbert S. Klein. 1974. "O Crescimento da População Não-Europeia antes do Inicio do Desenvolvimento: O Brasil do Século XIX." *Anais da Historia* 6: 51–70.

Levine, Robert. 1971. "Some Views on Race and Immigration during the Old Republic." *The Americas* 27 (Apr.): 373–80.

———. 1978. *Pernambuco in the Brazilian Federation, 1899–1937*. Stanford.

Lewis, W. Arthur. 1954. "Economic Development with Unlimited Supplies of Labour." *The Manchester School of Economic and Social Studies* 22, no. 2 (May): 139–91.

Lotz, J. R., and E. R. Morss. 1970. "A The Theory of Tax Level Determinants in Developing Countries." *Economic Development and Cultural Change* 18 (Apr.): 328–41.

Luz, Nícia Villela. 1961. *A Luta pela Industrializacão do Brasil*. São Paulo.

Manchester, Alan K. 1933. *British Preeminence in Brasil*. Durham, N.C.

Mandell, Paul. 1971. "The Rise of the Modern Brazilian Rice Economy." *Food Research Institute Studies* 10 (June): 161–219.

Mundell, Robert A. 1961. "A Theory of Optimum Currency Areas." *American Economic Review* 51 (Sept.): 657–65.

Onody, Oliver. 1960. *A Inflação Brasileiro*. Rio de Janeiro.

Prado, Caio, 1963. *The Colonial Background of Modern Brazil*, 7th ed. Suzette Macedo, trans. São Paulo.

Reigelhaupt, Joyce, and Shepard Forman. 1970. "Bodo Was Never Brazilian: Economic integration and Rural Development Among a Contemporary Peasantry." *Journal of Economic History* 30 (Mar.): 100–16.

Saes, Flávio Azevedo Marques de. 1976. "Expansão e Declíno das Ferrovias Paulistias: 1870–1940." In Carlos Manuel Pelaez and Mircea Buescu, eds., *A Moderna Historia Economica*. Rio de Janeiro.

Schumpeter, Joseph A. 1942. *Capitalism, Socialism, and Democracy*. New York.

Simonsen, Roberto. 1962. *Historia Economica do Brasil*, 4th ed. São Paulo.

Stein, Stanley J. 1970. *Vassouras: A Brazilian Coffee County, 1850–1900*. Cambridge, Mass.

————. 1957. *The Brazilian Cotton Textile Manufacture.* Cambridge, Mass.

Usher, Dan. 1968. *The Price Mechanism and the Meaning of National Income Statistics.* London.

Webb, Kempton. 1959. "Origins and Development of a Food Economy in Central Minas Gerais." *Annals of the Association of American Geographers* 49 (Dec.): 409–19.

Wirth, John. 1977. *Minas Gerais in the Brazilian Federation, 1889–1937.* Stanford.

CHAPTER 3

A Macroeconomic Interpretation
of Nineteenth-Century Mexico

ENRIQUE CÁRDENAS

The Mexican economy stagnated throughout the first half of the nine-teenth century. The available estimates indicate a drop in per capita gross domestic product (GDP) of 37 percent from 1800 to 1860. It was not until the second half of the nineteenth century that the economy once again began to grow, slowly at first through the 1860's and 1870's, then accelerating during the final decades of the century.[1]

This chapter is concerned with explaining the lackluster performance of the Mexican economy during the first part of the nineteenth century as well as with elucidating the factors that reignited growth during the second half of the century. In part, the analysis presented here borrows from earlier historiographic traditions that stress inadequate means of transport, politi-cal instability, and inefficient institutions that "amplified instead of reduced the difference between private and social economic benefits" in explaining Mexico's nineteenth-century decline.[2] This chapter also stresses macroeco-nomic elements that have received less attention in much of the literature to date.[3] By necessity it considers only one segment of the whole economy, namely, that which operated through the monetary market, as opposed to the barter economy and the self-sufficient sector. Therefore one must re-alize at the outset that it is only a partial approach, but one that has the potential to shed light on the origins of Mexico's underdevelopment. This chapter will show that the performance of the export sector, and its several linkages to the rest of the economy, both real and monetary, played a major role in retarding and then promoting Mexico's economic growth during the nineteenth century.[4]

The basic argument advanced here is that, after the War of Indepen-dence, the Mexican economy fell into a vicious cycle: the contraction of the mining sector and the capital flight that occurred during the colonial period and the war, along with the separation from Spain in 1821, generated monetary astringency and left little financial capital available to the rest of the economy. That, in turn, decreased the volume of domestic and international trade by creating a scarcity of foreign exchange. Political instability, coupled with the virtual destruction of some of the most important mines and the difficulties in rehabilitating them in the following two decades, reduced the availability of means of payment and diminished economic activity in general. This reinforced the lack of financial resources available for investment. The drastic restriction in trade then eroded the main source of financial savings for most productive activities, including mining itself and the rehabilitation of the transportation system. This erosion of saving for productive activities limited further trade and the creation of a domestic market that could take advantage of new technologies and expand economies of scale. Output thus fell drastically during the first two decades after Mexico's independence.

This chapter also argues that the gradual recovery of the mining sector and the surge of protoindustry towards the middle of the century, coupled with the development of the railroads in the 1880's, consolidated Mexico's growth toward the last quarter of the nineteenth century. Indeed, the export recovery and the development of railroads facilitated the economic boom of the Porfiriato. This growth set the basis for the integration of the internal market along with the creation of modern industry, a primitive financial system, and an increasingly monetized economy. However, the impact of the export boom on the whole economy would have been greater had it not been for a dramatic fall in the terms of trade, particularly during the last fifteen years of the Porfiriato.

From Colonial Boom to Independence Depression

Mexican economic growth had begun to slow even prior to the War of Independence that began in 1810. It was during the first decade of the nineteenth century, however, that growth began to falter seriously as a consequence of Spain's financial difficulties, which drained economic resources from Spanish America. The growth process was then completely interrupted by the War of Independence. The economic crisis that followed was a result of the shutting down of the mines, the flight of financial capital, and Mexico's separation from Spain in 1821.

The economic collapse started with the first battles for independence and the takeover of the mines by revolutionary armies. Guanajuato was the first victim; other mining centers were hit soon afterwards. Most mining activities were interrupted at first and later destroyed:

Disaster struck the industry with the War of Independence in 1810–21. Raids destroyed mine towns, the workings, the mints, and the archives. Transportation of bullion and supplies was hazardous at best. Mines filled with water, timbers rotted, shafts collapsed, roads fell into disrepair, and isolated mines were forgotten while prospectors left off their work. Finally, the Peninsular-born Spaniards and wealthy Creoles (American born whites), who held the best mines and most of the capital, were either expelled from Mexico by discriminating laws passed by the new government or confirmed in their predilection for landowning. "Mexico's greatest fount of wealth" had ceased to flow.[5]

During the first decade of the century, total silver extraction reached 5,538 tons. During the ten years of fighting between 1811 and 1820 it fell 44 percent, to 3,120 tons. Gold and silver coinage also collapsed during the war, falling 59 percent during the same period. Foreign trade declined by 41 percent in those years as a consequence of the disruption of trade routes and the reduction of domestic income. Table 3.1 shows some major indicators of the crisis.

A second major impact of the war was the continued drainage of financial capital. This process began in 1804 as a consequence of the Spanish

TABLE 3.1
Indicators of Mexico's Economic Crisis, 1800–30

Indicator	1800–10 (1)	1811–20 (2)	1821–30 (3)	Percentage change	
				(2)/(1)	(3)/(2)
Silver production (tons)	5,538	3,120	2,468	−43.7	−20.9
Volume of trade (imports & exports) (millions of pesos)	304.3	180.5	204.2[a]	−40.7	13.1
Imports (millions of pesos)	140.9	93.3	120.4[a]	−33.8	29.0
Exports (millions of pesos)	163.4	87.2	77.3[a]	−46.6	−11.3
Silver and gold exports (millions of pesos)	124.3	67.3	59.7	−45.9	−11.3
Coinage of gold and silver (millions of pesos)	226.7	92.7	96.6	−59.1	4.2
Available money supply[b]	102.4	25.4	36.9	−75.2	45.3

SOURCES: For silver production, González Reyna 1956:96. For coinage of gold and silver, Howe 1949:457–59. For figures on trade, 1801–28, Lerdo de Tejada 1853, 1829–30, Stevens 1991:20.

[a]Actual figures for 1823–30 are expanded to cover ten years. For 1823 and 1824, figures are underestimates, because they consider trade through the ports of Veracruz and Alvarado only.

[b]Coinage of gold and silver minus exports of gold and silver.

crown's need to finance the Napoleonic wars. The crown mandated loans via the *Consolidación de Vales Reales*. By 1811, 18 million pesos had already left New Spain to finance the mother country. Naturally, the war itself created further strains on the availability of money. Many Spaniards with capital left. Taxes and loans increased, and the public debt jumped threefold in six years to reach 68.5 million pesos by 1814. José María Luis Mora, a major liberal ideologue of the nineteenth century, stated, perhaps with some exaggeration, that the war had eroded half of Mexico's fixed and liquid capital.[6] For this reason there was substantial capital flight. Exports of gold and silver reached 131.9 million pesos between 1807 and 1820, a figure that does not include the "ordinary" royal net remittances to Spain.[7] Other authors estimate that between 80 and 140 million pesos left the country in those years.[8] Comparing that figure with mining exports, which in the whole decade previous to the war had reached 163.4 million pesos, capital flight was clearly substantial.[9]

The economic effects of the war were compounded by the disruption created by Mexico's separation from Spain in 1821. Though no annualized GDP series exists for this period, John Coatsworth's estimates indicate a 4.1-percent drop in real GDP and a 23.3-percent drop in real GDP per capita between 1800 and 1845.[10] Figures on mining output and money coinage suggest a powerful contraction of the economy during the period 1820–40. Mining exports declined from 124.3 million pesos in 1801–10 to 59.7 million in 1821–30. Silver production fell from 5,538 to 2,468 tons, and the coinage of money was reduced from 226.7 to 96.6 million pesos during the same periods (see Table 3.1).

What made the recession so long and severe? What major factors prevented a quicker recovery? When did the level of economic activity regain its colonial level?

Several explanations of the causes of continued economic crisis have validity. There is no doubt that, for the first 70 years of the nineteenth century, the lack of adequate means of transportation constituted a major problem for the creation of a domestic market. Also, many institutional arrangements, such as the lack of a general incorporation law and the absence of modern banking and credit laws, were not conducive to economic growth. However, one must consider other factors that created severe macroeconomic problems that retarded the resumption of economic growth. Political instability and the decline of the mining sector were two major obstacles to economic recovery.

Political instability gave rise to volatility in public policies. Changes in economic policy and priorities caused economic fluctuations and sometimes had other concrete repercussions. For example, the government-development bank, the Banco de Avío, founded in 1830 to help introduce industry in the country, was never able to raise sufficient capital. After 12 years of operation it had to close its doors when the government seized its resources to finance the army.[11] As Carlos Marichal discusses in his chapter on Mexico's capital markets, the new state was similarly unable to raise sufficient fiscal revenues to run the government, much less to finance the maintenance of roads and the other basic public services conducive to economic activity. The government even had to contract road maintenance and postal service to private companies and allow such firms to collect duties or taxes because it was unable to do so.[12] Without entering into the intricacies of explaining Mexico's political difficulties at the beginning of the nineteenth century, it is clear that political turmoil was not conducive to economic growth.

Mining activity, by far the most important sector of Mexico's market economy, stagnated for much of the century. During the 1820's silver production reached its lowest level since the last third of the eighteenth century, standing at only 44.6 percent of its pre-1810 tonnage. Silver exports contributed to the bulk of New Spain's foreign earnings. Although international trade had begun to recover as a consequence of capital inflows, its volume during the 1820's was nevertheless at only 67.1 percent of the level attained from 1801 to 1810. By the same token, silver coinage during the same time was still at 42.6 percent its level of the first decade of the century. Every effort was made to stimulate the mining sector, from lowering taxes and allowing the entrance of foreign investors to exploit existing mines to bringing in the most sophisticated technology available. Nonetheless, the mining disaster, which continued for several decades in spite of private investment and government efforts to rehabilitate the old mines, constituted one of the most important sources of economic contraction in the postwar period.[13]

Most mining enterprises, which were mainly owned by British firms, failed. Mines were destroyed during the War of Independence, and many were abandoned. As a consequence, the mines had to be re-excavated, in the hope that the old productive mines would still have significant amounts of ore to make them profitable. If one were to extrapolate from the case of Real del Monte, a major mining center near Pachuca, it would become clear that foreign miners did not have a thorough understanding of Mexican mining conditions. They imported everything from technicians and administration systems to equipment and technology. They overestimated their capabilities and skills and underestimated local labor and geological conditions, in particular the drainage problem. During the first fifteen years of British investment in mining, large amounts of silver were extracted, but at a high cost. Only a few small firms reported profits.[14]

Once it became possible during the 1830's to exploit new mines and rehabilitate old ones, silver production began to recover slowly. However, it would take another 40 years before silver-mining output reached pre-independence levels.[15] Of course, the mining crisis had drastic negative repercussions on the economic environments of the mining centers, reducing the derived demand for food for animals and miners, their clothing and housing, as well as other materials and transportation facilities. The crisis in mining also created a macroeconomic recession by reducing the money supply, the amount of trade, and fiscal revenues. All of these factors hindered government action to promote economic growth.

Although barter still occurred in many isolated places, Mexico's most important means of exchange, since the appearance of the conquistadors, was silver and gold coins. In fact, Mexico had been a highly monetized economy since the sixteenth century, because, according to royal ordinances, most silver had to be minted in order to pay taxes.[16] There was a close correlation over time between silver output and silver coinage: a reduction in silver production implied a corresponding decrease in coinage.[17] Therefore, ceteris paribus, one would expect that the disaster in the mining sector must have caused a severe scarcity of money, with all the macroeconomic effects of a restrictive monetary policy. In order to compute an estimate of the new money available to the market economy one must subtract coin exports from the coinage figures, because the behavior of silver exports affects the amount of money available to the domestic economy.

Table 3.2 clearly suggests that there was a dramatic reduction in the means of payment. Although coinage did not decrease until 1811, once the first attacks on the mining centers occurred, the drop in the available money supply actually started as a consequence of the *Consolidación* in 1804 and continued during the War of Independence. Between 1796 and 1806, the new money supply diminished from an estimated 16 million pesos per year on average to an estimated 3.1 million per year during the 1807–20 period, the height of capital drains and war violence. These figures do not include royal net remittances to Spain. If we include those remittances, then the annual difference would drop from 10 million pesos in 1796–1806 to negative 2.9 million pesos in 1807–20.[18]

The situation worsened somewhat in the 1820's. An average of only 2.8 million pesos a year was "available" for domestic use. No wonder there were so many complaints about high interest rates and the emergence of

TABLE 3.2

Indicators of the Mexican Money Supply, 1796–1850

(*millions of pesos*)

Period	Coinage of gold and silver		Exports of gold and silver		Difference	
	Accumulated	Annual average	Accumulated	Annual average	Accumulated	Annual average
1796–1806	253.1	23.0	77.0	7.0	176.1	16.0
1807–20	175.9	12.6	131.9	9.4	44.0	3.1
1823–30	80.9	10.1	58.3	7.3	22.6	2.8
1831–40	121.7	12.2	86.8	8.7	34.9	3.5
1841–50	159.3	15.9	96.2	9.6	63.1	6.3

SOURCES: For coinage, Howe 1949: 458–59. For exports of gold and silver, Lerdo de Tejada 1853: Tables 14, 52.

NOTES: Export figures from 1796 to 1820 do not include royal net remittances to Spain, estimated to be 6 million pesos a year on average, by Lerdo de Tejada (1853: 27). If this estimate is considered, the average annual difference is reduced from: 16 to 10 million in 1796–1806 and from 3.1 to −2.9 million in 1807–20.

Figures for 1821 and 1822 are not available.

"voracious" money lenders to finance the government as well as private ventures. The scarcity of money plagued not only the government, as Barbara Tenenbaum argues, but the private sector as well. Money lending in those conditions became such a profitable activity that the most successful *agiotistas* (moneylenders) accumulated fortunes large enough to permit them to enter other businesses, including mining and industry, as the nineteenth century progressed.[19]

The monetary crisis continued in the 1830's and into the early 1840's, with somewhat less strength (see Figure 3.1). Even considering royal remittances abroad, the new money supply had not regained its preindependence level by the middle of the century. This lack of money had strong depressive macroeconomic effects on the market economy, which spilled over to the subsistence-agriculture sector to some extent.

A second major effect of the mining recession was the fall in the volume of trade, because silver and gold served as foreign exchange and constituted the most important export commodity.[20] The decrease of mining production implied a drop in exports and foreign earnings. This, in turn, meant fewer imports. The volume of trade (imports plus exports) dropped from 304.3 million pesos in 1801–10 to 180.5 million during the war decade, but it started to recover in the 1820's. The recovery occurred because imports began to rise in spite of the decline in exports, which was only possible due to increasing capital inflows from foreign debt[21] and new foreign investment in the mining sector.[22]

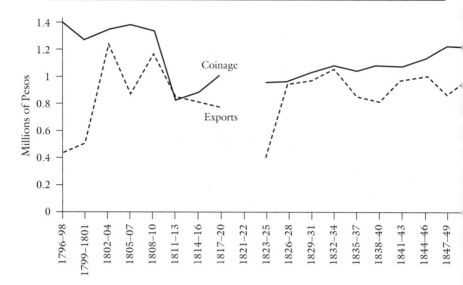

Figure 3.1. Mexican money supply from 1796 through 1851. Coinage is shown by the solid line; exports of gold and silver are shown by the broken line. The gap in the data from 1817 to 1825 is a result of independence. The vertical axis shows millions of pesos. Data on coinage are taken from Howe 1949: 458–59; data on exports of precious metals are taken from Lerdo de Tejada 1853: Tables 14, 52.

The volume of foreign trade was not very different in the 1830's from its reduced level of the 1820's, and it continued a slow downward trend through most of the 1840's. It fell approximately 7 percent from the 1830's to reach a trough the year of the war with the United States (see Table 3.3).[23] The fall in the volume of trade in the 1840's was caused entirely by the 29-percent drop in imports, which more than offset the estimated 12- to 13-percent increase in exports. However, the "available money supply" kept growing at increasing rates in the 1840's, which must have had a positive impact on the domestic economy.

In the case of cotton textile imports, however, the story was somewhat different. From the early 1820's to the late 1830's, cotton textile imports from the United States, including reexports, increased rapidly and reached levels not attained again until the end of the century. During the period from 1821/2 to 1839/40, annual cotton textile imports from and through the United States averaged 1.6 million pesos, the equivalent of 41 percent of the total Mexican import bill from the United States.[24] Such a flood of textile commodities made life very difficult for the emerging Mexican textile factories in their first years.

TABLE 3.3
Mexico's Volume of Trade, 1831–50
(*millions of pesos*)

Volume of trade	1831–40	1841–50[a]	Percentage change
Imports and exports I[b]	209.2	196.2	−7.2
Imports	95.5	67.8	−29.0
Exports[b]	113.7	128.4	12.9
Imports and exports II[c]	197.5	182.3	−7.7
Imports	95.5	67.8	−29.0
Exports[c]	102.0	114.5	12.3

SOURCE: Lerdo de Tejada 1853: Tables 14, 52.
[a]The figures for 1841–49 are expanded to cover ten years.
[b]The figures in exports I are based on a 0.746 share of silver exports in the total.
[c]The figures in exports II are based on a 0.850 share of silver exports in the total.

As a whole, imports declined at a fairly rapid pace after 1836. In spite of the fact that the economy was slowly beginning to recuperate, imports dropped approximately 29.4 percent between the decade 1826–35 and the decade 1836–45.[25] Richard Salvucci suggests that the reduction in imports was essentially a consequence of Mexico's protective policies and the difficult situation with Texas and the United States.[26] In the case of American cotton textile exports to Mexico, the fall was very dramatic. During the period from 1840/1 to 1846/7, those "domestic and foreign" American exports to Mexico averaged only 0.3 million pesos, an 81.4-percent reduction from the earlier eighteen-year period.[27]

The fall in the volume of trade had a negative impact on other sectors of the economy. In particular, there were no incentives to construct new roads or other transportation facilities, or even to take care of the existing ones. The sources of funding for financial intermediaries, a sector that had traditionally obtained its resources from foreign trade, became increasingly scarce and concentrated as a result of the recession.[28] In addition, because merchant capital had traditionally been a major source of savings to finance other areas of the economy, its contraction had a long-term impact on the availability of lendable funds and on the investment process. There were numerous complaints by nascent entrepreneurs of the 1830's regarding the scarcity and cost of loans.[29]

A third major impact of the mining crisis, related to that of the volume of trade, was its repercussion on public revenues. The Spanish crown based its taxation system on such monopolies as the production of silver; as long as mining was flourishing, royal revenues would also increase. The deterioration of the mining sector, however, prompted the first Mexican governments to make customs duties a major part of the tax base. The contraction of trade therefore had a detrimental effect on government revenues, making life very difficult for the first Mexican leaders. While tax revenues averaged 24 million pesos annually during the last twenty years of the colonial period, they amounted to only 12 million a year during the first decade after independence.[30] Tax collections increased somewhat in the 1830's and 1840's, to a yearly average of 14.3 million pesos, because of higher tariffs and increasing exports.[31]

Fiscal income was insufficient to pay for the expenses of the state, which were composed primarily of the military and the Ministry of the Treasury, 33.3 percent and 45.5 percent respectively in the 1822–45 period. The decline in fiscal revenues affected the government's capacity to maintain the roads and other basic infrastructure, which in turn had a detrimental effect on overall economic performance.

The first independent government had to supplement its revenues with foreign and domestic loans. The only two foreign loans that were granted in those years, however, amounted to 32 million pesos, of which only 17 million arrived in Mexico. The balance was absorbed in advance interest payments and commissions. In addition, the loans were not used productively but to pay operational expenses and to buy a boat and weapons to defend Mexico's national sovereignty. Then, in 1827, the government stopped servicing the foreign debt. New foreign loans to the government dried up.[32] The government had to rely increasingly on local money lenders to supplement its income. In the 1825–45 period, public domestic borrowing amounted to 97 million pesos, which was equivalent to 21.1 percent of total public income in those years. The use of these funds for nonproductive activities created a "crowding out" effect by which economic resources were drained from the private sector, thus tending to raise the cost of lendable funds whenever they were available.

Political turmoil in early republican Mexico, the separation of Texas, and the war with the United States were important obstacles to economic recovery. The contraction of mining and its effects on the real sector, the volume of international trade, the money supply, and the availability of financial capital were also important factors that not only retarded economic growth but made the whole economy collapse during the first two decades after the War of Independence. Let us now turn to the beginnings of recovery.

Indicators of Recovery

Without aggregate output figures, it is impossible to determine with precision the timing of recovery after the economic collapse that occurred during the War of Independence. Some sectors, like mining and manufacturing, seem to have started their recovery a decade after independence. As mentioned previously, silver mining began to grow again in the 1830's and 1840's at an average annual rate of 2.3 percent. Then its rate of growth diminished drastically to only 0.8 percent a year during the 1850's. By 1860–70, the level of silver production was still about 10 percent below the prewar level.[33]

Manufacturing, on the other hand, began to take advantage of the technological advances of the industrial revolution and mass production as early as the late 1830's. The first efforts promoted by the Banco de Avío are well known and need not be reviewed here.[34] It should be mentioned, however, that the *seed* money that was invested in the textile industry by the bank during its twelve years of operation seems to have been quite productive; more than half of the projects were still in operation by the mid-1840's.[35] Therefore, in spite of the difficulties in establishing the first modern factories, by 1845 there existed 52 cotton textile firms, with a capacity of 113,813 spindles, fourteen times more spindles than the number only eight years before. These firms were located in Puebla (37.6 percent), Mexico City (19.2 percent), Veracruz (17.4 percent) and in other important cities where the largest consumer groups were concentrated, qualified labor and energy was available, and raw materials were accessible.[36]

This first phase of industrial growth responded to an expanding money supply in the 1840's and to a commercial policy that protected domestic firms from foreign competition. We noted above that overall imports began to decrease in the second half of the 1830's in spite of increments in silver production and coinage, which constituted a source of recovery in the market economy. Despite a few sporadic jumps, cotton textile imports from the United States were kept at a relatively low level throughout the 1850's by a series of revisions of the tariff. Domestic industry responded very well to this tariff shield and started a modest process of import substitution.

One can understand this process by looking at raw cotton imports and at the establishment of new textile firms. Raw cotton was imported for the first time, in small quantities, in the early 1840's, just when several modern firms were being established. From 1851/2 on, when it was difficult to import cotton textile goods, raw cotton imports became significant and in many years even surpassed manufactured cotton product imports. During the decade from 1851/2 to 1860/1, the average value of raw cotton imports from the United States reached 0.8 million pesos.[37] Although the number of textile firms did not increase much in the 1860's, the number of spindles grew from 113,813 in 1845 to 152,332 in 1865, while the number of mechanical looms increased from 2,609 in 1843 to 4,393 in 1854.[38] The government was clearly successful in promoting economic development through commercial policy.

Just as the tariff was a protective expedient, so too was the transportation cost from the producer to the consumer; high costs acted as a restrictive tariff. Unfortunately, they also segmented the domestic market. Moving large volumes of low-value merchandise long distances was unprofitable. In fact, as Coatsworth pointed out many years ago, the lack of good roads and canals (like those built in Great Britain and the United States) and the delay in the construction of the railroads constituted two of the most important factors retarding Mexico's economic growth and persistently segmenting its domestic market.[39] The economy would have to wait until the 1870's to begin the process of modern economic growth.

The mining sector broke the economy's sluggish trend. During the second half of the 1860's and through the 1870's, silver production began to grow more rapidly. Average annual rates of growth increased from 0.8 percent in the 1850's, to 2.0 percent in the second half of the 1860's, and to 2.3 percent in the second half of the 1870's.[40] This development was made possible by the discovery of new silver deposits, which increased the industry's profitability. Gold and silver continued to be the only metals that were extracted, however, because transportation costs were still too high to exploit others.

The new expansion of the mining sector, and therefore of trade and money coinage, gradually broke the cycle of economic torpor that plagued the country for over 50 years. The mining centers, such as Pachuca, Zacatecas, and Guanajuato, were the first regions to feel the boom of the economy, which then spread to the rest of the country. Just as mining output increased, so did foreign trade. This generated a greater volume of economic transactions that stimulated domestic trade, manufacturing, and other economic activities.

Available figures on Mexico's trade with the United States suggest that the volume of trade increased rapidly in the second half of the 1860's: on average 4 percent annually with respect to the previous decade.[41] Mexican coinage of gold and silver also started to grow rapidly, reaching an average annual rate of growth of 3.1 percent in the second half of the 1860's, thereby stimulating the market economy and increasing the availability of investable resources.[42]

The economic recovery that began in the late 1860's can also be seen in the continued expansion of the cotton textile industry. By 1879 there were 258,458 spindles and 9,214 looms installed, more than double the number of spindles and looms in 1865. Raw cotton consumption, a good proxy for output, grew at an average annual rate of 2.9 percent.[43] Data on U.S. exports of raw cotton to Mexico corroborate this interpretation; raw cotton imports averaged $700,000 during the 1855–80 period. The size of the industry would have been larger still had imports of cotton cloth not surged as well in the 1870's. The annual value of imported cotton goods during that decade reached $1.4 million, 57 percent more than during the period 1850–69.[44] In any event, the combination of an increase in domestic production and an increase in imported goods clearly implies an increase in the consumption of manufactured products, indicating that national income had grown.

This economic expansion coincided with the founding of the first commercial bank, the Banco de Londres y México, in 1864. At the same time, tax revenues grew with increases in foreign trade, allowing the government to expand its financial capabilities. During the period from 1867/8 to 1877/8, yearly average fiscal revenues amounted to 18.2 million pesos, almost 100 percent above the average of the 1840's.[45] Once mining began to expand its output significantly, more money was clearly available, more imports could be acquired, and the government had, through greater taxation, a larger capacity to promote economic development. The government did precisely that during the Porfiriato.

The Resumption of Economic Growth

The reactivation of mining played the central role in the economy's resumption of growth. It created a more prosperous environment, sources of public and private funds became available again, and through an indirect fiscal linkage it helped build the railroads. The direct benefits of the expansion of the railroads included decreased transportation costs and an increased volume of trade. The main cities were linked with the mining centers, seaports, and border towns, while augmented passenger transportation contributed to the development of new areas of the country. With these improvements came growth of the export sector, an increase in fiscal revenues, development of the financial sector, and the establishment of modern firms with state-of-the-art technology.

The construction of the railroads was the most important event of the last third of the century. The Ferrocarril Mexicano, which linked Mexico

City with the seaport of Veracruz on the Gulf coast with 424 kilometers of track, was finally opened in 1873, more than 40 years after the first concession to build it had been granted. The transportation cost between the capital and the most important port decreased substantially and the volume of trade increased immediately. Between 1871 and 1877, foreign trade through Veracruz increased almost 60 percent.[46]

While the years that followed were characterized by a series of studies and discussions dealing with the ways in which the transportation network should grow, who should build it, how it should be financed, and so on, actual railway construction progressed at a very slow pace. When Porfirio Díaz assumed power in 1877, the railroad network had only 684 kilometers, of which 424 were from the Ferrocarril Mexicano. By 1880 it increased by 400 more kilometers, including several short sections under local management, such as the lines Mexico City–Cuautla, Mexico City–Toluca–Cuautitlán, Mérida–Progreso, and Celaya–León.[47]

Toward the end of the first Díaz administration (1877–80) and during the term of President Manuel González (1881–84), the government finally had the funds or the public credit to launch an aggressive program to expand the railroad network; 4,780 more kilometers of track were built in that four-year period. By 1892, there were 10,266 kilometers of track in operation, 9,400 of which operated under federal concession.[48]

The government made a significant effort to construct the railways, eventually putting severe pressure on public finances. During the 1881–84 period, public deficits averaged 19.3 percent of total expenditures. This deficit was financed with domestic debt. After 1888, the deficits were financed with foreign debt as well.[49] The government directly subsidized the construction of most of the railroads through tax exemptions, land grants, and even cash subsidies, which created a "crowding in" effect on private investment. The subsidies paid as much as 8,500 pesos per kilometer, which amounted to between 20 and 35 percent of the cost of construction. The funds were given to the companies in cash and government bonds that paid 6-percent interest. The issue of these bonds was eventually termed the "railroad debt" and the bonds were guaranteed with rights over customs duties. By 1890, when this debt was first renegotiated, its standing value was 36.8 million pesos, which was equivalent to 49.4 percent of the internal debt and 28.9 percent of all public debt at that time.[50]

The first spurt in the construction of the railroads, which was from 1880 to 1892, linked the main cities, the most important mining centers, and the most relevant seaports and border towns.[51] By 1894, almost all the most important cities and towns listed in the first population census of

TABLE 3.4

Exports Through Selected Mexican Border Towns or Ports
Linked by the Railroads, 1878–1900

(accumulated millions of dollars)

Place	1878–80	1881–85	1886–90	1891–95	1896–1900
Veracruz	36.4*	88.1	72.7	76.3	61.1
Tampico	3.5	5.0	3.0	24.3*	82.7
Progreso	4.8	16.1*	22.3	23.1	36.9
Ciudad Juárez	—	12.6*	49.7	47.4	42.8
Nogales	—	1.5*	2.3	4.8	16.2
Laredo	0.6	3.6*	7.1	13.4	11.2
Sum	45.3	126.9	157.1	189.3	250.9
Total exports	82.6	172.6	205.9	255.1	307.3
Exports through these customs	54.8%	73.5%	76.3%	74.2%	81.7%

SOURCE: INEGI 1985: Tables 18.1, 18.5, 20.6.
NOTE: An * indicates the period in which the port or town was incorporated into the railroad system. Original figures in pesos have been converted to current dollars.

1895 were already linked by the railroad system.[52] Also, a profound diversification of export outlets took place as the new railroads linked different areas of the country. From 1878 to 1880, 55 percent of total exports were shipped through Veracruz, which was the only port connected by the railways at the time. Laredo, Tampico, and Progreso in Yucatán had very little traffic. Once they were linked by the railroads, however, their operations grew enormously (see Table 3.4). One specific case is worth noting. Tampico, a seaport on the Gulf of Mexico that had very little traffic in 1880, surpassed all other ports by the end of the century, even before the oil boom affected it. By the turn of the century, 82 percent of the outward traffic was channeled through the above four ports linked by the railroads. Freight tonnage increased substantially. The average rate of growth of tonnage carried between 1880 and 1895 was 20.5 percent, and 9.5 percent between 1895 and 1910. The railroads were used more intensively as time passed (see Table 3.5).

Passenger operations were important as well. The railroads transported 1 million passenger in 1880; by 1895, that number had increased to 5.7 million. The total population of the country was 12.6 million at that time. By 1910, the number of passengers increased to 17.7 million, while total population was 15.2 million. The linkage of the most important consumer and production centers by the railroads and its increasing use implied that, for the first time in Mexico's history, the domestic market began its integration in a profound way and new areas of the country were developed.

TABLE 3.5

Mexican Railroad Indicators, 1885 –1910

				Average ratio of growth (%)		
Indicator	1885	1895	1910[a]	1880–95	1895–1910	1880–1910
Track[b]	963	10,537	19,748	17.3	4.3	10.6
Passengers[c]	1,018	5,653	17,670	12.1	8.5	10.3
Freight[d]	250	4,073	14,440	20.5	9.5	15.0
Total population[e]	9,000	12,632	15,160	2.3	1.2	1.8

SOURCE: INEGI 1985: Tables 1.1, 15.14.
[a]For passengers and freight, figures are for 1909.
[b]In kilometers.   [d]In thousands of tons.
[c]In thousands.   [e]In thousands.

Stephen Haber estimates that by 1895 the internal market had grown more than threefold since 1861 and was composed of more than 5 million people with purchasing power to acquire manufactured goods. This created important economies of scale and positive externalities for the rest of the economy. Nevertheless, the strong concentration of wealth and the low level of wages for the common citizen limited the effective demand for cheap manufactured commodities.[53]

The construction of the railroads generated the export boom that characterized the Mexican economy through the last three decades of the nineteenth century. In opposition to the conventional view that the depreciation of the exchange rate was the major impulse for the export boom during the Porfiriato, a recent study shows that it was the railroads that permitted such export expansion. The railroads suddenly brought closer the huge American and European markets that had been "too far" in terms of transportation costs for exporting many of Mexico's minerals and other agricultural products. The reduction in transportation costs caused industry to react as if the railroads suddenly lowered the equivalent of export taxes in a drastic way. This statement is based on the estimation of an export function for the 1895–1910 period, performed by V. de Allende and L. López, which shows that the "availability-of-track" elasticity is 1.058, while the real exchange-rate elasticity is only 0.301, both being statistically significant. Export demand measured by the U.S. domestic product was not significant.[54]

The construction of the railroads made more profitable some mining centers that otherwise would have had low productivity or might not have been exploited at all due to lack of transportation. This created the possibility of exporting large quantities of several minerals other than precious metals for the first time. For instance, the exploitation of minerals such as copper, zinc, and lead finally became profitable. So too did the export of agricultural products such as cotton, coffee, tobacco, and sisal. This occurred at the time when foreign demand for some of these products was growing, partly because of the so-called second industrial revolution.[55]

The economy's engine of growth from the 1870's until the end of the Porfiriato was undoubtedly the export sector (see Table 3.6). According to recent estimates, exports measured in dollars increased at an average rate of 3.9 percent in the 1878–95 period and then accelerated to 6.9 percent

TABLE 3.6

Indicators of Mexican Economic Growth, 1878–1910

(annual average rates of change)

Indicator	1878–95	1895–1910	1878–1910
Real gross national product	n.a.	2.9	n.a.
Agriculture	n.a.	1.5	n.a.
Manufacturing[a]	3.1	5.8	4.1
Mining[b]	5.4	6.1	5.6
Exports (current dollars)	3.9	6.9	5.3
Export quantum	7.0	8.4	7.6
Imports (current dollars)	3.7	6.6	5.0
Import quantum	6.0	4.0	5.1
Terms of trade	−0.7	−3.7	−2.2
Capacity to import	6.2	4.4	5.3
Nominal exchange rate (pesos per dollar)	3.4	0.3	1.9
Real exchange rate (pesos per dollar)	2.5[c]	−2.9	−0.9[d]
Nominal money supply	2.4[e]	5.0	3.8[f]
Nominal fiscal revenues[g]	4.6	6.1	5.3
Nominal public expenditure[g]	4.9	5.1	5.0
Nominal public investment	5.4	7.4	6.3

SOURCES: Real gross national product; agriculture; manufacturing; mining: INEGI 1985: Table 8.2. Cotton consumed for 1878 manufacturing index: INEGI 1985: Table 13.6.

Silver and gold production for 1878 mining index: INEGI: 1985: Table 10.1

Exports, export quantum, imports, import quantum, terms of trade: Catão 1991: Tables A.2.1, A.2.2. Capacity to import: calculated by the author with figures above.

Nominal exchange rate: INEGI 1985: Table 20.6. Real exchange rate, Mexico wholesale prices: INEGI 1985: Table 19.2.

U.S. prices: U.S. Bureau of the Census 1970. Money supply: Catão 1991: Table A.3.1. Fiscal revenues and expenditures: INEGI 1985: Table 17.2. Public investment: INEGI 1985: Table 16.1.

NOTE: n.a. indicates data are not available.

[a]Manufacturing output for 1878 was estimated from figures on raw cotton consumed then linked to the manufacturing GDP series of 1895.

[b]Mining output for 1878 was estimated from gold and silver production values obtained by taking the weighted average of their rates of growth, with 1880 relative weights. Then this index was linked to the extractive industry GDP series of 1895.

[c]Period 1886–95.

[d]Period 1886–1910.

[e]Period 1882–95.

[f]Period 1882–1910.

[g]Effective revenues and expenditures.

from 1895 to 1910. Although aggregate output data are not available prior to 1895, some isolated indicators show that the economy was growing. Mining and some agricultural commodities, like sisal and coffee, were expanding along with exports. Tonnage of gold and silver increased 5.4 percent from 1877 to 1895. The number of spindles installed and the amount of raw cotton consumed in the textile industry increased at an annual average rate of 3.1 percent in the 1877–95 period.[56]

After 1895, the process of economic growth accelerated, but in a very unbalanced way. Real aggregate output increased at an average rate of only 2.9 percent in the 1895–1910 period, basically because agriculture, by far the largest component of output at the time, grew at only 1.5 percent per year, apparently as a consequence of weakening demand. Meanwhile, mining grew at 5.9 percent annually and manufacturing at 5.8 percent.

The economy could have done much better if the terms of trade had been more favorable in those years. They diminished 43.4 percent during the 1895–1910 period, an average of 3.7 percent a year. Therefore, Mexico's capacity to import, defined as the export value over the price of imports, only increased 4.4 percent in that period vis-à-vis the 8.4-percent growth of the export quantum and the 6.9-percent increase of nominal exports (see Table 3.6).

The export boom naturally generated larger quantities of tax revenues, private savings, and foreign exchange in spite of the fact that most export firms were foreign owned. This statement can be indirectly corroborated by the fact that the differential in growth rates of exports and imports was relatively small: 0.2 percentage points in the 1878–95 period and 0.3 percentage points in the 1895–1910 years. Therefore, the availability of dollars and the growth of the economy reactivated the importation of goods, which increased at an annual rate of 3.7 percent between 1878 and 1895 and 6.6 percent between 1895 and 1910 (see Table 3.6). In addition, the composition of trade also changed rapidly. Imports of capital goods grew from 47 to 57 percent of total imports between 1889 and 1911. During the 1895–1905 period, which was characterized by a strong process of industrialization, capital-goods imports increased 21 percent on average per year.[57]

Fiscal revenues in nominal terms increased at an average annual rate of 4.2 percent in the 1870–95 period and 5.7 percent between 1895 and 1910. This enabled the government to finance public works and services that were linked to other productive sectors of the economy. As a whole, public investment in nominal terms is estimated to have increased on average 6.3 percent a year from 1878 to 1910. The government was devoting increasing resources to productive investment, both in absolute and relative terms.

A financial sector was finally able to develop within this environment of economic growth. As Haber argues in this volume, the banking system appeared very late for three reasons: the small size of the Mexican economy, the politicized nature of defending property rights and enforcing contracts, and the lack of appropriate legislation. The impact of the growing banking system did not play a major role in the development of industry. Firms used very little financial capital even when stockholders also had interests in the banks. The banking system was led by an in-group of financiers closely related to the Díaz government. This elite group used its political influence to build barriers to entry into the financial sector which, in turn, created a more concentrated industrial structure, at least in the case of cotton textiles.[58] To a large extent, the first banks were a new version of the *agiotistas* of the beginning of the century, because their most important client continued to be the government.[59] However, at least short term credit was more readily available to help carry out the day-to-day transactions of the economy. From 1882 to 1895, the money supply in nominal terms increased at an average rate of 2.4 percent and then accelerated its growth through the end of the Porfiriato at a rate of 5.0 percent per year.

In addition to the development of the railroads, the depreciation of the exchange rate also dynamized the economy. In the early 1870's, the international price of silver relative to gold began to fall. Higher worldwide production of silver as a consequence of technological improvements in mining, as well as greater demand for gold as more countries moved from silver or bimetallic regimes to the gold standard, made the price of silver fall 32.3 percent between 1872 and 1891. The nominal exchange rate of the silver peso relative to the gold dollar or the pound sterling depreciated in the same proportion. Starting in 1892, the nominal and the real exchange rate depreciated even more quickly. Between 1892 and 1899 the nominal and the real exchange rate depreciated 44.4 percent and 56.8 percent, respectively.[60] The real depreciation occurred essentially because of high prices of manufactured goods and sticky prices of nontradables (mostly high bulk-to-value agricultural goods) at a time of nominal depreciation. This promoted a strong impulse for import substitution.[61] Big firms often supplied a large share of the domestic market, further pushing out traditional artisanal workshops. Among those firms that covered a large segment of the market were Fundidora Monterrey, San Rafael y Anexas (paper), Compañía Industrial de Orizaba and Industrial Veracruzana (textiles), El Buen Tono and Tabacalera Mexicana (tobacco), Compañía Industrial Jabonera de la Laguna (soap), Vidriera Monterrey (glass), Cementos Hidalgo, Cementos Cruz Azul and Cementos Tolteca (cement), and the breweries Cuauhtémoc and Moctezuma, among others.[62]

In this fashion, the industrial sector began a new phase of modern development starting in the 1890's. New firms employing modern technology designed to capture scale economies were established, both in the consumer sector and in the intermediate goods sector. The market was growing, there was sufficient foreign exchange to import technology and raw materials, and profits were high because the real exchange rate was depreciating. Manufacturing output increased 106 percent in real terms between 1895 and 1910, 5.1 percent annually. In the last decade of the nineteenth century, import substitution contributed to over 30 percent of manufacturing growth, especially in the textile industry.[63] For the first time in Mexico's economic history, the industrial sector began to play an important role in the growth of the economy, although it would have to wait until the 1930's to become the actual engine of Mexico's economic growth, again through a process of import substitution.

In the early years of the nineteenth century, and especially during the War of Independence, the Mexican economy suffered a crippling blow. Productive capacity was severely damaged, capital flight emptied the country of cash and credit resources, and political instability and traditional forms of organization created an unfavorable environment for businesses.

The first two decades after Mexico became independent were particularly painful to the economy. Mining output continued to be depressed despite heavy foreign investments. As a result, and as a consequence of the capital and monetary drain suffered since early in the century, a major scarcity of money made the economy's recovery more difficult. The government had to turn to money lenders to finance its operations.

Nevertheless, modern factories were established by the late 1830's, incorporating new technologies and forms of organization, and flourishing under a tariff umbrella and the recovery of the money supply. Other economic activities seem to have been unable to develop, partly because capital financing was scarce and partly because markets were small and segmented due to the lack of a good transportation network.

From the end of the War of Independence in 1821 until the 1860's, economic activity did not attain its level of colonial times. The eventual recovery of the mining sector reactivated the economy through increases in the money supply and the expansion of foreign trade. This started to produce public and private savings that, along with foreign investment, helped to finance the construction of the railroads. The opening of the railroads is the major factor explaining the export boom of the Porfiriato, which led the rest of the economy.

The railroad network linked the most important urban centers; it connected mining and other production areas with towns, cities, and export outlets, integrating the domestic market for the first time and allowing for greater exports. Profits increased and markets expanded, creating the conditions for economic growth. The creation of a sufficiently large domestic market, along with a real depreciation of the exchange rate, established the basis for large-scale, modern industrial development in the 1890's. In the last decade of the century, import substitution was a driving force of industrial growth.

The role that mining and the railroads played in nineteenth-century Mexico is of the utmost importance. Mining provided the economy with surplus money and foreign exchange needed for economic growth. The railroads reduced barriers to the mobilization of goods, services, and factors of production. According to Coatsworth's estimates, the railroads contributed at least one-quarter of the productivity growth in Mexico during the Porfiriato, as a consequence of substantial savings from lower transportation costs. The spurt in productivity growth was actually concentrated in the second half of the Díaz administration, when at least 36.4 percent of output growth is explained by the construction of the railroads.[64] Economic growth would have been much greater, however, had it not been for a dramatic decrease in the terms of trade that accompanied the export boom in the last third of the century. While the export quantum increased at an annual average rate of 8.4 percent from 1895 to 1910, the capacity to import increased at only 4.4 percent a year. The Mexican economy nevertheless increased output more during the last 20 years of the Porfiriato than it had during the previous 70 years of independence.

Appendix

Table 3.7 shows volume of trade figures for the 1826–49 period, which were calculated as follows. Imports were taken directly from D. Stevens,[65] who considers imports coming from the United States, Great Britain, and France, which provided almost all Mexican imports. With regard to exports, two estimates are provided, both based on Mexico's silver exports. Although there is room for inaccuracies regarding silver and gold registered exports, as mentioned by Salvucci,[66] they seem to provide a general trend, as compared to that of Mexico's silver exports to the United States, which are regarded as more sound. Then, the two estimates consider a dif-

TABLE 3.7

Estimation of Mexico's Volume of Trade, 1826–49

	Imports[a] (1)	Exports I[b] (2)	Exports II[c] (3)	Volume of Trade I (4) = (1) + (2)	Volume of Trade II (5) = (1) + (3)
1826	9.1	7.2	6.8	16.3	15.9
1827	10.6	12.7	11.4	23.3	22.0
1828	6.4	16.2	14.6	22.6	20.0
1829	5.8	15.7	14.1	21.5	19.9
1830	14.4	13.7	12.4	29.1	26.8
1831	13.9	9.6	8.6	23.5	22.5
1832	7.1	18.6	16.7	25.7	23.8
1833	10.5	17.7	15.9	28.2	26.4
1834	10.0	10.6	9.5	20.6	19.5
1835	14.5	16.6	14.9	31.1	29.4
1836	9.2	11.1	10.0	20.3	19.2
1837	8.4	2.0	1.8	10.4	10.2
1838	6.6	3.9	3.5	10.5	10.1
1839	7.7	15.2	13.6	22.9	21.3
1840	7.6	8.4	7.5	16.0	15.1
1841	6.7	15.3	13.1	22.0	20.5
1842	5.7	11.1	10.0	16.8	15.7
1843	6.9	13.9	12.5	20.8	19.4
1844	7.0	15.3	13.8	22.3	20.8
1845	6.4	14.7	13.3	21.1	19.7
1846	5.1	12.7	11.4	17.8	16.5
1847	1.4[d]	1.2	1.0	2.6	2.4
1848	8.8[d]	14.9	12.9	23.7	21.7
1849	13.0[d]	16.5	14.4	29.5	27.4

SOURCES: Imports: Stevens 1991: 20. Exports of silver: Lerdo de Tejada 1853: Table 52.
[a]Imports from the United States, United Kingdom, and France only.
[b]Estimated considering 0.746 share of silver in total exports.
[c]Estimated considering 0.85 share of silver in total exports.
[d]United Kingdom and United States only.

ferent ratio of silver to total exports, providing in that way upper and lower bounds. The first estimate, an upper "conservative" bound, considers a silver share of 0.746 in total exports, which is the actual average in the 1796–1820 period provided by M. Lerdo de Tejada.[67] This share is actually higher than that observed from 1796 to 1804, when silver exports were booming. The second estimate, a lower bound, is calculated by assuming a corresponding share of 0.85, which is quite large compared to historical figures during the colonial period. The exports of silver are provided by Lerdo de Tejada.[68]

Notes

Partial research funds were granted by the UDLA–Brown Program and the Instituto de Estudios Avanzados of the Universidad de las Américas–Puebla. I am indebted to the participants' comments during the conference, particularly to Stephen

Haber, who made extensive written comments and suggestions. The usual disclaimers apply. I am also grateful to Maria Carmen Dircio for research assistance, to Elia Solis for typing part of the material, and to the hospitality of the Latin American Studies Program and the Economics Department at Brown University.

1. Coatsworth 1978: 82.

2. Coatsworth 1978: 92. Also see Stevens 1991: 25–27; Tenenbaum 1986.

3. For an exception, see Salvucci, chap. 8, this volume.

4. Indeed, since colonial times, the Mexican market economy has been heavily dependent on the foreign sector. The most typical transmission mechanisms of export crisis or boom to the rest of the economy, before the Keynesian revolution, are the following: a fall in foreign demand affects the domestic economy by reducing the actual demand for domestic exportable goods, and that of other sectors directly or indirectly related, thus having a real negative impact on aggregate production. A similar outcome would occur when the export sector declined as a consequence of supply deficiencies. Given the fact that most fiscal revenues originated from international trade duties during the nineteenth century, a fall in trade volumes would also reduce public revenues and consequently public expenditures or increase indebtedness to finance the deficit. Finally, an export crisis would affect negatively the current account of the balance of payments and consequently the monetary base, thus affecting the supply of money in circulation. The reverse effects would occur in the event of an export boom. Therefore, there would be both real and monetary consequences when the foreign sector faced either dramatic booms or recessions. The relationship between the behavior of the export sector and its impact on the Mexican domestic economy in a long-term perspective is explored in Cárdenas 1989.

5. Bernstein 1964: 12. For a full description of the impact of the war on mining, see Gortari 1989.

6. Cited in Cárdenas 1984: 13.

7. Lerdo de Tejada 1853: Table 14.

8. This is a very conservative estimate, because registered exports excluding net royal remittances (revenue less the cost of running the colony) almost reached the upper bound of the estimate.

9. Gortari 1989: 138; Marichal 1989: 103–30.

10. Coatsworth 1978: 82–86.

11. Potash 1986.

12. Tenenbaum 1986: 34, 59–60.

13. Gortari 1989: 149–61.

14. Bernstein 1964: 13–14; Randall 1972: 86–108; Gortari 1989.

15. González Reyna 1956: 96.

16. Gibson 1964: 246–56; Bakewell 1971: 125–26.

17. The correlation coefficient for these two variables over the 1700–1810 period is .994, and .983 for 1700–1830. Calculated by the author, with production and coinage figures taken from González Reyna 1956: 96; Howe 1949: 455–59, respectively.

18. The estimate of new money supply availability for domestic uses is the differ-

ence between mining production, using gold and silver coinage as a proxy, and their exports. This figure does not include royal net remittances to Spain, estimated to be between 5 and 6 million pesos a year before independence, according to various authors (Lerdo de Tejada 1853: 26–28; TePaske 1989: 65–66). This estimate is only an indicator because other uses of gold and silver, such as service payments to foreigners for shipping and insurance, unregistered exports as contraband, or other reasons are not accounted for. Therefore, these figures constitute an upper-bound estimate.

19. Tenenbaum 1986: 108–13.

20. During the 1796–1820 period, silver represented 76.4 percent of total exports. Lerdo de Tejada 1853: Table 14.

21. Two British loans were contracted in 1824/5 for 32 million pesos, although Mexico only received a little over 17 million in cash. Tenenbaum 1986: 21–22.

22. For example, the Real del Monte company raised in London the equivalent of 4.9 million pesos for its operations in Pachuca between 1824 and 1840. Randall 1972: 81.

23. Those estimates come from incomplete data, but they show the correct trends. See the appendix for the data and methodology in their calculation.

24. Cotton textile import figures are taken from Statement of Commerce, various years, while total imports are in U.S. Bureau of the Census 1975: series U321, p. 904.

25. Stevens 1991: 20.

26. Salvucci 1991: 710–14.

27. Statement of Commerce, various years, U.S. Bureau of the Census 1975: series U321, p. 904.

28. Tenenbaum 1986: 58.

29. Potash 1986. The Catholic Church, a traditional moneylender throughout the colonial period, also tended to diminish such operations as the government became more hostile and when people were legally exempted from paying the tithe in 1833.

30. Rodríguez 1989: 12.

31. These and the following public revenue figures are taken from Tenenbaum 1986: 178–82.

32. Bazant 1968: 24–35.

33. González Reyna 1956: 96. The microeconomic reasons for the growth trend of mining extend well beyond the scope of this chapter.

34. The standard reference is Potash 1986.

35. The financing from the bank to the whole industry by the early 1840's was only partial. Haber 1989: 64.

36. Potash 1986: 216, 219–20. Figures in parentheses indicate the percentage of spindles in each city.

37. Statement of Commerce, various years.

38. Sandoval 1976: 19–21, cited in Cardoso 1980: 152. It is interesting to note that the boom in mechanized manufacturing did not completely exterminate traditional artisan workshops. It has been estimated that by 1862 207 factories pro-

duced approximately the same output as 21,320 traditional workshops, yet, at the same time, in the textile and clothing industries there were still 3,555 artisanal shops in addition to 84 modern factories. Cardoso 1980: 153–60.

39. Coatsworth 1978: 90–92.

40. González Reyna 1956: 96.

41. U.S. Bureau of the Census 1975: 904, 907.

42. INEGI 1985: 845.

43. The 1878–79 textile census seems to understate the size of the industry. Therefore, the rate of growth mentioned could be somewhat higher. Sandoval 1976, cited by Cardoso 1980: 152.

44. Statement of Commerce, various years.

45. INEGI 1985: 643.

46. Pletcher 1950.

47. Coatsworth 1981: 358.

48. INEGI 1985: 592; Coatsworth 1981: 35–38.

49. Mexico's foreign debt service had been temporarily resumed during the Maximilian period, but then had fallen in moratoria again in 1867, when the new republican government repudiated the Second Empire's debt. In 1886 the so-called *Conversión de Dublán,* named after the then minister of finance Manuel Dublán, was signed, by which all former and accumulated debt was recognized obtaining a 37.3 percent discount. In this way, foreign credit was reestablished. De Allende and López 1991: 69–71.

50. De Allende and López 1991: 33–34, 98–99.

51. There was a second great impulse between 1896 and 1909, when 8,362 more kilometers of track were added to complete a grand total of 19,205 kilometers by 1910. Coatsworth 1981: 35–38.

52. The only towns that were listed but had no railroad are Colima, Cuernavaca, Culiacan, Chilpancingo, La Paz, Tlaxcala, Tuxtla Gutierrez, and Villahermosa, with an aggregate population of 72,700 inhabitants. On the other hand, among the many cities and towns connected by the railroads, the following list shows the point clearly: Mexico City, Puebla, Guadalajara, Querétaro, Morelia, Pátzcuaro, Veracruz, Orizaba, Córdoba, Jalapa, Perote, Apizaco, Atlixco, Toluca, Celaya, León, Guanajuato, San Miguel de Allende, Irapuato, Silao, Aguascalientes, San Luis Potosi, Saltillo, Monterrey, Zacatecas, Durango, Torreon, Monclova, Lerdo, Fresnillo, Chihuahua, Hermosillo, Ciudad Juárez, Nogales, Laredo, Tampico, Ciudad Victoria, Ciudad Valles, Pénjamo, Tulancingo, Pachuca, Mérida, Campeche, Oaxaca, Tehuacán, Izúcar de Matamoros, Cholula, and many others. INEGI 1985: Table 1.4; Secretaría de Comunicaciones 1895.

53. Haber 1989: 27–29.

54. The value of exports was made a function of the real exchange rate, the foreign demand, and railroad track availability. The function was specified in logarithmic terms, and the period used was 1895–1910. De Allende and López 1991: 180–84.

55. In most Mexican mines, zinc, lead, and copper were extracted along with silver and gold, but the nonprecious minerals were not actually exploited because

their cost of transportation was unprofitably high. Once these mining centers were linked by railroad to the export markets, the mines' productivity increased radically.

56. INEGI 1985: Table 10.1, 13.6.

57. De Allende and López 1991: 34–35.

58. See Haber, chap. 6, this volume.

59. The largest commercial bank, the Banco Nacional de México, acted as the government's bank and financial agent in exchange for privileges and certain prerogatives. Sánchez Martínez 1983: 61–62; Haber, chap. 6, this volume.

60. Catão 1991: 153–55.

61. Catão 1991: 173–82.

62. The concentration of those firms was enormous. For example, the soap company mentioned controlled 90 percent of the national market; the two textile firms mentioned covered 20 percent of the whole textile production; El Buen Tono covered 50 percent, while Tabacalera Mexicana supplied 20 percent, of the cigarette and cigar market. For a more profound discussion see, Haber 1989: chap. 4.

63. Catão 1991: 180.

64. Coatsworth 1981: 116–19.

65. Stevens 1991: 20.

66. Salvucci 1991: 706–7.

67. Lerdo de Tejada 1853: Table 14.

68. Lerdo de Tejada 1853: Table 52.

References

Bakewell, P. J. 1971. *Silver Mining and Society in Colonial Mexico: Zacatecas 1546–1700*. Cambridge, Eng.

Bazant, J. 1968. *Historia de la deuda exterior de México*. Mexico City.

Bernstein, M. 1964. *The Mexican Mining Industry 1890–1950: A Study of the Interaction of Politics, Economics, and Technology*. New York.

Brading, D. 1971. *Miners and Merchants in Bourbon Mexico 1763–1810*. Cambridge, Eng.

Cárdenas, E. 1984. "Algunas cuestiones sobre la depresión mexicana del XIX." *Revista Latinoamericana de Historia Económica y Social* 3: 3–22.

Cárdenas, E. 1989. "Contemporary Economic Problems in Historical Perspective." In Dwight S. Brothers and Adele E. Wick, eds., *Mexico's Search for a New Development Strategy*, pp. 1–25. Boulder, Colo.

Cardoso, C. 1980. "Las industrias de transformación (1821–1880)." In C. Cardoso, ed., *México en el Siglo XIX (1821–1910). Historia económica y de la estructura social*. Mexico City.

Catão, L. A. V. 1991. "The Transmission of Long Cycles Between 'Core' and 'Periphery' Economies: A Case Study of Brazil and Mexico, c. 1870–1940." Ph.D. diss., Darwin College, Cambridge University.

Coatsworth, J. H. 1978. "Obstacles to Economic Growth in Nineteenth Century Mexico." *The American Historical Review* 83, no. 1: 80–100.

Coatsworth, J. H. 1981. *Growth Against Development: The Economic Impact of Railroads in Porfirian Mexico.* De Kalb, Ill.

De Allende, V., and L. López. 1991. "La economía mexicana durante el Porfiriato. Análisis macroeconómico e interacción entre los sectores público y privado." Licenciatura thesis, Universidad de las Américas, Puebla, Mexico.

Gibson, C. 1964. *The Aztecs under Spanish Rule: A History of the Indians of the Valley of Mexico, 1519–1810.* Stanford.

González Reyna, J. 1956. *Riqueza minera y yacimientos minerales de México,* 3rd ed. Mexico City.

Gortari, H de. 1989. "La minería de México durante le guerra de independencia, 1810–1824." In J. Rodriguez, ed., *The Independence of Mexico and the Creation of the New Nation.* Los Angeles.

Haber, S. 1989. *Industry and Underdevelopment: The Industrialization of Mexico, 1890–1940.* Stanford.

Haber, S. 1991. "Industrial Concentration and Capital Markets: A Comparative Study of Brazil, México and the United States, 1830–1930." *Journal of Economic History* 51, no. 3 (Sept.): 559–80.

Howe, W. 1949. *The Mining Guild of New Spain and Its Tribunal General 1770–1821.* Cambridge, Mass.

INEGI [Instituto Nacional de Estadística, Geografía, é Informática]. 1985. *Estadísticas Históricas.* Mexico City.

Lerdo de Tejada, M. 1853. *El comercio esterior de Mexico desde la conquista hasta hoy.* Mexico City.

Marichal, C. 1989. "La Iglesia y la crisis financiera del virreinato, 1780–1808; apuntes sobre un tema viejo y nuevo." *Relaciones, Estudios de Historia y Sociedad* 10, no. 40 (fall): 103–30.

Pletcher, D. M. 1950. "The Building of the Mexican Railway." *Hispanic American Historical Review* 30 (Feb.): 26–62.

Potash, R. A. 1986. *El Banco de Avío de México, El fomento a la industria 1821–1846.* Mexico City.

Randall, R. 1972. *Real del Monte: A British Mining Venture in Mexico.* Austin, Tex.

Rodríguez, J. E. 1989. "Down from Colonialism: Mexico's Nineteenth-Century Crisis." In J. E. Rodríguez, ed., *The Mexican and Mexican American Experience in the 19th Century,* pp. 7–23. Tempe, Ariz.

Salvucci, R. 1991. "The Origins and Progress of U.S.-Mexican Trade, 1825–1884: 'Hoc opus, hic labor est.'" *Hispanic American Historical Review* 71, no. 4: 697–735.

Sánchez Martínez, H. 1983. "El sistema financiero mexicano bajo una perspectiva histórica: el Porfiriato." In J. Quijano, ed., *La banca: pasado y presente.* Mexico City.

Sandoval, R. 1976. "Industria textil mexicana: siglo XIX." *Estadísticas Económicas del siglo XIX.* Mexico City.

Secretaría de Comunicaciones y Obras Públicas. 1895. *Reseña histórica y estadística de los ferrocarriles de jurisdicción federal, 1837–1894.* Mexico City.

Stein, S., and B. Stein. 1970. *The Colonial Heritage of Latin America.* Oxford.

Stevens, D. 1991. *Origins of Instability in Early Republican Mexico*. Durham, N.C.

Tenenbaum, B. 1986. *The Politics of Penury: Debts and Taxes in Mexico, 1821–1856*. Albuquerque.

TePaske, J. J. 1989. "The Financial Disintegration of the Royal Government of Mexico During the Epoch of Independence." In J. Rodriguez, ed., *The Independence of Mexico and the Creation of the New Nation*. Berkeley.

U.S. Bureau of the Census. 1975. *Historical Statistics of the United States, Colonial Times to 1970. Bicentennial Edition*. 2 vols. Washington, D.C.

Statement of Commerce (and Navigation of the United States). Various years. The publication changes its name slightly during the century.

CHAPTER 4

Transport Improvements and Economic Growth in Brazil and Mexico

WILLIAM SUMMERHILL

In contrast to the North Atlantic economies that enjoyed impressive increases in per capita income in the nineteenth century, Latin American economies proved to be laggard. Institutional and technological innovations experienced in the industrializing countries in the late eighteenth and early nineteenth centuries often did not take hold in Latin America until the late nineteenth and early twentieth centuries, making for relatively poor economic performance. However, when such changes did eventually come about in Latin America their consequences were far-reaching. Thanks to both the adoption of new techniques of production and distribution and institutional changes designed to unfetter the economy, the pace of economic growth picked up dramatically by the end of the nineteenth century in many Latin American countries, including Mexico and Brazil. It is unlikely that any single technological innovation or improvement in economic organization was more important in the transition to economic growth in these countries than railroads.

In areas that suffered from backward prerail transport systems and high transport costs, railroads dramatically improved the efficiency and affordability of inland transportation. By providing for the low-cost overland movement of goods, the new technology effected a tremendous increase in the supply of transport services to Latin American economies. That the railroad was more efficient than preexisting sources of overland transportation meant that these economies could reduce the inputs required to provide a given level of transport services. Railroads freed capital and labor previously employed in producing overland transport services, permitting these factors of production to be used in other activities, thereby raising national income. In this way railroads served as an important stimulus to economic growth in Latin America. As will be shown below, the magnitude of the gains afforded the two largest Latin American countries by railroads was unprecedented by international standards. It is an outcome that holds unparalleled significance for the region's economic history.

This chapter examines Mexico and Brazil as major examples of the degree to which railroads transformed the economies of Latin American countries that suffered from backward transportation systems. It focuses on three main issues. First, where were railroads located and how were they financed? Second, how important were the direct savings that railroads afforded the users of freight and passenger transport services to the growth of these economies? Third, what was the nature of the linkages from railroads to those sectors of the economy that provided the inputs necessary for their operation?

It is surprising that relatively little attention has been devoted in the literature on Latin America to analyzing the railroad's role in spurring economic growth.[1] The historiography has treated the role of railroads less analytically than descriptively, more often than not attempting to characterize native business culture, the role of government, and the nature of foreign business involvement in the region.[2] The absence of more theoretically and empirically informed work on the economic consequences of railroads in the region is even more surprising when one considers the ready availability of sources for such studies.[3]

Of all of the changes that characterize the transition to accelerated rates of economic growth in Brazil and Mexico in the nineteenth century, railroads were certainly the most visible.[4] They were widely heralded before their construction as the solution to the problems posed by the high cost of freight transport in the region. While shippers all too typically found their services less affordable after the advent of railroads than they had hoped, the new technology still made for tremendous cost savings for the regions they served. Because it is the character of the prerail transport sector that accounts for the high cost of moving goods, it is appropriate to pass first to a description of the transport conditions that prevailed on the eve of the railway age.

Overland Transport Before Railroads

By the early nineteenth century Great Britain and the United States possessed an impressive array of navigable rivers, canals, and wagon roads. In those countries important improvements in prerail transport were made possible by a favorable topography and were aided by institutions that served to ameliorate the problems of cooperation inherent in coordinating large investments in infrastructure. Lacking a similar topography and institutional environment, many Latin American economies maintained relatively backward transport sectors. The limited public resources of the newly independent Latin American countries made it difficult to improve the quality or capacity of the transport sector. While colonial Cuba enjoyed the fruits of cheap railroad transport before midcentury, by and large it was not until the second half of the century that Latin American nations began to construct rail networks in earnest.[5]

A description of the transport conditions in Latin America during the first part of the nineteenth century provides a sense of the strength of the brake on economic growth arising from backward prerail transport systems. In Colombia, for example, railroads first began to carry freight across the Isthmus of Panama in 1855, but the country did not place another line in operation until 1871.[6] Until then, freight was carried by river wherever possible, but most of it was shipped overland across steep terrain on the backs of humans and mules.[7]

Mexico also had no significant railroad until the completion of the line between Veracruz and Mexico City in 1873.[8] Mexico's steep mountain ranges physically partitioned the country, making for natural divisions that were extremely difficult to traverse. Lacking navigable rivers, Mexico had long relied on a combination of wagons, mules, and human porters to move freight through the country. The Spanish colonial government, seeking to improve transport conditions, had grafted a road network on top of the existing indigenous transport routes in order to link the major population centers, the mines, and ports. By the end of the eighteenth century Mexico's colonial transport system had fallen into disrepair, and there were few stretches of road where wheeled traffic could even pass. Wagons continued to carry freight wherever possible, but the bulk of the goods shipped in the nineteenth century was hauled over Mexico's steep terrain by mule.[9]

Contributing to the challenge posed by slow, inefficient transportation in nineteenth-century Mexico were a frequent lack of physical security and the dissipation of public funds that could have been used to maintain and improve the highways. Before the advent of the Porfiriato, internal strife diverted resources from public-works improvements. In the context of an ongoing struggle to control the state, it proved difficult to pursue and support consistently policies designed to enhance communications. Moreover, warfare and brigandage increased the risk, and thereby the cost, of overland transportation.[10] The Porfirian state succeeded in securing and controlling the main routes of communication, and it vigorously promoted the construction of railroads.

Brazil enjoyed its first railroad in 1854, but major lines were not in place until the 1860's. Even with its natural endowment of rivers, Brazil possessed a prerail transport system at least as backward as that of Mexico. Few Brazilian rivers were navigable in any commercially significant sense, and many were of limited relevance to all but the most localized trade. Indeed, the absence of cheap, long-haul, waterborne transport in inland areas, and the lack of an active colonial road-building scheme, conditioned early settlement patterns. By the nineteenth century, Brazil's population concentrated itself near the littoral. Interior settlement of any importance existed only in areas that were relatively accessible or in regions possessing readily marketable, high value-to-weight goods (such as the gold and diamond fields of Minas Gerais). Coastal mountains, extending from the northeast to the south, presented an imposing obstacle to overland communication with the interior. With the third largest river in the world, one might expect Brazil to exhibit a prerail transport pattern similar to that found in the United States with the Mississippi River and its tributaries. However, insalubrious tropical conditions inhibited development in the Amazon basin, the region was unsuitable for the production of many commercial crops, and most settlement occurred in proximity to the coast.[11]

Problems with riverine transport elsewhere in the country hindered internal communication as well. Other than the Amazon, the only important water route to the interior was the Rio São Francisco. It too presented problems; its upper portion, limited to vessels with a draft of three meters or less, was "much impeded by rapids and falls."[12] Steamships first traveled the navigable portions in 1867, but the river's long-term importance hinged on a connection by rail to coastal populations. Far in the interior, overland shipment by mule proved cheaper than overcoming the natural barriers to navigation. Rivers in the economically more vibrant south-center and south were of limited use in carrying freight. For example, the Paraìba do Sul, at the heart of the coffee-producing region, presented a poor means of transport, "the river being so broken by rocks in many places, requiring a skillful navigation."[13] Rivers in western São Paulo Province flowed toward the Rio Paraná, rather than toward the Brazilian coast, and the eastward flowing rivers of Paraná Province were "of no importance."[14]

Due, then, to the locus of production and the nature of terrain, overland shipment by mule became the predominant means of freight transportation in Brazil. The colonial government did not inherit a native overland transport network as had the Spanish in Mexico, and little effort was expended to create a trafficable series of roads. The few good roads constructed in the nineteenth century, such as the União e Indústria, connecting Petrópolis to Juiz de Fora, were the exception rather than the rule. Purveyors of overland freight services relied almost solely on mules as beasts of burden.[15] The animals traversed sinuous routes over steep terrain to make the trip from the interior to the coast. By 1855, some 200,000 mule trips per year were being made from the São Paulo hinterland to the port of Santos alone, long before Santos became the preeminent gateway to the hinterland. Demand for mules in Brazil's largest market remained strong until the rapid expansion of railroads in the 1880's.[16] Even after railroads supplanted mules as the predominant means of long-distance freight transport, muleteers remained prominent in a complementary role, carrying goods between railroads and areas yet unserved by rail.

That Brazil and Mexico suffered from such poor transport conditions meant that the cost of transporting freight and passengers was high. When added to the costs of other inputs to production, transport costs were high enough to eliminate any chance of profit for potential producers of a wide variety of crops and manufactures in many areas. Consumers were unable to purchase many goods that became prohibitively expensive only after the transport bill was added, and they were frequently limited to purchasing only the most basic of necessities. Confronted with long, arduous journeys by foot, animal, or coach, many Brazilians never ventured far from their immediate locale. One of the consequences of this was a sharply limited opportunity for material progress. An economy marked by high transport costs manifests lower levels of economic activity, and thus lower levels of national income, than it would if transport costs were lower. With the relative price of transportation so high, it is little wonder that farmers, mine owners, nascent industrialists, and governments sought to improve transport conditions and lower the cost of transportation by implanting a more efficient technology from abroad.

Origins of the Railroads and Sources of Finance

In spite of the overwhelming advantages offered the economy by railroads, so obvious to many contemporary observers, the new technology was slow to be adopted in Mexico and Brazil. In a region with badly underdeveloped capital markets, the sources for the huge investments required to finance the construction of railroads were few and far between. With their high fixed costs and uncertain future profits, railroads required large initial outlays to construct and operate. In countries virtually devoid of financial institutions capable of collecting large amounts of private savings and converting them into lendable funds, financing railroad construction proved to be a tremendous challenge. As a result, the early railroad history of both Brazil and Mexico is marked by government railroad concessions that never bore fruit.[17] Various sources of capital drawn from domestic and foreign capital markets financed the construction of the earliest lines. However, given the institutional constraints on the domestic financial sector, both Brazil and Mexico were ultimately forced to turn to the far more sophisticated capital markets of the industrializing North Atlantic economies, which they tapped for funds to supplement domestic railroad financing. Due to the great uncertainty over the profits to be generated by the railroads, central and provincial governments in Mexico and Brazil offered blandishments in the form of subsidies and profit guarantees to attract railroad investors. The variety of financing schemes employed meant that, by the turn of the century, each country had a railroad sector that drew funds from the personal savings of single owners, local stock and bond issues, foreign stock and bond issues, and state coffers.

Early regional lines in Mexico were financed by local entrepreneurs using sundry mechanism to raise funds, including a lottery. However, U.S. firms garnered the concessions to build the largest, and most trafficked, lines in the country in the late nineteenth century, and U.S. investors ultimately financed much of Mexico's railroad construction. "Mexicanization" of the nation's railroads by the government after the turn of the century also drew on foreign capital markets to raise loans, enabling the government to buy controlling shares of the major lines and better control rates and service.[18]

In Brazil, the early lines were built similarly, using funds drawn from local and foreign markets. The legendary entrepreneur Irieno Evangeliste de Souza, Visconte de Mauá, completed the first line, but the second and more important railroad, the Dom Pedro II, bogged down financially. The Brazilian government interceded, buying out the shareholders and becoming the sole owner of the line, which it extended in the ensuing decades, ultimately making it the largest and most important railroad in the country.[19] The next wave of railroads, built in the late 1850's and 1860's in the northeast and in São Paulo, were British companies, financed initially by stock issues, and later by bonds, in London.[20] Brazilians also financed railroads through local stock issues, as was the case of the Companhia Paulista and the Companhia Mogiana in São Paulo, and the Leopoldina, in Minas Gerais. Even there, local funds eventually dried up, and to finance expansion Brazilian-owned lines throughout Brazil later turned to London to obtain loans.[21]

The location of rail lines in both Mexico and Brazil was a function of the political and financial strength of local interests and concession practices designed to keep those interests content. *Fazendeiros* and hacendados, for example, seeking to add to their wealth, worked to ensure that a railroad would pass near their properties in order to raise the value of their land.[22] That landowners sought to have access to cheap transport meant that disputes over the trace of a given line were likely, potentially slowing concessions and construction.[23] Ultimately the result for each country was a rail system with a layout closely tied to extant areas of settlement. Mexico possessed a well-integrated rail grid by 1910, linking the major population centers to the coasts and the United States. By the turn of the century Brazil had two large regional concentrations of connected railroads: one in the northeast, which connected the interior to major ports, and a network linking the cities, farming areas, and ports of the south and south-center.

Once rail lines were constructed, landowners continued to play a central role in shaping the course of public transport policies. Complaints from landowners over high railroad freight charges were common. In the United States, agrarian populists complaining about rail rates had to await state-level regulation and the passage of the Interstate Commerce Act in 1887. By way of contrast, Brazilians and Mexicans had recourse to government intervention in rate setting from the outset. Rates were regulated in both countries, and officials responded to farmers' complaints and continually pushed rates down. In addition, both governments sought to satisfy regional interests by adopting a liberal concession scheme. In Mexico the central government passed concessions to state governments, while in Brazil provinces could concede routes within their borders while the central government granted concessions to both intra- and interprovincial lines. Moreover, while both Brazil and Mexico were traditionally high-tariff countries, railroad equipment was typically imported at reduced rates, or duty free altogether. The scheme of concessions and guarantees pursued in Mexico and Brazil meant that, even with their late start, their rail systems grew at a relatively fast rate, particularly with the fall in the price of steel rails worldwide in the 1880's. Without such policies, the pace at which cheap transport diffused in these countries would have been far slower.

Railroads and Economic Growth

How, and to what extent, did the cheaper transport provided by railroads promote economic growth in Mexico and Brazil? There were two potential channels by which railroads raised national income. The first came about through the cost savings on transporting goods and people by rail ("forward linkage," or the "social saving"). The second arose through the demand for inputs necessary for the construction and operation of railroads ("backward linkage"). In Mexico and Brazil the forward linkage was of greater magnitude, and greater importance, than the backward linkage. The total impact of the railroad is partitioned into the resource savings produced through the two main categories of transport services: the savings on freight shipment, and the benefits of passenger travel. The freight social saving of railroads is defined as the difference between the actual cost of shipping goods in one year by rail and the cost of shipping the same goods over the same distances by an alternative means of transport in the absence of railroads. Passenger social savings is similar, defined as the difference between the costs of passenger rail travel and the cost of traveling by non-rail modes.

The resource savings that railroads created on these two types of service result in an addition to total output, via the employment of these freed resources in other sectors of activity. Total output in the economy (that is, national income) with railroads is equal to the final output of the transport sector and the output of the sector that produces all other goods and services. In the case of freight shipment, using wagon or mule transport to produce the output of the transport sector means that labor and capital must be drawn from the production of other goods. Thus, under the prerail transport system, the output of the "other goods" sector of the economy will necessarily be reduced, as will national income, as a large amount of resources are tied up in producing transport services. Likewise, producing freight transport service with railroads would release labor and capital involved in transport by mule to other activities in the economy. As a rough approximation, the freight social saving achieved by shifting from wagons or mules to railroads may be taken as equivalent to the hypothetical loss in national income that would be incurred by switching back from a rail transport system to a mule transport system. Passenger social savings arise in a very similar fashion and are equal to the resources saved by transporting people by rail rather than the alternatives (walking, riding, coaching). The social-savings approach captures the direct economic impact of a shift from a relatively inefficient mode of transport to a more efficient one.[24]

The application of this model in the literature on railroads has been met with skepticism by critics of "hypothetical" or "counterfactual" history of this sort. This criticism, focusing on the way social savings are computed rather than on how resources are saved by the railroad, has been misplaced. When one considers exactly what the social saving measures, the approach emerges not as "hypothetical" history but as a static approximation of the dynamic gains arising from the increased availability of cheap transport. Low-cost transport saves resources by improving product- and labor-market integration and promoting regional specialization. With the construction of a railroad, the cost of transporting goods between two locations declines. Thus, the wedge posed by transport costs between the prices of goods in the two regions shrinks, and prices for the same goods tend toward uniformity. The affected areas enjoy gains from trade and the specialization in production.

In the case of agriculture, for example, product-market integration induces farmers to specialize in the cultivation of those crops they can produce more efficiently than farmers in other areas, purchasing goods they no longer produce at a price that is lower than the cost of producing them themselves. A similar process unfolds in all areas served by the new form of transport; each farm, and region, specializes in those activities that it can pursue most efficiently. In this way, railroads, by providing low-cost transport, improve allocative efficiency and raise the level of output and income. Furthermore, if market integration dampens the oscillations of what were previously fluctuating prices, small farmers ("peasants") who are confronted with less risk will devote more resources toward producing crops that have high market value and will expend fewer resources on insurance-related ("safety-first") activities.[25]

In the case of the labor market, railroads enhance the geographic mobility of workers, making it possible for free workers to go to jobs over distances previously considered prohibitive. In the case of slave labor, the reduced cost of transport increases the ability of slave owners to participate in slave-labor rental markets and creates new opportunities for capital gains by selling slaves in distant markets. The railroad is coldly yet efficiently undiscriminating in this regard. Cheap transport thus released resources, making the economy larger, irrespective of the free or slave status of the worker.

The resource gains from market integration and regional specialization clearly occur through time. As the railroad network expands, cheap transport becomes available on an increasingly larger scale. Moreover, railroads become more efficient over time, producing output at a lower unit cost as they operate at higher levels of capacity utilization. This process repeats itself and is extended with each new section of railroad track opened to traffic. Hence, the gains to the economy, operating through market integration and regional specialization, are dynamic in nature. Unfortunately, the limitations posed by sources and incomplete data make it impossible to measure these gains dynamically, and a static approximation is used. The social-saving approach is the best available means to measure the cumulative dynamic gains of market integration afforded the economy by low-cost railroad transport.[26]

The magnitude of the direct economic effect of railroads—the social saving—depends on two components: declining unit transport charges, which are associated with the shift to a more productive mode of transport; and the volume of freight transport services produced, which itself is a function of the responsiveness of the sector producing transportable goods to the fall in transport costs. In Mexico and Brazil the prevailing prerail overland transport costs were high, and railroad expansion resulted in large unit savings on freight services. With the growth of each nation's rail system during the second half of the nineteenth century, direct social savings became quite large. Depending on what assumptions one wishes to apply to the "counterfactual" economy without railroads, by 1900 freight social savings accounted for as much as one-quarter of Brazilian gross domestic product (GDP), while in Mexico they were around 20 percent of GDP. Passenger benefits were much less than freight savings in both countries, but larger in Brazil than in Mexico.

The discussion of the railroad's direct effects proceeds from here in two stages. The first addresses freight services while the second focuses on passenger benefits. As did many other countries, Mexico and Brazil experienced a veritable transportation revolution during the nineteenth century. Mexico moved from an economy employing wagon and mule transport to one with 20,000 kilometers of track operating under federal concession in 1910. Brazil went from a nation that relied largely on pack mules for freight transport to one that by 1913 had some 24,000 kilometers of railroads, including those operating under provincial concession.[27] Constructing the social-savings estimates requires a specification of the relevant alternative transport mode that is employed in the absence of these railroads. In the case of Mexico, the alternative was wagon roads. Table 4.1 simply reproduces the results of John Coatsworth's estimates of freight social savings for all federally conceded lines in Mexico in 1910 and for a sample of fifteen lines in 1895, 1900, and 1905.[28] The social-saving estimates for Mexico are quite large, rising to almost 40 percent of GDP in 1910, in spite of the presence of a number of downward biases in the estimating procedure. Had the Mexican economy been denied its railroads and forced to operate with wagon roads in 1910, the loss to the economy would have been huge. By this measure, railroads had succeeded in freeing an enormous quantity of labor and capital from transport, which was then employed in other sectors.

TABLE 4.1
Upper-Bound Estimate of Direct Social Savings on Railroad Freight Service in Mexico, 1895–1910

Year	DSS	DSS/GDP (%)
1895	109.8	14.6
1900	211	19.8
1905	345.5	30.4
1910	455.4	38.5

SOURCE: Coatsworth 1981: 113–19.
NOTE: DSS is the direct social savings expressed in pesos of 1900. DSS/GDP is the direct social savings expressed as a percentage of GDP.

For Brazil, the appropriate substitute means of transport used for railroads is a combination of mule trains and cartage, because these were the historically feasible alternatives. An analysis of another technologically possible alternative, wagon roads, might be of interest, but few major road companies emerged in the nineteenth century, so their historical relevance is in doubt. Moreover, the observed charges on prerail freight service by wagon afford little advantage over mules. The mule freight rates culled from the literature are high relative to the known rail rates, and certain steps are taken to attempt to bias downward the social-saving estimates. Because the mule rates come from an era in which rail competition was not yet present, they are the relevant counterfactual rates for pricing nonrail transport services. Higher rates may be found in the 1880's in Brazil's south-center, but they likely reflect mule transport as a costly source of short-haul service, complementary to rail transport. For the Brazilian estimates of freight social saving, the prerail mule rate employed is a simple average of rates from five major routes in the province of São Paulo in 1864, drawn from the contemporary financial press. It is substantially lower than most of the other contemporary citations of prerail transport costs. Beyond selecting the low mule rate, other assumptions further bias the social-saving estimates downward. All hidden costs of shipping by mule, such as insurance and uninsured losses, additional handling charges, and inventory costs arising from slower, wet-season transport, are ignored.

In Table 4.2 tentative benchmark estimates of the freight social saving of Brazilian railroads are presented for five different years. In 1913 the figures are for lines that account for more than 80 percent of the total track in service in Brazil.[29] The social-saving estimates presented in Table 4.2 warrant several qualifications.[30] No ideal price index exists for the purpose of adjusting freight charges. Freight charges are deflated using an index

TABLE 4.2

Upper-Bound Estimate of Direct Social Savings on Railroad
Freight Service in Brazil, 1869–1913

Year	Ton/km freight service[a]	Cost for mule carriage[b]	Rail freight revenues[c]	DSS[d]	GDP[e]	DS/GDP (%)
1869	32.7	27.2	8.4	18.8	1,225	1.5
1887	142.2	118.5	31.3	87.2	1,953	4.5
1898	586	488.1	95.5	392.5	1,504	26
1907	1,004	836.3	121.5	714.8	3,156	23
1913	1,697	1,413.6	164.6	1,249	5,679	22

SOURCE: Summerhill 1995: chap. 3.
NOTE: All units in millions.
[a] "Ton/km freight service" is the quantity of rail freight transport service produced.
[b] The cost for mule transport of that freight is in 1913 mil-réis; one ton-kilometer of mule freight service cost 0.393 mil-réis at 1864 prices, adjusted to 0.833 mil-réis in 1913.
[c] Railroad freight revenues are adjusted to 1913 prices by the Rio wholesale price index.
[d] The upper-bound direct social savings (DDS) is the cost for mule carriage minus rail freight revenues.
[e] GDP from Contador and Haddad 1975, in millions of 1913 mil-réis.

of wholesale prices in Rio de Janeiro, extended backwards using an index of consumer prices in Rio de Janeiro.[31] Had an index of the wages of common day labor—the best available proxy for the labor cost conditions faced by muleteers, and a likely lower bound on the opportunity cost of their own work—been used, the adjusted nonrail freight charges would have been even higher in 1913.[32]

For 1869 and 1887, railroad freight operating data in units of ton-kilometers for the entire rail sector were not available. The output figures here are derived from a sample of the sector, which in 1869 consisted of just two major railroads. The 1887 ton-kilometer figures are understated as well, based on only the six most important railroads.

The increase in the social saving as a share of GDP by 1898 reflects both the increasing output of freight service and the more complete reporting of operating data. The magnitudes reported here employ necessarily synthetic estimates of Brazilian GDP.[33] Had an alternative measure of real product been used instead, the share of national income attributable to railroad social saving would have been larger still. In broad terms, the increasing importance of low-cost rail transport is apparent in the rising share of GDP afforded the Brazilian economy by cheap transport services between 1869 and 1913. Deprived of its railroads and forced to rely on its prerail transport technology, the Brazilian economy would have lost more than 20 percent of its output had it been required to produce the same level of transport services as it did in 1913.

The upper-bound social-savings estimates reported for Brazil in 1898, 1907, and 1913 may be unrealistically large, in spite of using a conservative estimate of the unit savings on transport costs. One key assumption of the model applied thus far in measuring the social savings is that the price elasticity of demand is zero. That is, the change in the price of freight transport service that accompanies the shift from the rail mode to mules is held to have no effect on the quantity of transport services demanded. However, prior to railroads the high cost of transport no doubt meant that the volume of transport services demanded was much less than in the economy with railroads. Thus, the upper-bound estimate of social savings may well be too high. Some adjustment is warranted to account for the lower demand for transport services in the prerail economy.

Such an adjustment is feasible given some information about the sensitivity of transport demand to changes in the price of transport. This sensitivity—the price elasticity of demand—can be roughly measured using the extant information on the market for transport services in the late nineteenth century. Hence, the social-saving estimate is rendered more exact by applying a realistic value of the price elasticity of demand for transport service. Modifying the assumption of a zero price elasticity of demand for freight transport service permits a more plausible lower-bound estimate of the direct benefits provided the economy by railroads. To derive a lower-bound measure, the demand curve for freight transport services must be estimated statistically.

In the Mexican case the elasticity has been estimated to be in the range of (−0.5).[34] The sensitivity of the social savings in Mexico to different assumptions about the value of the elasticity are reported in Table 4.3. While

TABLE 4.3

*Direct Social Savings on
Railroad Freight Service in Mexico, 1910*

(adjusted for the price elasticity of demand)

Elasticity	DSS[a]	DSS/GDP[b] (%)
0	455.4	38.5
−0.5	196.9	16.6
−0.75	135.8	11.5
−1.0	95.6	8.1

SOURCE: Coatsworth 1981: 113.

[a]DSS is the direct social savings in 1910 expressed in pesos of 1900.

[b]DSS/GDP is the direct social savings expressed as a share of GDP.

the share of GDP afforded by the railroad drops precipitously with the increase in the absolute value of the elasticity, it is still quite large over the range of probable elasticity estimates. Had the Mexican economy adjusted, in the absence of railroads, to the high cost of transport by demanding fewer transport services, the social savings would still be greater than 8 percent of GDP in 1910. It would be difficult to find any other innovation that offered such a large gain to the economy.

Because no single true price elasticity of demand exists, several different specifications of the demand function for railroad freight services in Brazil are estimated. A range of values for the price elasticity of demand, derived from five variants of a demand function for freight transport service are reported in Table 4.4.[35]

The first three specifications use data from a sample of six major railroads from 1861 to 1913. In expression I the demand for freight service (Q_D), in units of ton-kilometers, is modeled as a function of the real

TABLE 4.4

Alternative Specifications of the Demand
for Freight Transport Services in Brazil, 1861–1913

[I] $\ln Q_D = (-11.9) - 0.02 \ln P - 0.01 \ln Y + 1.5 \ln N + 0.8 \ln T$
          $(-1.4)\ (-0.07)\quad (-0.06)\qquad (2.2)\qquad (8)$
          R2 = 0.95   D.W. = 2.2   Rho = 0.65

[II] $\ln Q_D = (-9.8) - 0.92 \ln P + 0.06 \ln Y + 1.3 \ln N + 0.81 \ln T$
          $(-1.2)\ (-0.28)\qquad (0.77)\qquad (2.23)\qquad (8.9)$
          R2 = 0.96   D.W. = 2.2   Rho = 0.62

[III] $\ln Q_D = (-5.7) - 0.07 \ln P + 0.073 \ln X + 1.0 \ln N + 0.92 \ln T$
          $(-1.1)\ (-3.6)\qquad (0.91)\qquad (2.7)\qquad (13.8)$
          R2 = 0.99   D.W. = 1.9   Rho = 0.61

[IV] $\ln Q_D = (-5.2) - 0.22 \ln P + 0.44 \ln Y + 0.93 \ln N$
          $(-0.1)\ (-0.56)\qquad (0.32)\qquad (0.2)$
          R2 = 0.95   D.W. = 1.9

[V] $\ln Q_D = -16 - 0.24 \ln P + 0.19 \ln Y + 1.8 \ln N + 0.07 \ln T$
          $(-0.8)\ (-1.0)\qquad (0.41)\qquad (1.0)\qquad (0.09)$
          R2 = 0.95   D.W. = 1.9

NOTE: For data sources, and assumptions behind the different specifications, see Summerhill 1995: chap. 3. The price elasticity of demand for freight transport service, α, is given by

$$\alpha = \frac{\partial \ln Q_D}{\partial \ln P}$$

which is the parameter estimate of $\ln P$ in the demand functions.

(inflation-adjusted) unit freight charge (P), real income (Y), population (N), and rail track (T).[36] A Cochrane-Orcutt procedure, using time, income, population, and track as instruments, yields a price elasticity of demand with the correct sign, but which is almost completely inelastic. The estimated income elasticity takes on the wrong sign, probably reflecting the weakness of the GDP series in the early decades. Expression II also uses instrumental variables and corrects for serial correlation, but substitutes real exports (X) for income on the assumption that in early decades export earnings better represent the income of shippers of freight.[37] These results also indicate highly inelastic demand for freight services. Expression III takes the price of freight services as wholly exogenous, assuming that prices (rates) were set in the political arena. It is estimated without instruments using the AR1 technique and provides further support for the claim that the demand for freight services was inelastic.

The sample series may well understate the strength of the relationship between the fall in freight charges and the rise in the quantity of freight services. While the sample lines very likely capture adequately the fall in freight rates experienced by the sector as a whole, they understate the rise in output for the sector. To test the sensitivity of the results to the use of sample data, equations IV and V use data from the entire sector. Expression IV is estimated using OLS regression, with time, track, and the real price of coal as instruments.[38] Equation V takes the price of freight services as exogenous and employs no instruments. While both equations exhibit somewhat greater elasticity with respect to price than do the estimates from the longer sample series, demand is still quite inelastic.

Given the rather tentative nature of measuring the price elasticity of demand for freight service, the various lower-bound social-savings figures for 1913 are estimated by varying the elasticity of demand from 0 to -1, in Table 4.5. By applying these elasticity estimates to the demand curve for freight services it is possible to establish some bounds on the probable value of the resources saved by railroad freight transport in Brazil. Adjusting the social savings for different elasticities of freight transport service gives results ranging from 6.2 percent to 22 percent of Brazilian GDP in 1913, depending on which assumptions one wishes to impose on the nature of demand. However, even if the relevant elasticity was four times as large as the highest one estimated here, the resulting lower-bound social-savings estimate of 6.2 percent of GDP still represents a significant cost savings to the Brazilian economy, even after allowing for an adjustment to the large change in the relative price of freight transport service. It is unlikely that any other single innovation or improvement in economic or-

TABLE 4.5

Lower-Bound Social Savings for
Alternative Values of the Price Elasticity of Demand for
Freight Transport Service in Brazil, 1913

α	Lower-bound social savings (LBSS) (millions of mil-réis)	LBSS as a percentage of GDP
0	1,249	22
−0.5	635.5	11.2
−0.75	468.7	8.3
−1.0	354	6.2

SOURCE: Elasticities have been derived from different specifications of the demand function for freight transport services between 1861 and 1913, and 1898 and 1913, as reported in Table 4.4 and described in the text.

NOTE: To calculate the LBSS, output is related to price by the demand function.

$$Q = DP^{\alpha}$$

where Q is the quantity of freight service demanded, in ton/kilometers, P the unit charge for freight service, α is the price elasticity of demand for freight service, and D is a shift parameter. The LBSS is derived by integrating the demand function with respect to price. For $\alpha \neq -1.0$,

$$\int_{P_R}^{P_M} DP^{\alpha} dp = D \frac{P^{\alpha+1}}{\alpha + 1} \bigg|_{P_R}^{P_M}$$

where P_M is the charge for one ton/kilometer of freight service by mule, adjusted to 1913 prices, and P_R is the charge for one ton/kilometer of freight service by rail.
For $\alpha = -1.0$, LBSS is given by

$$\int_{P_R}^{P_M} DP^{\alpha} dp = D(\ln P_M - \ln P_R)$$

ganization had such an impact on the economic growth of Brazil in this period. The lower transport costs made possible by Brazilian railroads impelled the transition from low rates of economic growth in the nineteenth century to improved economic performance in the twentieth.

Table 4.6 shows that the magnitude of railroad freight social savings in Brazil and Mexico is roughly similar when the same elasticities of demand are applied to them, although direct comparison is difficult because the Mexican case is based on a technologically feasible counterfactual means of freight transport.[39] The significance of these levels of social saving may be better understood in a broad comparative context. Table 4.7 presents direct savings estimates on railroads in a variety of countries at various times. Direct comparisons among countries are difficult to make here as well, because of the differing assumptions employed in the estimates in each

TABLE 4.6

Social Savings on Freight Services for Mexico (1910) and Brazil (1913)

Elasticity	Mexico	Brazil
0	38.5	22
−0.5	16.6	11.2
−0.75	11.5	8.3
−1.0	8.1	6.2

SOURCES: Table 4.3, Table 4.5.
NOTE: Figures are given as a percentage of each country's GDP for various measures of the price elasticity of demand for transport services.

TABLE 4.7

Estimates of Freight Social Savings for Various Countries

Country	Year	Social savings as a percentage of GDP	Country	Year	Social savings as a percentage of GDP
England and Wales	1865	4.1	Spain	1878	11.8
England and Wales	1890	11.0	Spain	1912	18.5
United States	1859	3.7	Belgium	1865	2.5
United States	1890	8.9	Belgium	1912	4.5
Russia	1907	4.6	Mexico	1910	38.5
France	1872	5.8	Brazil	1913	22.0
Germany	1890s	5.0			

SOURCES: Mexico, Table 4.1; Brazil, Table 4.2; all others, O'Brien 1982: 336–67.

case. Note, however, that in contrast to the results derived from studies of railroads in North Atlantic economies, and even from some backward economies in which prerail transport was relatively efficient, the freight social saving from railroads in Latin America was large.

Passenger savings estimates reveal a different story. Relative to the North Atlantic economies the resources released by railroad passenger services in Brazil and Mexico are positive and appreciable in magnitude, but are not especially large. The resources released by passenger services depend on two separate channels of cost savings. The first is the savings on direct travel fares, the second is the value of the time spent on the journey for working passengers that was obviated by faster travel. The details of the calculation are suppressed here.[40] Both cases share two assumptions. The first is the nonrail mode of travel. For first-class railroad passengers the alternative mode was the stage coach, while for second-class travelers the alternative mode was walking. The second assumption is the nature of de-

TABLE 4.8

Passenger Social Savings in Mexico (1910) and Brazil (1913)

	Savings	Percent
MEXICO		
On first-class passenger services as a share of GDP		1.05
On second-class passenger services as a share of GDP		0.33
Total savings on passenger savings		1.38
BRAZIL		
On first-class passenger services as a share of GDP		3.7
On second-class passenger services as a share of GDP		0.33
Total savings on passenger services		4.03

SOURCE: Summerhill 1995: chap. 4.

mand. For first-class service, demand is taken as completely inelastic; the total level of first-class passenger service is unchanged in the face of higher travel fares. For second-class service, demand is held to be perfectly elastic; at any increase in the rail fare, all travelers walk. Table 4.8 presents the final results of the fare and time savings for both countries.

For Mexico in 1910, the estimated passenger savings are less than 2 percent of GDP. For Brazil in 1913, the estimates are somewhat higher, at 4 percent of GDP. The difference between the two cases stems in part from the greater savings on first-class fares in Brazil and in part from the higher levels of first- and second-class passenger services. In both cases, the passenger benefits are of secondary importance to the economy relative to the freight benefits. Small as those savings were, railroads nonetheless improved labor-market efficiency in both countries to an appreciable degree and provided travel-cost savings to leisure or nonworking travelers.

Other Linkages

The construction of railroads in Latin America has long been viewed as increasing the export orientation of the region's economies. It is widely held that the character of forward linkages from railroads in Latin America contributed significantly to the process of export-led growth. To date, the Mexican case has been seen as the relevant example of what happens when railroads are constructed in backward economies that suffer from poorly developed transport systems. Interestingly, Brazilian railroads differed markedly from those of Mexico with regard to their forward linkage effects and their impact on the output mix of the economy. In Mexico, market conditions and railroad transport rate policies worked to favor export-sector growth. In 1885 on Mexico's most important railroad less than 25 percent of freight was export bound. By 1910 more than 50 percent of the tonnage on that same line was export-sector produce. Moreover, export-bound transportables were especially railroad intensive, using a large share of rail transport capacity.[41] While this was not the sole factor in altering the output mix of the economy, the results were still dramatic. In 1877 some 9.3 percent of Mexican output was exported. By 1910 the share of exports in GDP had risen to 17.5 percent.[42]

The forward linkage to the output mix of the Brazilian economy operated quite differently than it did in Mexico. By referring to the available railroad operating statistics and macroeconomic series for Brazil, one sees how generalizations relating export growth and late nineteenth-century economic modernization must be qualified. The expansion of Brazil's railroads was accompanied by a declining share of export-sector freight and a slowly declining ratio of exports to GDP. If the freight data of fifteen lines reporting their figures in 1887 may be taken as indicative, the share of export-sector tonnage was, at most, 60 percent—and this assumes that all enumerated agricultural staples transported were exported. Under the same assumption, the share of export-sector freight in total tonnage had declined to 30 percent by 1913. With respect to national income, the share of exports fluctuated from 18 percent to 26 percent between 1870 and 1913. It must be further cautioned that the share of exports in GDP reported here may be too high; Nathaniel Leff makes a case for an export share no greater than 15 percent in this period. The trend rate of growth of the export share of Brazilian GDP is estimated using an AR1 regression as:[43]

$$\ln(\text{exports}/\text{GDP}) = 28.8 - .016/\text{year}$$
$$(10.3) \quad (-10.7)$$
$$R_2 = .73 \quad F = 116 \quad \text{D.W.} = 1.9$$

On average, the share of exports in Brazilian GDP declined at an annual rate of slightly more than 1.5 percent from 1870 to 1913.[44] This result shows that the supply of domestic-use agricultural goods and manufactures grew at least as fast as production for export. Brazilian railroads were intended to foster export growth from their inception, but, in fact, they also spurred dramatic growth in the domestic-use sector of the economy.

Backward linkages from railroads to the Mexican and Brazilian economies were weak and provided little economic stimulus beyond the magnitude of the social savings. Material inputs, engineering skill, and even labor often came from abroad. Over time, some inputs, namely fuel and refitted rolling stock, came to be provided domestically. In general, however, the original rolling stock, track—and in the Brazilian case, even coal—were imported. The value of these imported inputs was large. In Mexico, it is estimated that around 60 percent of railroad revenues in 1910 were spent abroad on railroad inputs.[45] In Brazil for 1908, for example, the value of railroad equipment and fuel imported was greater than 62 million mil-réis, or about 89 percent of freight revenues from federally conceded lines that year.[46] That so many inputs came from abroad may be interpreted to mean that railroads somehow caused the Latin American economies to miss an important opportunity to develop a manufacturing base and industrialize. By the turn of the century, for example, Mexico had only one steel mill.[47] In Brazil, no domestic iron and steel manufacture grew up around railroads, a nascent coal sector in the south received little stimulus from railroad operation, and few items of rolling stock came to be manufactured domestically during this period.

There is little reason to expect railroads in Latin America to have created around them an entire manufacturing sector, because they did not do this in the North Atlantic economies. In the United States, backward linkages from railroads to industry were of limited importance, because domestic iron, steel, and coal activities were already large and well developed, part of a generalized process of industrialization predating the construction of railroads.[48] By contrast, such linkages were unimportant in Brazil because the domestic iron sector was so backward and domestic coal was woefully inadequate in terms of quantity and quality. Identifying the specific reasons for the absence of stronger backward linkages from railroads in Mexico and Brazil requires an analysis looking beyond railroads to the conditions of industry itself.

Another effect not encompassed by the social-savings calculation is the possibility of improvements in efficiency in transport-using activities resulting specifically from railroad-induced economies of scale. Such changes arise if the lower cost of transport changes the cost conditions of factories and farms in a way that permits them to produce more output from the same inputs. For example, the Brazilian textile sector in the early twentieth century exhibited detectable economies of scale.[49] Sugar manufacturing in Brazil's northeast may have enjoyed increasing returns to scale in this period as well.[50] While the importance of railroad transport in altering the efficient scale of production in these activities cannot yet be gleaned with acceptable precision, it is plausible that at least part of the scale economies enjoyed by these industries in Brazil during this period resulted from the extension of the railroad system. For example, sugarcane must be moved quickly to the mill after harvesting. By lowering the cost and increasing the speed of transport, railroads made it possible for sugar mills to expand their feasible margins of cane supply and thereby increase their capacity. The reduced cost of cotton at the factory gate may have had similar effects in the cotton textile manufacture and in other industries as well. The presence of such effects will only increase the magnitude of the resource savings afforded the economy attributable to railroads.

The examination of the relationship between the low-cost freight and passenger transport services provided by railroads and the question of economic growth in this chapter reveals the importance of the new technology to Latin American countries. The extant results for Mexico, and new research on the Brazilian case, suggest that these countries, like other economies that had especially backward prerail transport systems, experienced significant gains from the construction and operation of railroads. Railroad expansion in Latin America removed one important impediment to the process of economic growth: high internal transport costs. By integrating markets and creating gains from regional specialization and improved interregional terms of trade, railroads spurred per capita income growth in both the domestic and external sectors of the Mexican and Brazilian economies. Moreover, at least in the Brazilian case, the railroads and freight rate regulation contributed to the emergence of an especially vibrant internal sector of the economy; Brazil's internal sector grew more quickly than its export sector, even during the period that is widely held to be one of export-led economic growth. In contrast to what is asserted in much of the economic historiography of Latin America, railroads in Brazil diminished the relative importance of the export sector, if anything reducing the degree of foreign economic "dependence."

Notes

1. Rigorous assessments of the railroad's role in Latin American economies is limited to the Colombian and Mexican cases; see McGreevey 1971; Coatsworth 1981.

2. A large body of modern research, some of it still unpublished, exists on Latin American railroads. On Cuba, see Zanetti Lecuona and García Alvarez 1987. For Mexico, see Schmidt 1987. On Chile, see Przeworski 1980. For Argentina, see Lewis 1983. For Brazil, see Mattoon 1971.

3. Examples of the railroad operating data required for such treatments, and the sources of such data, may be found for Cuba in Zanetti Lecuona and García Alvarez 1987; for Chile in Vallejos 1986.

4. Cortés Conde 1974.

5. Concessions in such countries as Brazil and Mexico were first made in the 1830's, but only Cuba executed its plans to build lines before midcentury.

6. McGreevey 1971: 253.

7. Ibid., 43–45.

8. Schmidt 1987: 1–11.

9. Coatsworth 1981: 17–24.

10. Haber 1989: 13–15, 24–25.

11. On the navigability of Brazilian rivers, see Lima 1922: 710–23.

12. Hartt 1870: 292.

13. Agassiz 1868: 121.

14. Hartt 1870: 506.

15. On mule transport in Brazil, see Goulart 1961: 165–80; Momsem 1964; Agassiz 1868: 114; Hartt 1870: 130–31.

16. Klein 1989: 347–69.

17. Coatsworth 1981: 33–38. For Brazil, one need only to compare the long list of concessions granted as of the early 1890's with the lines actually in operation in the early twentieth century; see Castro 1893; Brazil, Ministério da Viação e Obras Públicas 1914.

18. Coatsworth 1981: 37–38, 44–46.

19. El-Kareh 1982: 117–28.

20. Graham 1968: 51–72.

21. Saes 1981: 165–67; Lewis 1991: 35–51.

22. The increasing value of farmland, resulting from lower transport costs and new opportunities for profit, provides precisely the incentive to grab land from politically less powerful smallholders, as occurred in Mexico in the 1870's and in southern Brazil in the early twentieth century; see Coatsworth 1974: 48–71; Diacon 1991. Note that the increase in land values alone is not sufficient to account for the actual usurpation of smallholders. Such actions stem from the manner in which property rights in land are defined and enforced.

23. Competing traces of the Companhia Paulista in São Paulo were disputed by various parties; see Mattoon 1971: 50–60.

24. The version here is drawn from Fogel 1979: 1–59.

25. Note that this supply response to the diminished price variation that results from low-cost transport presupposes no change in peasant mentality or rationality that would be characterized as "profit maximizing." If the extension of railways did lead to such a change in peasant mentality, then the gains to the economy from having railways would be greater still.

26. See Metzer 1972: 3–26. To measure the social savings from railways and then claim that it does not include the effects of market integration is to miss the point of the exercise altogether; see Coatsworth 1979: 939–60.

27. For Mexico, see Coatsworth 1981: 36–37; for Brazil, see IBGE 1990: 457.

28. Reported here is Coatsworth's "A" measure of freight social savings; Coatsworth 1981: 113, 118–19.

29. More detail on the operating data and the computations that follow may be found in Summerhill 1995.

30. The national income figures (GDP) used here and in Table 4.2, along with the population figures, are taken from Contador and Haddad 1975: 407–39. These have been corrected and revised in Contador 1978: 379–401.

31. Catão 1992: 519–33.

32. Index in Lobo 1978: Table 4.43.

33. For national income and population estimates, see Contador and Haddad 1975; revised in Contador 1978.

34. Coatsworth 1981: 110–16. The demand for freight transport in the Mexican case is modeled as a function of the price of freight service, the amount of track, population, and national income (or exports where income is not available). Railway supply characteristics are not modeled or estimated separately.

35. The sample series comprises data from six of the most heavily trafficked lines, distributed through different regions.

36. Details on the sources of the data employed in this analysis are found in Summerhill 1995.

37. For all equations, *t* statistics are reported in parentheses. Many of the parameters here, while important theoretically, lack convincing statistical significance. Hence the use of multiple specifications of the demand function to check the sensitivity of the results.

38. The price of coal was that paid by the Companhia Paulista from 1898 to 1913 and taken from its annual operating reports. It is deflated by the Rio wholesale price index.

39. See Coatsworth 1979, where upper-bound savings in 1910 were as high as 38 percent of GDP.

40. Details of these computations for Mexico are found in Coatsworth 1981: chap. 3; for Brazil they are presented in Summerhill 1995: chap. 4.

41. Coatsworth 1981: 13–34.

42. Coatsworth 1989.

43. The OLS regression exhibited a strong positive autocorrelation, which affects the magnitude of the *t* statistics. The AR1 technique corrects for the problem. A Dickey-Fuller test confirms the absence of a unit root in the ln (export/GDP) series.

44. GDP from Contador and Haddad 1975. Brazilian exports drawn from IBGE 1941.

45. Coatsworth 1981: 143–44.

46. Value of imports calculated from Wileman 1909: 340–43.

47. Haber 1989: 30–37.

48. Fogel 1964: 190–210; Fishlow 1965: 141–43.

49. Denslow 1978: 23–24; Haber, chap. 6, this volume.

50. Denslow 1974.

References

Agassiz, Louis. 1868. *A Journey in Brazil*. Boston.

Brazil, Ministério da Viação e Obras Públicas. 1914. *Estatística das Estradas de Ferro de União Relativo ao Anno 1911*. Rio de Janeiro.

Castro, João Chrockatt Pereira de. 1893. *Brazilian Railways: Their History, Legislation, and Development*. Rio de Janeiro.

Catão, Luis A. V. 1992. "A New Wholesale Price Index for Brazil During the Period 1870–1913." *Revista Brasileira de Economia* 46, no. 4 (Oct.-Dec.): 519–33.

Coatsworth, John H. 1974. "Railroads, Landholding, and Agrarian Protest in the Early Porfiriato." *Hispanic American Historical Review* 54, no. 1 (Feb.): 48–71.

———. 1979. "Indispensable Railroads in a Backward Economy: The Case of Mexico." *Journal of Economic History* 39 (Dec.): 939–60.

———. 1981. *Growth Against Development: The Impact of Railroads in Porfirian Mexico*. De Kalb, Ill.

———. 1989. "The Decline of the Mexican Economy." In Liehs Reinhard, ed., *América Latina en la época de Simon Bolivar: La Formación de las economias nacionales y los intereses económicos europeos, 1800–1850*, pp. 27–54. Berlin.

Contador, Cláudio. 1978. "Crescimento, Ciclos Econômicos e Inflação: Uma Descrição do Caso Brasileiro." *Revista Brasileira de Mercados dos Capitais* 4, no. 12: 379–401.

Contador, Cláudio, and Cláudio Haddad. 1975. "Produto Real, Moeda, e Preços: A Experiência Brasileira no Periodo 1861–1979." *Revista Brasileira de Estatística* 36: 407–40.

Cortés Conde, Roberto. 1974. *The First Stages of Modernization in Spanish America*. New York.

Denslow, David. 1974. "Sugar Production in Northeastern Brazil and Cuba, 1858–1908." Ph.D. diss., Yale University.

———. 1978. "As Exportações e a Origem do Padrão de Industrialização Regional do Brasil." In Werner Baer, Pedro Pinaha Geiger, Paulo Roberto Haddad, and Michael Webb, eds., *Dimensões do Desenvolvimento Brasileiro*, pp. 21–63. Rio de Janeiro.

Diacon, Todd A. 1991. *Millenarian Vision, Capitalist Reality: Brazil's Contestado Rebellion, 1912–1916*. Durham, N.C.

El-Kareh, Almir Chaiban. 1982. *Filha Branca de Mae Preta: A Companhia da Estrada de Ferro D. Pedro II, 1855–1865*. Petrópolis.

Fishlow, Albert. 1965. *American Railroads and the Transformation of the Ante-Bellum Economy*. Cambridge, Mass.

Fogel, Robert William. 1964. *Railroads and American Economic Growth*. Baltimore.

———. 1979. "Notes on the Social Saving Controversy." *Journal of Economic History* 39, no. 1 (Mar.): 1–54.

Goulart, Jose Alipio. 1961. *Tropas e Tropeiros na Formação do Brasil*. Rio de Janeiro.

Graham, Richard 1968. *Britain and the Onset of Modernization in Brazil, 1850–1914.* Cambridge, Eng.

Haber, Stephen H. 1989. *Industry and Underdevelopment: The Industrialization of Mexico, 1890–1940.* Stanford.

Hartt, Fred. 1870. *Geology and Physical Geography of Brazil.* Boston.

IBGE [Instituto Brasileiro de Geografia e Estatísticas]. 1941. *Repertório Estatístico do Brasil, Quadros Retrospectivos No. 1.* Rio de Janeiro.

IBGE. 1990. *Estatísticas Historicas do Brasil.* Rio de Janeiro.

Klein, Herbert S. 1989. "A Oferta de Muares no Brasil Central: O Mercado de Sorocaba, 1825–1880." *Estudos Econômicos* 19, no. 2 (May-Aug.): 347–69.

Lewis, Colin. 1983. *British Railways in Argentina, 1857–1914.* London.

———. 1991. *Public Policy and Private Initiative: Railway Building in São Paulo, 1860–1889.* London.

Lima, Armando. 1922. "Rios navigaveis do Brasil." In Instituto Histórico e Geográphico Brasileiro, *Diccionário Histórico, Geográphico e Ethnográphico do Brasil.* Rio de Janeiro.

Lobo, Eulália Maria Lehmeyer. 1978. *História do Rio de Janeiro. Do Capital Comercial ao Capital Industrial Financeiro,* vol. 2. Rio de Janeiro.

Mattoon, Robert Howard. 1971. "The Companhia Paulista de Estradas de Ferro, 1868–1900: A Local Railway Enterprise in São Paulo, Brazil." Ph.D. diss., Yale University.

McGreevey, William Paul. 1971. *Economic History of Colombia.* Cambridge, Eng.

Metzer, Jacob. 1972. "Some Economic Aspects of Railroad Development in Tsarist Russia." Ph.D. diss., University of Chicago.

Momsem, Richard. 1964. *Routes over the Serra do Mar.* Rio de Janeiro.

O'Brien, P. K. 1982. "Transport and Economic Growth in Western Europe, 1830–1914." *Journal of European Economic History* 11, no. 2 (fall): 336–67.

Przeworski, Joanne Fox. 1980. *The Decline of the Copper Industry in Chile and the Entrance of North American Capital, 1870–1916.* New York.

Saes, Flávio Azevedo Marques de. 1981. *As Ferrovias de São Paulo, 1870–1940.* São Paulo.

Schmidt, Arthur. 1987. *The Social and Economic Effect of the Railroad in Puebla and Veracruz.* New York.

Summerhill, William. 1995. "Railroads and the Brazilian Economy Before 1914." Ph.D. diss., Stanford University.

Vallejos, Sonia Pinto. 1986. "Historia de los Ferrocarriles de Chile: Volumenes de Carga y Cantidad de Pasajeros Transportados (1901–1929)." *Cadernos de Historia* 6 (July): 49–66.

Wileman, J. P. 1909. *The Brazilian Year Book.* London.

Zanetti Lecuono, Oscar, and Alejandro García Alvarez. 1987. *Caminos para el azucar.* Havana.

CHAPTER 5

Obstacles to the Development of Capital Markets in Nineteenth-Century Mexico

CARLOS MARICHAL

The late development of modern financial markets in nineteenth-century Mexico is a rather striking phenomenon not only in terms of comparison with the more advanced economies of the United States and Europe but also with reference to the economies of other Latin American nations such as Brazil, Argentina, or Chile. In the latter countries the birth of banking networks and of small but institutionalized capital markets took place from the 1860's, whereas in Mexico these same processes only began in the 1880's and 1890's.[1] The time lag is difficult to explain exclusively in economic terms. In this regard, the recent literature on Mexican economic history suggests that political instability, the financial weakness of the national government, low per capita income, and institutional restrictions jointly constituted the major obstacles that impeded the modernization of Mexican financial structures.[2]

The slow process of growth of capital markets necessarily influenced the pace of overall economic development in Mexico in the nineteenth century, and it is, in fact, the premise of this chapter that financial backwardness was one of the key factors contributing to economic underdevelopment. Without access to medium- or long-term sources of credit or investment funds from a formal capital market, miners, agriculturalists, industrialists, and merchants had to rely on informal mechanisms of raising capital, in most cases based on kinship networks of credit. Such circumstances inevitably limited the mobility of capital and restricted its efficient allocation. In addition, the lack of formal capital markets tended to impel entrepreneurs to move into speculative activities that could allow them large capital windfalls with which to obtain sufficient funds for their investment plans in diverse sectors. Such speculative trends only contributed to further limiting and, indeed, destabilizing money markets.

Having said this, it is the specific aim of the first part of this chapter to explore how the evolution of government finance affected local money markets, arguing that it was the state's fiscal and credit policies that were most directly responsible for the instability of Mexican financial markets and, therefore, for many of the difficulties in development of modern capital markets during the greater part of the nineteenth century. In the second part, attention is devoted to analyzing how the vicious circle of financial underdevelopment finally *began* to be broken in the mid-1880's.

In this chapter it is argued that two basic preconditions for the development of capital markets in nineteenth-century Mexico were the stabilization and broadening of short-term money markets and the creation of a relatively open, internal market for public securities. These conditions, however, were not met until the end of the century and, even then, were met in limited ways. During the first half-century following independence, interest rates for short-term commercial loans tended to be quite high (12 to 40 percent) and frequently were much higher in the case of government loans (fluctuating wildly between 30 and 200 percent). As a result, most potential investors could not be attracted to long-term investments, which offered lower rates. It should be noted in particular that the high rates on the leading money market—that of Mexico City—were in good measure the negative effect of the extremely unstable debt policies of the federal government, which therefore stymied the effective development of a short-term capital market as well the birth of a stable and open market in long-term public and private securities. The prime indicators of this situation were the lack of banking institutions, the erratic fluctuations of exorbitant interest rates, the lack of *modern* commercial and financial legislation, and the nonexistence of a formal stock market.

In this regard, it seems worthwhile recalling that the historical experience of advanced economies indicates that the operation of a broad and stable market for public securities was one of the key preconditions for the development of capital markets. A review of the financial evolution of England, Holland, and the United States in the late eighteenth and nineteenth centuries, to cite only three cases, suggests that the creation of a broad market for low-interest and low-risk government securities attracted increasing numbers of investors (large and small) to financial markets.[3] The general acceptance of public securities provided depth and stability for short-term money markets and for banks; treasury bills, for instance, were extremely useful instruments for merchants, bankers, and industrialists operating on the short-term money market, whereas government bonds were ideal for providing a substantial portion of bank reserves and portfolios.[4] The stable operation of markets for public securities also had a positive impact on long-term markets for private securities, leading to a growing spillover of investors who moved from government bonds to railway bonds and subsequently to other private stocks.[5]

In other words, in the first countries to develop modern capital markets, historical experience indicates that securities markets have tended to grow following the development of a stable market for public debt. Only after individuals realize that holding a piece of paper (in the form, for instance, of a treasury note) can be as secure an investment as a house, farm, mine, or factory are they willing to accept stocks and bonds. Thus, the widespread sale of government bonds (which are *honored* by the state treasury) has been essential to the long-term growth of a market for corporate securities.

In nineteenth-century Mexico, in contrast, the trend was almost exactly the reverse. The government had such irregular sources of revenues and so many short-term financial obligations that it did not honor many of its long-term debts and constantly rolled over or repudiated short-term debts. The general lack of acceptance of public debt instruments resulting from such policies inevitably obliged finance ministers to offer extremely high interest rates on internal debts, thereby distorting the routine operations of the Mexico City money market for almost half a century.

In addition, the frequent suspensions of payment on both short- and long-term public securities made them unattractive instruments for most potential small- and medium-sized investors and made them extremely risk-prone instruments as components of the portfolios of financial firms or other enterprises with surplus capital. The reasons for these distortions in Mexican public finance were the result of a combination of supply and demand factors, which are the subject of the following section. It is important to note in this context that the interplay of these factors in the Mexico City money market was repeated in some cases in the existing small regional credit markets. The implications of this situation for an understanding of Mexican economic history in the nineteenth century would thus appear to be considerable.

The Mexico City Money Market, 1830–80

By midcentury there had developed in Mexico City a money market with some rather singular characteristics. In the first place, it should be noted that it was a highly concentrated market, controlled by 20 to 25 merchant houses, engaged in the import/export business as well as in mining and textile enterprises and, naturally, in the provision of loans for the impecunious government.[6]

While these private financial houses lent money to merchants, miners, and property owners (as David Walker has demonstrated in the most important, in-depth study of one of these firms), the larger part of their credit transactions consisted in the buying and selling of a variety of government securities. Among these were short-term securities such as the *certificados de aduanas* (certificates that could be used to pay customs duties), which were popular among merchant bankers because of their liquidity as a result of the considerable demand that existed for them from importers. The volume of *certificados de aduanas* that circulated from the 1830's onwards was large and continued to be so for many decades.[7] Other relatively short-term securities included a variety of treasury bills and bonds—*pagarés, vales de alcance,* and *vales de amortización*—which were mostly advances on salaries to public employees, military officers, and soldiers, or promissory notes paid to merchants who had provided supplies to the government or army. It should be noted that much of this paper was relatively difficult to liquidate.[8]

Apart from short-term securities, there were also several types of longer-term government securities in which the moneylenders invested; these included shares and bonds of the Banco de Avío (a public industrial bank that only operated between 1830 and 1840), stock of the state tobacco monopoly (leased between 1839 and 1844 as a private enterprise), and shares in mining companies controlled by the government, such as the Fresnillo silver mines of Zacatecas. However, the financiers involved in these enterprises were mostly the same individuals who had previously advanced large sums to the government, and they tended simply to practice the lucrative business of exchanging old debt paper for control over the more productive fiscal milch cows of the state.[9]

Although the number and variety of securities sold was considerable in the 1830–60 period, it would be erroneous to conceive of these transactions in terms of a stable or open money market. Rather, they were part of what Albert Fishlow has called a "forced market."[10] Indeed, the Mexico

City money market was not free but rather *closed*, being limited on the supply side to a small group of private financial firms that held most of the liquid money capital (basically silver coin) in Mexico City, as well as most public debt instruments.[11] On the demand side, one entity, namely the federal government, took the bulk of the loans offered by the local circle of financiers, although, it so happened, the treasury not only ran large and constant deficits but also had great difficulties paying off even its short-term debts. As a result, finance ministers were frequently "forced" to accept the extortionate rates charged by the oligopoly of moneylenders. Moreover, *instability* was the hallmark of most financial transactions, making it almost impossible to anticipate real, probable returns on investments efficiently.

The effects of this situation on financial operations were striking. In the first place, rates of interest on virtually all government loans were extremely high and volatile, ranging from 30 to 200 percent per year.[12] These rates were conditioned both by the leverage exercised by the oligopoly of private bankers and by two structurally debilitating fiscal factors: first, the abrupt fluctuations of foreign trade, which had a critical impact on the income of the government, because it relied so heavily on customs revenues; and, second, the incapacity of finance ministers to find stable, alternative sources of tax income. As a result, risks on most credit to the fiscally poor government were abnormally large, a factor that also explains the high level of bankruptcies among moneylenders from the 1840's onwards. These risks, moreover, were caused not only by the extreme fluctuations in government income but also by the unstable military and political situation, the rapid turnover of finance ministers, and an established pattern of temporary repudiation of debts in times of crisis or war.

The fact that the merchant bankers who handled the bulk of government loans were also those who controlled most sources of money capital bespeaks the underdevelopment of Mexican money markets at the time. Their cash resources flowed from oligopolistic positions of control over the principal cash-rich sectors of both the private and public economy. In the private sphere, these bankers retained large market shares of the textile business (including both legal imports and contraband) and at the same time had major participation in the acquisition of most silver produced by the numerous Mexican mines; their control of money circulation (essentially silver coin), and especially of the state mints (*casas de moneda*) allowed them in turn to dominate both monetary circulation and much trade.[13] Equally important was their control of key state economic agencies, the state tobacco monopoly, the Fresnillo silver mines in Zacatecas (which were leased by the government), the salt-mining administration (also leased by the state), toll routes, and other public concessions won as a result of loans provided to the finance ministry, all of which reinforced their control over the principal money-making firms and entities in the country.[14]

Most merchant bankers reaped their largest profits from government business, but they also lent or invested substantial sums in trade, mining, manufactures, and real estate.[15] According to the most detailed case study of one of these merchant banking firms, interest rates on short-term loans by these private bankers to the private sector (mostly to other merchants) averaged between 12 and 30 percent in the late 1830's in Mexico City, somewhat lower than rates on money lent to the government.[16]

Long-term private investments consisted mainly of the acquisition by merchant bankers of fixed properties rather than securities: ranches, houses, textile factories, and some silver mines. Generally speaking, these were family firms, because joint-stock enterprises were infrequent except in the case of a few of the larger mining companies. In the latter case, the largest Mexican mining enterprise at midcentury, the Real del Monte silver mining company, sold stock to a fairly broad number of individuals, but in practice the firm was controlled by two wealthy financial houses of Mexico City, those of the Escandóns and the Beísteguis.[17]

The small number of long-term securities placed on the Mexico City financial "market" were therefore not usually private but public debt instruments, most of them a variety of bonds on which interest was paid irregularly. They were, in fact, basically speculative (rather than investment instruments), being attractive insofar as they could be exchanged for new bonds or customs certificates at a heavy discount or for a variety of government concessions. Indeed, it would be questionable whether there was any rational possibility of calculating earnings on the basis of interest rates, because speculative gains were almost always equally or more important.[18]

In this sense, it is clear that while the eminently imperfect money market of Mexico City in the first half of the nineteenth century did allow for a considerable number of transactions in public securities, it did not constitute a capital market as such.[19] Apart from the high interest rates, the great risks involved, and the multifaceted collection of government paper and bills in circulation, it should be noted that by the 1850's a very large amount of the government's debt was in a state of virtual moratorium, or nonpayment, a circumstance that drastically reduced the negotiability of public securities.

Two quite different solutions to this problem were sought by the

moneylenders. The first consisted of transforming their holdings of internal government debt into external debts, guaranteed by England, France,
or Spain.[20] The second lay in exchanging their bonds and other public
credits for real estate as a result of the new legislation, established in 1856–
57, disentailing the properties of the Catholic Church.[21] These operations
made the money and credit market more complex, and undoubtedly broadened its realm of activities, but, once again, there is considerable doubt
about whether this implied a process of modernization of the market.

For the period 1860–80, the paucity of secondary studies makes it
unwise to make any categorical affirmations about the evolution of the
Mexico City money market. Certainly the establishment of the Bank of
London and Mexico in 1864, during the Empire of Maximilian, suggests
that some important changes were taking place, especially with regard to
international financial transactions. Then again, while initially successful,
this bank later had to limit the scope of its activities, and no other banking
institutions followed in its steps in the nation's capital until the 1880's.[22]
The risks of carrying on a regular banking business were still high, and
therefore it may be presumed that most local credit transactions continued
to be handled by a score of merchant houses. Nonetheless, it is important
to keep in mind that the latter firms were, to a substantial degree, different
from the moneylenders who had dominated prior to 1860 and that at this
time there began to become manifest a process of financial specialization,
with the growth of small, specialized firms of brokers, commission agents,
and specialists in exchange and insurance dealers, suggesting a gradual
broadening of the money market.[23]

Regional Credit Markets, 1830–80

While the Mexico City money market was the largest in the republic,
it was not the only operating credit market. A more balanced assessment of
the nationwide situation may be garnered from a comparison of the Mexico City market with the existing case studies of regional credit markets
during this period. Apart from the smaller scale of business, it is first important to note that these local markets operated with considerable autonomy from those of the capital; in other words, most loan transactions
were carried out by *local* merchants who provided funds to *local* entrepreneurs and property owners. Second, it is worthwhile observing that the
bulk of operations in the field of public finance were with the respective
state governments, which suffered from considerable fiscal limitations, although perhaps not so grave as those of the federal government.

While the study of regional credit markets is still in its infancy, there are several important studies that provide insights into their workings and possible parallels or contrasts with the financial market of Mexico City. In the case of the silver-rich state of San Luis Potosí, Barbara Corbett has described the workings of a close-knit network of merchant/financiers in the 1830's and 1840's who derived their greatest earnings in the financial sphere from their control of local customs, silver exports, and the tobacco and salt administration. Thus Corbett's studies suggest that the transactions of financial entrepreneurs like Cayetano Rubio were similar in origin to those of his counterparts in Mexico City, and that those financiers also benefitted from the high interest rates that characterized the relatively underdeveloped local money markets. In fact, Rubio eventually became so important in regional finance that he established a banking house in the nation's capital and soon rivaled Escandón and the other prominent *agiotistas* (moneylenders) who vied for control over federal finance at midcentury.[24]

A relatively similar situation with regard to public credit transactions is found in the case of the scarcely populated but economically dynamic northern state of Nuevo León, which depended heavily on ranching production and on increasing trade with Texas. In the years 1858–62, when governor Santiago Vidaurri was consolidating the provincial administration, evidence of expansion of credit markets is provided by a review of regional loan transactions, the bulk of which went to finance the 5,000-man regional army that Vidaurri had built up and that served as his power base. These loans—studied in detail by Mario Cerutti—were provided by a small coterie of merchants who quickly accumulated a considerable mass of money capital by charging rates that ranged from 11 to 50 percent per year.[25] Whether such rates were accurate indicators of financial returns is somewhat doubtful, because a large portion of the funds advanced were covered with import certificates that fluctuated substantially in value. Government lending was risky but highly profitable and according to Cerutti provided the original basis of capital accumulation for the regional merchant elite, which subsequently began investing a substantial part of its money capital in productive activities.

Rates on private commercial transactions were lower than government loans and tended to decline. By the 1870's, for instance, interest rates on loans advanced by Monterrey-based merchant bankers to cotton growers in the region of La Laguna averaged between 12 and 18 percent per year. Given the relative scarcity of credit in most of Mexico, these appear to be reasonable levels, but in fact the loan contracts also included numerous onerous clauses that made the costs of the loans far higher in real terms. Lending money thus tended to be a gainful business, so much so that the majority of the most successful industrial entrepreneurs of Monterrey at the turn of the century could trace their success back to a lucrative loan business in previous decades.

In the case of the state of Veracruz, where the government borrowed less than its counterparts elsewhere in the country, local credit was oriented basically toward agricultural and mercantile activities. Nonetheless, interest rates were high and fluctuated markedly, and there was little in the way of the development of a capital market. According to an excellent study by Eugene Wiemers of credit markets in Veracruz between 1820 and 1870, loans were generally available to medium and large landowners in this agriculturally rich region from the decade following independence. He notes, "This analysis shows a functioning credit market in Córdoba and Orizaba where the terms facing most debtors, the requirements of property to secure debts, and the ability of most debtors to meet those terms were well-defined and related to risk."[26]

Wiemers observes that despite the fact that traditional legislation continued to be in force, placing a nominal ceiling of 6 percent on interest rates in loan contrasts, actual interest costs were higher as a result of hidden charges.[27] Thus, long-term mortgages paid 8 to 9 percent per year, while short-term rates on commercial loans ranged from 12 to 40 percent. The cost of money for short-term operations was therefore high but not prohibitive. As Wiemers argues, "For most of the time before the railway was completed in the region, debt contracts for sale of property and for loans for agriculture were regularly liquidated and repayments were predictable. . . . That the market functioned as well as it did, despite warfare and economic chaos at the national level, is remarkable."[28]

In sum, it would be wrong to argue that money and credit markets did not exist in different regions of Mexico before 1880.[29] It is evident, however, that there were no equity markets and it is clear that the single most important money market—that of Mexico City— had numerous peculiarities that were a function of its heavy engagement in the unstable finances of the federal government. But, as the Mexican economy began to experience a phase of sustained expansion from the 1870's, the pressures for financial and fiscal reform as well as for the creation of a modern banking system gained strength.

The Birth of a Banking Network in the 1880's

While historians have traditionally emphasized the role of foreign investments, particularly in the construction of railways, as a key to the expansion and process of market integration experienced by the Mexican economy in the 1880's and 1890's, they have tended to neglect the importance of investments in banks, both by foreign and domestic investors. It is my view that the establishment in the 1880's of a modern banking network based initially in Mexico City (but with links to all the economically dynamic regions) had key significance, because it helped to lower and stabilize interest rates and gradually to promote the integration of the various regional credit markets. Bringing interest rates down to more reasonable levels, both in the capital and nationwide, was probably the single most important factor in both broadening the short-term money market and stimulating longer-term investments, both of which helped spur real growth rates of the Mexican economy upwards.

In this regard, it is necessary to underline the role of the government in providing a new institutional framework conducive to the modernization of financial transactions. The institutional reforms carried out by the state in this regard included (1) new commercial legislation (the commercial codes of 1884 and 1889) that progressively guaranteed the operations of joint-stock enterprises, (2) the resolution of the old debt quandary in the years 1886–88, a prerequisite to the operation of a modern money market, and (3) the provision of concessions and financial subsidies for new companies, especially banks.

The decline of interest rates in the 1880's on commercial loans, and most notably on short-term advances to the government, was the single most important indicator of the success of the financial reforms, the Banco Nacional de México's discount rates in that decade averaged between 6 and 10 percent, setting the basic parameters for short-term credit in the financial markets.[30] These, for instance, were the rates paid by merchants on good commercial paper and were also the going rates for the government when it borrowed on its regular account at the Banco Nacional. This meant that for the first time in the nineteenth century, public and private short-term credit transactions began to operate within the same general parameters of the money market rather than in different, segmented markets with quite different interest rates, as had been the case for decades.

The creation of a banking network in Mexico City in the 1880's is especially revealing of the mix of public and private factors that characterized the more ambitious economic projects of the Porfirian administration. Until 1880, as has been noted, only one commercial bank existed in the capital, namely the Banco de Londres y México, although it should be kept in mind that a number of wealthy merchant houses operated as private bankers to the mercantile and mining community. It was precisely from this circle of merchant/financiers that the impetus came to form two new banking institutions, the Banco Nacional Mexicano and the Banco Mercantil Mexicano, both established in 1881. The Banco Mercantil was founded basically with the capital of a group of wealthy merchants of Spanish origin, who controlled much of the wholesale business in Mexico City in textiles and food products. The Banco Nacional, on the other hand, was formed primarily with foreign capital (French, British, and German financiers were heavily involved), with a minority position taken by wealthy Mexico City merchants.[31]

In 1882, a subsequent group of entrepreneurs established the Banco Internacional Hipotecario, an institution intended to open up a new line of financial business, namely mortgages on urban and rural real estate. In addition, two other credit institutions existed in the capital: the Monte de Piedad (the national pawnshop), which received deposits on a fairly large scale and had the right to issue bank bills for a maximum sum of 9 million pesos; and the Banco de Empleados, a semipublic entity intended to receive deposits from government employees, although it was never successful in this venture.

By the year 1883, therefore, the Mexico City money market had changed dramatically. A variety of banking institutions, which had issued a total of over 15 million pesos in bank bills, was now operating. The clients of these banks included import/export firms, the new railway companies, shipping firms, and a variety of local wealthy customers. The discount of commercial paper was expanding and rates had dropped to an average of 6 to 8 percent annually on the paper of the better known firms.[32] The government was also able to get advances from the banks at similar rates, a fact which notably decreased its reliance on the old moneylender circle. Nonetheless, as we shall see, when the finance ministry sought larger sums, it was obliged to pay higher rates, with discounts running as high as 25 percent on customs certificates, which were the main type of public securities exchanged for the larger advances obtained from the banks and from private financiers.

In November 1883, for instance, the Banco Nacional, in conjunction with seven allied merchant houses in Mexico City and the Paris-based Banque Franco-Egyptienne, finally agreed to advance 700,000 silver pesos to the treasury in exchange for 1 million pesos in customs certificates.[33] The increasingly difficult financial position of the government, however, could not be resolved merely with one loan. The deficits caused by the large subsidies paid to private railroad companies were the main cause of this problem; the amounts of subsidies surpassed 7 million pesos in 1882/83 and 3 million pesos in 1883/84, which went to the Ferrocarril Central, Mexicano y Interoceánico. These subsidies, as well as those for port works and shipping companies, were paid with customs certificates, which implied that a great percentage of customs revenues was mortgaged to the privately owned firms, thus reducing regular tax income.[34] As a result, government authorities were forced to increase the "floating debt" (short-term debt), taking new advances from the Banco Nacional, which provided the huge sum of 5 million pesos during the year 1884, in exchange for which the bank was to take over virtually the entire administration of customs certificates.[35] Yet this was too large a task for the bank as constituted, and without additional capital, the government credit requirements could not be met.

The solution to these problems lay in the fusion of the Banco Nacional with the Banco Mercantil into one large bank, known from then as the Banco Nacional de México (Banamex).[36] Even though the new bank was quite a powerful private financial entity, however, it alone could not support the continual financial requirements of the state treasury. Indeed, it is possible to argue that only a broad capital market could have provided the solution, and such a market did not yet exist.

The Financial Crisis of 1885 and the Conversion of Mexican Public Debts

By the early summer of 1885 public finances were approaching bankruptcy. On June 22, Treasury Minister Manuel Dublán took emergency action. Declaring that the government was faced with a potential deficit of 25 million pesos, he announced a suspension of payments on all short-term government debts at the same time as he ratified a proposal for the conversion of all the outstanding bonded debt, internal and external. Jointly, these measures constituted a financial revolution.

The suspension of payments on short-term debt included a huge backlog of credits due to the Banamex, to the three leading railway companies, and to a wide array of public contractors and local creditors. The prestigious Mexico City newspaper, *The Mexican Financier*, described the measures as a *golpe de estado* (coup d'état), suggesting that massive commercial bankruptcy would be the inevitable consequence. In fact, there was a bank panic, as clients of the Banamex rushed to take their money out of the accounts of a bank they believed would fail without government support. But the Banamex survived, paying out over 1 million pesos in Mexico City in the course of a few days until, finally, wary depositors became convinced that the institution was so solid that it would not fall.[37]

One of the most interesting features of the 1885 financial crisis can be found in the fact that for the first time in Mexican history it was possible to follow the evolution of the crisis on the basis of weekly changes in bank discount rates and stock market quotations as published in the brand-new financial press. A second interesting feature was the increasing interaction of Mexican private and public finances with international capital markets.[38] That the Boston, London, and even Paris stock exchanges should respond to movements in the financial markets of Mexico City indicates the intensification of international capital flows, but also signals the increasing importance of the Mexican capital markets themselves.

In any event, Dublán's emergency measures suspending payments on short-term debts and obligations allowed the Mexican government a financial respite, and during the following years public deficits declined somewhat. The railway investors received a considerable amount of new internal bonds (*certificados de construcción de ferrocarriles*) to guarantee future payments on their subsidies.[39] Banamex worked out a series of new financial arrangements with the government that assured it a regular percentage of fiscal income in order to liquidate a portion of the money it had advanced to the government.[40] Thus, the country's financial situation stabilized and its prospects of being able to raise a large foreign loan improved markedly as a result of the successful conclusion of negotiations with national and foreign bondholders for the conversion of the bulk of a considerable volume of internal and external debts and an equally large sum of unpaid interest that had accumulated over the decades.

The great £10,000,000 foreign loan of 1888 marked the successful conclusion of the process of debt conversion and also signaled the formal reentry of Mexican government securities into European capital markets.[41] A spate of external bond issues were subsequently placed on the London and Berlin exchanges in 1889, 1890, and 1893. The increased flow of capital to Mexico had a positive impact on local financial markets, as can be observed in the trends of quotation of the shares and bonds of the Banco Nacional de México from 1887 to 1892. In the following year, however, the economic crisis in Mexico caused by agrarian problems, the steep drop in silver prices, and the slowdown in the U.S. economy led to an abrupt decline in prices, as witnessed during the crisis of 1893.

The Mexican Market for Public Securities in the 1890's

While the Porfirian government was clearly successful in gaining access to European money markets after 1888, it is less clear to what extent it was able to stimulate local demand for public securities. In fact, at first glance it would appear that finance minister Dublán and his successors Matías Romero (1891–93) and Yves Limantour (1893–1910) relied essentially on foreign funds to cover the credit needs of the Mexican government. This is not an entirely adequate description of the situation, however, because a series of policies were adopted that aimed precisely at the possibility of raising an increasing volume of funds internally to finance the domestic public debt.

Our review of the years 1886–90 indicates that the finance ministry devoted most of its attention to the conversion of internal debts rather than to the sale of securities that presumably could have provided a fresh flow of long-term funding. The conversion of the panoply of outstanding internal debts consisted basically of a process of exchanging old bonds and certificates for new 3-percent internal bonds, payable in silver.[42] Holders of old government paper (who had bought this paper at huge discounts because of the decades-long suspension of debt service) were willing to convert because they could reap huge speculative gains. These conversions therefore did not imply much buying or selling of public securities and were less the product of a functioning market than of an arbitrary attempt by the government to establish such a public securities market.

Although it is clear that the actual sales (as opposed to conversion) of new long-term public securities was limited, it is also evident that by 1890 a large volume of new internal bonds (as well as customs certificates and railway subsidy bonds) were in circulation and that the government was now making interest payments on a fairly regular basis. The government, nonetheless, continued to require fresh sources of credit. The market, however, would not absorb new issues of internal debt (payable in silver), precisely because silver prices had long been falling. Thus the government once again sought recourse from the Banamex, which advanced funds on current account to the finance ministry and also provided short-term loans, which were rolled over to become medium-term credits of two or three years. In order to be able to count on the support of Banamex, the government eventually had to liquidate such credits in gold. As a result, a considerable percentage of its foreign loans of the period went to this purpose: over 10 million pesos of the great foreign loan of 1888 went directly to Banamex to pay off public debt, close to 30 percent of the 1890 loan of £6 million went for the same purpose, and so did almost 60 percent of the 1893 loan issued by the German banker Bleichroder.[43]

The lessons of the extremely expensive foreign loan of 1893 were not lost on Limantour, who proceeded in September 1894 to restructure the Mexican debt and to initiate new policy aimed at finally creating a market for long-term internal bonds, payable in silver. His principal objective was to reduce dependence of the treasury on advances by Banamex and, at the same time, force railway and public works contractors to accept payments in long-term internal bonds rather than customs certificates or other short-term liabilities. According to the decree ratified on September 6, the government created a new type of 5-percent silver-denominated bonds to be issued in various tranches of 20 million pesos.[44] The bulk of these new bonds went to the railway companies and contractors in successive issues (September 6, 1894, December 10, 1895, January 3, 1898, December 23, 1899, and June 9, 1902), and reached a total of 100 million pesos by the turn of the century.

The bulk of the bonds was initially placed with companies involved in public works projects, which accepted them at a discount and attempted to find ways of selling them (largely with the assistance of Banamex), although as long as silver prices remained depressed the market was weak for these securities. By 1898, however, as silver prices recovered, Mexican private bankers (such as the house of Hugo Scherer) found means of placing large blocks on primary and secondary financial markets throughout Europe.[45] Investors who bought the bonds at 75 percent of nominal value at a time of rising silver prices could expect to reap significant profits, although the risks were clearly considerable.[46]

In summary, the new policies of promoting the issue of internal bonds after 1894 were a partial success, although it seems questionable whether Limantour actually stimulated the creation of a broad, domestic market for public securities, because, in fact, most of the 5-percent silver bonds ended up in Europe. What he did manage to accomplish was virtually to eliminate the fiscal deficits of the government from the mid-1890's onward, and he therefore generated confidence in the capacity of the state treasury to cover the debt service on new internal or external bond issues.

Expansion of Mexican Markets for
Private Securities, 1890–1913

While local markets for Mexican public securities remained limited, must the same be said of the markets for stocks and bonds of private enterprise? Did not the process of economic expansion promote new forms of long-term domestic investment? And, indeed, was such a process linked to the restructuring of public finance? These are questions that clearly go beyond the limits of this essay, but it seems worthwhile to comment briefly on some aspects of them in order to link the financial and debt reforms of the period with the growth of Mexican capital markets.

I have already argued that money and credit markets expanded quite rapidly after the 1870's in a process closely tied to the growth and multiplication of the banking system, but the growth of commercial banks specializing mainly in the discount of commercial paper and short-term loans did not necessarily result in the development of dynamic capital markets (basically, markets for medium or long-term investment). Little systematic or statistical research has been done in this field in Mexico, a fact that makes most comments on the subject propositional. Moreover, the existing published sources (essentially the financial press) do not provide estimates of volume turnover in stocks and bonds, although they do indicate that by the 1890's there was already a considerable variety of private securities being issued or traded, which certainly suggests that capital markets were expanding.

Among the many factors that contributed to this development, three stand out. The first was the impact of foreign capital, which forcefully introduced the *modern* joint-stock company into the Mexican economy. It is worthwhile recalling that already in the 1840's and 1850's a few large mining and textile companies (with a fair number of stockholders) existed, but it was not until the establishment of the Banco de Londres (1864), the Banco Nacional de México (1884), and of the large railway companies in the 1870's and 1880's that the new models of company administration and finance became a marked feature of the national economic landscape.

A second important advance was the ratification of legislation that defined and protected joint-stock companies, thereby assuring potential investors of the safety of putting their money into such ventures. Much of this legislation initially revolved around the creation of the first Mexican banks, as can be seen in the relevant legislation in the first commercial code of 1884, the reforms in the code of 1889, and the sweeping definitions in the banking law of 1896. Advances were made simultaneously in legislation with respect to mining and industrial companies.

Finally, a third key factor was the growth of a native investing public, which became increasingly attuned to the potential interest and profit to be gained by investing in new enterprises. The views of this new class of investing capitalists were shaped and reflected by the contemporary financial press, which has already been mentioned and which flourished after the mid-1880's, the most notable organs being *La Semana Mercantil, El Economista Mexicano,* and *The Mexican Financier.*

These factors stimulated the growth of a small capital market in Mexico City that also attracted entrepreneurs from other regions. Nonetheless, there was no authentic stock market in the capital. Brokers had long met in favorite spots, at a given cafe, pastry shop, at the *Lonja* (commodities market)—all located in a small web of downtown streets and corners—but they did not actually carry out their buying or selling of stock there.[47] The actual trading of stock was usually over-the-counter and involved personal visits to the interested parties, whether this meant handling public securities for the Finance Ministry or placing private securities among wealthy clients. Finally, in 1895, a formal institution known as the Bolsa came into existence, but it still did not truly fulfill the functions of a stock exchange. As Pablo Macedo noted a few years later, the Bolsa housed no formal stock exchange but rather a considerable number of informal, private transactions handled by brokers.[48]

Macedo's pessimistic evaluation is misleading in several regards. It suggests that trading in stock was limited—which was true—but this should not obscure the fact that considerable advances had been made since 1880. By the first decade of the twentieth century, there were regular quotations cited in the Mexico City press for an average of 80 mining companies, some 25 industrials, and some 20 banks. The trade in mining stocks was the most active, there being considerable speculation at times of both rising silver or gold prices as well as financial crisis, when heavily indebted investors played the market to the hilt in order to attempt to recoup losses.[49] It should be recalled, nonetheless, that this speculation was basically in small, Mexican-owned companies; the large U.S. and British mining concerns did not usually sell stock locally, preferring to rely on the New York and London markets for their capital needs.

A second, although less important, area of stock transactions was that connected with industrial firms. The first important group of joint-stock industrial firms in Mexico dates from the 1890's, and by the turn of the century there were some 25 large-scale concerns operating in the textile, tobacco, brewing, and metalurgical sectors. These enterprises were established by several circles of wealthy individuals who had been involved in trade, moneylending, or railroad contracting. They promoted the first large industrial enterprises and, apparently, continued to hold most of the stock. A recent study by Stephen Haber suggests some of the key characteristics of the financing of industry at the time:

By the turn of the century, in order to enter large-scale manufacturing in Mexico, one had to be first a financier and, prior to that, to have been a merchant. This explains, in large part, the notable absence of Mexicans among the major stockholders of manufacturing companies. In effect, the merchant-financier-industrialist nexus excluded the Mexican born from industry, because large-scale commerce had been historically dominated by foreigners.[50]

Haber's analysis overemphasizes the foreign monopoly in the import/export sector, and consequently underestimates native Mexican participation in some large industrial concerns, but his basic argument is convincing, for indeed, the circle of new industrialists was not large, and, while they did issue stock and sell some of it to friends, the market for such securities was not broad.[51]

A somewhat different situation existed in northern Mexico, especially in Monterrey, where an independent capital market developed rapidly in the 1890's. Here local merchant/financiers stimulated a quite extraordinary process of heavy investment in mining, metalurgical, brewing, and glass firms from the 1890's, establishing the basis for the formation of the most innovative and aggressive sector of the Mexican industrial bourgeoisie. The information provided by the studies of Mario Cerutti suggests that the development of the joint-stock company in the north of Mexico was probably the most rapid in the nation, although it would also appear that the local market for private securities was quite limited, because most firms were controlled by an oligopoly of wealthy families who reinvested profits systematically in their most promising concerns.[52]

A third and final area in which markets for private securities gradually developed was that related to banking companies. In the 1880's there were only two important commercial banks in Mexico City and a handful of regional banks, but from the 1890's on the number of new banks and bank branches multiplied. By the turn of the century, the bigger banks, like Banamex, had more than a dozen regional branches and some 50 agencies and correspondents. At the same time, local banks sprang up in practically every state.[53] All of these institutions were private companies that were created on the basis of the sale of stock.

The placement of Mexican bank stocks and bonds had two singular characteristics that distinguished it from that in the fields of mining and industry. First, the larger Mexico City banks sold their stock simultaneously in Mexico and abroad, mainly on European capital markets. In fact, the majority of the capital in institutions like Banamex, Banco de Londres y México, and the Banco Central was held abroad, although as much as 30 to 40 percent of the stock was acquired by Mexican capitalists, and the administration of the banks remained clearly in Mexican hands.[54] These banks were—to use modern terminology—joint ventures, in which private native and foreign capital collaborated, with the acquiescence and favorable support of the Porfirian government. Second, the numerous privileges held by the leading banks allowed them considerable economic advantages, a fact that was reflected in the trends of their quotations, which were among the most stable in local markets and also among the highest money earners of all Mexican private securities.

The regional banks sold shares to both wealthy local elites and to some wealthy financiers from Mexico City, a fact that tended to reinforce the trends toward financial oligopoly, with a few exceptions. Nonetheless, as Haber has argued, restrictive government regulations did not favor the growth of small banks that would have broadened the financial market. Furthermore, "the [Mexican] credit market could not serve as a source of finance for speculation on the stock exchange as it had in the United States (and as it would in Brazil)."[55] This is an important point, for it is indicative of the main thrust of the policies of powerful finance minister Limantour, who—during his tenure of almost two decades (1892–1910)—remained committed above all to providing secure sources of credit for the federal government and to assuring economic stability rather than to stimulating the expansion of possibly dynamic but also potentially unstable stock markets.

It is possible, finally, to suggest that there was one unexpected and rather paradoxical benefit to the lack of depth and breadth of Mexican capital markets; namely, that the outbreak of the revolution in 1910 did not, initially, provoke a major financial panic. During the years 1910–13, the traditional small volume of transactions continued on the Mexican stock market, and these trades continued to be handled by the small circle of capitalists who were the only regular investors. Even the collapse of Mexican banks and banking networks after 1914 did not appear to have as cataclysmic an effect on the Mexican economy as it would have had in a more advanced economy.[56]

Nonetheless, after the end of the revolution (1920), the reconstruction of the banking system would take almost two decades, and the development of dynamic and institutionalized capital markets much longer. This fact, in itself, might help explain why the role of government was so important in providing the financial thrust behind the strong phase of industrialization that took place in Mexico from the mid-1930's to the 1970's. Hence, it would appear that the legacy of the underdevelopment of capital markets in the nineteenth century, and in particular the relationship between state finances and money markets, should be reconsidered by historians and economists in order to understand its impact on the secular trends of the Mexican economy in the twentieth century.

Notes

1. The best history of a Latin American stock exchange in the nineteenth century is Levy 1977. For a comparative view of the birth of Latin American banking, see Marichal 1986.

2. Haber (1991: 566–67) argues that the three principal obstacles to modernization of Mexican financial markets were (1) the low per capita income, (2) the political nature of enforcing property rights and contracts, and (3) the lack of modern commercial legislation. On the role of institutional restrictions in the Mexican economy, also see comments by Coatsworth 1990: 95–106; Rodríguez 1989: 7–23; Cárdenas 1985: 3–22. For a study that underlines government fiscal and financial instability in the first half of the nineteenth century, see Tenenbaum 1986.

3. On the origins and growth of capital markets, and particularly on the role of government securities, see Neal 1990; Riley 1980; Ferguson 1961.

4. For the classic study on financial modernization and the growth of public securities markets in eighteenth-century England, see Dickson 1967. On bank acquisition of government bonds in the United States in the nineteenth century, see James 1978: 74–88.

5. For a classic analysis of capital markets in the United States in the last third of the nineteenth century, see Davis 1965.

6. "The agiotistas (merchant bankers) . . . frequently met at the Sociedad de Comercio or at the Lonja de México at the Palacio de Ayuntamiento. The Escandóns, the Garays, the Martinez del Rios, Felipe Nerri del Barrio, Manuel Nicod and Juan B. Jecker were all members of the Sociedad as was former Treasury Minister, Manuel Gorostiza": Tenenbaum 1986; 74. For case studies of these merchant banking houses, see Bernecker 1992; Walker 1981; Cardoso 1968.

7. So considerable were these transactions that in 1836 the government created a special fund that guaranteed the various holders of the customs certificates payment of the 15 percent of the annual revenues of all the Mexican customs houses; in 1837 another fund, which mortgaged 17 percent of the Veracruz customs revenues, was created for the same purpose. In later years additional funds from other customs revenues were set up: among them were the 8-percent fund of 1838,

the 10-percent fund of 1839, the 17-percent fund of 1840, and the 11-percent fund of 1841. Finally in 1843 all these funds were consolidated into one sinking fund, which paid 26 percent of all Veracruz customs-duty income to the bondholders.

8. The best contemporary study of the Mexican internal debt is Payno 1865. However, it should be complemented by the excellent recent historical study of Tenenbaum 1986.

9. An excellent case study is Walker 1984, which analyzes the "Empresa del Tabaco," a private enterprise set up to administer the public tobacco monopoly. The financiers involved made large profits by carrying out complex speculative transactions that involved not only tobacco bonds but also stock of the Fresnillo mines, customs certificates, and special concessions for cashing silver export duties.

10. In his comments in a colloquium, Fishlow characterized "forced markets" as those in which rates are very high and fluctuate erratically. Also see Fishlow 1985.

11. It is perhaps worthwhile noting that the international price of silver remained basically stable until 1870, a fact that stimulated a high level of both legal and illegal export of silver coin, leading to constant shortages of coin in the Mexican economy. Because there was no paper money, those merchants who held or controlled the trade in silver bullion had distinct economic advantages, a fact that is notoriously evident when reviewing negotiations between moneylenders and the government. Not surprisingly, the latter was generally willing (or obliged) to pay extremely high premiums for metallic currency.

12. Already by 1839 the outrageous rates charged by private bankers (*agiotistas*, or usurers, as they were then called) led the government to ratify a law declaring 12 percent to be the maximum interest rate to be charged. The real effect of the law, nonetheless, was nil. See Lagunilla 1981: 37.

13. The control of certain merchant bankers over the mints (both those of Mexico City and of mining centers like Guanajuato or San Luis Potosí) was crucial to their control over silver circulation and gave them monopoly advantages in this sphere. The extraordinary fortune accumulated by the Beísteguis (second only to the Escandóns in midcentury in Mexico) can only be attributed to their control of the Mexico City mint and their large stakes in the biggest silver-mining firm, that of Real del Monte. For details, see Meyer 1978: 108–39.

14. On the tobacco monopoly, see Walker 1981; on the salt administration, see Flores Clair 1992; on the toll routs, see Urias 1978.

15. In the early 1840's the Martínez del Río firm obtained 45 percent of its profits from government loans, which constituted only 10 percent of its working capital. See Walker 1981: 230.

16. The data are on loans by the Martínez del Río firm to local clients in the years 1836–37: Walker 1981: 151.

17. Information on this topic was provided to me by Rocío de la Barrera, who is currently preparing her doctoral dissertation on the Real del Monte company.

18. A review of the information in Tenenbaum 1986 on the large and complex number of debt instruments issued by the Mexican government suggests that there was no such thing as a standard long-term interest rate on such securities.

19. A review of notarial records of the period indicates that there were few transactions involving the sale of shares of firms, because these were mostly family enterprises. Among private enterprises, it would appear that only mining companies, and to a lesser extent a few textile firms, actively promoted the sale of stock. On notarial records, see Gonzalbo and Vázquez 1986–87.

20. These were the "Convention" debts, which allowed foreign merchants residing in Mexico to define debt against the government as external claims. To avail themselves of such benefits, numerous native merchants "acquired" foreign citizenship. See Wynne 1954: 55–62.

21. For the standard history of disentailment, see Bazant 1977, which has much information on these transactions.

22. For an interesting if brief company history, see Banco de Londres y México 1964.

23. An interesting portrait of the "new" commercial and financial bourgeoisie of the capital can be found in Ludlow 1990 and in Ludlow's doctoral dissertation, currently in progress.

24. Corbett (1989, 1991).

25. See Cerutti (1986: 141–50) for a chart of loans to the Vidaurri government, covering the years 1858–62.

26. Wiemers 1985: 545.

27. The traditional legislation, which was the inheritance of church law against usury, established a ceiling of 6 percent on interest on loans and continued formally in force in the state of Veracruz until 1867. The law was observed in notarial contracts, although not in actual practice. See Wiemers 1985.

28. Wiemers 1985: 546.

29. Additional studies on regional credit markets at midcentury may be found in studies on Michoacán by Chowning (chap. 7, this volume) and on Puebla by Cervantes 1986.

30. The Banco Nacional de México dominated the banking market throughout the period 1884 to 1910, but its weight was particularly marked in the first decade of this period because of the small number of other existing banks and because it had the greatest network of branches and agencies. See Ludlow 1986.

31. For detailed lists and analysis of shareholders, see Ludlow 1990.

32. The expansion of the Mexico City money market and the lowering of rates on short-term capital in the 1880's even allowed for *initial* operations of a long-term capital market on which—according to the first financial journal, *El Economista Mexicano*—the stock of a handful of large enterprises (the Central Mexican Railway, the National Railway, and the Banco Nacional), in conjunction with some public securities, was quoted. Separate sections of the financial press provided occasional information on mining stocks, suggesting that these still belonged, in a sense, to a separate market, which had special and traditional characteristics.

33. The Banque Franco-Egyptienne was a leading foreign-based stockholder of the Banco Nacional. The Mexico City merchant/financiers involved in this deal included Bermejillo Hnos., Benecke Sucs., Felix Cuevas, Gutheil y Cia., Ramón G.

Guzmán, Lavie y Cia., and Antonio de Mier y Celis. The customs certificates were to be cashed in at the customs offices of the Mexican Pacific ports. See AHBAN-AMEX B, Contrato no. 1, "Sindicato 'Ordenes del Pacífico.'"

34. In his financial report, Minister De la Peña stated in September 1884 that an estimated 60 percent of the customs revenues of the port of Campeche, 90 percent of those of Tampico and Matamoros, and 84 percent of those of Veracruz were mortgaged to private companies, merchant houses, and the Banco Nacional. Secretaria de Hacienda 1884: lxx–lxxix.

35. See discussion by the bank directors of the government proposal in AHBAN-AMEX A: January 24, 1884.

36. For details on the bank fusion, see Ludlow 1986.

37. The Banamex also paid out 150,000 pesos to Puebla clients in those same days. *Semana Mercantil*, July 6 and 13, 1885.

38. *Semana Mercantil* reported that the Boston newspapers had reported a panic on the local stock exchange on June 25 and 26 as a result of the news arrived from Mexico regarding the suspension of the payment of the customs certificates held by the Mexican Central Railway (which was controlled by investors from Boston). The response on the London stock exchange (where there were large numbers of stockholders of the Mexican National Railway as well as large quantities of old, unpaid, external bonds of the Mexican government) was more mixed because of initial positive reports on the debt-conversion plan. But all Mexican securities soon fell on the London market as the financial press began to insist on the negative effects of the suspension of the railway guarantees.

39. For regulations on amortization of these *certificados*, see Secretaría de Hacienda 1885–86: 250–51.

40. See AHBANAMEX B, Contratos nos. 9, 10, and 11, between the Banco Nacional de México and the government, signed October 21, 1885, January 11, 1886, and February 4, 1886.

41. In order to guarantee the external debt conversion, Dublán made arrangements with the Banamex for the transfer of the biannual debt payments from Mexico to London, and throughout 1887 the Mexican bank advanced the sum required and placed them with Glyn, Mills. It was from this time that Banamex became the government's formal agent for all its foreign-debt operations and payments, a role it would continue to exercise until 1913. It should also be noted that it was Eduoard Noetzlin, head of the Banamex board in Paris, who was charged by the Mexican government with the negotiation of the foreign loan. Noetzlin was able to pull off a major financial coup by arranging the issue of the 1888 conversion loan in London and Berlin.

42. Creditors simply presented their claims and titles (including all kinds of government paper from different periods of the nineteenth century) to the public debt office and, in case of favorable judgment, received the new bonds. These procedures also were similar in the case of the railway companies, which received certificates and 5-percent railway construction bonds (between 1885 and 1890); they used these to pay import taxes on the equipment they imported or, alternatively, sold the certifi-

cates at a discount to the Banamex, which in turn placed them among importers. Much information on these questions is found in AHBANAMEX.

43. The bulk of this loan went to liquidate the old, unpaid subsidies due to the Central and National Railways, which received 17 million pesos in exchange for 23 million pesos in claims. But an additional 9,283,000 pesos went to Banco Nacional de México to pay off the loans it had advanced. Secretaría de Hacienda 1890: xxx–xxxi.

44. For details on the loan restructuring of 1894, see Castillo 1903: 274–304.

45. On the role of Scherer and Co. in placing Mexican securities in Europe, there are some data in Poidevin 1970: 13–14, 212, 333–35, 716–17.

46. The price of silver on international markets hit bottom in January 1895, after which it made a notable recovery that lasted until mid-1896. For the next five years silver prices tended to stabilize, with small fluctuations making the Mexican bonds attractive investments because of the discounted prices at which they were offered by the government.

47. For a review of the meeting places of the brokers of Mexico City, see Lagunilla 1973.

48. "Aunque en la ciudad de México han organizado hace años los principales corredores de la plaza una Bolsa mercantil de valores, no se ha implantado la costumbre de hacer en ella la contratación; y si los corredores se reunen cada día es simplemente para comunicarse los tipos a que han hecho operaciones de cambio, compras o ventas fuera de la Bolsa y publicar los tipos en un Boletín especial. Carecemos, pues, de una Bolsa propiamente dicha, y las operaciones a descubierto o a término son desconocidas." Macedo 1905, I: 126.

49. A fascinating description of the extravagant speculation in mining stocks in times of crisis is recounted by the British Consul in Mexico City. See CFBH, microfilm, F.O. 203, roll 72, L. Jerome, British Consul in Mexico City to the Foreign Office, August 3, 1903.

50. Haber 1989: 79–80.

51. Haber (1991) has also demonstrated that the shallowness of Mexican capital markets tended to stymie the emergence of small- and medium-sized textile firms and therefore reinforced industrial concentration.

52. Cerutti has published more than a half dozen monographs on the subject and a recent synthesis (1992).

53. There were 27 regional banks with state charters in 1908, according to the *Mexican Yearbook* 1908: 258–315.

54. The only detailed research on stockholding in a leading Mexico City bank is Ludlow (1989). According to Cerutti (1992) practically 100 percent of the stock of the Banco Mercantil de Monterrey, as well as of other local financial institutions, was held by capitalists from Monterrey and other northern regions.

55. Haber 1991: 568.

56. In this sense, it would appear that the Mexican economy had a hidden resilience due to traditional rather than modern factors, a fact that would appear to confirm the view of Womack (1978).

References

PRIMARY SOURCES

AHBANAMEX [Archivo Histórico de Banamex] A. *Libro de Actas—Acuerdos del Consejo de Administración, 1881–1886.* Mexico City.

AHBANAMEX B. *Libro de Contratos Originales con el Gobierno Federal, 1883–1914.* Mexico City.

Cámara de Diputados (Mexico) 1885. *Diario de Debates, Cámara de Diputados (Doceava Legislatura), 1884–1885.* Mexico City.

CFBH [Council of Foreign Bondholders]. Newspaper Clippings on Mexico, 1873–1940. Microfilm. El Colegio de México.

Economista Mexicano, El. 1886–93. Mexico City.

Secretaría de Hacienda y Crédito Público. 1880–81, 1883–84, 1884–85, 1885–86, 1890. *Memoria.* Mexico City.

Semana Mercantil, La. 1884–85. Mexico City.

SECONDARY SOURCES

Banco de Londres y México. 1964. *100 Años de Banca de México: Primer Centenario del Banco de Londres y México, S.A., 1864–1964.* Mexico City.

Bazant, Jan. 1968. *Historia de la deuda exterior de México.* Mexico City.

———. 1977. *Los bienes de la Iglesia en México, 1856–1875.* Mexico City.

Bernecker, Walther L. 1992. *De Agiotistas y Empresarios: en torno de la Temprana Industrialización (Siglo XIX).* Mexico City.

Bulnes, Francisco. 1885. *La deuda inglesa.* Mexico City.

Cárdenas, Enrique. 1985. "Algunas cuestiones sobre la depresión mexicana del siglo XIX." *HISLA, Revista Latinoamericana de Historia Económica y Social* 3: 3–22.

Cardoso, Ciro, ed. 1968. *Formación y desarrollo de la burguesía en México.* Mexico City.

Casasús, Joaquín. 1885. *Historia de la deuda contraída en Londres.* Mexico City.

Castillo, Juan. 1903. "Colección-de leyes, decretos, reglamentos, contratos, supremas resoluciones y noticias referentes al crédito público y correspondientes a los años 1883 a 1903, epoca del arreglo definitivo de la deuda nacional." Mexico City.

Cerda, Luis. 1990. "Causas económicas de la revolución mexicana." Manuscript, Instituto Tecnológico Autónomo de México.

———. 1991. "Exchange Rate and Monetary Policies in Mexico: From Bimetallism to the Gold Standard, 1890–1910." Manuscript, Instituto Tecnológico Autónomo de México.

Cerutti, Mario. 1986. "El préstamo prebancario en el noreste de México: la actividad de los grandes comerciantes de Monterrey, 1855–1890." In L. Ludlow and C. Marichal, eds., *Banca y poder en México, 1800–1925*, pp. 119–64. Mexico City.

——. 1992. *Burguesía, capitales e industria en el norte de México: Monterrey y su ámbito regional, 1850–1910*. Mexico City.

Cervantes, Francisco. 1986. "La Iglesia y la crisis del crédito colonial en Puebla, 1800–1814." In L. Ludlow and C. Marichal, eds., *Banca y poder en México, 1800–1925*, pp. 51–74. Mexico City.

——. 1992. "La Iglesia y la economía en Puebla, 1820–1856." Diss., El Colegio de México.

Coatsworth, John. 1990. *Los orígenes del atraso: nueve ensayos de historia económica de México en los siglos XVIII y XIX*. Mexico City.

Corbett, Barbara M. 1989. "Soberania, elite politica y espacios regionales en San Luis Potosí (1824–1828)." *Secuencia*, no. 15 (Sept–Dec.): 7–27.

——. 1991. "Libre de derechos: la politica fiscal y el liberalismo potosino en los años 40." Paper at Conferencia de Historia Económica del Gran Norte Oriental, Monterrey, Feb. 21.

Cosío Villegas, Daniel, ed., 1964. *Historia moderna de México: vida económica*, 2 vols. Mexico City.

Davis, Lance 1965. "The Investment Market, 1870–1917: The Evolution of a National Market." *Journal of Economic History* 25: 335–99.

Dickson, P. G. M. 1967. *The Financial Revolution in England: A Study in the Development of Public Credit, 1699–1756*. London.

D'Olwer, Nicolau. 1964. "Las inversiones extranjeras." In D. Cosío Villegas, ed., *Historia moderna de México: vida económica*, vol. 2, pp. 973–1177. Mexico City.

Eichengreen, Barry, and Peter Lindert, eds. 1989. *The International Debt Crisis in Historical Perspective*. Cambridge, Mass.

Ferguson, E. James. 1961. *The Power of the Purse: A History of American Public Finance, 1776–1790*. Chapel Hill, N.C.

Fishlow, Albert. 1985. "Lessons from the Past: Capital Markets during the Nineteenth Century and the Interwar Period." *International Organization* 39, no. 3 (summer): 420–60.

Flores Clair, Eduardo. 1992. "Fuentes para el estudio de la renta de la sal." *Boletin de Fuentes para la Historia Económica de México*, no. 7 (Aug.): 17–24.

Gonzalbo, Pilar, and Josefina Vazquez, eds. 1986–87. "Guia de Notarias de la Ciudad de México, 1849" and "Guia de Notarias de la Ciudad de México, 1875." El Colegio de México.

Haber, Stephen H. 1989. *Industry and Underdevelopment: The Industrialization of Mexico, 1890–1940*. Stanford.

——. 1991. "Industrial Concentration and the Capital Markets: A Comparative Study of Brazil, Mexico and the United States, 1830–1930." *The Journal of Economic History* 51, no. 3 (Sept.): 559–80.

James, John A. 1978. *Money and Capital Markets in Postbellum America*. Princeton.

Lagunilla, Alfredo Iñarritu. 1973. *Historia de la Bolsa de México, 1895–1970*. Mexico City.

———. 1981. *Historia de la banca y moneda en México.* Mexico City.

Levy, María Bárbara. 1977. *Historia da Bolsa de Valores do Rio de Janeiro.* Rio de Janeiro.

Lewis, W. A. 1983. *Crecimiento y fluctuaciones, 1870–1914.* Mexico City.

Ludlow, Leonor. 1986. "La construcción de un banco: el Banco Nacional de México, 1881–1884." In L. Ludlow and C. Marichal, eds., *Banca y poder en México, 1800–1925,* pp. 299–345. Mexico City.

———. 1990. "El Banco Nacional Mexicano y el Banco Mercantil Mexicano: radiografía social de sus primeros accionistas." *Historia Mexicana* 39, no. 4 (Apr.–June): 979–1027.

Ludlow, Leonor, and Carlos Marichal, eds. 1986. *Banca y poder en México, 1800–1925.* Mexico City.

Macedo, Pablo. 1905. *La evolución Mercantil. Comunicaciones y obras públicas. La hacienda pública; tres monografías que dan idea de una parte de la evolución económica de México.* Mexico City.

Marichal, Carlos. 1986. "El nacimiento de la banca mexicana en el contexto latinoamericano: problemas de periodización." In L. Ludlow and C. Marichal, eds., *Banca y poder en México, 1800–1925.* Mexico City.

———. 1989a. *A Century of Debt Crises in Latin America, 1820–1930.* Princeton.

———. 1989b. "The Banco Nacional de México and the Modernization of Mexican State Finances, 1880–1900." Paper presented at the colloquium on Latin American Debt in Historical Perspective, Ibero-Amerikanisches Institut, Berlin, November 15–18.

———. 1991. "Tres etapas de la elite financiera de la ciudad de México, 1780–1880." In A. Hernández and M. Miño, eds., *Cincuenta Años de Historia,* pp. 433–55. Mexico City.

The Mexican Yearbook. 1908. London.

Meyer, Rosa Mariá. 1978. "Los Beistegui, especuladores y mineros, 1830–1869." In C. Cardoso, ed., *Formación y desarrollo de la burguesía en México,* pp. 108–39. Mexico City.

Neal, Larry. 1990. *The Rise of Financial Capitalism.* Cambridge, Eng.

Ortiz de Montellano, Mariano. 1886. *Apuntes para la liquidación de la deuda contraída en Londres.* Mexico City.

Poidevin, Raymond. 1970. *Finance et relations internationales, 1887–1919.* Paris.

Riley, James. 1980. *International Government Finance and the Amsterdam Capital Market, 1740–1815.* Cambridge, Eng.

Rodríguez, Jaime, ed. 1989. *The Mexican and Mexican American Experience in the 19th Century.* Tempe, Ariz.

Stallings, Barbara. 1987. *Banker to the Third World: U.S. Portfolio Investment in Latin America, 1900–1986.* Berkeley.

Tenenbaum, Barbara. 1986. *The Politics of Penury: Debts and Taxes in Mexico, 1821–1856.* Albuquerque.

Thomson, Guy. 1989. *Puebla de los Angeles: Industry and Society in a Mexican City, 1700–1850.* London.

Urias, Margarita. 1978. "Manuel Escandón: de las diligencias al ferrocarril, 1833–

1862." In C. Cardoso, ed., *Formación y desarrollo de la burguesía en México*, pp. 25–56. Mexico City.

Walker, David. 1981. "Kinship, Business and Politics: The Martínez del Rio Family in Mexico, 1824–1864." Ph.D., diss., University of Chicago.

———. 1984. "Business as Usual: The Empresa del Tabaco in Mexico, 1837–1844." *Hispanic American Historical Review* 64, no. 4 (Nov.): 675–705.

Wiemers, Eugene. 1985. "Agriculture and Credit in Nineteenth Century Mexico: Orizaba and Córdoba, 1822–1871." *Hispanic American Historical Review* 65, no. 3 (Aug.): 519–46.

Womack, John. 1978. "The Mexican Economy During the Revolution, 1910–1920: Historiography and Analysis." *Marxist Perspectives* 1, no.4: 80–123.

Wynne, William. 1954. *State Insolvency and Foreign Bondholders*. New Haven, Conn.

CHAPTER 6

Financial Markets and Industrial Development

A Comparative Study of Governmental Regulation, Financial Innovation, and Industrial Structure in Brazil and Mexico, 1840–1930

STEPHEN HABER

Historians of the United States and Western Europe have long been interested in how capital was mobilized for industrial development during the nineteenth century. One result of this interest is a mature literature addressing the impact of governmental regulatory regimes on the development of financial markets, the transformation of kinship-based financial networks into modern financial institutions, and the relationship between the structure and size of capital markets and the structure and size of industry, among other issues.[1] Three themes emerge from this literature. First, governmental regulatory policies played a critical role in structuring capital markets. Second, the development of impersonal sources of capital (banks, stock exchanges, bond markets) were crucial for industrial success in the nineteenth century. Third, imperfections in capital markets strongly influenced the geographic location and productive organization of industry.[2] In short, the literature on advanced industrial economies suggests that the growth of institutional sources of capital was not itself a necessary outcome of the larger process of economic growth; regulatory policies and the legal tradition had important independent effects, which were felt in both the financial and industrial sectors.

Comparatively speaking, Latin American historians have done very little work on any of these issues, except for a few recent studies on the history of banking in Brazil, Mexico, and Peru and a single study of the Rio de Janeiro stock market. Moreover, most of what has been done is of an institutionalist nature.[3] Surprisingly little of this literature directly addresses the question of how the growth of capital markets affected the region's industrial development.[4]

This chapter therefore employs the tools and techniques of economic analysis to study one of nineteenth-century Latin America's most salient obstacles to economic growth and structural transformation: the absence of well-developed capital markets. It addresses two interrelated questions. First, what impact did governmental regulatory policies have on the development of financial markets in Brazil and Mexico? Second, what was the relationship between the development of capital markets and the development of industry? That is, how well do the different experiences of Brazil and Mexico in the development of institutional sources of finance account for differences in the two countries' rate of growth and structure of the cotton textile industry?

I focus on Brazil and Mexico because they were the two most industrialized economies of Latin America during the period under study.[5] Moreover, focusing on Brazil and Mexico allows for the testing of hypotheses about the impact of institutional innovations in finance on the growth and structure of industry. Both countries followed repressive financial-market regulatory policies throughout the nineteenth century, and both, therefore, had small capital markets that provided little in the way of industrial finance. In 1890, however, Brazil created a less repressive regulatory environment, opening up new sources of finance for its textile industry. Because Mexico did not undertake these kinds of regulatory reforms, the Brazil-Mexico comparison provides a counterfactual test case for understanding the effects of these regulatory changes on Brazil's industrial development and allows us to measure the loss to Mexico when it failed to enact similar, less-repressive policies and failed to lower the costs of obtaining information.

I focus on the cotton textile industry for two reasons. First, the cotton goods manufacture was the most important manufacturing industry in Mexico and Brazil during the period under study.[6] Second, there are compelling theoretical reasons to focus on cotton textiles. In underdeveloped economies, numerous factors, such as large economies of scale or technological barriers to entry, can condition the development of many industries. Separating the effects of access to institutional sources of capital (that is, capital from impersonal institutions such as banks, bond markets, and stock exchanges) from among these other factors is difficult across the entire industrial sector. In the cotton textile industry, however, these other factors did not come into play: the capital equipment was easily divisible, the minimum efficient scale of production was small, and nonfinancial barriers to entry were largely absent. The only important barrier to entry was access to finance.[7] The textile industry therefore provides an excellent test case of the relationship between the development of the financial markets that provide capital to an industry and the development of the industry itself.[8]

The argument I advance runs in the following terms. The size and structure of financial markets played a crucial role in determining the size and structure of the textile industry. In Mexico, where the banking system was small and concentrated, the distribution of bank loans among potential textile industrialists was narrow; banks could only monitor a limited number of borrowers. Differential access to bank capital, in turn, gave rise to differential access to equity capital; entrepreneurs with the proven ability to obtain loans for working capital had a significant advantage over their competitors when it came to selling equity in the securities markets. In short, a small group of powerful financiers was able to obtain all the capital it needed, while everyone else was starved for funds.

The results were twofold. First, the textile industry was highly concentrated, because access to impersonal sources of capital served as a barrier to entry. Second, because the ability to mobilize capital from banks and the securities markets was a scarce talent, financial capitalists played an important role in the development of the cotton textile industry.

In Brazil, where the institutional rules of the game after 1889 created larger and less-concentrated capital markets, the distribution of funds among potential textile industrialists was broader. Access to institutional sources of finance did not, therefore, serve as a barrier to entry, which in turn meant that the textile industry in Brazil tended to be less concentrated. In fact, as the capital markets broadened in Brazil during the last decade of the nineteenth century and the first decade of the twentieth, industry tended to become increasingly less concentrated. This is precisely the opposite outcome that obtained in Mexico. In the Mexican case, differential access to capital created by the limited opening of the capital markets during the 1880's and 1890's actually gave rise to an increase in concentration.

The reason for these differences between Mexico and Brazil was largely political. In Brazil, the abolition of slavery in 1888, the overthrow of the monarchy in 1889, and the formation of the First Republic brought about a liberalization of the policies regulating financial markets, which spurred the growth of the banking sector, the stock exchange, and the bond market. Mexico did not undergo such a transformation; it continued to be ruled by the Porfirio Díaz dictatorship (1876–1911), which relied on the financial and political support of a small group of politically powerful financial capitalists. This financial elite used its political power to erect legal barriers to entry in the banking industry. This gave some firms an advantage in obtaining short-term working capital from banks, because banks tended to lend only to those entrepreneurs with whom they had direct connections. This differential access to working capital, coupled with the difficulty in obtaining information on the financial state of firms, meant that only the enterprises of well-known financial capitalists had much hope of attracting outside equity investors. The corporate form of ownership therefore spread much more slowly than in Brazil.

The first section of this chapter compares the institutional history of financial intermediaries and textile-mill financing in the two countries over the period 1840 to 1930. The second section then examines the rate of industrial investment in the two countries and measures the level of industrial concentration in each country over time through the estimation of four-firm ratios and Herfindahl indices, assessing changes in the size and structure of the textile industry in the light of institutional innovations in textile finance. It also develops a counterfactual model to estimate the loss to Mexico of its repressive financial market regulatory policies. The third section concludes.

Capital Markets and Textile Finance

There are five ways that entrepreneurs can mobilize capital for industrial investment. The first and most common is for an entrepreneur to borrow money from his network of kin relations and business associates. The disadvantage of this approach is that, should the enterprise fail, the entrepreneur is personally liable for the firm's debts. In addition, this method has the drawback that the amount of capital that can be raised is limited by the wealth and willingness to invest of an entrepreneur's social network. This severely limits the scale of investment that may be undertaken.

In order to partially overcome these disadvantages, an entrepreneur may use his social network to raise capital through a second avenue: providing his kin and business associates with an equity stake in the firm by forming a partnership or privately held joint-stock company. This spreads risk among all of the principals, but the amount of capital that may be mobilized is still limited by the wealth and willingness of the entrepreneur's family and business network.

Third, an entrepreneur may reinvest the profits of an already extant enterprise. The disadvantage of this method is that it is slow; new investment is limited by the amount of profits in previous years. In addition, it presumes that the original investment capital can be generated through some other means, such as the two methods discussed above.

Fourth, entrepreneurs may borrow money from an institutional source, such as a bank, or from a group of investors they do not personally know through the sale of bonds. This avenue can only be used, however, if banks and bond markets exist and if bankers and bondholders are willing to lend money to businesses in which they have no direct knowledge or control. An added disadvantage of this approach is that a sole proprietor or partnership will still be legally responsible for the debts to these institutional investors if the business fails.

A fifth method of capital mobilization solves this liability problem. An entrepreneur may sell equity in an enterprise to impersonal investors by forming a publicly traded, limited-liability, joint-stock company. This company may also sell bonded debt. This method can mobilize large amounts of capital quickly and spreads risk among a large group of investors. Moreover, stockholders in a limited-liability company are not personally responsible for the debts of that company should it fail. This approach to capital mobilization may only be employed, however, if there is a stock market on which to sell shares and if investors perceive that owning shares in a business that they know relatively little about is a secure way to invest their savings. Like the sale of debt to impersonal investors, this avenue of finance requires the existence of institutions that bring together those with capital with those who need it. It also requires that mechanisms exist to provide useful and reliable information about the financial health of firms to potential investors. In short, in order to mobilize capital through impersonal sources, specialized institutions must be developed (stock exchanges, bond markets, banks) whose purpose is to connect savers and investors, overcome information asymmetries, and reduce transaction costs.

BRAZIL

Until the last decade of the nineteenth century, Brazilian textile entrepreneurs were limited to the first three methods of capital mobilization. Brazilian firms could neither sell equity on the stock exchange nor appeal to the banking system for loans; industrialists therefore had to rely on their extended kinship groups and reinvested profits in their search for finance.

Throughout most of the nineteenth century, institutions designed to mobilize impersonal sources of capital were largely absent in Brazil. An organized stock exchange had functioned in Rio de Janeiro since early in the century, but it was seldom used to finance industrial companies. During the period from 1850 to 1885, only one manufacturing company was listed on the exchange, and its shares traded hands in only 3 of those 36 years. Neither could Brazil's mill owners appeal to the banking system to provide them with capital. As late as 1888, Brazil had but 26 banks, whose combined capital totaled only 145,000 *contos*—roughly $48 million. Only seven of the country's twenty states had any banks at all, and half of all deposits were held by a few banks in Rio de Janeiro.[9]

The slow development of these institutions can be traced in large part to public policies designed to restrict entry into banking and limit abuses of the public by unscrupulous corporate promoters. The imperial government, which held the right to charter banks, was primarily concerned with creating a small number of large superbanks that could serve as a source of government finance and that would promote monetary stability. Unfortunately, its continual changes in regulatory policies prevented the development of even a tightly controlled, centralized banking system along the lines of many Western European countries. The result was that Brazil forwent the tremendous advantages that accrued to other countries through the expansion of banking systems designed to channel funds from traditional enterprises into other economic activities.[10]

What is perhaps more important, the imperial government created regulations designed to discourage the spread of the corporate form of ownership. Brazil's 1860 incorporation law required the promoters of joint-stock companies to obtain the special permission of the imperial government, prohibited investors from purchasing stocks on margin, and restricted banks from investing in corporate securities. In addition, it did not permit limited liability. In fact, under Brazilian law an investor could be held liable for a firm's debts even after he had sold the stock.[11]

The last decade of the nineteenth century witnessed a dramatic and sustained transformation of Brazil's capital markets. Driving the expansion of the credit system were changes in regulatory policies. The government's purpose in putting these policies into effect was to speed Brazil's transition from an agrarian economy run with slave labor to a modern industrial and commercial economy. In order to do that, Brazil's policy makers were willing to forgo their traditional inclination to value monetary stability over credit creation. The result was a credit boom and a speculative bubble, known as the *Encilhamento*, that had important and lasting consequences for the Rio de Janeiro stock exchange and the enterprises that sold their securities there.[12]

The opening of Brazil's capital markets began in 1888, when the treasury abandoned monetary orthodoxy by awarding concessions to twelve banks of issue and providing seventeen banks with interest-free loans. The easy credit policies of 1888 were not enough, however, to stem the tide of Brazil's republican movement, which saw the monarchy and its policies as inimical to the creation of a modern economy and society. In 1889 the imperial government of Dom Pedro II was overthrown and a federal republic was created. The new government quickly moved to open the banking system and free the securities markets from the regulations that had dampened their activities. In 1890 the government modified the 1888 law, creating three regional banks of issue whose currency was backed by treasury bonds. Next, the government deregulated the banking industry; banks could now engage in whatever kind of financial transactions they wished. Other reforms permitted limited liability, eased the formation of joint-stock companies, and encouraged securities trading by permitting purchases on margin. Finally, new industrial ventures were exempted from taxes and customs duties.[13]

This is not to argue that the First Republic completely deregulated the capital markets. In fact, the government continued its policy of requiring publicly traded corporations to produce financial statements and reprint them in public documents (such as the *Diario Official* or the *Jornal do Commercio*). In addition, corporate reports had to list the names of all stockholders and the numbers of shares each controlled. Investors could thus obtain reasonably good information on the health of firms and the identities of their major shareholders.[14]

The results of these reforms were dramatic. Brazil's money supply, which had grown at a rate of scarcely 1 percent per year since the 1870's, grew fourfold in the twelve months between December 1889 and December 1890. The nation's newly formed banks, flush with investable funds and free to employ them without restrictions, plunged into the Rio de Janeiro stock exchange, purchasing large numbers of corporate securities. The Rio exchange, which had been a staid and sleepy affair throughout the nineteenth century, now saw wild securities trading as well as an expansion of the number of firms listed. In the first year of the *Encilhamento* alone, it saw almost as much trading as it had in the previous 60 years.[15]

In the short term, the speculative bubble created by the *Encilhamento* created large numbers of banks, some of which provided capital for the textile industry. Bank-financed industrial development was not, however, to be long lasting in Brazil. The boom created by the *Encilhamento* created a speculative bubble, which burst in 1892, bringing down many banks with it. The government in 1896 therefore once again restricted the right to issue currency to a single bank acting as the agent of the treasury.[16] These more restrictive regulations, coupled with the already shaky financial situation of many of the country's banks (exacerbated by a significant amount of foreign-exchange speculation) produced an almost complete collapse of the banking sector. In 1891 there were 68 banks operating in Brazil. By 1906 there were but ten, and their capital was only one-ninth that of the 1891 banks.[17] The banking sector then began to expand, led and controlled by a semiofficial superbank, the third Banco de Brasil, which acted both as a commercial bank and as the treasury's financial agent.[18]

By international standards this was an extremely modest banking system. Moreover, Brazil's banks, such as they existed, lent very little money for productive investment. As Anne Hanley and Gail Triner have independently demonstrated, most banks' assets were held in cash and notes receivable (used to facilitate commercial transactions). Loans made up a small part of their portfolio.[19] In fact, an analysis I have made of the balance sheets of fifteen large-scale, publicly traded textile manufacturers reveals that circa 1900–07 only three had any itemized bank loans on their balance sheets at all, and these debts were a very minor portion of their total liabilities.[20]

The more important, long-term effect of the *Encilhamento* was that it financed the creation of large numbers of joint-stock manufacturing companies. In 1888 only three cotton textile enterprises were listed on the Rio stock exchange; by 1895 twelve of the country's operating textile firms were publicly traded. This grew to 21 operating firms in 1905 and to 32 in 1915, where it leveled off. Thus, in 1915, 32 of Brazil's 180 operating cotton textile companies (18 percent) were publicly traded joint-stock, limited-liability corporations. These 32 companies controlled 38 percent of installed capacity and 34 percent of output.[21]

More striking than the existence of an equity market in Brazil was the simultaneous development of a market for long-term debt. As early as 1895 four of Brazil's operating firms sold debentures on the Rio exchange. This increased to 13 firms by 1905 and to 24 firms by 1915 (13 percent of all firms in operation).[22]

These debt issues raised significant amounts of capital. A comparison of the 1905 and 1915 censuses indicates that new debt issues accounted for 32 percent of all new investment during that ten-year period (see Table 6.1). Thus, from 1905 to 1915, the average debt-equity ratio grew

TABLE 6.1

Capital Structure of the Brazilian Textile Industry, 1882–1934

(*millions of current mil-réis*)

PANEL I

Year	1 Paid-in capital[a]	2 Retained earnings	3 (1 + 2) Equity	4 Debt issues	5 (3 + 4) Total capital
1882	—	—	—	—	7.3
1895	—	—	—	—	47.4
1905	—	—	177.1	28.3	205.4
1907	—	—	—	—	214.6
1914	—	—	—	—	314.1
1915	236.4	39.5	275.9	74.5	350.4
1924	383.9	272.5	656.4	69.9	726.3
1925	462.0	349.7	811.7	99.6	911.3
1926	557.7	383.1	940.8	147.3	1,088.1
1927	606.8	411.1	1,017.9	134.8	1,152.7
1934	659.2	292.0	951.2	245.4	1,196.6

PANEL II

Year	6 (1/5) Paid-in/ total capital	7 (4/5) Debt/ total capital	8 (2/5) Retained/ total capital	9 (3/5) Equity/ total capital	10 (4/3) Debt- equity ratio	11 New debt/ new capital
1905	—	.14	—	.86	.16	—
1915	.67	.21	.11	.79	.27	.32
1924	.53	.10	.38	.90	.11	−.01
1925	.51	.11	.38	.89	.12	.16
1926	.51	.14	.35	.86	.16	.27
1927	.53	.12	.36	.88	.13	−.19
1934	.55	.21	.24	.79	.26	2.52

SOURCES: Estimated from Borja Castro 1869: 3–73; Commissao de Inquerito Industrial 1882; Branner 1885; Ministerio da Indústria 1896; Vasco 1905; Centro Industrial do Brasil 1909; Centro Industrial do Brasil 1915; Centro Industrial do Brasil 1917; Centro Industrial de Fiação 1924; Centro IIndustrial de Fiação 1925; Centro Industrial de Fiação 1926; Centro Industrial de Fiação 1928; Centro Industrial de Fiação 1935; Stein 1957: appen. 1.

from 0.16:1.00 to 0.27:1.00 for Brazilian cotton textile firms as a whole. This seriously understates the importance of debt finance, because it includes all firms (not just those with access to the bond markets) and because it does not include suppliers' credits, bank loans, or other short-term liabilities. In Table 6.2 I estimate financial ratios for fifteen publicly traded textile firms from information in their balance sheets. The balance-sheet data indicate that circa 1900 the typical debt-equity ratio of a large, publicly traded firm was 0.40:1.00. By 1914, the debt-equity ratios of these firms had grown to 0.64:1.00. During the seven years from 1907 to 1914,

TABLE 6.2

Capital Structure of Large-Scale, Publicly Traded Brazilian Cotton Textile Firms, 1900–34

(in current mil-réis)

Year	Total liabilities	Paid-in capital	Retained earnings	Total equity	Total debt	Bonded debt	Short-term debt
1900	101,996,071	50,600,000	16,520,462	67,120,462	27,059,903	17,056,260	9,003,643
1905	104,902,338	52,100,000	24,048,338	76,148,338	20,891,179	13,486,180	6,404,999
1907	97,327,434	50,150,000	19,021,633	69,171,633	21,551,213	13,093,800	5,157,413
1914	150,243,610	64,950,000	21,762,395	86,712,395	55,913,446	34,963,460	19,149,986
1915	160,658,519	68,550,000	24,474,488	93,024,488	59,562,774	34,118,420	23,644,354
1924	333,197,005	107,000,000	105,011,357	212,011,357	101,587,402	30,991,600	68,535,802
1927	379,087,305	111,000,000	115,696,047	226,696,047	125,798,097	51,101,571	72,816,526
1934	371,681,541	109,900,000	102,968,621	212,868,621	131,624,822	50,254,318	69,285,237

Year	Long-term debt other than bonds	Paid-in capital/ debt + equity (%)	Retained earnings/ debt + equity (%)	Debt-equity ratio	Short-term debt/ debt + equity (%)	Bonded debt/ debt + equity (%)	Other long-term debt/ debt + equity (%)
1900	1,000,000	53.7	17.5	0.40	9.6	18.1	1.1
1905	1,000,000	53.7	24.8	0.27	6.6	13.9	1.0
1907	3,300,000	55.3	21.0	0.31	5.7	14.4	3.6
1914	1,800,000	45.5	15.3	0.64	13.4	24.5	1.3
1915	1,800,000	44.9	16.0	0.64	15.5	22.4	1.2
1924	2,060,000	34.1	33.5	0.48	21.9	9.9	0.7
1927	1,880,000	31.5	32.8	0.55	20.7	14.5	0.5
1934	12,085,267	31.9	29.9	0.62	20.1	14.6	3.5

SOURCE: Calculated from balance sheets of firms listed in note 20.

42 percent of additions to capital in these publicly traded firms were financed by bond sales, greater than the 28 percent financed through additional issues of equity and the meager 5 percent financed out of retained earnings.

The use of the Rio de Janeiro Bolsa as the principal means to finance new companies began to slow after 1915, when the number of operating firms selling equity reached 32. By 1924 the number of such firms had fallen to 27. This occurred at the same time the industry's installed capacity increased by 45 percent and the total number of firms increased from 180 to 202. This trend continued through the rest of the 1920's. Between 1924 and 1927 only one new firm sold equity on the Rio Bolsa, at the same time that installed capacity grew by an additional 21 percent and that 68 new firms entered the industry. During this three-year period new equity issues by already-existing firms came to a virtual halt as well.

The bond market displays a similar pattern. The number of operating firms raising capital through the sale of debt grew from 4 in 1895, to 13 in 1905, 14 in 1907, 22 in 1914, and 24 in 1915. After that it went into abrupt decline, falling to 16 firms by 1924, 14 in 1927, and 13 in 1934. As Table 6.1 demonstrates, the percentage of total capital invested in the industry (not including short-term liabilities) accounted for by bond debt declined from its peak of 21 percent in 1915 to 12 percent in 1927.[23] The more complete balance sheet data from the 15-firm sample tell much the same story; bonds as a percentage of total debt and equity hit its peak of 24.5 percent in 1914, declined to 9.9 percent in 1924, and then slowly grew to 14.6 percent by 1934 (see Table 6.2).

The decline in the use of the Rio de Janeiro Bolsa to mobilize capital for the textile industry is something of a mystery. There are three possible explanations. The first is that World War I dealt a severe blow to investor confidence. Financial losses during the war might have dampened the enthusiasm of investors to hold securities in firms of which they did not have direct knowledge or control.[24] For that reason, established firms with proven records could still obtain capital through new issues of debt and equity, but new entrants could not. The second hypothesis centers on the shift of the textile industry to São Paulo after 1915 because of the technical advantages to producing textiles there. High transactions costs would have discouraged the capitalization of São Paulo firms in the faraway Rio de Janeiro market, while São Paulo's securities market was too thin to mobilize the required funds. A third hypothesis would also focus on the shift of the industry toward São Paulo, but would focus on the development of the São Paulo Bolsa as a source of debt and equity capital. Certainly by

1907 São Paulo textile producers were beginning to sell equity in the local securities market, and by 1909 two of the biggest producers in the state were publicly traded. In this scenario there was no decline in the use of formal securities markets to mobilize capital, simply a relative decline of Rio de Janeiro in favor of the São Paulo Bolsa. Research in progress will evaluate each of these hypotheses systematically.

Even considering the slowing of the use of formal securities markets after 1915, however, Brazil still had an extremely large and well-integrated capital market by the standards of developing countries. The result was that institutional sources of capital were widely available to potential textile industrialists.

MEXICO

Mexico's experience stands in stark contrast to that of Brazil. Like their Brazilian counterparts, Mexican textile entrepreneurs could only mobilize capital though kinship networks and reinvested profits until the end of the nineteenth century. Unlike those in Brazil, however, the opening of the capital markets in Mexico at the end of the century was far more limited.

Institutional lending to industry was largely absent in Mexico until the 1880's. A rudimentary banking system with specialized institutions and stable practices did not even begin to develop until 1864, with the opening of the Banco de Londres y México. By 1884 only 8 banks were in operation, and as late as 1911 Mexico had but 47 banks, only 10 of which were legally able to lend for terms of more than a year. The few banks able to make long-term loans existed primarily to finance urban and rural estate transactions; in fact, they had a great deal of difficulty generating their own capital.[25]

Not only were there few banks, but the level of concentration within this small sector was very high. In 1895, three banks—the Banco Nacional de México, the Banco de Londres y México, and the Banco Internacional Hipotecario—accounted for two-thirds of the capital invested in the banking system. The first two banks issued 80 percent of the bank notes in circulation. Even as late as 1910 the same two banks dominated the credit market, accounting for 75 percent of the deposits in Mexico's nine largest banks and roughly one-half of all bank notes in circulation.[26] If anything, the years after 1910 saw an increase in concentration, as the Mexican Revolution in that year threw capital markets into disarray, destroyed the public's faith in paper money, and put a brake on the development of the banking sector until the late 1920's.[27]

The result of Mexico's slow and unequal development of credit inter-mediaries was that most manufacturers could not obtain bank financing. Even those that could succeeded only in getting short-term loans to cover working capital costs. Thus the Banco Nacional de México provided credit to a number of large industrial establishments in which its directors had interests, but even these insider loans constituted a small part of the total capital of those manufacturing firms. An analysis of the balance sheets of three of the country's largest cotton textile producers during the period 1907 to 1913 indicates debt-equity ratios averaging 0.09 : 1.00. Recall that similar, large-scale Brazilian textile firms had debt-equity ratios seven times this value. Moreover, all of this debt in the Mexican firms was short-term. Unlike their Brazilian counterparts, they raised no funds from the sale of bonds.[28]

Equity financing through the creation of a publicly held joint-stock company was also unknown in the Mexican textile industry until the 1890's. Even after the first industrial companies appeared on the Mexico City stock exchange, however, the use of the exchange to raise equity capital re-mained limited. In fact, during the entire period from 1890 to 1940 there were only four publicly traded joint-stock cotton textile companies listed on the Mexico City exchange. All four were founded during the last decade of the nineteenth century. Thus, at the time of the 1912 cotton textile census, only 4 percent of firms (4 out of 100, operating 148 mills) repre-sented publicly traded joint-stock companies, a small fraction of the 18 percent of textile firms that were publicly traded in Rio de Janeiro.[29]

The reason that capital markets were so late in developing in Mexico and then grew in such a limited way was largely owing to four factors. The first, as Carlos Marichal makes clear in his contribution to this volume (chapter 5), was the fact that through much of the nineteenth century the Mexican government did not repay its debts to its bondholders. This de-layed the widespread holding of paper securities by the public, and hence the development of securities markets. Simply put, the Mexican public learned precisely the opposite lesson that holders of U.S. government bonds did; a piece of paper was not as secure an investment in Mexico as a house, farm, or bag of coins.[30]

The second factor was the politicized nature of defending property rights and enforcing contracts. Personal ties to members of the govern-ment were essential for entrepreneurs to obtain the rights to official monopolies, trade protection, government subsidies, or favorable judicial rulings. Indeed, it was almost impossible to do business without resort-ing to political machinations.[31] Thus, only well-established financiers with clear ties to the Díaz regime appear to have been successful in floating equity issues.[32]

The third factor impeding the growth of capital markets was the loose enforcement of financial reporting requirements. In fact, publicly traded manufacturing companies often failed to publish balance sheets in public documents (such as the *Diario Official* or the financial press) in many years, even though the law required them to do so. The result was that individuals tended to invest only in those enterprises controlled by important financial capitalists. In this sense, Mexico's major financiers played the same role as individuals like J. P. Morgan in the financing of U.S. heavy industry. Their presence on the boards of companies signaled the investment community that a particular enterprise was a safe bet.[33] Two characteristics of the Mexico City stock exchange are particularly striking in this regard. First, almost all of the publicly traded industrials had well-known, politically well-connected financial capitalists like Antonio Basagoiti, Hugo Scherer, or León Signoret as directors. Second, there was very little entry and exit in the stock exchange. It was not the case that small firms tried to float issues and failed, or that small firms succeeded in selling equity and then went out of business. Rather, the pattern was for a few large firms to be capitalized through the sale of equity. These firms then dominated their respective product lines well into the 1920's and 1930's.[34]

The fourth factor slowing the development of impersonal sources of finance was Mexico's regulatory environment. Throughout the early and mid-nineteenth century, the lack of modern commercial and incorporation laws retarded the development of banks and joint-stock companies. No body of mortgage credit laws was written until 1884, and it was not until 1889 that a general incorporation law was established. Thus for most of the century it was extremely difficult to enforce loan contracts and establish joint-stock companies.

Even when those laws were in place, however, new restrictive banking regulations prevented the widespread development of credit institutions. The Mexican government favored the nation's largest bank, the Banco Nacional de México, with all kinds of special rights and privileges. These included reserve requirements that were half those demanded of other banks, the sole right to serve as the government's intermediary in all its financial transactions, a monopoly for its notes for the payment of taxes or other fees to the government, an exemption from taxes, and the sole right to establish branch banks. At the same time that the government created this privileged, semiofficial institution, it erected significant barriers to entry for competing banks, including extremely high minimum capital requirements (originally 500,000 pesos, later raised to 1,000,000), high reserve requirements (banks were required to hold one-third the value of their bank notes in metallic currency in their vaults and an additional third in the treasury), a prohibition on creating new banks without the authorization of the secretary of the treasury *and* the Congress, a prohibition on foreign branch banks from issuing bank notes, a 5-percent tax on the issue of bank notes, and the restriction of bank notes to the region in which the bank operated.[35] Making the situation even more problematic was the revision of these banking laws every few years. The result was a legal environment that was not only restrictive but arbitrary as well.

The motivation behind these restrictive banking policies was essentially twofold. First, the Mexican government was more concerned about establishing a secure, stable source of finance for itself than it was in creating large numbers of institutions designed to funnel credit to manufacturers. Second, the group of financiers that controlled the Banco Nacional de México also happened to belong to the inner clique of the Díaz regime and had used its political influence to obtain a special concession that restricted market entry.

The tight regulation of banking had three important ramifications. The first was that the number of banks and the extent of their operations remained small; industrial companies could not therefore generally rely on them as a source of finance. The second was that the credit market could not serve as a source of finance for speculation on the stock exchange as it had in the United States (and as it would in Brazil). The third was that financiers with proven abilities to mobilize capital from the banking system or the small network of Mexico City merchants had an advantage when it came to raising long-term capital through the sale of equity.

One might think that foreign capital would have made up for the lack of a well-developed Mexican capital market. After all, foreign investors were pumping billions of dollars into Mexican oil wells, mines, railroads, utilities, and export agriculture. There was in fact some foreign portfolio investment in Mexico's cotton textile industry, but the phenomenon was not widespread. In any event, to the extent that foreigners invested in the textile industry, they invested in the large, well-established firms that already had privileged access to the Mexico City stock exchange, thereby reinforcing the problem of differential access to capital. The reason for this lack of foreign investment in textiles was that manufacturing enterprises sold their output domestically, and thus earned their incomes in Mexican silver pesos. Silver, unfortunately, lost 50 percent of its value against gold during the period from 1890 to 1902, meaning that the rate of return in foreign, gold-backed currency, was halved once an investor converted his Mexican dividend payments back into sterling, dollars, or francs. In fact, the one foreign company that specialized in Mexican manufacturing investments, the Société Financière pour l'industrie au Mexique, fared very poorly for precisely this reason. Its franc-denominated rates of return were embarrassingly low, and its annual reports read like an apologia to its shareholders for the depreciation of the Mexican peso.[36] It was largely for this reason that foreign investors tended to focus on enterprises in which income was earned in foreign, gold-backed currencies, like oil extraction, mining, and export agriculture, or where the Mexican government offered sizable subsidies, like railroading.

In short, throughout its first 100 years of existence, the Mexican cotton textile industry had to rely on informal networks for its financing. When institutional innovations in the capital market created new opportunities for firms to obtain impersonal sources of finance, only a small group of entrepreneurs was able to benefit.

Finance and the Structure and Growth of the Textile Industry

What effects did these differences between Brazil and Mexico with regard to financial intermediation have on the development of the textile industry? One would expect at least three. First, the Mexican textile industry should have grown more slowly than Brazil's after 1890, because the vast majority of Mexican firms had to finance their expansion out of retained earnings, while their Brazilian counterparts had access to institutional sources of capital. Second, the limited opening of Mexico's capital market should have provided firms that had access to institutional finance with a sizable advantage over their competitors. The result should have been an increase in concentration in the Mexican textile industry. Third, the more generalized access to impersonal sources of capital in the Brazilian case should have resulted in a significant drop in concentration. The net result should have been lower levels of industrial concentration in Brazil than in Mexico.

An examination of the development of the textile industry in the two countries bears out these hypotheses. In regard to the rate of growth of the textile industry, the Brazilian textile industry surpassed Mexico's after its capital markets opened up. As late as 1882, the entire modern sector of the Brazilian cotton goods industry numbered only 41 firms running just over 70,000 spindles, less than one-third the size of Mexico's cotton goods in-

TABLE 6.3

Size and Structure of the Brazilian Cotton Textile Industry, 1866–1934

Year	Active firms	Firms with useful data	Estimated active spindles	Estimated four-firm ratio[a]	Estimated Herfindahl index[a]
1866	9	9	14,875	0.766	0.1773
1882	41	30	70,188	0.376	0.0631
1883	44	33	65,937	0.371	0.0582
1895	43	27	169,451	0.349	0.0585
1905	98	80	734,928	0.207	0.0279
1907	117	115	—	0.203	0.0250
1914	227	210	—	0.143	0.0144
1915	180	168	1,492,822	0.161	0.0165
1924	202	162	2,161,080	0.212	0.0222
1925	226	186	2,469,247	0.179	0.0182
1926	272	213	2,504,339	0.166	0.0155
1927	273	231	2,634,293	0.162	0.0141
1934	266	247	2,700,228	0.173	0.0168

SOURCES: same as Table 6.1.

[a]Concentration, by estimated value of sales, measured at the firm level. See note 41. A detailed discussion of the estimation procedures used is available from the author.

dustry (see Tables 6.3 and 6.4). This relative size relationship continued into the mid-1890's, but over the following ten years widespread access to impersonal sources of capital in Brazil meant that its cotton textile industry was able to outgrow Mexico's by a factor of five, producing for the first time an absolute size difference in favor of Brazil. By the outbreak of World War I, Brazil's industry was roughly twice the size of Mexico's, a gap which grew to three to one by the onset of the Great Depression.

This is not to argue that access to capital was the only factor influencing the rate of growth of either country's textile industry. There were numerous other constraints to the development of industry in Brazil and Mexico.[37] The data suggest, however, that problems of capital mobilization played an important role in the slow development of industry in both countries during the nineteenth century. First, the fact that the textile industries in both countries witnessed a spurt of growth after impersonal sources of finance became available indicates that their lack was a constraint before 1890. Second, the fact that Brazilian industry was able to outgrow Mexican industry rapidly after its capital markets opened up certainly suggests an important role for impersonal sources of finance in a country's rate of industrial growth.

One might argue that capital immobilities had little to do with the rate of growth of the textile industry; demand factors were far more important in influencing industry growth. Mexico's industry was smaller and grew

TABLE 6.4

Size and Structure of the Mexican Cotton Textile Industry, 1843–1929

Year	Firms listed	Firms with useful data	Estimated active spindles	Estimated four-firm ratio[a]	Estimated Herfindahl index[a]
1843	52	51	95,208	0.376	0.0524
1850	51	51	135,538	0.449	0.0686
1853	36	36	121,714	0.430	0.0677
1862	40	40	129,991	0.319	0.0490
1865	52	52	151,722	0.342	0.0501
1878	81	81	249,294	0.160	0.0209
1883	83	83	—	0.189	0.0225
1888	110	91	249,561	0.217	0.0249
1891	80	78	—	0.228	0.0268
1893	89	83	351,568	0.284	0.0355
1895	85	85	411,090	0.363	0.0480
1896	97	83	397,767	0.371	0.0513
1902	109	109	595,728	0.381	0.0637
1906	106	106	688,217	0.338	0.0486
1912	100	100	749,949	0.271	0.0343
1919	88	88	735,308	0.374	0.0592
1929	123	123	839,109	0.278	0.0335

SOURCES: Secretaría de Hacienda 1977: 81; Ministerio de Fomento 1854: table 2; Ministerio de Fomento 1857: docs. 18-1, 18-2; Dirección de Colonización e Industria 1851; Pérez Hernández 1862; Ministerio de Fomento 1865: 438–40; Secretaría de Hacienda 1880; García Cubas 1885; Secretaría de Fomento 1890; García Cubas 1893; Secretaría de Fomento 1894; Secretaría de Fomento 1896; Secretaría de Hacienda 1896a; Secretaría de Hacienda 1896b; Archivo General de la Nación, Ramo de Trabajo, caja 5, legajo 4; Secretaría de Hacienda 1919: second semester; Secretaría de Hacienda 1920: first semester; Secretaría de Hacienda 1930: Jan.; *Semana Mercantil*, June 23, 1902, June 25, 1906; Haber 1989: 125, 158.

[a]Concentration, by estimated value of sales, measured at the firm level. See note 41. A detailed discussion of the estimation procedures used is available from the author.

less quickly than that of Brazil because it had a smaller, poorer population. A comparison of national income and population estimates for the two countries indicates, however, that demand factors cannot explain differences in observed industry size. True, Brazil's population, which was roughly equal to that of Mexico in the early 1870's (9.9 million and 9.1 million, respectively) grew at almost twice Mexico's rate up to 1910 because of Brazil's policy of subsidizing European immigration. Mexican national income, however, outgrew Brazilian national income at a similar rate during this same period. Circa 1877, Mexican national income was only 55 percent that of Brazil. By 1910, it was within 6 percent of Brazil's. More important, Mexican income *per capita* outgrew that of Brazil by a factor of ten. In 1877, Mexican per capita income was 75 percent that of Brazil. By 1910, Mexican income per capita was 140 percent that of Brazil.[38] Given that the income elasticity of demand for textiles was very high, Mexico likely had a much higher per capita demand for textile products

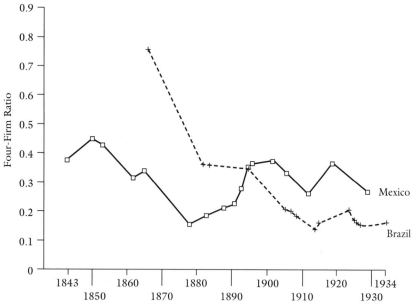

Figure 6.1. Four-firm ratios for Mexico and Brazil, 1843–1934. Data are taken from Tables 6.3, 6.4.

than the differences in per capita income would indicate.[39] In short, it is hard to reconcile a demand-side explanation with Brazil's lower absolute levels of per capita income and lower rates of growth of both per capita and national income.[40]

As for the effects of capital immobilities on industrial concentration, the data are unequivocal; access to capital had a significant effect on the level of concentration. Tables 6.3 and 6.4 and Figures 6.1 and 6.2 present estimates of four-firm concentration ratios (the percentage of the market controlled by the four largest firms) and Herfindahl indices (the sum of the squares of the market shares of all firms in an industry) for both countries. There are two striking features of the data.[41]

The first is that the opening of Mexico's capital markets actually produced an increase in concentration. The trend in Mexico from the 1850's to the late 1880's was a gradual decrease in concentration: exactly the trend one would expect in an expanding industry characterized by constant returns to scale technology. As Figures 6.1 and 6.2 indicate, Mexico's four-firm ratio fell from a high of .449 in 1850 to a low of .160 in 1878, while the Herfindahl dropped from a .0686 to .0209 over the same period. Beginning in the middle to late 1880's, the trend reversed, even though the

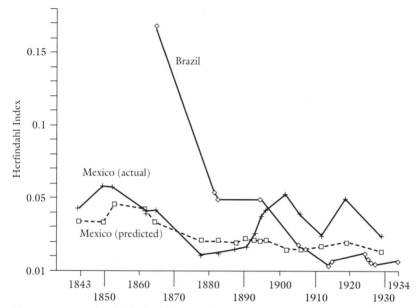

Figure 6.2. Predicted Herfindahl index for Mexico in the absence of the intervening variable, in comparison to actual Herfindahl indices for Mexico and Brazil, 1843–1934. Data are taken from Table 6.6.

industry was witnessing rapid growth. By 1902, both the four-firm ratio and the Herfindahl had nearly regained their 1853 levels, standing at .381 and .0637 respectively. Concentration then began to decrease again until 1912, when the revolution interceded and again reversed the trend.

The second striking feature of the data is that they indicate that the more profound opening of Brazil's capital markets produced exactly the opposite result than that obtained in Mexico (see Figures 6.1 and 6.2). The sharp drop in concentration from 1866 to 1882 is clearly a mathematical identity, having to do with the small size of the industry in 1866 when there were only nine firms. What is more relevant for our purposes is that this rapid date of decrease in concentration took off again during the years from 1895 to 1907, and then slowed only slightly until 1915, when it began gently to level off. By 1915, the estimated Herfindahl index for Brazil stood at approximately one-quarter of its 1882 value.[42]

Compared to Mexico, Brazil's textile industry was surprisingly unconcentrated and became increasingly less so over time. Prior to the 1890's, Brazil's relatively small textile industry displayed higher levels of concentration than Mexico's. By 1905, however, relatively widespread access to institutional sources of capital in Brazil drove concentration down to roughly 60 percent of that in Mexico. Just prior to the onset of the Great Depression, the level of concentration in Brazil was only 58 percent of that in Mexico measured by the four-firm ratio and only 42 percent of that in Mexico measured by the Herfindahl index.

One might argue that Mexico's higher concentration ratios had little to do with capital immobilities; high levels of concentration were produced by demand, not supply, factors. Mexico had higher levels of concentration and a different trajectory of concentration because it had a smaller textile industry than Brazil. There are three problems with this line of argument.

The first is that Mexico's industry leaders were tremendous operations in an absolute sense. Mexico's leading firms were not simply large relative to the small Mexican market, they were enormous operations, even by U.S. standards. Mexico's largest firm in 1912, for example, the Compañía Industrial de Orizaba (CIDOSA), was a four-mill operation employing 4,284 workers running 92,708 spindles and 3,899 looms. Had it been located in the United States, it would have ranked among the 25 largest cotton textile enterprises.

The second problem with this argument is that it assumes that Mexico had a small number of very large firms because there were technical advantages to being large. That is, the industry was concentrated because only a small number of firms could operate at the minimum efficient scale of production given the small size of the Mexican market. The problem with this assumption is that it does not stand up to empirical evidence on the relationship between total factor productivity (TFP) and firm size. I have estimated TFP by firm size for Mexico in two different census years (1896 and 1912). These estimates were constructed by first estimating Cobb-Douglas production functions, normalizing the labor and capital coefficients to 1, and then using the adjusted coefficients to weight the capital and labor inputs to calculate TFP. Two different specifications of the production function were tried for each cross section. All specifications yielded the same qualitative results; the minimum efficient scale of production in Mexico was reached at a firm size that corresponded to a market share of less than 1 percent. That is, the publicly traded firms that were the industry leaders in terms of market share did not have a productivity advantage over their competitors.[43]

The third problem with this line of argument is that it cannot explain why Mexican concentration increased during a period when the industry was experiencing rapid growth, the years 1878–1902. Without some supply factor intervening during this period, Mexican concentration should have continued to decline, instead of jumping back up to its 1850 level.

In order to test this hypothesis in a formal manner, I estimated a simple OLS regression that measures the elasticity of concentration with respect to industry size. The logic behind the estimation is the following. In an industry characterized by modest returns to scale, with no significant technological changes that would raise the minimum efficient scale of production in a discontinuous way, one should be able to predict the level of concentration simply by knowing the size of the industry. Similar regression results for Brazil and Mexico would indicate that concentration was simply a function of industry size. If, however, similar specifications of the regression for each country yield different results, then some intervening variable (like an imperfection in a factor market) must have been at work.[44]

Table 6.5 presents three specifications of the regression. The first uses the number of firms as the proxy for industry size, the second employs the number of spindles as the proxy, and the third employs both firms and spindles. All values are converted to natural logarithms in order to capture how changes in the size of the industry affect the change in concentration. Concentration is measured as the Herfindahl index.

All three specifications of the regression produce the same qualitative results. The level of concentration in Brazil was a function of the size of the industry. The regressions explain virtually all of the movement in industry structure as a result of changes in industry size. In Mexico, however, exactly the opposite results obtained; there is little statistical relationship between industry size and industry structure. A glance at Tables 6.3 and 6.4 and Figures 6.1 and 6.2 quickly indicate why it was not; in many years in post-1890 Mexico, concentration actually increased as industry size grew.

TABLE 6.5

Alternate Specifications of Industrial Concentration Regressions,
Mexico (1843 – 1929) and Brazil (1866 – 1934)

	Mexico			Brazil		
	Spec. 1	Spec. 2	Spec. 3	Spec. 1	Spec. 2	Spec. 3
Intercept	−1.28	−1.92	−3.83	−.31	2.09	−.08
(ln) firms	−.44		−1.29	−.72		−.60
	(−1.73)		(−2.58)	(−22.66)		(−3.12)
(ln) spindles		−.09	.50		−.42	−.07
		(−0.74)	(1.97)		(−13.80)	(−.59)
R^2	.17	.04	.38	.98	.95	.98
N	17	15	15	13	11	11

SOURCES: Same as Tables 6.1 and 6.4.
NOTE: The dependent variable is the natural logarithm of the Herfindahl index. *T* statistics are shown in parentheses.

Some other intervening variable—which I argue was a highly imperfect capital market—influenced concentration in Mexico.

What would Mexican industry have looked like, in terms of its structure, had this other intervening variable not been operating? Assuming that in the absence of this intervening variable the same relationship between industry size and industry structure would have held for both Brazil and Mexico, estimating Mexico's predicted level of concentration is a straightfoward operation. It simply entails estimating a predicted Herfindahl series using the Brazilian coefficients from the first specification of the regression (see Table 6.6) and the actual Mexican data on the number of firms.[45]

Table 6.6 and Figure 6.2 present these predicted Herfindahl values for Mexico, as well as the actual Mexican and Brazilian series. There are two features about the predicted series that are notable. The first is that until the early 1890's the fitted series does a reasonably good job of predicting the movement of concentration in Mexico, indicating that the statistical relationship between industry size and concentration observed in Brazil held in Mexico as well until Mexico's capital markets opened up. The second is that after 1893 Mexico's actual and predicted Herfindahl values moved in entirely different directions. By 1902, the actual level of concentration in Mexico was more than twice its predicted value.

What mechanisms were at work causing Mexico's level of industrial concentration to increase during a period of rapid expansion? Why did the trajectory of concentration in Mexico reverse in the 1890's, and why did it resume its fall after 1902?

The answer to these questions basically turns on the effects of the limited opening of Mexico's capital markets. In the years after 1889, Mexico's big, multiplant industry leaders—the Compañía Industrial de Orizaba (CIDOSA), Compañía Industrial Veracruzana (CIVSA), Compañía Industrial de Atlixco (CIASA), and Compañía Industrial de San Antonio Abad—were founded with capital provided by the Mexico City stock exchange. These firms were able to purchase newer, more efficient equipment faster than their smaller competitors, who did not have recourse to the sale of equity. The result was increasing levels of concentration.

Why then did concentration drop in the years from 1902 to 1912? Why did the industry leaders not continue to exercise market dominance? The answer is that after they achieved control of the market, Mexico's industry leaders dramatically slowed their rate of new investment. A comparison of the 1895 and 1912 censuses indicates that firms that had access to the capital market did not purchase new machinery at a faster rate than did non–capital market firms. In fact, a comparison of firms extant in both

TABLE 6.6

Actual and Predicted Herfindahl Indices,
Mexico and Brazil, 1843–1934

Year	Actual Mexico	Predicted Mexico	Actual Brazil
1843	.0524	.0432	—
1850	.0686	.0432	—
1853	.0677	.0556	—
1862	.0490	.0515	—
1865	.0501	.0426	—
1866	—	—	.1773
1878	.0209	.0310	—
1882	—	—	.0631
1883	.0225	.0305	.0582
1888	.0249	.0285	—
1891	.0268	.0318	—
1893	.0355	.0305	—
1895	.0480	.0299	.0585
1896	.0513	.0305	—
1902	.0637	.0250	—
1905	—	—	.0279
1906	.0486	.0255	—
1907	—	—	.0250
1912	.0343	.0266	—
1914	—	—	.0144
1915	—	—	.0165
1919	.0592	.0292	—
1924	—	—	.0222
1925	—	—	.0182
1926	—	—	.0155
1927	—	—	.0141
1929	.0335	.0229	—
1934	—	—	.0168

SOURCES: Actual data from Tables 6.3 and 6.4. The predicted Mexico series uses the parameter estimates for Brazil from
specification 1 in Table 6.5 and the information on the number of
firms with useful data from Table 6.4, and predicts Mexico's level
of concentration had the same relationship held between industry
size and industry structure as in Brazil.

censuses indicates that, if anything, firms that did not have access to impersonal sources of capital purchased new machinery at a rate 13 to 35 percent
faster (depending on how new investment is measured) than firms that had
access to the capital market.[46]

In short, the data suggest that the handful of firms that were able to
mobilize capital through institutional sources gained a one-time advantage
over their competitors. They then sat back and watched their rents dissi-
pate as their smaller competitors gradually closed the size gap through the
reinvestment of retained earnings. Why they pursued this strategy is some-

what of a mystery at this point. It may have been that their managers perceived (incorrectly) that their ability to mobilize institutional sources of capital would serve as a disincentive to new entrants. Potential new entrants would, according to this rationale, have seen that the industry leaders could rapidly install excess capacity, thereby increasing production and lowering prices below the potential entrant's long-run average cost curve. Or it may have been that stockholders did not trust the management of the enterprises or were operating with a short time horizon. They therefore demanded that all profits be paid out as dividends. It might also have been that the rates of return available from the big, multiplant mills were disappointing to the investment community. New infusions of equity capital may therefore have dried up after 1902. Evidence from the Mexican financial press lends considerable support to this last interpretation. Of the four firms that were able to raise capital through the securities markets (CIDOSA, CIVSA, CIASA, and San Antonio Abad), two paid dividends on an extremely irregular basis. One of them, San Antonio Abad, failed to pay anything from 1899 to 1906. Though the two industry leaders, CIDOSA and CIVSA, paid steady dividends, the real value of CIDOSA's dividends fell by two-thirds after 1900 and stayed at this lower level for the rest of the decade.[47] Work in progress hopes to shed additional light on this issue.

Whatever the source of this peculiar behavior by the industry leaders, the lack of new investment on their part, coupled with the relatively slow rate of growth of new investment implied by the need to finance new plant and equipment purchases out of retained earnings by their competitors, suggests that the overall rate of growth of investment and productivity in Mexico was likely lower than that of Brazil and its other international competitors.

What lessons are there to be drawn from this story about government regulation, capital market development, and the growth and structure of industry?

The first is that governmental regulatory policies had a significant effect on the growth of capital markets in Brazil and Mexico. The divergence in capital-market development between the two countries was clearly the result of different policies regarding the formation and operation of banks, the reporting of financial data, and the reporting of stockholder identities. In short, capital-market development was not completely endogenous to the process of economic growth; government regulation exerted powerful independent effects.

Second, differences in capital-market development had a significant impact on the rate of growth and structure of industry. Mexico's financial system, in which a small group of entrepreneurs could get access to impersonal sources of capital while most entrepreneurs could not, gave rise to a small textile industry relative to Brazil's. The rapid expansion of the Brazilian textile industry after the opening up of the capital markets in 1890 underlines the important role played by access to finance in industrial growth. In sum, lack of access to institutional sources of capital because of poorly developed capital markets was a serious obstacle to industrial development in the nineteenth century.

Third, imperfections in capital markets also had a significant effect on the structure of industry. The much more limited opening of the Mexican capital market gave rise to higher levels of concentration than in Brazil, suggesting that Mexican textile firms operated in a less competitive environment.

Fourth, the data analyzed to date suggest that Mexico's peculiarly uncompetitive structure of industry may have created disincentives to new investment by its industry leaders. In addition, the need to rely on retained earnings to finance most new investment would suggest that in general Mexico's rate of growth of investment was much slower than in countries, such as Brazil, that had more open capital markets. The result may well have been much slower rates of growth of productivity in the Mexican case, meaning that Mexican industry may have become increasingly less competitive over time.

Fifth, a great deal of the difference between Mexico and Brazil was political. Mexico followed repressive capital market regulatory policies in large part because it was a centralized dictatorship. Banks were slow to develop because of restrictions on their founding and operation in order to protect the interests of an in-group of financial elites. Similarly, the politicized nature of doing business in Porfirian Mexico, coupled with the lack of good financial and stockholder information, meant that individuals were reluctant to invest in enterprises in which they lacked direct knowledge or control. The only way around these problems was to invest in enterprises directed by entrepreneurs with clear ties to the reins of political power. As a result, the corporate form of ownership spread slowly. In short, there may well have been economic, as well as social, costs to the Díaz regime.

Notes

This chapter was made possible through support provided by the U.S. Agency for International Development under Cooperative Agreement No. DHR-0015-A-00-0031-00 to the Center on Institutional Reform and the Informal Sector (IRIS) and administered by the Office of Economic and Institutional Reform, Center for Economic Growth, Bureau for Global Programs, Field Support and Research. Additional support for this research was generously provided by the Center for U.S.-Mexican Studies at the University of California, San Diego, the Social Science Research Council, the Stanford University Center for Latin American Studies, and the Stanford University Institute for International Studies. I am indebted to Lance E. Davis, Nathaniel Leff, Jean-Laurent Rosenthal, Kenneth L. Sokoloff, and William Summerhill for their comments on an earlier draft of this paper. The usual caveats apply.

1. On capital markets and industrial structure, see the seminal articles by Davis 1963; Davis 1966. On the role of regulatory regimes in structuring financial markets, see Sylla 1975; Lamoreaux 1986; McKinnon 1973. On the distributive effects of capital market imperfections, see Roe 1979.

2. The term *capital market* refers to the organized process by which funds for long-term investment are raised, distributed, traded, and valued. During the period under study, this process typically took place through banks, stock exchanges, and bond markets. In a "perfect" capital market, all enterprises with a rate of return that exceeds the rate of interest will receive financing. All capital markets depart from this ideal. In highly imperfect markets, however, the tendency for profitable firms to lack access to institutional sources of finance is highly pronounced, because the institutions that channel the savings of people who have liquid wealth to those who need it for investment in business enterprises are poorly developed. In a highly imperfect capital market, therefore, there are many potentially profitable enterprises that cannot obtain access to external financing and many savers who earn lower rates of return on their investments than they would otherwise. For an excellent discussion of capital markets in history, see Smith and Sylla 1993.

3. Marichal 1986; Ludlow 1986; Levy 1977; Quiroz 1993. For a recent study that links government policies directly to the development of financial markets in Mexico, see Marichal, chap. 5, this volume.

4. This lack of a theoretically informed literature on the historical development of Latin American financial markets is particularly peculiar given the interest of Latin Americanists in such issues as the region's late and incomplete industrial development, its modest degree of social and economic mobility, the concentration of economic power in the hands of small and persistent elites, and the tendency to high levels of monopoly and oligopoly—all of which are directly related to the existence of capital-market imperfections. For an exception, see Hanley 1995.

5. The term *industrialized* here refers to the spread of the mechanized factory. By the mid-nineteenth century, mechanized factories were producing cotton goods in both countries, and by early in the twentieth century the mechanized factory

system had spread into other products, including cement, steel, paper, glass, beer, chemicals, explosives, shoes, and wool textiles. The arrival of the mechanized factory in most product lines appears to have occurred earlier in Mexico than in Brazil, but both countries led the rest of the region, where most industrial goods continued to be produced in workshops and nonmechanized manufactories until the 1920's. For a discussion of the industrial histories of the two countries, see Suzigan 1986; Haber 1989.

6. As Simon Kuznets pointed out, textiles tend to be the first manufacturing industry to develop as economies modernize. Mexico and Brazil conformed to this general pattern. See Kuznets 1971: 111–13.

7. This does not mean that scale economies were insignificant in textile production. Indeed, had economies of scale been negligible, access to capital could not have served as a barrier to entry, and the argument developed here would not hold. It does mean, however, that scale economies in textiles were exhausted at relatively small firm sizes compared to such industries as steel, cement, and chemicals. In these industries, scale economies were so large that they precluded more than a few firms from operating at the optimal level of production.

8. While I focus on cotton textiles, it is quite likely that the same mechanisms at work in that industry held throughout the rest of the industrial sector.

9. Topik 1987: 28; Peláez and Suzigan 1976: chaps. 2–5; Saes 1986: 73; Levy 1977: 109–12; Stein 1957: 25–27.

10. Topik 1987: 28; Paláez and Suzigan 1976: chaps. 2–5; Saes 1986: 22, 73, 78–86; Levy 1977: 109–12; Stein 1957: 25–27.

11. Levy 1977: 117; Peláez and Suzigan 1976: 78–83, 96–97; Saes 1986: 22, 86.

12. Topik 1987: 28–32.

13. Topik 1987: 28–29; Paláez and Suzigan 1976: 143; Stein 1957: 86.

14. Shareholder lists were not published in the abbreviated reports reprinted in the *Jornal do Commercio* or the *Diario Official,* but they were published in the original semiannual reports.

15. Topik 1987: 29–31.

16. Triner 1990: 4.

17. Neuhaus 1975: 22.

18. Triner 1990: 7.

19. Triner 1990; Triner 1994; Hanley 1995.

20. The fifteen firms were among the largest in the country, accounting for 77 percent of total installed capacity in 1895. They are: Companhia de Fiação e Tecidos Alliança, Companhia America Fabril, Companhia Brasil Industrial, Companhia de Fiação e Tecelagem Carioca, Companhia de Fiação e Tecidos Industrial Campista, Companhia de Fiação e Tecidos Cometa, Companhia de Fiação e Tecidos Confiança Industrial, Companhia de Fiação e Tecidos Corcovado, Companhia de Fiação e Tecidos Industrial Mineira, Companhia de Fiação e Tecidos Mageénse, Companhia Manufactora Fluminense, Companhia Petropolitana, Companhia Progresso Industrial do Brasil, Companhia de Fiação e Tecidos Santo Aleixo, Companhia Fabrica de Tecidos São Pedro de Alcantara.

21. Data on all firms in 1915 come from Centro Industral do Brasil 1917. Information on publicly traded firms comes from stock tables of the *Jornal do Commercio*. Note that this understates the number of publicly traded textile firms because it includes only those in operation at the time of the censuses. There were other firms that were founded and went bankrupt between census years. The total number of cotton textile firms listed in the *Jornal do Commercio* in 1915 was 57.

22. Data from the 1905 and 1915 censuses indicate that there were other markets for debentures besides Rio de Janeiro. The 1905 census enumerates 31 firms that indicated debt financing on their returns, only 13 of which were listed on the Rio de Janeiro Exchange. The value of the debt of the 18 firms not listed on the Rio de Janeiro exchange was almost as large as the value of the 13 firms that were traded there (43 percent of debt listed on the census was in firms not traded in Rio). The 1915 census indicates a similar pattern; 53 firms listed long-term debt, only 24 of which were traded in Rio de Janeiro. The debt of firms not traded in Rio de Janeiro was 48 percent of total outstanding long-term debt enumerated in the census. See Table 6.1 for sources.

23. Calculated from Vasco 1905; Centro Industrial do Brazil 1917; Centro Industrial de Fiação 1924; Centro Industrial de Fiação 1935.

24. For an analysis of rates of return to firms, stockholders, and bondholders, see Haber 1995b.

25. Marichal 1986: 251; Sánchez Martínez 1983: 60, 76–77; Haber 1989: 65.

26. Sánchez Martínez 1983: 81–82; Marichal 1986: 258.

27. Cárdenas and Manns 1989.

28. Sánchez Martínez 1983: 86; Haber 1989: 65–67.

29. The activity of the Mexico City stock exchange was followed by Mexico's major financial weeklies: *La Semana Mercantil* 1897–1914; *El Economista Mexicano* 1896–1914; *Boletín Financiero y Minero* 1916–1938. The behavior of the shares of these firms is analyzed in Haber 1989: chap. 7. The total number of firms is from textile-industry manuscript censuses in Archivo General de la Nación, Ramo de Trabajo, caja 5, legajo 4 (also see caja 31, legajo 2).

30. Marichal, chap. 5, this volume.

31. Coatsworth, 1978: 98. For a discussion of the politicized nature of the legal system, see Walker 1986: chaps. 1, 4–5, 7–8.

32. For a discussion of the activities of these entrepreneurs, see Haber 1989: chaps. 5, 6.

33. On the U.S. case, see Davis 1963; De Long 1991.

34. Examples can be found in the steel, beer, soap, dynamite, cigarette, wool textile, and paper industries, in addition to cotton textiles. See Haber 1989: chaps. 4, 5.

35. When the first minimum was established in 1897, it was equal to $233,973. The increase in 1908 brought the minimum capital requirement up to $497,265, roughly five times the minimum for nationally chartered banks in the United States. For a discussion of these various privileges and barriers to entry, as well as changes in banking laws, see Sánchez Martínez 1983: 43, 61–62, 67; Ludlow 1986: 334–36; Bátiz 1986: 286, 287, 293.

36. The annual reports of the Société Financière pour l'industrie au Mexique can be found in *Semana Mercantil*, Aug. 8, 1903; *Economista Mexicano*, Oct. 11, 1902, July 6, 1904, Aug. 4, 1904, Oct. 21, 1905, Aug. 18, 1906.

37. For a discussion of these constraints in Mexico, see Haber 1989: chaps. 3–5; for a discussion of the Brazilian case see Stein 1957; Suzigan, 1986.

38. National income data from Coatsworth 1978: 82. Population data from Instituto Nacional 1985: 9; Instituto Brasileiro 1990: 33.

39. Contemporary observers noted this high income elasticity of demand for textile products. Their observations can be found in Haber 1989: 28–29.

40. Accounting for imports and exports of textiles would not affect these results. Neither country exported much in the way of textile products, their national industries being no match for British and American manufacturers. Both countries were also highly protectionist, with tariffs exceeding 100 percent. In both countries, imports accounted for roughly 20 percent of consumption by 1910, and this proportion declined thereafter. These imports were almost entirely high-value, fine-weave goods.

41. These estimates of concentration are all calculated at the firm level. This involves combining the market shares of all mills held by a single corporation, partnership, or sole proprietor. Market shares were calculated from estimates of the actual sales or value of output of mills. In years where data on installed capacity only were available, I calculated the distribution of installed capacity and used these data to estimate market shares. These estimates were based on a regression of market shares on the distribution of installed capacity for those years where both variables were available.

42. These ratios were constructed to bias the results against the hypothesis that Mexico had higher levels of concentration than Brazil. A detailed discussion of the method is available from the author. One might argue that these differences in concentration would disappear if imports of foreign textiles were accounted for, but that argument does not stand up to the empirical evidence on textile imports. Indeed, both Brazil and Mexico followed highly protectionist policies after 1890, virtually eliminating imported cloth except for fine-weave, high-value goods.

43. Haber 1995a.

44. The model makes the reasonable assumption that there were no discontinuous jumps in minimum efficient scales in either country, though it does allow for a gradual increase in minimum efficient scales. For this reason, it is unlikely that the elasticities of the size variables will sum to unity. Observations by contemporaries indicate that there were no discontinuous jumps in textile manufacturing technology during the period that affected the Brazilian or Mexican industries. The only major innovation was the Northrup automatic loom, which was developed in the 1890's, but was not widely adopted in either country (there were only 25 of them in service in Mexico as late as 1910). Moreover, to the extent that there were technological jumps, these would be more pronounced in the Brazilian regressions than in those for Mexico, because of Brazil's faster purchase of new capacity. This would tend to bias the results against the hypothesis advanced here.

45. This is an upper-bound prediction. The model assumes that Mexico's indus-

try size would have been the same in the presence of a better-developed capital market, which is highly unlikely. Had the size of the industry been larger, the predicted concentration ratios would be even lower than those estimated here. The first specification of the regression was used because it provided the best fit for both the Mexican and Brazilian data.

46. The method employed involved measuring the change in the number of looms and spindles in firms listed in both censuses and then dividing by the number of machines listed in the 1895 census. For sources, see Table 6.4.

47. Haber 1989: 115.

References

Archivo General de la Nación, Ramo de Trabajo. Mexico City.

Bátiz V., José Antonio. 1986. "Trayectoria de la banca en México hasta 1910." In Leonor Ludlow and Carlos Marichal, eds., *Banca y poder en México, 1800 –1925,* pp. 267–98. Mexico City.

Boletín Financiero y Minero. 1916–38. Mexico City.

Borja Castro, Agostino Vioto de. 1869. "Relatorio do segundo grupo." In Antonio José de Souza Rego, ed., *Relatorio da segunda exposição nacional de 1866,* pp. 3–73. Rio de Janeiro.

Branner, John C. 1885. *Cotton in the Empire of Brazil.* Washington, D.C.

Cárdenas, Enrique, and Carlos Manns. 1989. "Inflación y estabilización monetaria en México durante la Revolución." *Trimestre Económico* 56: 57–80.

Centro Industrial de Fiação (e Tecelagem de Algodao). 1924–26. *Relatorio ao diretoria.* Rio de Janeiro.

———. 1928. *Estatisticas da industria, commercio e lavoura de algodao relativos ao anno de 1927.* Rio de Janeiro.

———. 1935. *Fiação e tecelagem: censo organizado pelo centro industrial de fiaçaõ e tecelagem de algodão.* Rio de Janeiro.

Centro Industrial do Brasil. 1909. *O Brasil: suas riquezas naturaes, suas industrias.* Vol. 3: *Industria de transportes, industria fabril.* Rio de Janeiro.

———. 1915. *Relatorio.* Rio de Janeiro.

———. 1917. *O Centro Industrial na conferencia algodoeira.* Rio de Janeiro.

Coatsworth, John H. 1978. "Obstacles to Economic Growth in Nineteenth Century Mexico." *American Historical Review* 83: 80–101.

Commissão de Inquerito Industrial. 1882. *Relatorio ao Ministerio da Fazenda.* Rio de Janeiro.

Davis, Lance E. 1963. "Capital Immobilities and Finance Capitalism: A Study of Economic Evolution in the United States, 1820–1920." *Explorations in Economic History* 1: 88–105.

———. 1966. "The Capital Markets and Industrial Concentration: The U.S. and U.K., A Comparative Study." *Economic History Review* 19: 255–72.

De Long, J. Bradford. 1991. "Did J. P. Morgan's Men Add Value? An Economist's Perspective on Financial Capitalism." In Peter Temin, ed., *Inside the Business Enterprise: Historical Perspectives on the Use of Information,* pp. 205–50. Chicago.

Dirección de Colonización e Industria. 1851. *Memoria 1850*. Mexico City.

Economista Mexicano, 1896–1914. Mexico City.

García Cubas, Antonio. 1885. *Cuadro geográfico, estadístico, descriptivo e histórico de los Estados Unidos Mexicanos*. Mexico City.

———. 1893. *Mexico: Its Trade, Industries, and Resources*. Mexico City.

Haber, Stephen H. 1989. *Industry and Underdevelopment: The Industrialization of Mexico, 1890–1940*. Stanford.

———. 1995a. "Financial Market Regulation, Imperfect Capital Markets, and Industrial Concentration: Brazil, Mexico, and the United States, 1830–1930." Manuscript, Stanford University.

———. 1995b. "Capital Markets in the Early Stages of Industrialization: The Brazilian Cotton Textile Manufacture, 1866–1934." Paper presented at the Conference of the Cliometrics Society, Lawrence, Kans., April 4.

Hanley, Anne. 1995. "Capital Markets in the Coffee Economy: Financial Institutions and Economic Change in São Paulo, Brazil, 1850–1905." Ph.D. diss., Stanford University.

Instituto Brasileiro de Geografia e Estatísticas. 1990. *Estatísticas históricas do Brasil*. Rio de Janeiro.

Instituto Nacional de Estadística, Geografia, e Informática. 1985. *Estadísticas históricas de México*. Mexico City.

Kuznets, Simon. 1971. *Economic Growth of Nations: Total Output and Production Structure*. Cambridge, Eng.

Lamoreaux, Naomi. 1986. "Banks, Kinship, and Economic Development: The New England Case." *Journal of Economic History* 46: 647–67.

Levy, María Bárbara. 1977. *História da Bolsa de Valores do Rio de Janeiro*. Rio de Janeiro.

Ludlow, Leonor. 1986. "La construcción de un banco: el Banco Nacional de México, 1881–1884." In Leonor Ludlow and Carlos Marichal, eds., *Banca y poder en México, 1800–1925*, pp. 299–346. Mexico City.

Marichal, Carlos. 1986. "El nacimiento de la banca mexicana en el contexto latinoamericano: problemas de periodización." In Leonor Ludlow and Carlos Marichal, eds., *Banca y poder en México, 1800–1925*, pp. 231–66. Mexico City.

McKinnon, Ronald I. 1973. *Money and Capital in Economic Development*. Washington, D.C.

Ministerio da Industria Viação e Obras Publicas. 1896. *Relatorio, 1896*. Rio de Janeiro.

Ministerio de Fomento. 1854. *Estadística del departamento de México*. Mexico City.

———. 1857. *Memoria del Ministerio de Fomento*. Mexico City.

———. 1865. *Memoria del Ministerio de Fomento*. Mexico City.

Neuhaus, Paulo. 1975. *História monetária do Brasil, 1900–45*. Rio de Janeiro.

Peláez, Carlos Manuel, and Wilson Suzigan. 1976. *História monetária do Brasil: análise da política, comportamento e instituçoes monetárias*. Brasilia.

Pérez Hernández, José María. 1862. *Estadísticas de la República Mexicana*. Guadalajara.

Quiroz, Alfonso W. 1993. *Domestic and Foreign Finance in Modern Peru, 1850–1950.* Pittsburgh, Pa.

Roe, Alan R. 1979. "Some Theory Concerning the Role of Failings of Financial Intermediation." In V. V. Bhatt and Alan R. Roe, eds., *Capital Market Imperfections and Economic Development.* World Bank Staff Working Paper No. 338. Washington, D.C.

Saes, Flávio Azevedo Marques de. 1986. *Crédito e bancos no desenvolvimento da economia paulista, 1850–1930.* São Paulo.

Sánchez Martínez, Hilda. 1983. "El sistema monetario y financiero mexicano bajo una perspectiva histórica: el Porfiriato." In José Manuel Quijano, ed., *La banca, pasado y presente: problemas financieros mexicanos,* pp. 15–94. Mexico City.

Secretaría de Fomento. 1890. *Boletín semestral de la República Mexicana 1889.* Mexico City.

———. 1894. *Anuario estadístico de la República Mexicana, 1893–94.* Mexico City.

———. 1896. *Anuario estadístico de la República Mexicana, 1895.* Mexico City.

Secretaría de Hacienda. 1880. *Estadística de la República Mexicana.* Mexico City.

———. 1896a. *Estadística de la República Mexicana.* Mexico City.

———. 1896b. *Memoria, 1895.* Mexico City.

———. 1919–30. *Boletín de estadística fiscal.* Mexico City.

Secretaría de Hacienda y Crédito Público. 1977. *Documentos para el estudio de la industrialización en México, 1837–1845.* Mexico City.

Semana Mercantil. 1902–14. Mexico City.

Smith, George David, and Richard Sylla. 1993. "The Transformation of Financial Capitalism: An Essay on the History of American Capital Markets." *Financial Markets, Institutions and Instruments* 2 (May): 1–61.

Stein, Stanley J. 1957. *The Brazilian Cotton Textile Manufacture: Textile Enterprise in an Underdeveloped Area.* Cambridge, Mass.

Suzigan, Wilson. 1986. *Indústria brasileira: origem e desenvolvimento.* São Paulo.

Sylla, Richard. 1975. *The American Capital Market, 1846–1914: A Study of the Effects of Public Policy on Economic Development.* New York.

Topik, Steven. 1987. *The Political Economy of the Brazilian State, 1889–1930.* Austin, Tex.

Triner, Gail D. 1990. "Brazilian Banks and the Economy, 1906–1918." M.A. thesis, Columbia University.

Triner, Gail D. 1994. "Banks and Brazilian Economic Development: 1906–1930." Ph.D. diss., Columbia University.

Vasco, Cunha. 1905. "A industria do algodão." *Boletim do Centro Industrial do Brasil.* Dec. 30.

Walker, David W. 1986. *Kinship, Business, and Politics: The Martínez del Río Family in Mexico, 1824–1867.* Austin, Tex.

CHAPTER 7

Reassessing the Prospects for Profit in Nineteenth-Century Mexican Agriculture from a Regional Perspective: Michoacán, 1810-60

MARGARET CHOWNING

The wars for independence that began with the Hidalgo rebellion in 1810 crippled estate agriculture in much of the colony of New Spain, but perhaps nowhere more than in the province of Michoacán. Property destruction and abandonment, disruption of the work force, and near paralysis of commercial networks characterized the decade of insurrection. After independence was finally achieved in 1821, economic recovery was impeded by the sluggish revival of silver mining, by the flight of Spanish capital (which had begun with the Hidalgo rebellion and continued through the expulsions of Spaniards in 1827 and 1829), and by the inability of governments after independence to secure peace in the countryside.

Under these circumstances it is small wonder that after 1810 hacienda agriculture, along with the rest of the economy, is usually presumed to have entered a prolonged period of retraction, which did not begin to lift until the Pax Porfiriana in the late 1870's and 1880's. As Simon Miller put it, with the outbreak of the Hidalgo rebellion, "crisis and insolvency returned to the hacienda."[1] Not only was there little "progress" or "capitalist transformation" in the agricultural sector (according to a recent collection of essays on the *cuestión agraria* in Mexican history), but per capita agricultural production declined (according to one estimate, by 12.5 percent between 1800 and 1860) as landowning elites, caught in a "cycle of decline," yielded ground in a literal sense to sharecroppers and tenants.[2]

My first doubts about the notion that the rural economy remained moribund for some three generations after the Hidalgo rebellion came from weekend trips taken to old hacienda sites in Michoacán in the early 1980's. In line with my expectations, many of the ruins dated from the Porfiriato, but a surprising number of impressive buildings were constructed in the 1830's and 1840's. In time, my research confirmed that as early as the mid-1820's the rebuilding of productive capacity was well underway and that by the time of the midcentury reforms (the disentailment of the church and the attempt to create modern property rights in land), often seen as the juridical prerequisite to economic growth, the rural economy of Michoacán was by many measures fully recovered.[3]

The goal in this chapter is to go beyond the fact of recovery to an exploration of the process by which recovery took place, through an analysis of the rate of return on agricultural investment. I focus on the rate of return because profits are the ultimate measure of success in a capitalist economy. I focus on estate agriculture because the economy of Michoacán was overwhelmingly agrarian. I ask what effect the political and economic changes that flowed from the insurgency/independence period had on the profitability of large estates. Was it more difficult to earn good returns on agricultural investment after 1810 than it had been before, as the conventional wisdom has it? Why or why not?

As any student of the rural economy in Latin America will attest, hacienda profitability is extremely difficult to define. Even for the closely studied and fairly well-documented colonial period, there is no consensus; on the one hand is David Brading's often-repeated "hacienda as sinkhole" hypothesis, and on the other is the ample research demonstrating that hacendados were maximizers.[4] These views can be reconciled, but only by a Promethean interpretation in which hacienda owners grasped every possibility to make their estates profitable, but consistently threw good money after bad, century after century. For the long period between the wars for independence and the Porfiriato, with only a handful of exceptions, the profitability issue dwells even more in the realm of speculation and assertion than it does for the colonial period.[5] Brading tried to follow through on his own hypothesis but became disappointed with the lack of hacienda account books, the only direct sources of information about profitability. As he put it, "the scholar may propound his questions, but it is the sources which prescribe the limits of the answers." These sources, for him, "precluded any sustained treatment of . . . the rate of agricultural profit and its relation to capital investment."[6]

Brading was correct, of course; the sources available for the study of profitability are not good. There are no detailed farm surveys and very few contemporary discussions of any aspect of agriculture. Hacienda account books or production records are extremely rare, and those that have survived are often biased in the direction of low or nonexistent profits, having been preserved as evidence in bankruptcy proceedings or as part of a lawsuit involving the administration of an estate on behalf of a minor heir. Tithe records, which are particularly valuable for colonial Michoacán because they allow historians to reconstruct the structure of production and cash flow on individual haciendas, cease to be useful for estimating production or estate income in any systematic way after 1810, because many hacendados refused to pay the tithe.

Yet the issue is important enough to rethink, whether or not we must throw up our hands and give in to the paucity of data, especially in light of the many indications that the regional economy was on a trajectory of recovery by 1830, prompting the hypothesis that hacienda profitability, too, regained pre-1810 levels and perhaps exceeded them. In fact, there are sources of economic data that can be mined for answers or at least insights into the profitability question: the virtually complete runs of notary records and mortgage account books (*libros de becerro*) for the capital city of Morelia and the two other important cities in the state, Pátzcuaro and Zamora; the records of tithe collections, which contain good commodity price data and the odd hacienda record with material on production and/or profits; and the miscellaneous lawsuits and other judicial records collected by the cities of Morelia and Pátzcuaro and by the state courts.[7] From these documents we can derive trends in commodity prices and hacienda prices and rents, gain an understanding of the credit and distribution links between merchants and hacendados and between haciendas and markets, determine the degree and nature of capital investments made by hacienda owners, and reconstruct the career patterns and social backgrounds of hacendados. None of these materials will give us definitive answers, but taken together and approached with some aggressiveness, they allow us to advance the debate on hacienda profitability beyond its current state.

To make the best use of these not-entirely-satisfactory materials, I have built my argument along two lines. In the first part of this chapter, I present evidence from Michoacán that suggests that haciendas were more profitable in the 1830's and 1840's than in the alleged heyday of the great estate in the late colonial period. In the second part, I try to explain how this could be so. I focus first on changes in factor and commodity markets in the decades after the Hidalgo rebellion. The intent here is to question the common assumption that insurgency and independence necessarily brought about an enduring decline in profitability and to suggest instead that at least some of the changes that occurred in the wake of these dramatic events may have heightened the potential for profit rather than reduced it. Then I explore some ways in which hacendados took advantage of favorable structural conditions and adjusted to unfavorable ones; in other words, I ask how hacendado behavior intersected with market forces to improve profitability.

Profits in Estate Agriculture in Michoacán

I, like Brading, have found few detailed hacienda records for the period 1810–60, and from the three sets of records and one summary of such a record I have located, it is impossible to generalize; one hacienda earned a 30-percent annual net return on the current market value of the estate; one earned 10.5 percent; another earned 4.4 percent; another earned no profit at all.[8]

There is ample circumstantial evidence, however, to suggest that many hacendados commanded quite respectable profits. First, hacienda prices and rents rose more or less steadily beginning around 1830. Hacienda prices had dropped from over 43,000 pesos in 1800–10 to under 25,000 pesos in the 1810's and 1820's. But from 1830, prices jagged upward until, by the decade of the 1850's, the average hacienda sold for 44,400 pesos, slightly more than in the decade before 1810. Rents followed a generally similar pattern; after a precipitous drop following the Hidalgo rebellion, they began in the late 1830's to climb and in the early 1850's reached 3,250 pesos, almost exactly the pre-1810 level (see Table 7.1). This return to pre-1810 prices and rents is particularly impressive in light of the fact that political turmoil and uncertainty had never ceased to be a factor that prospective buyers and renters had to take into account. Thus even after prices and rents had been discounted for risk, they were still as high or higher than the levels of the calmer days before 1810. Furthermore, by 1850 the ratio of rents to prices had for all intents and purposes returned

TABLE 7.1

Hacienda Sales and Rentals, Michoacán, 1800–56

(in pesos)

Years	Mean sale price	Mean rental price	Ratio of prices to rents
1800–10	43,200 ($n = 31$)	3,300 ($n = 18$)	13.1:1
1811–29	24,600 ($n = 21$)	1,200 ($n = 38$)	20.5:1
1830–39	32,000 ($n = 35$)	2,000 ($n = 33$)	16.0:1
1840–49	30,200 ($n = 41$)	2,100 ($n = 40$)	14.4:1
1850–56	44,400 ($n = 31$)	3,250 ($n = 28$)	13.7:1

SOURCES: AHMCR, ANM, AHMM, AHCP, AGN, AHPJ.

to its pre-1810 level, suggesting that buyers and renters were making judgments about the ability of their investments to produce profits over the short and long term that were in line with those of the palmy preinsurgency period.

Second, there was an improvement over time in the ratio of portable capital (livestock, crops, tools) to nonreproducible wealth (land), indicating the willingness and ability of hacendados to accept higher risk in exchange for the rewards of higher productivity. In the decade before 1810, movables on ten inventoried haciendas accounted for just over 27 percent of the total appraised value of the estate.[9] For the three decades after 1810, the proportion on eleven inventoried haciendas fell to 21 percent of the total value of inventoried estates. Because the overall value of these estates had fallen as well, the absolute decline in the value of producers' capital is even more impressive, from an average of over 20,000 pesos in the pre-1810 period to about 7,000 pesos in the next 30 years. For the two decades from 1840 to 1860, however, movables as a percentage of total value rose to over 35 percent on 27 haciendas, a proportion that was not regained until the decade 1900–10.[10] Because an increasing proportion of reproducible capital generally implies a faster pace of and greater potential for economic growth, the significance of a movables-to-nonmovables ratio that was even higher in the 1840's and 1850's than in the decade before 1810 is obvious.

Finally, a profile of 113 buyers of haciendas during the period from 1810 to 1855 suggests that there was growing interest in the agricultural sector and that this interest was not motivated solely by the perception that there were opportunities for land speculation, nor by the traditional view of land as the most stable of investments—though these elements were no doubt present in some degree—but also by the conviction that estate agriculture, properly approached, offered good opportunities for profits (see Table 7.2).

Several relevant points emerge from this profile of hacienda purchasers. One is that successful merchant/capitalists continued, as they had done before 1810, to invest in agriculture. If anything, merchants who purchased haciendas after independence were even more aggressively entrepreneurial than the earlier generation, and they were overwhelmingly successful. Of the 113 hacienda buyers, at least 19 started out as retail merchants, and 13 of them at least doubled the value of the properties, primarily by means of expensive improvements. (Four others were modestly successful, one failed, and one's success or failure is unknown.)

TABLE 7.2

Profile of Hacienda Buyers, Michoacán, 1810–55

Profile	Began in agriculture	Began in trade	Total
Nonelites			
Highly successful	14	9	23
Modestly successful	19	3	22
Failed	24	1	25
Unknown	6	1	7
TOTAL	63	14	77
Elites			
Highly successful	6	4	10
Modestly successful	17	1	18
Failed	5	0	5
Unknown	3	0	3
TOTAL	31	5	36

SOURCES: AHMR, ANM, AHMM, AHCP, AGN, AHPJ.

NOTE: *Elite* is defined as households with gross wealth of 20,000 pesos or more. Wealth is usually derived from estate inventories formed during probate of wills, but occasionally an estimate is derived from a particularly specific will or from the amount of heirs' share in the estate, where that information has been found.

Many of the merchants who invested in agriculture seem to have kept a hand in trade, but this was by no means true of all. Ignacio Arriaga, for example, abandoned trade altogether in 1844, when he sold the contents of his store for 23,244 pesos and rented the storefront in his house to the buyer. He had three years earlier rented the hacienda of Tejamanil in partnership with José María Bocanegra, an arrangement that ended in 1847 when Bocanegra bought the hacienda, but in the meantime Arriaga had rented another sugar hacienda, Santa Efigenia, from its creditors in 1843, and this became the focus of his energies.[11] Another merchant who left trade altogether was José María Ibarrola, who sold the inventory of his store and rented out its location in 1845; ten years earlier he had rented the hacienda of Coapa from the bishopric, and Coapa now became his sole business operation.[12]

The most spectacular example of a merchant who abandoned retail trade for agriculture was Cayetano Gómez, Michoacán's first millionaire. The timing of Gómez's abandonment of trade is not clear. In 1840 he was still the city's leading retail merchant, though by this time he had already purchased two haciendas. In the inventory of his estate carried out in 1858, however, there were no store effects; his three haciendas, by contrast, were worth over 850,000 pesos and constituted approximately 70 percent of his estate.[13] Even when merchants continued to maintain a retail outlet, it usually represented a small portion of their estates. Fernando Román, for example, left an estate in 1851 worth over 616,000 pesos, of which only 5,300 pesos was in a store. The rest was in his hacienda of La Huerta, worth over 285,000 pesos, and in money owed him by his several partners in *compañías de campo*, including two sons-in-law.[14]

There was a similar tendency for business partnerships that had centered on trade to shift into agriculture and sometimes out of trade altogether. Castañeda and Company, for example, sold its store in 1857 for 27,038 pesos and rented the hacienda of Tepenahua; later the company rented the hacienda of Urundaneo as well.[15] In 1847, after four years in trade, Magaña and Company rented, and three years later bought, the sugar hacienda of La Loma; in 1854 the company bought the hacienda of Pedernales.[16] Zacanini, Losano and Company is another partnership that began exclusively as a trading company and moved into agriculture, buying one-fourth of the hacienda of Corralejo near Pénjamo in 1849 and the hacienda of Turicato in *tierra caliente* (lowland areas) in 1853.[17]

The fact that those with mercantile capital and connections invested in agriculture and were successful during this period is only part of the picture, however. In some ways an even more compelling argument for hacienda profitability is the success of those who had no accumulated mercantile capital when purchasing a hacienda, who financed rebuilding and new capital investments mainly out of profits, with occasional recourse to credit markets. Over 80 percent (94) of all hacienda purchasers between 1810 and 1855 were men who never appeared in the records as retail or wholesale merchants. Some were members of old landowning families, but two-thirds (63) were men with nonelite social origins, who had inherited little or nothing from their own parents, and thus started out in agriculture without benefit of capital, collateral (other than the hacienda they had just purchased), or connections. Most of them were apparently former administrators or renters who took advantage of a relaxation in the rules of the purchase game, which allowed them to buy with no down payment and no schedule of amortization. These measures had been prompted initially by the desperation of sellers in the post-Hidalgo environment and were probably perpetuated by some combination of inertia and unwillingness on the part of buyers to return to stricter purchase conditions.

Of the 94 purchasers with agricultural backgrounds, at least 56 succeeded (that is, held or improved their properties), and at least 29 failed. (The success or failure of the other nine cannot be determined.) The rate of failure was predictably much higher among those who came from nonelite backgrounds; at least 40 percent of nonelites with agricultural backgrounds failed, compared to 16 percent of those with elite backgrounds. Both groups had higher rates of failure than those with mercantile backgrounds (who were, incidentally, overwhelmingly nonelite in social background). All the same, even if we assume that all of the unknowns were failures, it is impressive that at least half of those with the least promising (nonelite, nonmercantile) backgrounds succeeded in agriculture, despite risk and uncertainty. If such buyers could at least hold onto their properties in such troubled times, it is not surprising that almost 30 percent (33) of all hacienda buyers managed to achieve spectacular success, more than doubling the value of their original purchases.

Explaining Hacienda Profitability: Factor Markets and Owner Behavior

If it seems relatively clear that many hacienda owners earned good returns in agriculture, it is much less clear precisely how or why. We can approach this question in two ways: first, by examining changes in market conditions after 1810 that might have favored hacienda agriculture and, second, by exploring changes in the behavior of hacendados.

Elsewhere I have estimated that returns on late colonial cereal-livestock haciendas were around 7 percent (see Table 7.3 for a summary of my reasoning). This estimate squares in a general way with evidence from other regions during the same period.[18] It is harder to estimate returns on sugar haciendas, which were an important aspect of the rural economy in Michoacán, but the average in the late colonial period may have been as high as 10 percent. There is some consensus about the market conditions that allowed agriculturalists working in the late colonial period to earn these respectable returns on their investments. Most historians agree that the late colonial period was characterized by continued population growth (especially in such relatively sparsely populated regions as Michoacán, where growth occurred naturally and by immigration from overcrowded areas) and urbanization, the latter especially notable and rapid in the mining zones to the north of Michoacán. These demographic factors contributed to two phenomena that were highly favorable to hacendados: rising commodity prices and falling real wages.[19]

A somewhat more ambiguous element was the behavior of capital markets, which, according to preliminary analysis of data from Valladolid notary records, shrank some 20 percent between the 1790's and the first de-

TABLE 7.3

*Model of Profitability on Late Colonial
Cereal-Livestock Haciendas in Michoacán*

	Pesos
Hacienda value	100,000
Income	
Sales of tithable commodities	20,000
Additional income	
(from fees, rents, store)	3,000
TOTAL	23,000
Expenditures	
Production costs	10,000
Distribution costs	2,000
Tithe	2,000
Debt service	2,000
TOTAL	16,000
Profit	7,000 (7%)

SOURCES: AHMCR, ANM, AHMM, AHCP, AGN, AHPJ.
NOTE: This model is a composite based on published and unpublished hacienda records, mainly the latter. Production figures, for example,
come from tithe records for central Michoacán for the period 1794–1804.
A full discussion of methods is available from the author on request.

cade of the nineteenth century, rather clearly as a result of increased fiscal
exactions by the penurious colonial state, especially during the Consolidation (1804–08).[20] On the other hand, the constriction of capital markets
did not markedly hinder investment; rents and hacienda prices rose faster
than commodity prices, in large part because of investments in capital improvements such as dams, irrigation projects, storehouses, fences, etc.[21]

We might hypothesize that these considerable capital investments in
hacienda agriculture, sparked by the increasing opportunities for profit inherent in the combination of low wages and high prices, would eventually
have resulted in higher productivity (which was certainly the hacendados'
intent) and that higher productivity in turn would have driven down food
prices and raised real wages. But that development possibility—and I should
emphasize that it was only a possibility—was cut off by the wars for independence. The wars so disrupted both production and distribution in
Michoacán that commodity prices skyrocketed during the period 1810–
19. Prices of four major products (corn, wheat, sugar/*piloncillo*, and beef
cattle) averaged more than 60 percent above those of the decade 1800–09
(see Table 7.4). I have found evidence that many hacienda owners, in some
cases men and women who had abandoned production altogether in the

TABLE 7.4

Agricultural Price Index for Michoacán, 1800–59

Years	Maize	Wheat	Sugar and *piloncillo*	Beef cattle and calves	Weighted and combined
1800–09	100	100	100	100	100
1810–19	177	113	215	136	164
1820–29	98	77	148	159	110
1830–39	97	86	127	129	104
1840–49	102	73	95	110	97
1850–59	104	87	106	139	106

SOURCES: AHMCR, AHCP, AHMM, ANM, AHPG.

NOTE: The most important source of price data is from the sale of tithed commodities. Unfortunately, there are not complete runs of these records. After 1780 the tithe records are intermittent, and between 1810 and 1817 few collections were carried out because of disruption from the insurgency. From 1817 on the data are better, but still spotty until the mid-1830's. For years when tithe data are scanty, one is forced to supplement with material from unsystematic sources, chiefly notarized commodity sale transactions and appraisal values for commodities included in estate inventories. Although the correlations between the tithe prices and the prices from other sources—for years when good data was available for both—were not perfect, I decided to assume for the present purposes that the data could be collapsed into a single index. I then derived a general commodity price index by weighting the commodities, somewhat arbitrarily, in the following manner: maize, 0.5; wheat, 0.2; sugar and *piloncillo*, 0.15; cattle and calves, 0.15. My best guess is that these were roughly the proportions in which these commodities were produced in Michoacán. For a more detailed discussion of my methods, see Chowning: 1992.

early stages of the insurrection, struggled to return to production in order to take advantage of these extraordinarily high prices.[22] Not all were able to do so, of course, and many of those who did owned properties that had probably suffered only minor damage during the wars—but high wartime prices may have encouraged a more concerted effort to rebuild in the early stages than is usually assumed.

As the painful, often backsliding restoration of productive capacity proceeded, the agricultural profits that drove the recovery were boosted by some factors and undermined by others. One obvious profit-enhancing development was the elimination, at first de facto and after 1833 de jure, of the civil obligation to tithe. In the aftermath of the Hidalgo rebellion, the church simply could not orchestrate the collection of its share of what was being produced. Even the miniscule amounts that were collected aroused resentment; the tithe collector in Zamora, for example, noted in 1811 that "most producers pay what they owe with increasing repugnance."[23] Between the church's inability to collect and the great sacrifice that tithing represented in a period of unusual hardship, the habit of tithing, so ingrained during the long colonial period, turned out to be an easy one to break. This was all the more true after 1833. By 1837, when the bishopric requested from local tithe collectors a list of all those who refused to tithe, virtually every hacienda in the state was represented. "Bernardo García pays nothing for his hacienda on the outskirts of Zamora," one local official complained, "and he has informed me that I need not stop at his hacienda in the future, that he will pay when it suits him. The hacienda of Pedernales owes over 200 *panes* (loaves) of sugar and 80–100 *cargas* (a unit of measure equal to 91 kilograms) of *piloncillo* for the 1835 and 1836 harvests, but instead it proposes to satisfy its obligation with 60 *panes* of low weight and poor quality, which it did not turn over until last August."[24] In short, most of the 10 percent of cereal and livestock production and the 4 percent of sugar that had been turned over to the church during the colonial period now stayed in the hands of producers. For *tierra fría* (highland area) haciendas, this step alone would improve net returns from the estimated 7 percent in the late colonial period to 9 percent, if all other factors were equal.

The second factor that favored hacienda profitability was that, after the extraordinarily high commodity prices of the 1810's settled back over the decade of the 1820's, a new equilibrium was achieved at historically high, pre-1810 levels. This price level was maintained through the decade of the 1850's (see Table 7.4). Because high commodity prices had been an important stimulus to hacienda expansion and capital investments during the late colonial period, the fact that producers commanded similar prices in the post-1810 period forms a key part of the argument that good profits were possible in nineteenth-century estate agriculture.

High commodity prices in the 1810's and 1820's are probably best interpreted as indicative of reduced supply compared to the pre-1810 period; certainly there is every indication in the tithe records and other contemporary documents that agricultural production in these decades was substantially below the levels of the first decade of the nineteenth century. But by 1830, and with each decade thereafter, the best interpretation of price trends is that the pre-1810 markets that had supported increased production and high prices between 1790 and 1810 were being reconstituted. This view is consistent with evidence that by the late 1840's and probably before, per capita agricultural output of Michoacán's staple crops—corn, wheat, and sugar—had reached pre-1810 levels or even, in the case of sugar and wheat, exceeded them. This evidence comes primarily from secondhand summaries of agricultural surveys, which are of somewhat dubious reliability taken separately, but the fact that all point in the same direction partially compensates for their inadequacies. One contemporary report, for example, put the increase in maize production between 1808 and 1851 at over 40 percent, higher than the estimated 25 percent growth of the state's population during the same period.[25] Wheat production, too, appears at least to have kept up with population growth and probably to have exceeded it, increasing by at least 30 percent and perhaps as much as doubling during the period from 1810 to 1850.[26] In Pátzcuaro, the only district for which there exist contemporary reports of wheat production both before and after 1810, the increase between 1804 and 1849 was over 60 percent.[27] Finally, sugar production on haciendas in the districts of Ario and Pátzcuaro was around 85,000 *arrobas* (a unit of measure roughly equal to 25 pounds) in 1804; by 1849 these haciendas produced about 143,000 *arrobas*, an increase of some 70 percent.[28] At least one hacienda (Puruarán) doubled production, from about 21,500 *arrobas* of sugar in 1804 to about 45,000 *arrobas* in the early 1860's, when new techniques were introduced that enabled the hacienda to process cane around the clock.[29]

In part, increased agricultural production was a response to population growth in out-of-region markets that Michoacán had always served, especially Mexico City and the near-north mining districts.[30] One contemporary stated in 1849, for example, that Michoacán sent to Mexico City "considerable" quantities of wheat, *queso grande* (a type of cheese, also known as *queso de la Barca*), chile, fattened hogs, and beef cattle; to Guanajuato, all of the above, as well as almost all of the wood used in the mines; to Jalisco, flour; and to Zacatecas, Durango, and other northern states, large amounts of rice and sugar.[31] There were also two positive long-term market changes. One was the opening of western ports and the consequent post-1810 prosperity of Colima and Guadalajara, among other western cities, which surely spurred the rapid population growth, clearing of new lands, and urbanization apparent in western Michoacán, especially around Zamora. By 1860, Zamora, a sleepy village during the colonial period, is said to have enjoyed an "animated commerce" in *efectos del país* with Guadalajara, Guanajuato, and Morelia.[32] The other potentially important long-term trend was the growth of markets in the north, not only as the mining sector recuperated, but also as first Texas and later the U.S. southwest and California grew rapidly beginning (in the case of Texas) in the 1820's and increasing in the late 1840's and early 1850's.[33]

The third factor that affected hacienda profitability positively was that, by around 1830 if not earlier, labor costs seem to have settled back to pre-1810 levels or even dropped below them. Even in the colonial period, labor arrangements on haciendas are difficult to reconstruct, and after 1810 it is especially difficult to find good descriptions of how hacienda work was done. It is likely that the balance between sharecropping, multiple cash tenancies, and wage labor—the chief means of securing and holding a labor force before 1810—probably changed, along with the terms of tenancy contracts and the range of wages, but we must rely primarily on logical inference to conclude that adjustments in response to dislocations in the labor supply worked at least temporarily to the disadvantage of hacendados. Cash rents almost certainly went down in the aftermath of the Hidalgo rebellion, and there was probably more land made available for sharecropping on better terms, as owners withdrew from direct production. Wages must also have risen, perhaps even faster than commodity prices, although the data do not permit confidence on this point. In my examination of hacienda inventories, I have observed that appraisals of fencing, quite clearly an item whose inventory value represented mainly labor inputs, rose in the 1810's and 1820's above those of the pre-1810 period, from about 1.25 reales per *vara* (0.84 meters) in the period 1800–10 to 2 reales per *vara* in the 1810's and 1820's.[34] In short, there is good reason, for the first fifteen or twenty years after the Hidalgo rebellion, to accept the concept of "decompression" posited by John Tutino in his study of rural social relations in nineteenth-century Mexico.[35]

It appears, however, that population loss and disruption during the wars were not enough to boost wages permanently. Evidence from outside of the state indicates that as early as 1822, in some areas, the standard wage was 1.5 reales a day or less, about the same or perhaps even a bit lower than in the late colonial period.[36] My "fence-wage index" shows the appraised value of a *vara* of fence in the 1830's, 1840's, and 1850's to have fallen to 1 real per *vara*, 20 percent below that of the late colonial period. Thus there is good reason to operate on the assumption that by 1830 hacendados benefited from real wages that were at least as low as those of the late colonial period.

Hacienda profits must also have been boosted by the availability of haciendas for purchase and rent at very low prices for much of the period. As we have seen, the average price of a hacienda was less than 25,000 pesos in the twenty years after 1810, a decline of over 40 percent from the levels of the previous decade, and although prices began a jagged upward trend around 1830, distressed haciendas—many of them ceded decades earlier—continued to constitute a historically disproportionate share of the market, keeping prices low. It was not until the period 1850–56 that the proportion of total hacienda sales composed of distressed haciendas finally returned to precrisis levels. Also tending to keep prices down was the fact that the church, fearful of a governmental attack on its property, began in the mid-1840's to sell some of the haciendas it had owned since "time immemorial." In short, there were bargains available in hacienda markets through the 1840's. The situation in rental markets was similar; from an average of almost 3,300 pesos a year in the period 1800–10, hacienda rents dropped to 1,200 pesos between 1810 and 1830, finally beginning in the late 1830's the same sort of ratcheting upward movement as was characteristic of hacienda sale prices. This suggests, of course, that there were many producers who were earning subnormal profits for several decades after the insurrection of 1810–20. But it also suggests that there were agricultural entrepreneurs willing to purchase these properties and improve them.

Part of the fall in rents and prices was surely caused by property destruction, which meant that sometimes expensive repairs had to be carried out before production could resume. On cereal-livestock haciendas, the most pressing needs were restocking herds, especially oxen used for cultivation, and rebuilding fences, dams, irrigation systems, mills, and warehouses, for which labor had to be diverted. On sugar haciendas, the costs of returning to production involved not only restocking (here the main expense was for mules used to power *trapiches* or grinding mills) and diversion of labor to rebuild and refence, but also the purchase of new equipment.

To some extent, however, the drop in prices was caused by psychological factors and oversupply—because of the unusual number of owner deaths, flight to Europe, and especially pressure of debts—which meant that the need for capital investments in order to bring the estate back into production might be relatively minor. Although the balance between property destruction on the one hand and oversupply and lack of confidence on the other cannot be determined with any precision, there was surely a strong role for the latter factors. To the extent that this was the case, the significance for profitability might be fairly considerable. When Antonio Chávez purchased the hacienda of La Labor at auction from the church in 1843, for example, he paid only 8,000 pesos for the unimproved lands. At his death in 1857, these same lands had doubled in value to over 15,900 pesos. The net return on this property for the year after Chávez's death was approximately 10.5 percent of the current value of his estate, but because Chávez had purchased the hacienda at a discount, the return on the actual purchase price plus capital investments was over 12 percent.[37] In such cases as Chávez's, new owners who purchased when prices were low were earning a risk premium.

If we presume for the moment that risk aversion and oversupply were *entirely* responsible for the decline in prices and rents, then a buyer who bought into the market when hacienda prices were lowest and brought the

TABLE 7.5

Model of Profitability on a Hacienda Purchased or Rented in Michoacán Between 1810 and 1830 Requiring No Major Capital Investments

	Purchase	Rental
Pre-1810 value	100,000	100,000
Post-1810 purchase price	57,000	n.a.
Post-1810 value (rent capitalized at 5%)	n.a.	36,400
Income		
Sales of tithable commodities	20,000	20,000
Additional income	3,000	3,000
TOTAL	23,000	23,000
Expenditures		
Production costs	10,000	10,000
Distribution costs	2,000	2,000
Debt service		
(assumes buyer takes full purchase price as a mortgage)	2,850	n.a.
Rent	n.a.	1,820
TOTAL	14,850	13,820
Profit	8,150 (14%)	9,180 (25%)

SOURCES: AHMCR, ANM, AHMM, AHCP, AGN, AHPJ.

property back to pre-1810 levels of output might command as much as a 14-percent rate of return, even if he took the entire purchase price as a mortgage, which was the usual procedure during this period (see Table 7.5). An individual who rented before rents went up in the late 1830's and who brought the property back to full production would earn close to the equivalent of a 25-percent return. Given that property destruction was at least a minor factor in all known cases, these returns are clearly only hypothetical, but they serve to illustrate the larger point that risk premiums were a factor that surely widened the range of hacienda profits after 1810.

This view, that intangible factors played a strong role in driving down property values, can also be supported by use of the theory of net present value. Put simply, this theory holds that potential buyers and renters of haciendas (in this case) bid on properties based on the anticipated profitability of their investments; that is, they discounted into the future the net present value of the properties they were planning to buy or rent. Because the value of hacienda rentals fell farther than the value of sales (a 64-percent decline versus a 43-percent decline), we can infer that while agricultural entrepreneurs were uncertain about the ability of their investments to produce profits over the short term (such as the length of a rental agreement), they were somewhat more confident about the ability of their investments to produce reasonable returns over the long term.

Finally, in ways that are quite impossible to quantify, hacienda profits may have been boosted by the weakness of the state during this period, by its inability effectively to collect taxes, for example, and by the ability of landowners to manipulate state lawmaking bodies, if not actually to control them. My examination of the socioeconomic background of officeholders in Michoacán in the period after independence indicates that even during periods when the wealthy were a minority of state and national legislators, city councilmen, or executive appointees—in the 1820's and early 1830's—this did not prevent the state legislature of Michoacán from passing laws intended to bolster private landholding. Although these laws (especially the 1827 expulsion of Spaniards) often implicitly favored new landowners over old, the expansion-minded, ambitious hacendado—no matter what his social or even ethnic background—benefited. Two notable examples are an 1827 law mandating the division of Indian communal property among villagers (which would have had the effect of making Indian village lands available for purchase had the funds to enforce the law been available) and an 1829 vagrancy law that, among other things, was intended to put "unproductive" men to work on haciendas, thus helping to lower labor costs.

Despite all this, it was a gamble to purchase a hacienda during the period between the wars for independence and the Reform. Aside from the ever-present danger that localized warfare might prevent a harvest or a planting or cause the confiscation of a crop shipment, one factor that clearly undermined hacienda profitability after 1810 was the high cost and limited availability of capital for investment. Linked to this problem was a shortage of specie, due to hoarding and the decline in silver production. During the colonial period, even at times when capital markets were shrinking, interest rates were held down by the substantial ecclesiastical presence in loan markets, since the church was prohibited from lending at more than 5-percent interest. After 1810, however, the church never recovered its dominant position in capital markets; in fact, it was for a time reduced to borrowing at usurious rates of interest outside the bishopric, as its income from the tithe, bequests, and redemptions of old loans dried to a trickle.[38] Furthermore, the departure or death of most Spanish merchant/financiers thinned the ranks of nonecclesiastical lenders in a most dramatic fashion. From 135,000 pesos a year in loans notarized in Valladolid between 1800 and 1810 (an already-reduced level compared to the 1790's), notarized lending plummeted to under 15,000 pesos a year in the two decades following the Hidalgo rebellion, and revival of loan markets was painfully slow thereafter. Interest rates, as a consequence, by all accounts rose sharply.[39] It is no surprise that, as we shall see, much of the thrust of post-1810 agricultural arrangements, both external (with outside creditors and suppliers) and internal (with the labor force) was oriented toward finessing the cash and capital scarcity problems.

Another factor that is often thought to have undermined hacienda profitability after 1810 was high transportation costs. High freight costs were, of course, a perennial problem in Mexico, which the impecunious and Europe-oriented late colonial viceregal governments had done little to ameliorate. Transport costs almost certainly rose still further after 1810, given the government's inability to secure "public tranquility" and the prevalence of banditry along even major highways.

The extent to which higher transportation costs eroded hacienda profits, however, is open to question. It is necessary first to recall that in Michoacán there was a significant difference between the highland haciendas devoted primarily to grains and livestock, whose markets were mainly local and whose freight costs, as a result, were a relatively light burden, and the hot-country hacienda, whose products (sugar, rice, indigo, livestock) were shipped long distances out of region and whose transport costs were very high. Shipping the tropical products of the *tierra caliente* haciendas was complicated by the fact that rebellion was particularly rife in that part of the state. It is these hacendados, then, whose profits were most threatened by the dangers and expense of prerailroad transportation systems.

In theory, even though merchant/distributors and not the producers themselves were ordinarily responsible for arranging and paying freight costs for long-distance transport of tropical products and cattle, any increases in distributors' costs after 1810 might have been passed along to the producers in the form of lower prices. Yet, as we have seen, wholesale commodity prices did not fall vis-à-vis the late colonial period.

What can we conclude from all this? Are these changes in market conditions after 1810 sufficient to explain the success of hacienda agriculture? On the one hand, I have described conditions in which ecclesiastical taxes were substantially lower and civil taxation more ineffectively collected (even if higher than during the pre-1810 period), in which production costs were probably the same or lower, in which for an important period of time land prices and rents were considerably lower, and in which commodity prices were as high or higher than before 1810. On the other hand, I have described continuing political instability, significant losses of reproducible capital on the haciendas as a result of the wars, high costs of distribution, and ravaged capital markets that would not make it easy to replace stock and equipment by borrowing. In short, changes in structural conditions alone are probably not enough to explain the comeback in hacienda profitability after 1810; there were too many possible ways to fail, even if there were more ways to succeed than historians have generally thought. We need as well to ask how individuals mediated these conditions and whether (and if so, how) some of them adjusted their behavior to take advantage of changes in the climate of production.

I have identified several changes in hacendado behavior after 1810 that may help to clarify the matter. First, hacendados had to find a way around credit shortages and high interest rates. One obvious solution was to open lines of credit with merchant/financiers in Morelia and Zamora, who themselves often operated on credit lines from Mexico City houses. A similar chain of credit from Mexico City merchants to rural consumers had existed in the colonial period as well, of course, but the presence after independence of a growing number of foreign mercantile houses in Mexico City, all competing for regional markets and seemingly willing to open credit lines to all comers, appears to have expanded the practice. Charges on these accounts did not technically carry interest, but in lieu of interest, the hacendado might agree to purchase supplies exclusively from the regional house or to allow the regional house exclusive rights to market the hacienda's produce. Accounts would be settled from time to time and the balance, invariably in favor of the mercantile house, would be paid in staggered *libranzas* (bills of exchange), sometimes payable in kind.

A closely related variation on this theme was for a hacendado to request an advance from a merchant, with an agreement to repay the loan in kind at prearranged unit prices. The obligation to repay loans in kind was potentially devastating. In 1831, for example, the prominent merchant/speculator Fernando Román lent 9,750 pesos to the struggling owners of the hacienda of Araparícuaro, which they were to repay with 6,000 *arrobas* of sugar from the 1833, 1834, and 1835 harvests at 13 reales per *arroba* (there were 8 reales to a peso). But sugar from the nearby hacienda of Puruarán in 1832–34 commanded 19 to 24 reales per *arroba*. Thus the owners of Araparícuaro, the Menocal family, missed the chance to earn some 6,400 pesos in sales over three years, for an implicit annual interest rate of 22 percent. If they had been able to borrow the 9,750 pesos from the church, interest over three years would have amounted to only 1,461 pesos.[40] The alternative for the Menocals, however—going to loan markets—would have been equally unappealing, because their already heavily indebted hacienda would not be accepted as collateral by any knowledgeable lender, and as a result the terms of any conventional loan would likely have been even more onerous than the lost opportunities represented by the advance contract.[41]

Internally, there were three partial solutions to the capital shortage problem. One was to pay one's workers as little in wages and as much in kind as possible. Most haciendas paid workers a ration in maize, which workers expected and probably demanded, because it protected them from fluctuations in the price of this most-necessary foodstuff. If a hacienda did not grow maize, it was necessary to purchase it in outside markets. The maize ration had existed before the postindependence cash and capital shortages and was only loosely related to them, but payment of rations in other commodities besides maize may have been a postindependence innovation designed to help offset the largest cash requirement on all haciendas, the wage bill. The owner of the sugar hacienda of Puruarán, for example, besides paying his workers in sugar, *piloncillo*, and the alcoholic beverage *aguardiente*, produced on the estate, bought an average of 1,365 pesos a year in such commodities and manufactured items as soap, clothing, shoes, chiles, frijoles, and garbanzos, which he used to pay workers' rations. He also purchased almost 3,000 pesos a year worth of goods for the *tienda de raya* (company store).[42] Combined, rations and sales to *peones* (day laborers) from the store reduced the cash required for wage payments by almost one-third. Although the provenance of the goods purchased outside the hacienda is not known, the odds are very good that they were supplied by one of the merchants to whom the owner of Puruarán was indebted; the owner, in other words, was most likely paying his workers with goods that he then charged to his mercantile account.

The second internal solution was tenancy, either cash rents or sharecropping. I have not found any means of comparing rents per hectare before and after 1810, but given the precipitous decline in hacienda rents, it is surely safe to infer that unit rents also went down. Under prevailing conditions of relatively high commodity prices and low rents, owners probably turned to cash rents only when there was no other choice. The exceptions were large *arrendatarios* (renters) of whole ranchos within a hacienda. Sharecropping, on the other hand, for the hacendado was a means of benefiting from any productivity and/or price increases and required only a modest cash investment. Those costs that were usually borne by the hacendado (supervision, tools, animals, seed, distribution, and often half the costs incurred by the sharecropper in preparation of the land, and/or hiring seasonal labor, and/or harvesting) were still less than those of direct production, because of wage savings.[43]

As with cash rents, there is no systematic source of information about sharecropping in nineteenth-century Mexico, and the ways in which share-croppers show up in the written records that I have examined are quite confusing. At times the system seems most to resemble the one that appar-ently dominated the postbellum South of the United States, in which des-perate owners embraced sharecropping only because of capital and labor shortages. The Augustinians of Pátzcuaro, for example, owners of the ha-cienda of Sanabria, noted in 1831 with obvious regret that it had been necessary to give out the lands of the hacienda of Sanabria to sharecroppers because the convent did not have the funds to purchase mules, cattle, and oxen; as a result, they said, the harvests were poor and were sometimes lost altogether, "as often happens in these cases."[44] Other references to share-croppers also carry last-resort overtones; Domingo Torices, for example, manager of the rich but shaken hacienda of San Bartolomé near Morelia, decided to turn over all corn production on the hacienda to sharecroppers during the 1820's, after having engaged in direct production of maize for decades.[45]

In other cases, however, sharecroppers appear to have been valued ad-juncts to highly successful, and not particularly cash-poor, enterprises—not unlike the larger *arrendatarios*. Antonio Sierra, for example, divided his haciendas of Disparate and Rosario between just two *medieros* (share-croppers), who grew rice; their crops in 1847, 1848, and 1849 sold for well over 4,000 pesos, to be split with Sierra.[46] This kind of privilege share-cropper was given the irrigated maize lands to work, or was engaged in growing wheat, indigo, or other labor intensive crops—not in the stereo-typical maize production on marginal lands.[47] These sharecropping ar-rangements were more like business partnerships than they were means of immobilizing a labor force or ekeing out some income from marginal lands. In short, it seems likely that future researchers will make important distinc-tions between sharecropping types, as well as between *arrendatarios*. For our purposes, however, the point is that the system in both of the incarna-tions sketched here was well-suited to the hacienda's need to maximize income with as little cash outlay as possible.

Hacendados also seem to have learned to manage debt better than in the past. Late colonial hacendados were notoriously willing to tolerate high levels of indebtedness, regularly adding to debt that was inherited or accepted on purchase of the hacienda not only by borrowing cash but also by giving the church liens on property in lieu of paying cash for ecclesias-tical endowments or nuns' dowries. Mercantile loans were ordinarily paid off quickly, but these ecclesiastical obligations were extended, in effect, in perpetuity, and were redeemed only if it was convenient for the borrower to do so. After 1830 or so, however, a pattern of debt redemption, even of low-interest ecclesiastical loans, is apparent among the most successful hacendados, probably because of some combination of borrower prudence and pressure from nervous creditors. Furthermore, hacendados were far less likely to put an ecclesiastical lien on their property after 1810 than before. Bequests, foundations of chaplaincies, and female entrance into convents all went down. By the 1850's, the estates of the ten wealthiest landowners in Michoacán were encumbered to an average of under 30 percent of gross assets, compared to over 41 percent for the ten wealthiest landowners in the two decades before 1810. To the extent that Domenico Síndico is correct to argue that the most important constraint on nineteenth-century growth was debt, then there is some evidence that hacendados were aware of the disasters that had befallen their heavily indebted predecessors after the Hidalgo rebellion and sought to avoid such pitfalls.[48]

Toward midcentury there is some evidence that the tight credit markets characteristic of the early national period were easing. Although the capital-shortage problem was not resolved until the arrival of a banking system in the late Porfiriato (and not really even then), two of the solutions to the problem—cash advances by merchant/financiers to hacendados, which were to be repaid in kind, and extensive use of sharecropping—may have turned out, as hacendados hoped, to be temporary expedients. The evidence is strongest in the case of cash advances. Blessed by generally good weather, favorable commodity prices, expanding demand, and stable labor costs, many producers who had accepted advances in the 1830's were, by the 1840's, selling their crops on a buyer-pays-later basis, in which the producer took the risk and commanded the price advantage. In fact, even now, unestablished hacienda purchasers in the 1840's and 1850's did not find it so necessary to turn to merchants for cash advances as had those in the 1830's. By 1840, the heyday of this particularly profit-draining mechanism for recapitalizing haciendas had passed. The evidence for a decline by 1840 in sharecropping, or for a shift in the nature of sharecropping (described below), is far weaker; it consists only of the absence of any references to small-scale maize sharecropping in any of the documents I have consulted. Much more research remains to be done in this area.[49]

Ironically, one of the factors contributing to the widening and deepening of credit networks in Mexico was the increasing use of *libranzas*, traditionally an expedient used to circumvent cash shortages. In time, with usage and perhaps under the influence of the practices of foreign merchants in Mexico City, *libranzas* came to be convenient and liberating, not just bills of exchange extended because cash was short. *Libranzas* were not themselves notarized, but *protestas* (protests of nonpayment) were, and from an examination of these *protestas* in the 1850's it is clear that merchants from all over Mexico were not only accepting *libranzas* issued in Michoacán but that these *libranzas* were close to fully negotiable; that is, A would issue a note to B, who would use it to pay C, who would use it to pay D, and so on, ordinarily with a 2- to 4-percent discount. This conforms to Eugene Wiemers's view that, overall, credit markets during this period worked well, that debts were regularly liquidated, and repayments were predictable.[50] In sum, though the solutions were often problematic (as in the advance contracts with regional houses), hacienda owners found ways to adjust to high interest rates and cash scarcity.

Adjustments to tight credit markets were of supreme importance, but there were other changes in behavior initiated by hacendados after independence that meant to protect and enhance profits. One is related to the blurring of the lines between commerce and agriculture noted in the first section above. While the movement from trade into agriculture during the colonial period had been almost invariably a one-way street, a strategy undertaken by Spanish-born merchants to secure a lifestyle and income for their families that was not linked to the vicissitudes of trade, during the postindependence period there were far fewer barriers between trade and agriculture, now that virtually all merchants were creoles (Mexican-born). The social convention and economic exclusivity that had kept creoles out of trade before independence vanished almost overnight, and after 1810 creole sons of landowners frequently started out their careers in trade.[51]

A less clearly demarcated division between merchant/distributors and producer/processors, who were now more likely than before 1810 to be bound by ties of kinship and custom, meant that it was easier to link the processes of production, processing, and distribution, and this was the direction taken by all of the most successful individual entrepreneurs, whether they began in agriculture and moved into trade and speculation, or whether they began in trade and moved into agriculture. One of the merchant Cayetano Gómez's earliest moves, for example, was to manage a sugar hacienda that had been taken over by its creditors, to market the hacienda's produce in his own store, and to enlarge demand by financing manufacturers of *aguardiente*, who then agreed to buy raw materials only from him.[52] When a decade later Gómez bought the wheat-producing hacienda of San Bartolomé, he began to set up bakers in business, who then bought flour from his mills; in a vertical integration that worked the other way, he lent money to cotton growers in order to assure a regular supply of raw materials for his textile factory in Colima.[53] His brother-in-law Manuel Alzúa had agreements with cotton textile manufacturers, whom he supplied with cotton that he grew and/or purchased in his trading activities on the Pacific coast.[54] Fernando Román's two sons-in-law managed large cereal-livestock haciendas in the Puruándiro region, which supplied the *tocinería* that Román owned in Mexico City.[55]

This strategy of integration was feasible only for the largest individual producers, but landowners or renters of more modest means were able to tap the benefits of integration by forming business partnerships with capitalists or processors. These partnerships, not unknown in the late colonial period, were nonetheless far more common in Michoacán in the postindependence era. I have identified 23 partnerships concluded between 1830 and 1855 whose main business was managing a hacienda.[56] The potential for profit in agriculture if one had access to capital and means of distribution can be seen quite clearly in the profits of these partnerships. In nine cases for which documents detailing both the formation and the dissolution of partnerships could be found, thus making it possible to calculate an annual rate of return, profits averaged 23 percent a year (see Table 7.6). In several other cases for which only partial information is available, high rates of profit can be inferred. The partnership between second cousins Agapito and Augustín Solórzano, for example, in the sugar hacienda of Tomendán, produced 100,000 pesos in profit over a period of four years, from 1846 to 1850. A precise return on investment cannot be determined because the amount of Agapito's original investment is unknown, but even if it were as much as 75,000 pesos, making it by far the largest individual capital invest-

TABLE 7.6

Rural Business Partnerships in Michoacán, 1841–62

Duration of partnership	Partners	Annual rate of return (%)	Capital investment (pesos)
1841–47	Bocanegra-Arriaga	12.3	9,500
1836–43	Flores-Ibarrola	24.4	30,772
1851–53	Jaso-Orozco	8.9	23,000
1858–59	Sosa-Soravilla	22.8	20,438
1836–39	Román-Elorza	46.2	47,903
1848–50	Losano-Solórzano	27.4	4,000
1857–59	Lama-Vallejo	24.0	10,000
1850–55	Zacanini-Losano	24.3	6,733
1853–62	Alzúa-Alzuyeta-Huarte	14.9	100,000

SOURCES: AHMCR, ANM, AHMM, AHCP, AGN, AHPJ.

ment of the period, the average annual return would have been about 30 percent.[57]

Another changed element of hacendado behavior that helps explain an increase in profitability is experimentation with new, labor-intensive crops that were particularly well-suited to an era of high transport costs and low wages. In the valley of Indaparapeo, for example, haciendas had grown chile intermittently and as an adjunct to wheat farming in the late colonial period, but as early as the 1820's several haciendas that had returned to production were growing very large amounts indeed. When Fanny Calderón de la Barca visited the hacienda of San Bartolomé in Indaparapeo in the early 1840's, an estate that had been overwhelmingly devoted to grains and livestock production in the late colonial period, she was told that chile was its major crop.[58] There are hints of much-increased frijol and garbanzo production in the Zamora area, and we know that during the push by Lucas Alamán (secretary of domestic and foreign affairs) to industrialize, farmers in the western part of the state rushed to plant mulberry trees for silkworms and linseed for *molinos de aceite* (oil-pressing mills).[59] In the *tierra caliente*, there were experiments with coffee, cacao, and fruit production.[60] More widespread was the production of rice (the famous *arroz de Apatzingán*) and the dry, sharp cheese for which Michoacán is still noted.[61]

If hacendados managed in some ways to adjust to conditions detrimental to estate agriculture and to take advantage of those structural conditions that favored accumulation, there were also elements of hacendado behavior that did not change, or did not change much, after independence. It is useful to ask why further (and, by narrow economic standards, logical) changes were not forthcoming, because such conservatism is often held up as a reason for, or an indication of, agricultural "backwardness."

One aspect of hacendado decision making that changed little in Michoacán after 1810 concerned the subdivision and expansion of estates. It is true that, especially in the 1820's, there was some splitting up of haciendas undertaken by owners attempting to get out from under crushing debt burdens, but under the circumstances it was relatively rare, and cession or sale of the entire estate was a more likely means of dealing with indebtedness. Subdivision of property with the apparent purpose of creating more efficient units of production or of raising capital for investment in the core of the estate, while logical enough on the surface, simply was not much done. Part of the explanation may be that the church, almost invariably the main mortgage holder on rural properties, subverted the process of hacienda division in subtle ways, though there is ample evidence that it did not invariably oppose fractionalization.[62] Probably more persuasive was the conviction, based on both economic logic and cultural convention, that "dismemberment" would destroy the organic nature of the hacienda. An ideal hacienda was one which *could* (if necessary) revert to self-sufficiency in bad years. Put another way, the pasturage, or the *monte* (hill lands), or the fallow, or the marginal lands that could be rented out were seen as just as essential to the estate's ability to survive as the irrigated land or the *casco* (the central, high-quality portion of the hacienda). It was not until estate specialization progressed much farther than was the case during the period in question that division of large estates into intensively worked smaller units was seen as a sensible strategy.

Evidence of some consolidation of estates during the first half of the century is more plentiful than evidence of subdivision. Hacienda expansion seems to have occurred mainly at the expense of Indian communities, especially as the recovery gathered momentum in the 1840's, but even here the trend cannot be described as powerful.[63] The recovery was still young enough, the damage done during the insurgency great enough, and the Indian villagers "troublesome" enough that expansion within the limits of existing estates was seen as the most potentially profitable path, especially when combined with experimentation in new crops and new intensive methods of cultivation and processing. Thus there were political and cultural, as well as economic, reasons why the size of estates changed little between the late colonial period and the middle of the nineteenth century.

Furthermore, agriculture continued to absorb the vast majority of the state's labor force, and although output per worker probably increased slightly during the period, as we have seen, there is no evidence of a corresponding shift of population out of the agricultural sector or of a rise in rural wages. Moreover, there were several features of the climate in which estate agriculture operated that militated against such changes occurring any time soon. Highly unequal land distribution and population pressure kept wages down and lured even ambitious and entrepreneurial-minded hacendados into sidestepping the issue of worker inefficiency. Although, as noted above, by circa 1840 there may have been a decline in the use of sharecropping and cash tenancy from the levels of the 1820's and 1830's, continuing weak capital markets probably led hacendados to maintain, even if in somewhat attenuated form, tenancy patterns forged during the early years of the recovery.

These tenancy arrangements in turn may have encouraged hacendados to make available only cheap (but inefficient) oxen for plowing, rather than the more expensive draft horses and mules. Tenants and sharecroppers may have sacrificed yields by planting too close together on small plots.[64] The plows used by tenants and sharecroppers may have been more often wooden than iron, and some may not have used plows at all.[65] Tools owned by the hacienda that were used mainly by dependent cultivators may not have been replaced or maintained; in fact, part of the reason that tools and equipment constitute such a low proportion of movables on most haciendas is that they were *viejos* (old) or *maltratados* (worn-out). Thus sharecropping and tenancy, for all their advantages to the hacendado, probably contributed inherently to the retardation of structural change by discouraging technological and even technical change.[66]

Beyond these economic considerations, hacendados may not have addressed the low-productivity issue head-on because maintaining a large work force increased the number of privileged and presumably loyal permanent residents on one's estate, not an inconsiderable factor in a period of peasant and Indian rebellions, beginning with the Hidalgo rebellion. It also gave the hacendado political power by increasing the number of votes or armed men he could command.[67] Thus issues of power and control may well have dampened the willingness of hacendados to demand the kind and degree of productivity increases that might lead to evicting tenants or reducing the size of the labor force.

In sum, a recovery of estate agriculture was engineered in Michoacán by new men who took over haciendas from the virtually demolished late colonial elite and carved out new ways to make them profitable. To a point they succeeded by means of what we might call "progressive" strategies: reducing debt, reaching new markets, diversifying production, and modernizing operations. But the limits to which profits could be reconciled with uncontrolled growth in output must have been apparent almost from the beginning. This meant that profitability would have to depend as well on cornering capital, labor, and commodity markets, on integrating production, processing, and distribution, on building political power and control, and otherwise closing other ambitious newcomers out. In this, too, the extraordinary generation to come of age after the Hidalgo rebellion succeeded. By the 1850's, wealth inequality among the elite (defined as those with assets of at least 20,000 pesos) was even higher than during the late colonial period, implying that the most important roads to wealth—trade and agriculture—were increasingly blocked (see Table 7.7).

It is not surprising that pressure to change the rural status quo—by removing the Indian communities and the church as obstacles to the free movement of property, by building railroads to permit access to larger mar-

TABLE 7.7

Distribution of Wealth Among the Elite in Michoacán, 1790–1859

Share of elite wealth (by decile)	1790–1810	1811–29	1830–49	1850–59
91–100 (richest)	35.0%	39.6%	31.6%	43.8%
71–100	63.4%	62.1%	60.4%	69.6%
31–70	27.2%	26.4%	29.9%	22.0%
1–30	9.4%	11.5%	9.7%	8.4%
1–10 (poorest)	2.3%	3.3%	2.3%	2.1%
Total households	59	42	47	44
Total elite wealth (pesos)	5,681,000	3,092,000	3,714,000	5,842,000
Gini coefficient	0.44	0.42	0.41	0.50

SOURCES: AHMCR, ANM, AHMM, AHCP, AGN, AHPJ.
NOTE: *Elite* is defined as households with gross wealth of 20,000 pesos or more. See Table 7.2 for a more complete discussion.

kets, and by establishing a banking system that would extend credit on an impersonal basis—came not from those who had been most successful in manipulating extant conditions but from those members of the urban and rural middle classes who were increasingly denied the upward economic mobility that had characterized their parents' and grandparents' generations. This discussion of Mexican agriculture in the period before the Reform thus adds to Mexico's political history a sense in which the liberal frustrations were not based solely on invidious comparison of Mexico to Europe or the United States, or on ideological commitment to liberal individualism, or even on the political crisis brought about by the Mexican War. Instead, it suggests that, at least in Michoacán, the timing and the direction of the middle-class-led Reform movement emerged at least in part from the fact and nature of the recovery of the rural economy.

Notes

1. Miller 1984: 311.
2. García de León 1988: 83; Semo 1988: 88; Coatsworth 1990: 126; Tutino 1986: 215.
3. I developed this argument in an earlier article; see Chowning 1992.
4. "The Mexican hacienda was a sink through which drained without stop the surplus capital accumulated in the export economy"; Brading 1971: 219. On hacendados as maximizers, Coatsworth 1978: 87.
5. The chief exceptions are Brading 1978; Bazant 1975. See note 8 below for details. Simon Miller's two articles on sharecropping and grain production (1984,

1990) are certainly concerned with hacienda profitability, but mainly for the Porfiriato.

6. Brading 1978: xi.

7. For Morelia, notary registers alone were used. For Pátzcuaro, the *libro de becerro* covers the period from 1818 through 1853, and notary registers are also available for many years. AHCP, leg. 68, 1810–19, exp. 4, on front reads "Libro de hipoteca, 1818–26" but is inclusive through 1853. For Zamora, notary registers for 1842–49 and 1853–54 have been published by the Colegio de Michoacán; *libros de becerro* for 1830–45 and 1846–61 are found in the ANM.

8. For La Huerta, see ANM, Rincón, 1833, 7 Oct.; AHMM, 1839, "Convenio en arbitradores nombrados por los Ciudadanos Fernando Román y Agustín Elorza, para decidir las diferencias que les ocurrieron en la compañía que celebraron para el giro de la Hacienda de la Huerta propria del primero." For La Labor, see AHPJ, 1857, Primero Civil, legajo 1, "Cuenta de partición y división de los bienes pertenecientes a la Testamentaria de D. Antonio Chávez"; AHMM, Año de 1855, "Expediente instruido a instancia de D. Estevan García, alvacea del finado D. Antonio Chávez." For Paramuen-Istaro, see AHCP, legajo 95-D, notary register for 1856, undated document following entry for Nov. 20, 1856, "Cuenta de cargo presentada por el alvacea de D. Joaquin del Río y corre desde 1 febrero 1852 hasta la fecha 1 agosto 1856," and "Avalúo e inventario de Istaro y Paramuen." For Puruarán, see AHMM, 1831–34, records of the hacienda de Puruarán; ANM, José María Aguilar, 1825, 15 Jan. Bazant (1975: 192) shows average returns on capital on the hacienda of La Parada from 1843 through 1862 to be 5.7 percent. Brading (1978: 103, 105–06, 113) has calculated profits on three haciendas: Duarte, which earned the equivalent of a 4- to 5-percent return on capital value in 1811–18; Otates, which seems to have earned a return of about 7.7 percent in 1814 and 1815, before the hacienda was destroyed; and Sauz de Armenta, which earned under 1.5 percent a year for its owner in 1827–39. For Querétaro, making certain assumptions about labor costs, capital-output ratios, etc., Raso (1848: 38–45) hypothesizes a net return of around 10 percent, which assumes (apparently incorrectly, at least for Michoacán) that everyone tithed; using his figures, the rate of profit without deducting for the tithe would be 11.4 percent.

9. Structures accounted for another 18 percent of which approximately 40 percent was fencing.

10. Inventories filed between 1810 and 1850 so rarely break down *raíz* into land and structures that I cannot generalize about the value of structures. Structures on ten haciendas in the 1850's for which that information is available accounted for an average of approximately 11 percent of the value of the property.

11. ANM, Rincón, 1835, 30 Dec.; Rincón, 1843, 7 June; Valdovinos, 1843, 5 July; Valdovinos, 1844, 26 July; García, 1845, 31 May; García, 1847, 12 June; García, 1847, 1 July; García, 1851, 5 June.

12. ANM, Rincón, 1841, 16 Oct.; Valdovinos, 1845, 16 May; García, 1852, 6 Sept.

13. AGN, Alcabalas, misc. boxes containing *alcabala* (internal tariff) records for Valladolid and Pátzcuaro, 1817, 1818, 1821; ANM, Rincón, 1833, 11 Dec.; Rin-

cón, 1837, 11 Aug.; García, 1838, 13 Feb.; Valdovinos, 1842, 10 Oct.; AHMM, 1858, "Resumen general de todos los bienes pertenecientes a la Testamentaria [de D. Cayetano Gómez] y que existen tanto en esta Ciudad y en la de Colima como en las jurisdicciones de los pueblos de Yndaparapeo, Tarímbaro, Taretan, y de la Villa de Charo"; AHMM, 1840, "Expediente sobre igualas celebradas con algunos comerciantes por sus giros de comercio."

14. AGN, Alcabalas, misc. boxes containing *alcabala* records for Valladolid and Pátzcuaro, 1817, 1818, 1821; ANM, Valdovinos, 1839, 18 Mar.: García, 1851, 26 Feb. and 6 Mar.

15. ANM, Valdovinos, 1857, 11 Aug.; Cano, 1860, 27 Aug.; Cano, 1860, 10 Oct.; Valdovinos, 1866, 3 Nov.; Cano, 1866, 20 Feb.

16. ANM, García, 1843, 2 Dec.; García, 1847, 5 Nov.; Valdovinos, 1853, 20 June; Valdovinos, 1855, 22 Dec.

17. ANM, Salomo, 1849, 22 Feb.; Huerta, 1850, 6 Mar.; Pérez, 1852, 7 May; Valdovinos, 1857, 19 Jan.; Pérez, 1859, 14 June; AHMM, 1857, on cover is "Curaduría ad bona de la menor Dona Socorro Chávez" but contains inventory and liquidation of estate of D. Antonio Zacanini.

18. Van Young (1981: 224) has profits of 5 percent, 7 percent, and 7 percent on three haciendas in the late eighteenth and early nineteenth centuries before 1810; Tutino (1983: 363) says that profits averaged from 6 to 9 percent of capital value in the late eighteenth century; Brading (1971: 216) finds 5.6-percent and 7-percent returns on capital on two haciendas in the period 1800–5.

19. Good summaries of the relationship between rising prices, rising land values, and falling wages are Brading 1978: chap. 8; Van Young 1986.

20. Chowning 1989.

21. I am grateful to Frederick P. Bowser for providing data on hacienda prices and rents and commodity prices for the period before 1810. My calculations using his data show hacienda prices climbing from an average of 27,500 pesos in the 1770's and 1780's to 36,700 pesos in the 1790's and to 43,200 pesos in the 1800's. Rents rose from an average 1,200 pesos a year in the 1770's through the 1790's to 3,275 pesos in the period 1800–10. Commodity prices in general rose more slowly; maize prices went up approximately 38 percent between 1770 and 1804, wheat prices about 44 percent, *becerros* (calves) about 73 percent (livestock was slower than maize or wheat to recover after the severe droughts of the mid-1780's). Maize in Valladolid: 1770–84, 8 reales/*fanega* (a *fanega* equals 3.6 hectares); 1797–1804, 11 reales/*fanega*. Wheat: 1770–84, 5.70 pesos/*carga*; 1797–1804, 8.20 pesos/*carga*. *Becerros:* 1770–84, 15 reales/head; 1797–1804, 26 reales/head. Sugar prices have not yet been calculated from tithe returns for the late eighteenth century, but the general impression is of much more price stability than in any of the other commodities. The average price in 1804 was 16.5 reales/*arroba*, and it was probably not too much less than this earlier in the century. For the relationship between structures, movables, and land, see note 9 above.

22. AHMCR, Diezmos, legajo 11, "Cuenta general de cargo y data. . . La Piedad [1819–27]"; AHMCR, Diezmos, Varios, legajo 8, "Cuenta general de la Administración de Maravatío [1823–34]"; AHMCR, Diezmos, legajo 7, "Ario, Santa

Clara, Urecho. Ramo de dulces. 1820–35"; AHMCR, Diezmos, Varios, legajo 13, "Cuentas del Diezmatorio de Puruándiro del Año [1818–33]"; AHMCR, Diezmos, Varios, legajo 22, "Diezmos de Zamora. Año de 1811[–33]"; AHMCR, Diezmos, Varios, legajo 23, "Cuentas . . . del Diezmatorio de Zinapécuaro, 1819 [–33]."

23. AHMCR, Diezmos, Varios, legajo 22, "Diezmos de Zamora. Año de 1811[–33]."

24. AHMCR, Diezmos, Varios, legajo 9, 1837, no title. Contains the list of individuals in the bishopric who refused to tithe.

25. Romero (1862: 29), Gamboa Ramírez (1988: 226), and Brachet (1976: 103) have population increasing about 25 percent between 1810 and 1856.

26. Romero's agricultural survey taken in 1851 concluded that 12,000 *cargas* of wheat were sown in Michoacán in that year. Estimates of average wheat yields in central Mexico range from 1:10 to 1:20 and higher—Brading (1978: 67), for example, accepts Humboldt's very high ratio of 1:40 for wheat grown on irrigated land and calls a 1:15 ratio "low." If we assume that each *carga* sown in Michoacán around 1850 produced 15 *cargas* at harvest, this would mean a harvest of some 180,000 cargas. There is no contemporary estimate of the amount of wheat sown or harvested before 1810, but if each white or mestizo in the state consumed three-quarters of a carga of wheat a year (which is surely a very generous estimate, as it is based on estimates of urban consumption in wealthy Valladolid, while many rural whites and mestizos were primarily maize consumers), internal consumption of wheat would be only about 110,000 *cargas*. The intendant estimated that in 1810 Michoacán exported 30,000 *cargas* from the intendancy, chiefly to Mexico City, bringing total production to no more, and probably far less, than 140,000 *cargas*. An increase of 100 percent would occur if wheat yielded 20 *cargas* per *carga* sown, and if only 30 percent, rather than 40 percent, of the state's population consumed wheat at the level of Valladolid's per capita consumption in 1787. See Romero (1862: 29) for wheat sown; Humboldt (1966: 257) for wheat yields; Humboldt (1966: 167) for proportion of white and mestizos to Indians; Humboldt (1966: 38) for population of Valladolid in 1793; Morin (1979: 142) for wheat consumption in Valladolid in 1787; Bancroft Library, M-M 1830: 5, June 30, 1813, letter from Intendant of Valladolid, Manuel Merino, to Viceroy Calleja, f. 56, for out-of-province exports; Brachet (1976: 103) for population of the intendancy in 1810.

27. AHMCR, Diezmos, Varios, legajo 10, "Informes de los curas del diezmatorio de Pátacuaro . . . [1804]"; Piquero 1861: 173.

28. AHMCR, Diezmos, Varios, legajo 24, "Cuentas que el Br. D. Juan José Corral Farías . . . presenta por lo causado en el año de 1804"; Piquero 1861: 173. The accuracy of these figures is clouded by the fact that one is forced to compare tithe districts for 1804 to political jurisdictions in 1849, but I have tried to resolve this problem by checking to be sure that the same major haciendas were included in these districts for both periods.

29. AHMCR, Diezmos, Varios, legajo 24, "Ramo de dulces, 1804"; AHMM, 1857, misfiled document currently attached to "Información que para justificar en pobreza . . . José María y María Gertrudis Rodríguez," should be filed under 1864, "Laudo arbitral, D. Julián de Tarno contra la alvacea de D. Manuel de Alzúa."

30. Romero 1862: 44; Bancroft Library, M-M 1830:5, Merino to Calleja, f. 5.

31. Piquero 1861: 174–75.

32. González 1984: 88; González 1974: 19–20; Heredia Correa 1984: 124–26; Piquero 1861: 165.

33. Brading 1978: 202; Barrett 1970: 63; Voss 1982: 36–38, 68, 128; Harris 1975: 259–62.

34. The utility of fence prices to infer rural wage trends is supported by the fact that in the 1780's and 1790's, fences were appraised at an average of 1.66 reales/ *vara*; the decline in the period 1800–10 to 1.25 reales/*vara* is in line with more direct data on the decline of wages during the same period.

35. Tutino 1986, chap. six. See also Tutino 1975: 523–24.

36. For the late colony, Van Young (1981: 250–52) has seasonal workers at 2 reales/day at least until the end of the eighteenth century and probably into the nineteenth. Morin (1979: 260) calls a wage of 2 reales the "customary" wage but notes that wages of 1.5 or even 1 real/day were not uncommon. Konrad (1980: 223) has the standard daily wage of peones at 2 reales in 1739–51. Brading (1977: 37) has *peones* earning 1.3 reales/day with free pasture in Celaya in 1807; on page 38 he says 1.5 reales/day plus a maize ration was standard for the Bajío in the 1790's. For the postindependence period, Bazant (1973: 338) has seasonal labor at 1.5 reales/day in 1852. Raso (1848: 44) also puts seasonal labor at 1.5 reales/day. Brading (1978: 202) cites an 1822 pamphlet in which landlords in Querétaro were accused of taking advantage of a labor surplus to cut the wages of *peones* from 1.5 to 1 real/day. On the other hand, on the southern Michoacán sugar hacienda of Puruarán in early 1830's, *peones* earned 2.4 reales/ day (AHMM, 1831–34, records of the Hacienda of Puruarán. Wages specified in the "Estado Mensual de Frutos" for 1832). Still, sugar haciendas, generally located in more sparsely populated districts, seem always to have paid higher wages than cereal haciendas, so this case should not invalidate the argument that wages had fallen back to colonial levels by the early 1830's.

37. AHPJ, 1857, Primero Civil, legajo 1, "Cuenta de partición y división de los bienes pertenecientes a la Testamentaria de D. Antonio Chávez"; AHMM, Año de 1855, "Expediente instruido a instancia de D. Estevan García, alvacea del finado D. Antonio Chávez."

38. ANM, Birbiesca, 1812, 3 Nov.; Birbiesca, 1813, 10 Mar. and 9 Apr.

39. Interest rates were reportedly as high as 12 to 40 percent. The question is difficult, because after independence there remained legal impediments to charging rates above 6 percent, so that loan documents may conceal the true rate of interest, probably most often by overstating the amount that the borrower actually received.

40. ANM, Aguilar, 1831, 22 Sept.; AHMM, 1831–34, records of the Hacienda de Puruarán.

41. Tutino (1975: 511) notes the same phenomenon for the Chalco region, where a small number of grain merchants and bakers financed Chalco estate agriculture in the 1820's and 1830's, depriving the owners of the traditional means of exploiting precarious Mexican agriculture: holding produce off the market until prices were favorable.

42. AHMM, 1831–34, records of the Hacienda de Puruarán.

43. For cases in which hacendados shouldered half the costs of production, see AHCP, legajo 95-D, notary register for 1856, undated document following entry for 20 Nov. 1856, "Cuenta de cargo presentada por el alvacea de D. Joaquin de Río, y corre desde 1 febrero 1852 hasta la fecha 1 agosto 1856"; AHMM, 1856, "Sobre facción de inventario . . . D. Bacilio Páramo."

44. Bancroft Library, *Libro de Consultas [del Convento de Santa Catarina de Pátzcuaro, 1808–1848]*, f. 62, 15 Jan. 1831.

45. AHMCR, Diezmos, Varios, legajo 23, "Cuenta . . . del Diezmatorio de Zinapécuaro . . . 1819[–33]"; AHMCR, Diezmos, legajo 877, "Diezmos de Valladolid."

46. AHMCR, Diezmos, legajo 887, Apatzingán, 1835–63, "Cuentas que presentó el B. D. Manuel B. Gutiérrez por los efectos que recibió de la restitución de D. Antonio Sierra . . . 1847, 48, 49."

47. For the assumption that sharecropping was chiefly in maize, see Brading 1978: 12; Meyer 1984: 33. For other examples in which a hacienda administrator was also a sharecropper with the hacienda, see Bazant 1973: 333; AHMCR Diezmos, Varios, legajo 8, "Manifestación de D. Luis Delgado" in "Copias de manifestaciones presentadas al Administrador de Diezmos de Maravatío, por lo causado en los años de 1819 al 1822"; for the statement that irrigated lands were given out to sharecroppers, see AHMM, 1828, "Cuenta que presenta el Depositario Ciudadano Sergio Velasco de la parte embargada en la Hacienda del Rincón por el tiempo que ha corrido desde 12 de septiembre de 1827 hasta 18 de junio de 1828."

48. Síndico 1985: 20.

49. The best studies of sharecropping in nineteenth-century Mexico are by Miller 1984, 1990. But these articles, despite their titles, do not really cover the period before the Reform.

50. Wiemers 1985: 545–56.

51. The situation was evidently quite different in Mexico City, where Tutino (1975: 512) finds that "a merchant-landowner dichotomy, never an absolute division in Mexico, more nearly describes the Mexico City oligarchy after independence [than during the colonial period]." The reason for the difference between the two regions, apparently, is that the foreign domination of mercantile activities in Mexico City inhibited the convenient marriages between women from the landed elite and merchants that had characterized the colonial period both in Mexico City and in Michoacán and that continued to characterize Michoacán, where virtually all merchants were creoles.

52. ANM, José Maria Aguilar, 1825, 8 July; Valdovinos, 1841, 27 Oct.

53. ANM, Rincón, 1841, 6 Dec.; Rincón, 1842, 26 Sept.

54. ANM, Iturbide, 1831, 2 Dec.

55. ANM, García, 1851, 26 Feb. and 6 Mar.

56. The average capital investment, where data are available, was 23,410 pesos (12 cases); the average duration of the association (18 cases) was 5.5 years.

57. Given a rent of 5 percent of the value of the estate, as was customary. ANM, García, 1846, 28 Aug.; Salomo, 1850, 22 Aug.

58. AHMCR, Diezmos, legajo 877, "Diezmos de Valladolid"; AHMCR, Diez-

mos, Varios, legajo 23, "Cuenta . . . del Diezmatorio de Zinapécuaro . . . 1819 [-33]"; Calderón de la Barca 1966: 562. On the hacienda of San Bartolomé during the late colonial period, chile made up less than 2 percent of the average total value of production (37,000 pesos). Most other late colonial haciendas produced no chile at all, or very small amounts. In the 1820's, San Bartolomé's chile production still languished, but other haciendas in the region were already beginning to depend on chile for a substantial portion of their income. On the hacienda of Queréndaro, for example, 37 percent of total sales (an average of over 15,000 pesos a year) came from chiles; on the hacienda of La Bartolilla, 23 percent (1,544 pesos) came from chiles; and it is clear that other haciendas in an intermittent fashion were beginning to experiment with chile production on the hacienda account.

    59. Heredia Correa 1984: 122, 126, 129, 139.

    60. Romero 1862: 91; AHMM, 1836, "Expediente promovido por el Sr. General D. Mariano Michelena, sobre la aprobación de la acta de la junta extrajudicial y que se llevó a efecto la transacción que tuvo con el Sr. Prior del convento de Pátzcuaro para la entrega de la Hacienda de la Parota."

    61. AHMCR, Diezmos, legajo 887, Apatzingán, 1835–63, "Cuentas que presentó el B. D. Manuel B. Gutiérrez por los efectos que recibió de la restitución de D. Antonio Sierra . . . 1847, 48, 49"; AHCP, legajo 90-F, exp. 3, "Año de 1846. Expediente de arbitraje promovido por los Sres. D. Cayetano Villavicencio . . . y D. Agustín Luna"; AHMM, 1839, "Convenio en arbitradores nombrados por los Ciudadanos Fernando Román y Agustín Elorza, para decidir los diferencias que les ocurrieron en la companía que celebraron para el giro de la Hacienda de la Huerta propria del primero."

    62. Brading (1978: 202) says that one effect of the depression can be established beyond debate: the breakup of haciendas. He cites Chevalier and Bazant for the near north, his own examples for León and Pénjamo and the uplands of Jalisco and Michoacán. The example of the uplands of Jalisco and Michoacán is not strong, only consisting of one case of hacienda breakup. It does not seem to me that the issue is closed; instead, historians should be on the lookout for the regional variations that are so characteristic of Mexican history.

    63. AHPJ, 1847, Primera Civil, legajo I, "Común de indígenas del Pueblo de Indaparapeo contra la Hacienda de Naranjos"; AHPJ, 1839, Primera Civil, legajo I, "Lic. Clemente Munguía como apoderado de varios indígenas vecinos de Tarímbaro contra Ventura González [sobre despojo del potrero de San Francisco]"; AHPJ, 1839, Primera Civil, legajo I, "José Maria Ibarrola, arrendatario de la Hacienda de Coapa y como apoderado de la Sagrada Mitra contra el común de indígenas del pueblo de Jesús Huiramba"; AHPJ, 1839, Primera Civil, legajo I, "Indígenas del Pueblo de Santa Catarina Morelia sobre posesión de un terreno contra D. Mariano Mota como encargado de las rentas de los propios y arbitrios de Morelia"; AHPJ, 1845, Primera Civil, legajo I, "Promovido por D. Ventura Ortiz de Ayala sobre despojo de tierras, contra el común de indígenas del pueblo de Jesús del Monte"; AHPJ, 1848, Primera Civil, legajo I, no title, "Comunidad de Zaragoza [La Piedad] contra Lic. D. Pedro García por despojo de tierras"; AHPJ, 1848, Primera Civil, legajo I, "Común de indigenas de San Salvador Atecuario sobre apeo y

deslinde de sus tierras"; AHPJ, 1850, Primera Civil, legajo I, "Civil Ordinario promovido por . . . los Sres. Ponce de Ayimbo contra el común de indígenas del pueblo de Capula sobre propiedad de tierras"; AHPJ, 1853, Primera Civil, legajo I, "Yndígenas de Tacámbaro contra el Prior del Convento de agustinos;" AHPJ, 1855, Primera Civil, legajo I, "D. Antonio Homobono Cortes, contra el común de Yndígenas de Yndaparapeo, sobre perjuicios por haber impedido el trasporte de maderas"; AHPJ, 1856, Primera Civil, legajo I, "Común de Indígenas de Cuitzeo contra el convento de agustinos de Cuitzeo"; AHPJ, 1856, Primera Civil, legajo I, "Sres. Rubio y Dranes, condueños de los Montes de los Azufres y cuyo juicio se sigue con los Yndígenas de Gerahuaro."

64. Raso (1848: 42) observes that "en las lamas solo deben tirarse cuatro tercios de cebada en una fanega de tierra, pero algunos labradores siembran de cinco a diez."

65. Raso (1848: 39) states that in Querétaro the haciendas and their tenants used 8,000 wooden plows each year.

66. It is worthy of note, however, that outside of Michoacán Tutino has found evidence of glimmerings of interest in use of new techniques and technologies (manure, selection of seeds for high yields, artisian wells and other elaborate hydraulic systems) in the period before the Reform, and Bazant cities an interesting case in which a hacendado explained why he had decided to pay his workers wholly in *plata* (silver) and not half in cash and half in scrip good only at the hacienda store, as on other haciendas; although profits from the store were reduced, "no solo abunda la gente para las operaciones, sino que se ha hecho una baja en el precio del trabajo." Tutino 1988: 108–10; Bazant 1979: 384.

67. Bazant, Katz, and others have suggested that permanent residents of haciendas, even sharecroppers and tenants, saw themselves as occupying a privileged position within the rural socioeconomic structure and were thus less likely to rebel than those outside of the permanent hacienda population. See Bazant 1973; Katz 1974. Tutino (1986) amends this view slightly, suggesting that, under the right conditions, both dependence (lack of autonomy) and insecurity (lack of permanent role to play on the hacienda) might lead peasants to rebel.

References

PRIMARY SOURCES

AGN. Archivo General de la Nación. Mexico City.
AHCE. Archivo Histórico del Congreso del Estado.
AHCP. Archivo Histórico de la Ciudad de Pátzcuaro. Pátzcuaro, Michoacan.
ANM. Archivo de Notarías de Morelia. Morelia, Michoacan.
AHMCR. Archivo Histórico Manuel Castañeda Ramírez (Casa de Morelos). Morelia, Michoacan.
AHMM. Archivo Histórico Municipal de Morelia. Morelia, Michoacan.

AHPJ. Archivo Histórico del Poder Judicial. Mexico City.
Bancroft Library, manuscript collection. University of California, Berkeley.

SECONDARY SOURCES

Barrett, Ward. 1970. *The Sugar Hacienda of the Marqueses del Valle*. Minneapolis, Minn.

Bazant, Jan. 1973. "Peones, arrendatarios y aparceros en México, 1851–53." *Historia Mexicana* 23, no. 2 (Oct.–Dec.): 330–57.

———. 1975. *Cinco haciendas mexicanas. Tres siglos de vida rural en San Luis Potosí (1600–1910)*. Mexico City.

———. 1977. "Landlord, laborer, and tenant in San Luis Potosí, northern Mexico, 1822–1910." In Kenneth Duncan and Ian Rutledge, eds., *Land and Labour in Latin America*, pp. 59–82. Cambridge, Eng.

———. 1979. "El trabajo y los trabajadores en la Hacienda de Atlacomulco." In Elsa Cecilia Frost, Michael C. Meyer, and Josefina Zoraida Vásquez, eds., *El trabajo y los trabajadores en la historia de México*, pp. 378–90. Mexico City.

Boyer, Richard. 1977. "Mexico in the Seventeenth Century: Transition of a Colonial Society." *Hispanic American Historical Review* 57, no. 3: 455–78.

Brachet, Viviane. 1976. *La población de los estados mexicanos (1824–1895)*. Mexico City.

Brading, David A. 1971. *Miners and Merchants in Bourbon Mexico, 1763–1810*. Cambridge, Eng.

———. 1977. "Hacienda profits and tenant farming in the Mexican Bajío, 1700–1860." In Kenneth Duncan and Ian Rutledge, eds., *Land and Labour in Latin America*, pp. 23–58. Cambridge, Eng.

———. 1978. *Haciendas and Ranchos in the Mexican Bajío: León, 1700–1860*. Cambridge, Eng.

Brading, David A., John Coatsworth, and Hector Lindo-Fuentes. 1989. "Comments on 'The Economic Cycle in Bourbon Central Mexico: A Critique of the *Recaudación del diezmo líquido en pesos*,' by Ouweneel and Bijleveld." *Hispanic American Historical Review* no. 3: 531–49.

Calderón de la Barca, Frances Erskine. 1966. *Life in Mexico: The Letters of Fanny Calderón de la Barca*. Howard T. Fisher and Marion Hall Fisher, eds. New York.

Chowning, Margaret. 1989. "The *Consolidación de Vales Reales* in the Bishopric of Michoacán." *Hispanic American Historical Review* 69, no. 3: 451–78.

———. 1992. "The Contours of the Post-1810 Depression in Mexico: A Reappraisal from a Regional Perspective." *Latin American Research Review* 27, no. 2: 119–50.

Coatsworth, John. 1978. "Obstacles to Economic Growth in Nineteenth-Century Mexico." *The American Historical Review* 83, no. 1 (Feb.): 80–100.

———. 1990. *Los orígenes del atraso: Nueve ensayos de historia económica de México en los siglos XVIII y XIX*. Mexico City.

Gamboa Ramírez, Ricardo. 1988. "Campo y ciudad en México." In Enrique Semo, ed., *Historia de la cuestión agraria mexicana*, vol. 1. Mexico City.

García de León, Antonio. 1988. "Las grandes tendencias de la producción agraria." In Enrique Semo, ed., *Historia de la cuestión agraria mexicana*, vol. 1. Mexico City.

González y González, Luis. 1974. *San José de Gracia: Mexican Village in Transition*. Austin, Tex.

———. 1984. *Zamora*. Zamora, Michoacán.

Harris, Charles H. 1975. *A Mexican Family Empire. The Latifundio of the Sánchez Navarros, 1765–1867*. Austin, Tex.

Heredia Correa, Roberto. 1984. "Zamora y su distrito en 1844." *Relaciones* [*del Colegio de Michoacán*] 20: 121–40.

Hoberman, Louisa Schell. 1991. *Mexico's Merchant Elite, 1590–1660*. Durham, N.C.

Humboldt, Alexander von. 1966. *Ensayo político sobre el reino de la Nueva Espana*. Mexico City.

Katz, Friedrich. 1974. "Labor Conditions on Haciendas in Porfirian Mexico: Some Trends and Tendencies." *Hispanic American Historical Review* 54, no. 1: 30–47.

Konrad, Herman W. 1980. *A Jesuit Hacienda in Colonial Mexico: Santa Lucia, 1576–1767*. Stanford.

Meyer, Jean. 1984. *Esperando a Lozada*. Zamora, Michoacán.

Miller, Simon. 1984. "The Mexican Hacienda between the Insurgency and the Revolution: Maize Production and Commercial Triumph on the *Temporal*." *Journal of Latin American Studies* 15, no. 2: 309–35.

———. 1990. "Mexican Junkers and Capitalist Haciendas, 1810–1910: The Arable Estate and the Transition to Capitalism between the Insurgency and the Revolution." *Journal of Latin American Studies* 22, no. 2: 229–63.

Morin, Claude. 1979. *Michoacán el la Nueva Espana del siglo XVIII: crecimiento y desigualdad en una economía colonial*. Mexico City.

Ouweneel, Arij, and Catrien C. J. H. Bijleveld. 1989. "The Economic Cycle in Bourbon Central Mexico: A Critique of the *Recaudación del diezmo líquido en pesos*." *Hispanic American Historical Review* 69, no. 3: 479–530.

Pérez Hernández, José María. 1862. *Estadística de la república mexicana*. Guadalajara.

Piquero, Ignacio. 1861. *Apuntes para la corografía y la estadística del Estado de Michoacán* [*en 1849*]. In *Boletín de la Sociedad Mexicana de Geografía y Estadística*, no. 1. Mexico City.

Raso, Jose Antonio del. 1848. *Notas estadísticas del departamento de Querétaro*. Mexico City.

Reyes García, Cayetano, et al. 1983. *Protocolos notariales del Distrito de Zamora, 1842–1854*. Zamora, Michoacán.

Romero, Jose Guadalupe. 1862. *Noticias para formar la estadística del Obispado de Michocán*. In *Boletín de la Sociedad Mexicana de Goegrafía y Estadística*, no. 9. Mexico City.

Semo, Enrique. 1988. "Hacendados, campesinos y rancheros." In Enrique Semo, ed., *Historia de la cuestión agraria mexicana*, vol. 1. Mexico City.

Síndico, Domenico. 1985. "Azúcar y burguesía: Morelos en el siglo XIX." In Mario Cerruti, ed., *El siglo XIX en México: cinco procesos regionales: Morelos, Monterrey, Yucatán, Jalisco y Puebla*. Mexico City.

Tutino, John. 1975. "Hacienda Social Relations in Mexico: The Chalco Region in the Era of Independence." *Hispanic American Historical Review* 55, no. 3: 496–528.

———. 1983. "Power, Class and Family: Men and Women in the Mexican Elite, 1750–1810." *The Americas* 39, no. 3: 359–81.

———. 1986. *From Insurrection to Revolution: Social Bases of Agrarian Violence, 1750–1940*. Princeton.

———. 1988. "Agrarian Social Change and Peasant Rebellion in Nineteenth-Century Mexico: The Example of Chalco." In Friedrich Katz, ed., *Riot, Rebellion and Revolution: Rural Social Conflict in Mexico*. Princeton.

Van Young, Eric. 1981. *Hacienda and Market in Eighteenth-Century Mexico: The Rural Economy of the Guadalajara Region, 1675–1820*. Berkeley.

———. 1986. "Millenium on the Northern Marches: The Mad Messiah of Durango and Popular Rebellion in Mexico, 1800–1815." *Comparative Studies in Society and History* 28, no. 3 (July): 385–413.

Voss, Stuart F. 1982. *On the Periphery of Nineteenth-Century Mexico: Sonora and Sinaloa, 1810–1877*. Tucson, Ariz.

Wiemers, Eugene L. 1985. "Agriculture and Credit in Nineteenth-Century Mexico: Orizaba and Córdoba, 1822–71." *Hispanic American Historical Review* 65, no. 3: 519–46.

CHAPTER 8

Mexican National Income in the Era of Independence, 1800–40

RICHARD J. SALVUCCI

Did the lingering effects of Mexican independence slow Mexico's economic growth in the early nineteenth century? Our findings suggest that although independence imposed real costs on the Mexican economy it was by no means the only impediment to growth. Historians of eighteenth-century Mexico have generally argued that a Bourbon climacteric existed; growth slowed sharply in the century's final decades. In other words, growth first slowed before independence. The economic costs of independence were imposed on what was already a weakening economy.

What were the costs of independence, and why did they lead to prolonged stagnation? Our argument focuses on silver mining and its impact on liquidity. In essence, the collapse of silver production during the fighting of the 1810's explains why the economy stopped growing. After independence, silver exports, which had been growing since the 1780's, were driven up in the face of a growing demand for imports, the decline in output notwithstanding. Yet the terms of trade for silver were also lower in the 1820's than subsequently. In other words, after independence Mexico produced less silver, exported relatively more products and materials, but gained relatively less. Persistent trade deficits and continuing restrictions on the supply of domestic credit were the rule. Slower growth in the early nineteenth century was the result.

The historical consequences of Mexico's slow growth are clear. In falling behind other, more rapidly growing economies, Mexico lost ground that it was later unable to recover. Among historians of national income, the Mexican pattern is a familiar one. A gap opened between income levels in what would become the developed countries and the Third World between 1800 and 1860. This gap has proved difficult for Mexico, and for other countries, such as Cuba, to close.[1] The years following independence were a critical juncture in Mexico's long-term economic history.

The validity of this hypothesis depends on how reliable existing estimates of Mexican gross domestic product (GDP) are, yet few scholars have attempted to review and revise these estimates. Angus Maddison's recent monograph on national income growth yields no GDP figures for Latin America (Argentina, Brazil, Chile, and Mexico) before 1900. Lloyd Reynolds's comprehensive survey of the Third World ventures little on the subject before 1950.[2] The statistical Dark Ages end only with the twentieth century.

As a result, we first review estimates of Mexican national income between 1800 and 1840. In so doing, we find that the standard statistic for 1800, while plausible, has largely escaped scrutiny since 1817. The current estimate for the mid-1840's is also reasonable, but somewhat more tentative. Mexicans in the 1840's perceived no sustained decline. Some thought that GDP had grown since 1810, although only a little. Still, as our knowledge of the early nineteenth century improves, we are likely to revise our estimate of Mexico's GDP substantially.

Estimates of National Income: Quirós, His Contemporaries and Successors

We must first survey the existing estimates of Mexican national income around 1800. These estimates appear in Table 8.1. There are five variants, only two of which are truly independent. For convenience, we call them (1) the TePaske estimate, (2) the Coatsworth estimate, (3) the Quirós estimate, (4) the Quirós-Rosenzweig estimate, and (5) The Humboldt-Aubrey estimate. In addition, we employ Paul Bairoch's general rule (i.e.,

TABLE 8.1

Estimates of Mexico's Late Colonial National Product

Source	Date	Millions of pesos
TePaske	1806	251
Coatsworth	1800	240
Quirós	1817	228
Quirós-Rosenzweig	1810	190
Humboldt-Aubrey	1803	120–140
Bairoch-rule method	n.a.	241

SOURCES: see text.
NOTE: We have converted Coatsworth's estimate into current dollars.

per capita income is 200 times the daily wage) for estimating nominal GDP on the basis of the daily wage. In Table 8.1, this result is labeled the "Bairoch-rule method."[3] Angus Maddison has also estimated Mexican GDP around 1800 using the Humboldt-Aubrey estimate that Clark Reynolds employed.[4]

What are the sources of these estimates?

John TePaske's estimate is the largest. It embodies two steps. First, TePaske employs data on the taxation of legally registered silver to deduce silver production. Second, following John Coatsworth's lead, TePaske assumes that mining (of which silver mining constituted the lion's share) comprised 8 percent of national product. TePaske's result then follows directly.

There are two possible objections to the procedure. David Brading cautions that the treasury accounts on which TePaske's calculation of silver production rests often reflect carryovers of loans and debts from year to year.[5] TePaske contends that the reworked accounts on which he bases his estimate exclude carryovers and transfer income. Some silver evaded registration, a problem TePaske recognizes. A nineteenth-century analysis suggested that 20 percent of Mexican silver was neither registered nor minted.[6] In other words, the fiscal accounts present some unavoidable difficulties. TePaske's estimate may have a systematic bias whose direction is not immediately apparent.

John Coatsworth's estimates of national income are most familiar to historians. I have converted Coatsworth's calculation to U.S. dollars of 1800 and then to pesos using a market exchange rate of $1 = 1 peso. Coatsworth's basis for estimating income in 1800 was not specified in his original article. In a later essay, Coatsworth gives its source as José María Quirós's famous essay of 1817, "Idea de la Riqueza . . . de Nueva España."[7] Since Coatsworth's calculations are based on Quirós's, we pass on to Quirós.

José María Quirós, who was secretary of the *consulado* of Veracruz, is, in large part, the source of our "idea" of New Spain's national income at the turn of the century. Our estimate of New Spain's national product around 1800 is based on Quirós's estimate of 1817, and has hardly been updated. Quirós developed series that measured "typical" spending on agricultural and industrial goods. Quirós's efforts suffer from a number of defects, most then unavoidable. Much of his analysis is cast in terms of expenditure, although his discussion of mining switches abruptly to production. Moreover, as Fernando Rosenzweig observed in 1963, Quirós double counted. He included both raw materials and final product in his totals. For example, Quirós included both raw cotton (731,250 pesos) and finished cottons (3,000,000 pesos) in his final totals, rather than deducting input costs from final product to derive value added (i.e., 2,268,750 pesos rather than 3,731,250 pesos). Rosenzweig himself did not realize that Quirós made no explicit allowance for governmental purchases of goods and services. Rosenzweig does notice that Quirós made no allowance for private investment such as in housing or irrigation. These could not have represented trivial sums. Quirós did include all allowances for expenditure on bricks, lime, timbers, and gunpowder, all of which could have represented governmental spending or been used in private investment. Yet even Quirós recognized that his computations were fallible. He suggested that his results could have been a third higher.[8]

Fernando Rosenzweig's reading of Quirós is well known. For the most part, Rosenzweig does not stray far from Quirós's text. He sometimes supplements it with references to Humboldt or Viceroy Revillagigedo the younger. Rosenzweig's primary purpose was to correct Quirós's computations for value added. Rosenzweig is sketchy about his adjustments. Equally puzzling is his failure to deduct certain inputs—wheat, eggs, gunpowder, mules, and burros, for instance—from industry as raw materials. Yet Rosenzweig was observant. He realized that his computation of sectoral shares overestimated manufactures and underestimated agriculture. His results could yield the misleading impression that New Spain had reached a level of development roughly comparable to, say, mainland China in the mid-1960's.[9]

Perhaps more important, Rosenzweig argued that Humboldt was an unreliable guide to agricultural production. Rosenzweig noticed a huge disparity in the value of agricultural production reported by Quirós and Humboldt. Humboldt's figure is 29 million pesos; Quirós reports nearly 140 million pesos. Even adjusting for double counting, Rosenzweig could reduce Quirós's totals to no less than 90 million pesos. The difference is no less than 60 million pesos. How could the two authors have calculated so differently?

Rosenzweig suggested that Humboldt (by Humboldt's own acknowledgment) relied on the tithe as an indicator of production. Yet the tithe is an imperfect indicator of agricultural production. For example, Indians were never required to tithe on the maize they grew.[10] Such omissions are a significant source of error.

Humboldt put the average annual consumption of maize in New Spain at roughly 133 kilograms per person, or some 3 *fanegas* (a *funega* equals 3.6 hectares). For a population of 6 million inhabitants, this implies a domestic demand of 18 million *fanegas*. Humboldt put the average price of maize at a peso a *fanega*, so the market value of maize should have been 18 million pesos, a total that Rosenzweig (and Quirós) essentially accept.[11] Yet, as Rosenzweig suggests, it is inconceivable that the balance of Mexico's agricultural production could have been no more than 11 million pesos (29 million total − 18 million for maize = 11 for everything else). Indeed, if wheat accounted for another 5 million pesos, the remainder shrinks to about 5 or 6 million pesos. As Rosenzweig put it, "It is not possible that the rest . . . could have amounted to only five million pesos a year."[12] The difference between the Quirós-Rosenzweig and Humboldt-Aubrey estimates is attributable almost entirely to the 60 million pesos of agricultural production that Humboldt omitted. As it stands, then, the Humboldt-Aubrey estimate may be discarded as far too low. Estimates based on it, such as Angus Maddison's of 1983, must also be considered too low.[13]

We can summarize this discussion. There are, in essence, two estimates of Mexican national product around 1800. One of these estimates, first offered by José María Quirós in 1817, is the basis of the modern estimates of John Coatsworth, Fernando Rosenzweig, and John TePaske. The average of these estimates is 227 million pesos; their standard deviation is 23 million pesos. Rosenzweig's adjustment of Quirós's 1817 estimate is slightly more than one standard deviation lower than the mean, but, statistically, all these estimates are about equal, which is what one would expect, given their common source. The Humboldt-Aubrey estimate is much lower but can be reconciled with the Quirós estimate. The major difference between the two is Humboldt's smaller—and undoubtedly erroneous— value for agricultural production. Even the Bairoch-rule estimate, based on nothing more than a crude rule of thumb, yields 241 million pesos, a figure within one standard deviation of the computed mean of the Quirós-based estimates. By and large, Mexican national product around 1800 fell between 205 and 250 million pesos.

A contemporary estimate of income distribution yields an intriguingly similar picture. As we indicate in Table 8.2, in 1813, Manual Abad y Queipo concluded that 20 percent of Mexico's families had an annual income of at least 300 pesos. Of the remainder, a third of all families had an income of no more than 300 pesos, and fully two-thirds received no more than 61 pesos a year. To be sure, Abad y Queipo put Mexico's population at 4.5 million, which is too low. If we substitute Humboldt's 5.8 million, the total income implied by this distribution is not quite 200 million pesos, assuming a conventional family size of five.[14] This total conforms Quirós's estimate.

TABLE 8.2

Mexico's Late Colonial Income
according to Abad y Queipo

Number of families	Income group (pesos)	Total (pesos)
232,000	>300	69,600,000
306,240	62–300	91,872,000
621,760	≤61	37,927,360
TOTAL 1,160,000		199,399,360

SOURCE: Abad y Queipo 1813: 57–58.
NOTE: Abad y Queipo put New Spain's population at 4.5 million, which is plausible but considerably lower than Humboldt's 5.8 million. To be consistent, we have used Humboldt's figure rather than Abad y Queipo's in estimating the number of families, although we followed Abad y Queipo's usage in setting family size at five. The groupings were suggested to me by Rosenzweig's discussion (1989: 31–33), although Rosenzweig does not use the resulting frequency distribution as a means of computing income.

From Colony to Nation: Estimates by Alamán and His Circle

The historical evidence on national product in the early national period is thinner. Given the political circumstances of the era, the lack of contemporary estimates is not surprising, yet it would be a mistake to think that neither Quirós's nor Humboldt's estimates had no early national counterpart. They did. Indeed, there is one estimate directly linked to Quirós's. We may thus discover how contemporaries thought that national income had changed since the days of Quirós's 1817 calculations.

At first glance, the evidence is contradictory. Some anecdotal accounts suggested that the state of the economy had deteriorated between 1835 and 1837. Things, according to this view, were worse by the end of the 1830's than they had been in the waning years of the 1820's.[15]

José María Luis Mora similarly put national product in Mexico around 1836 at 137 million pesos, or far less than the total registered around 1800. On a per capita basis, Mora's estimate would be even lower than John Coatsworth's widely accepted figure for 1845. Yet it is clear that Mora could not have been correct. Mora used returns from domestic and foreign trade (the customs and excise) as a means of deducing the value of the product on which taxes were levied. Mora concluded that trade contributed 79 million pesos to national income, while domestic output contributed 58 million pesos. This is clearly absurd, for it implies that net exports drove an agricultural economy that basically produced nontradeable goods. Mora's estimate of domestic income is far too low. It assumes that the excise was levied on all goods and services produced. It was not. Sales of maize were traditionally exempt from the excise. After 1778, retail sales of less than a peso were as well. Yet maize was the nation's staple crop, and few workers earned as much as a peso per day. The effect of these omissions in estimating national consumption can well be imagined. Because consumption typically accounts for most of national product, Mora necessarily underestimated national product and overestimated the ratio of net exports to national income.[16]

Yet there are other avenues to follow to determine national product during this period. By 1842, Lucas Alamán had been appointed Director of the Dirección General de Agricultura e Industria. In his first "Memoria sobre el estado de la agricultura e industria de la Republica" in 1843, Alamán addresses the question of national income directly.[17] "Everything [induces] me to believe that the whole of agricultural production, considered in toto, is greater today than in the epoch that preceded 1810." Here Alamán explicitly compares agricultural production in 1842 to production before 1810. Mexico was an agricultural nation; if production in 1842 was larger than in 1810, national income must have been as large in 1842 as it had been earlier.

In his "Memoria sobre el estado de la agricultura e industria de la Republica en el año de 1845" (1846), Alamán returned to the same theme.[18] However much time and political factors—"including the upsets of the war of 1810"—had altered the composition and distribution of agricultural and industrial goods, "their consumption had not diminished, but rather, grown considerably." All in all, thought Alamán, agricultural production throughout the central regions of the Republic was "overabundant."

Finally, and perhaps most remarkably, we have an essay that appeared in the liberal journal *El Siglo Diez y Nueve* in April 1845.[19] Although the entire essay is interesting, its estimate of Mexican product is most relevant. After citing (and, in part, reproducing) the results of Quirós's paper of 1817, the anonymous author of the essay concludes, "The National Institute of Geography and Statistics says that, considering that the value of lands, homes, and commerce has increased a great deal since 1817, one can calculate that the production of [agriculture, industry, and mining] was in 1839 at least . . . 300,000,000 [pesos]."

In this context, then, the essay implies that income, measured against what we might call the "Quirós base-year" (i.e., around 1817) had grown by about a third in 22 years. Moreover, the population statistics the essay provides imply that per capita income had grown as well. If population in 1839 was, as the essay suggests, roughly 7 million, then per capita income, measured against an 1817 base, had grown some 4.7 percent. The context of the essay implies real per capita income had grown as well, albeit at the negligible rate of no more than 0.15 percent per year.

It is important to understand precisely how the anonymous author of "Situación financiera de México" reached his conclusions. While the author offers few clues about his sources and methods, a contemporary document resolves the mystery.[20] The Instituto de Geografía y Estadística, whose authority the anonymous author of the "Situacíon financiera" invokes, was established in 1833. It worked hand-in-glove with Lucas Alamán to compile reliable national statistics.[21] Its members knew that the precise data needed to compute "the general products of [the] soil" and the "value of each individual" (i.e., total and per capita product) were unavailable. Nevertheless, they found some evidence of growth in the late 1830's.

The Instituto had an ingenious way of estimating national product. It reasoned that national income is a stream of income produced by a nation's capital stock. As a result, if property values (i.e., the net present value of the stream of income) were rising, their increase was driven by a rise in the stream of income. Of course, this is a crude way of proceeding. Property values are affected by risk, and risk was greater after independence than before. The more slowly property values rose because of perceived risk, the greater the understatement in national income was apt to be.[22]

To construct an estimate, the Instituto examined changes in the assessed value of properties, and derived a coefficient based on their average increase. It then applied the coefficient to Quirós's estimate of late colonial product and used the product to approximate national product in 1839. For instance, four properties in the Valley of Mezquital had been assessed at 165,300 pesos in 1790, but at 275,600 pesos in 1829, for an increase of 66 percent. The Instituto presumably made numerous such calculations, for it termed the Mezquital example simply one of many. The resulting estimate, 300 million pesos, was considered a minimum.

Whether or not this estimate is strictly correct (it most assuredly is not) is not the point. What is striking from a historical standpoint is the changed tone of the discussion. In the 1820's and early 1830's, as Minister of Home and Foreign Relations, Lucas Alamán reported only that the statistics available to him were too poor to support analysis, or that there had been "considerable advances" in all branches of agriculture.[23] By the early 1840's, his tone was radically different. Alamán was never one to underplay the costs of Mexican independence or the losses of war that purchased it. In this context, his willingness to contemplate an advance over colonial levels of production is intriguing. Even Antonio López de Santa Anna, perhaps understandably, characterized his dictatorship in the early 1840's (1841–44) as a time of economic recovery. Political peace, no forced loans, and renewed public investment: this was San Anna's recipe for growth.[24]

From Colony to Nation: Conjectures

In short, the data on national product in early nineteenth-century Mexico are thin. Indeed, we have no useful estimates of national income at the end of the colonial period that are independent of Quirós's. The figures for the early nineteenth century are suggestive, but inconclusive. In light of recent research on the late eighteenth and early nineteenth centuries, can we improve on what we have?

The answer depends on the definition of improvement. We can certainly check the calculations of Quirós and the Instituto de Geografía indirectly and establish whether their calculations are reasonable. We can also pinpoint the effects of potential errors of measurement. But we cannot measure national income precisely, particularly in the early nineteenth century. We do not have the data for doing so, the intensive archival work of a generation of historians of Mexico notwithstanding.

Indeed, the data preclude estimating national product in the way that cliometricians find theoretically acceptable. The best illustration is Paul David's seminal paper on the growth of national product in the United States before 1840.[25] David's work has been influential, not to say definitive. But it requires data on labor force participation and industrial distribution that we do not have for Mexico—certainly not for the nineteenth century. Nor do we have proxies, even poor ones, that permit similar calculations, particularly decade by decade. To replicate David's work is a worthy goal, but we are a long way from doing it. Must we then remain agnostic about the size of Mexican product and about the many issues that depend on it?

More promising, if less theoretically satisfying, is Raymond Goldsmith's approach. It is worth explaining Goldsmith's approach in some detail, its strengths as well as its shortcomings. By weighing benefits and costs, we can better decide how much faith to put in the results.

Goldsmith's method has been described in a number of publications.[26] As Goldsmith saw it, estimating national income was largely a matter of estimating the income or expenditure of an average person or household, then deriving national totals by multiplying income or expenditure by the number of people or households in the nation. This is a crude procedure, but it is supported by a simple principle. National product can be measured in three ways: by expenditure, by production, or by income. If measured correctly, national income, product, and expenditure must be equal. Their equality is a simple accounting identity.

The appeal of Goldsmith's method is twofold. First, he depends less on theory than on intuition, and the results of a Goldsmith-style exercise are apt to be clearer to working historians than David's approach. The second consideration is pragmatic. The results of recent archival work are well suited to Goldsmith-style estimate, but much less so for a David-style estimate. Indeed, there is no way of using the data we have in David's framework without resorting to outright guessing. Whatever precision David's method promises is inevitably lost.

However, there are costs to using Goldsmith's approach. Although Goldsmith did not admit it, he used labor income as a proxy for net national income. But net national income includes both labor income (wages and salaries) and property income (rents, interest, and profits). He then used net national income as a proxy for gross national product as market prices, assuming that depreciation and indirect taxes could be neglected. Yet it is clearly risky to use labor income as a proxy for national income. In Britain, N. F. R. Crafts estimates that the share of labor income in national product was about 50 percent between 1700 and 1860. The explicit share of wages in French national income was somewhat smaller, although less so when mixed incomes are considered.[27] Clearly, labor income and national income are hardly the same thing.

With these caveats in mind, let us construct a Goldsmith-style estimate of Mexican national income around 1800.[28] We can start with expenditure. Michael Scardaville estimates that per capita subsistence income in Mexico City at the end of the eighteenth century was 34 pesos per year.[29] Of course, the cost of living in Mexico City was considerably higher than elsewhere in the colony. In general, cities of more than 10,000 persons accounted for little more than 6 percent of the population of New Spain.[30] If we base our constructed estimate on urban expenditure, it must overestimate rural expenditure. The result is an upper-bound estimate of national expenditure.

Humboldt put Mexico's population at 5.8 million persons, which implies that annual consumer expenditure was 197 million pesos (34 pesos/person/year × 5.8 million persons). We cannot estimate investment, but instead we follow Raymond Goldsmith in raising consumption by 10 percent to account for investment and government expenditure. This is a reasonable and accepted procedure.[31] National income is therefore 217 million pesos (197 + (0.1) 197).

To estimate national product by income, we follow Eric van Young. Van Young assumes that rural workers typically earned five pesos per month, while urban workers earned six.[32] If 6 percent of the population lived in cities, then Mexico's urban population was 348,000 persons [(0.06)5.8 million]. The remainder, 5,452,000 persons (5,800,000−348,000), were therefore rural.

To estimate the size of the labor force, we must also establish the labor force participation rate. People above the age of fifteen typically worked, although the employment of younger children was hardly unknown. In the 1790's, 40 percent of the population was under 15 years of age. If 10 percent of this group worked, the labor force participation rate was 64 percent of the population (i.e., 60 + (0.1)40).[33] Once we know the labor force participation rate, we can estimate the size of the labor force. If we multiply the size of the labor force by a typical annual wage rate, we have national product as measured by income.

If the urban population was 348,000 persons, the urban labor force was 222,720 persons [(0.64)348,000]. Assuming that urban workers earned an average of six pesos per month, or 72 pesos per year, urban income was 16,035,840 pesos yearly [222,720 persons × (72 pesos/person)/year]. If the rural population was 5,452,000 persons, then the rural labor force was 3,489,280 persons. Assuming that rural workers earned an average of five pesos per month, or 60 pesos per year, rural income was 209,356,800 pesos [3,489,280 persons × (60 pesos/person)/year]. At this rate, total income was about 225 million pesos per year (209 + 16). Our Goldsmith-style estimates thus far, by expenditure and income, respectively, are 217 and 225 million pesos. The average estimate based on Quirós's calculations were 227 million pesos.

On the expenditure side, using budget data from Mexico City clearly overestimates total expenditure. Rural families constructed their own shelters, raised their own food, received it from haciendas, or purchased it from haciendas at farmgate prices that were far lower than urban retail prices.[34] On the income side, patterns of work were extremely irregular, both in the city and the countryside. Simply multiplying the average daily wage by 24 days per month is apt to overestimate earned income considerably. In other words, the Goldsmith-style estimates are upper-bound estimates of labor income. Yet they are the only independent estimates of Mexican national income around 1800 that we have, and they point more in the direction of Quirós's estimate than Humboldt's.

Moreover, Querós evidently believed his estimate was correct. He made no subsequent effort to revise it, although he certainly had the opportunity to do so, even after independence.

In 1821, the *consulado* of Veracruz published a series of statistics on silver and merchandise flows through the port since 1796. One series, "Estado ó Balanza General del comercio . . . desde el [año] de 1796," was reproduced by Miguel Lerdo de Tejada in his history of Mexican foreign trade, *Comercio exterior de México*.[35] The *balanzas* normally carried explanatory notes, yet for some reason Lerdo did not include the note that appeared with this one in *Comercio exterior*.

Nevertheless, explanatory notes written by Quirós once existed. The British consul general Charles T. O'Gorman had a translation of them prepared for inclusion with the original table in his correspondence.[36] In note 3, Quirós observed that the average consumption of domestic agricultural produce and manufactures in New Spain was "32 3/8 [pesos]" per person, while the consumption of imports was "1 1/2 [pesos] for each individual." In other words, per capita consumption was 33.88 pesos. Quirós used a population of 6 million, which implies total consumption of 203,280,000 pesos. If, as before, we add 10 percent of consumption to account for government spending and investment, we reach national income of 223,608,000 pesos measured by expenditure.

This sum is nearly the same as Quirós's earlier estimate of national income. Indeed, if we take the sum of agricultural and industrial production from Quirós's "Idea de la riqueza . . . de Nueva España" and divide it by 6 million people, we find the source of Quirós's 1821 calculation of domestic consumption (i.e., (133,852,625 + 61,011,818)/6,000,000 = 32.47).

Obviously, Quirós did not "recalculate" per capita consumption in 1821, yet he clearly had no qualms about using his prewar figures to describe the size of the economy in 1821. Quirós plainly regarded his figures as reasonable estimates of typical expenditure and consumption. We may regard them in the same light—as orders of magnitude.

For the 1830's and 1840's, it is far more difficult to produce independent estimates of national income. The data that will enable us to make comparisons with the late colonial period are not yet available. We do have some estimates of a family budget for Mexico City, but they must be used cautiously. Historians have only recently turned their attention to the early nineteenth century, and these estimates may not be good ones.

In 1841, average consumer expenditure per person in Mexico City was said to be 1.5 reales per day, or 68 pesos per year.[37] If we multiply this sum by a national population of 7 million, total expenditure at Mexico City prices would have been 476 million pesos. We may again add 10 percent to account for government spending and private investment. The result is 524 million pesos. This seems very high, even allowing for substantial differences in the cost of living between urban and rural areas.

In fact, a total product of 524 million pesos reflects a rapidly rising price level. The cost-of-living data were inflated by the introduction of copper coinage by the state governments in the mid-1820's and by the national government in 1829. This copper coinage depreciated rapidly; its equivalent in silver was no more than 50 percent.[38] Converting from copper to silver yields 262 million pesos.

This constructed estimate is lower than the 300 million peso figure that the Instituto Nacional de Geografía e Estadística supplied for 1839, but only somewhat. On a per capita basis, the estimate amounts to roughly 37 pesos. This is essentially equal to the per capita income of the late colonial period that work based on Quirós's calculations implies (i.e., 227/6 = 37.8 pesos). By this standard, there had been no growth between 1800 and 1839.[39] On the face of it, this finding appears to lend strong support to John Coatsworth's "decline of the Mexican economy" thesis.

Yet contemporaries saw things somewhat differently. Around 1840, Lucas Alamán and his circle were arguing that national income was growing and that real per capita income was well over 4 percent larger than it had been in 1817. Recent historiography supports Alamán's view. Based on a review of notarial records in Michoacán, Margaret Chowning finds that, after 1820, the volume of loans, the level of rural rents, and the average value of urban and rural property sales all turned sharply upward, at least through 1835. Juan Carlos Garavaglia and Juan Carlos Grosso allude to the beginnings of an economic revival of the agrarian economy of the Tepeaca region around 1840. Mexico's increasingly restrictive commercial policy provided scope for a modest industrial expansion after 1837 as well.[40]

In sum, we now have three versions of what happened to per capita product in the early nineteenth century. One version, John Coatsworth's, argues that per capita product fell between 1800 and 1845. A second, based on the limited evidence presented here, finds virtually no growth in per capita product between 1800 and 1840. A third, supported by Lucas Alamán and several modern historians, points to stronger growth around 1840 than we normally assume. Yet none of these views indicates that Mexico did more than stagnate. At worst, the economy went into a Coatsworth-style decline. At best, it grew 4 percent over 23 years, which is very little indeed.

Quirós and the Costs of the Insurgency

Most descriptions of the costs of the insurgency are vague. Only José María Quirós offered a detailed accounting of the losses,[41] but his calculations are not entirely convincing. Quirós writes that "in times of peace, internal and external circulation [i.e., national income] was 227 million pesos. But this has largely disappeared, having been reduced to a third [of its former value]." And, indeed, Quirós calculates that agricultural production had fallen to 60 million pesos per year; industrial output to 20 million pesos per year; and mining to no more than 7 million. It is inconceivable that national product could have fallen by almost 70 percent, especially when much of the population lived at the margins of subsistence. Mass starvation would have been the result, not just dearth and hunger.

It is difficult to find a well-specified indicator of general economic activity that permits a test of Quirós's analysis. The *alcabala* or sales tax might be such an indicator, although, as we argued earlier, it is a crude one at best.[42] We can compare *alcabala* collections in the years leading up to the coup against Viceroy Iturrigaray with collections down to 1817. There is no statistically significant difference in average collections before and after the insurgency broke out. During the war years (here simply defined as 1810 through 1816), only one year, 1812, was much worse than average, that is, more than a standard deviation below the mean. On the basis of this crude test, it is not possible to identify a major decline in overall production, distribution, and consumption associated with the insurgency other than in 1812.

Yet there were local sharp declines in production, particularly in areas hard hit by the outbreak of the insurgency. Production in Querétaro's woolen manufactories fell by over 75 percent between late 1810 and early 1812.[43] It is not hard to judge the impact of this collapse on demand. Quirós, who followed the lead of Querétaro's famous *corregidor*, Miguel Domínguez, believed that textiles provided a livelihood for 10,000 in Querétaro.[44] If the city's population was about 40,000, and if the participation rate was 64 percent, Querétaro's labor force was about 26,000. By that standard, textile work employed about 38 percent of the city's labor force (i.e., $10/26 = 0.38$) By 1812, unemployment in Querétaro could have approached as much as 29 percent (i.e., $0.75(0.38) = 0.29$) because of the collapse of the woolen industry alone. This makes no allowance for a multiplier effect, so that 29 percent must be a lower-bound estimate. Of course, Querétaro's woolen industry was not typical. The woolen manufactories there were used to hold imprisoned insurgents.

Quirós also estimated the overall cost of the "revolution" in income sacrificed dating from 1808 and the overthrow of Iturrigaray. His total was nearly 1.3 billion pesos between 1808 and 1817, or about 216 pesos per person. It would have taken the typical Mexican nearly six years to earn that much. The figure is much too large to be credible, and, again, there is no evidence that there was a sustained fall in production after 1808.

In other words, Quirós's account of the costs of the insurgency is not convincing. Major disruptions of production and distribution did occur, but the disruptions seem to have been transient and localized. There may have been a sharp fall in per capita product for a year or two, but nothing that lasted for as much as a decade.

This perhaps explains why Quirós's analysis of the costs of the war was rejected by some contemporaries. The peninsular press apparently reproduced the results of Quirós's analysis in late 1824, alluding to what the *Times* of London called "a manifest decline in the agriculture, manufactures, and general prosperity of Mexico since the origin, and in consequence of its revolution." Deep in the throes of an enthusiasm for investments in the new states of Mexico and Central and South America, the *Times* called the analysis one of the many "gross and monstrous falsehoods of every kind published by the Spanish government in relation to America," and concluded, "Nothing published on such authority deserves a moment's credit."[45]

Yet it would be a mistake to conclude from this discussion that the insurgency had no enduring costs. There is widespread agreement that silver production was a victim of the violence.[46] Mines abandoned because of the insurgency quickly flooded and could be rehabilitated only at great expense.[47] As a result, the annual average volume of silver production fell to about 300,000 kilograms per year (1821–41) from 435,000 kilograms per year (1781–1800). If mining accounted for about 8 percent of national income around 1800, the collapse of mining accounted for a reduction in national product of 2.7 percent (i.e., a third of 8 percent), assuming nothing else changed. The fall in mining employment alone accounted for a decline of one percentage point in national income (i.e., nearly 40 percent of its total decline, or $1/2.7 = 0.37$).

It is important to put these figures in perspective. In the most pessimistic case, John Coatsworth argues that national income fell by 3 percent between 1800 and 1845. If silver mining alone could account for a fall of 2.7 percent in national income, then the drop in silver production accounted for 90 percent of the overall decline. If incomes were stagnant, the fall in mining production typically cost every inhabitant of Mexico about a peso—or 2.5 percent of per capita income around 1840. From this stand-point, much of the poor performance of the economy between 1810 and 1840 can be attributed to problems with silver mining, and these were very much a legacy of the violent rebellion of the 1810's.

Mining and Money: A Long-Term Crisis?

The relation between mining, the supply of money, and production in Mexico was complex. Silver was Mexico's principal export, the one commodity in which it had comparative advantage. This is why silver had always accounted for the largest part of Mexican exports under Spanish rule. It would long do so in independent Mexico as well.

At the same time, silver was money. Until the late nineteenth century, specie constituted the bulk of the Mexican money supply. Indeed, Mexico remained on the silver standard until 1905. There was consequently an inevitable tension between domestic and export uses of silver. Silver that was exported could not be used to purchase domestic production. Silver retained for domestic uses could not be used to purchase imports.

There was also a tension between the long- and short-run effects of retaining or exporting silver. In the short run, exporting silver made sense, for silver financed imports or could be used to purchase such financial assets as stocks and bonds. In the long run, however, exporting silver could reduce the size of the money supply and lead to a reduction in production and employment through restrictions in the supply of credit. If silver production grew more quickly than total output, the excess, unless exported, would drive up prices. Conversely, lagging silver production and substantial exports would produce deflation, and perhaps unemployment as well.

Of course, Mexico mined silver, so mining output mattered. When silver was exported, the terms of trade for silver mattered. Because Mexico was the largest silver producer in the world at the close of the eighteenth century, the impact of Mexican exports on the international price of silver was substantial. Large Mexican exports could make the terms of trade deteriorate.

The story of silver in late colonial and early national Mexico is then necessarily complex. Its history bridges the gap between the old regime and the new. For that reason, the monetary aspects of independence were deeply affected by the violence of the insurgency but were in no sense a unique product of it. A monetary crisis had been brewing in Mexico since the 1780's. The violence of the 1810's largely exacerbated it.

A number of historians have explored what we might term the Bourbon "climacteric," particularly its monetary roots. Of these, Richard Garner, Claude Morin, and Pedro Pérez Herrero anticipate our argument most directly, although Eric Van Young, Enrique Cárdenas, and John Coatsworth have also made important contributions.

In general, Coatsworth has suggested, the later Bourbons reduced rather than promoted economic growth. His argument is by no means simple, but misallocation plays a central role in it; "the [colonial fiscal] system distorted factor markets and diverted resources to less productive use." As the grasp of the fiscal system increased, the consequences of misallocation widened. As a result, during the first half of the eighteenth century, when Mexico was loosely governed, it grew rapidly. As the Bourbon state (in the sense of fiscal machinery) expanded, growth slowed.[48]

Richard Garner has developed a similar thesis, but one with a specific monetary content. Garner finds that, by 1780, exports of specie on royal account had surpassed those on private account and that the overall growth of specie exports on royal account accelerated substantially after 1770, and again in the 1790's. Garner ascribes increasing remissions on royal account to growing Bourbon fiscal pressure. Moreover, he suggests that rising exports of silver created growing monetary stringency. In essence, tight money discouraged investment and growth.[49]

Claude Morin also discusses what he terms the growing "weight of fiscal exaction." Pointing to large increases in the *alcabala* and the tribute in Michoacán under José Gálvez, Morin draws a distinction between "fiscality" and overall growth. Morin criticizes the tendency to equate the growth of the royal fisc with "general prosperity," a caution reiterated by Pedro Pérez Herrero. Moreover, even though the Bourbons spent a part of their growing collections in Mexico, Morin estimated that they shipped 40 to 60 percent of their take abroad. Morin believes that the Bourbons did much to expropriate what would have otherwise been invested in Mexican production. The result, he believes, was monetary stringency, high effective rates of interest (or "usury," as Morin prefers), and stagnant economic growth.[50]

The arguments of Coatsworth, Garner, and Morin are largely synthesized by Pérez Herrero in his study of the eighteenth-century money supply. Pérez Herrero concludes that "the fiscal apparatus [of the crown] subjected the economy of New Spain to a drain of capital that could not be reinvested in the productive process. . . . The reform of the Royal Treasury to increase the Crown's income was undeniably successful, but it also presupposed an evident drag on the economy of the viceroyalty."[51]

The general point—widely made by historians of the late eighteenth century, with variations in emphasis, chronology, and nuance—was that the later Bourbons viewed Mexico as a source of wealth to be appropriated by the Spanish Empire. The Bourbons transferred Mexican savings by draining the colony of specie, especially after 1780. The result, in economic terms, was decreasing liquidity. As a result, growth had already slowed by 1810 when the insurgency broke out.

This argument, and particularly its concern with liquidity, is also valid for the decades immediately following independence. Indeed, it is a central link between the macroeconomic history of the colony and the Mexican state that succeeded it. A few examples may make the connection clearer.

We have already indicated that silver output fell by a third after independence, but in the years immediately following independence there was little reduction in the export of specie. Indeed, in 1825, the British consul general Charles O'Gorman concluded that total exports (legal and otherwise) were still in the neighborhood of £1.6 million per year, or roughly what they had averaged between 1796 and 1823.[52] This implies a relative increase of roughly 50 percent in the ratio of specie exports to total silver output after independence (i.e., $1/0.67 = 1.49$). British exports to Mexico in the 1820's averaged about £1.3 million per year,[53] and accounted for perhaps two-thirds of Mexico's imports. At that rate, there was a residual flow of about £300,000 (i.e., 1.5 million pesos) per year in the 1820's. This may serve a crude estimate, perhaps, of capital sent abroad. The net outward transfer of resources during the 1820's (i.e., net of inflows of British capital from loans on London and mining operations) was £200,000.[54] This is in itself not a large sum. It is less than one-half of 1 percent of Mexican product. Capital outflows alone did not destabilize the Mexican economy in the 1820's.

Yet more than capital movements affected the balance of payments. The terms of trade in the 1820's stood at 81 (1840's = 100).[55] This implies that the imports of the 1820's could have been purchased for nearly 23 percent less at the terms of trade of the 1840's. Since the import bill in the 1820's was in the range of 10 to 11 million pesos yearly, the effect of the poor terms of trade was to reduce national income by about 1 percent (i.e., $0.23(10.5)/225 = 0.01$). Adding this to the outflow of capital represents a transfer of national income of about 1.5 percent. This may be a small number, but it is hardly a small sum.[56]

Contemporaries understood the consequences of pressure on the balance of payments. The results they described sound much like what we would call the Hume price-specie flow mechanism of international adjustment. Shipping silver abroad reduced the money supply, drove down prices, and caused commerce to stagnate. Specie was less important for its intrinsic value than as a means of facilitating transactions.[57] Small wonder that one observer called the "arrangement of foreign trade" the "moral basis for public prosperity in Mexico."[58] As Charles O'Gorman put it in early 1827, "the drain caused by the exportation [of silver] is beginning to be severely felt [and will continue] until the produce of the mines reestablishes an equilibrium between the currency and the demand for exportations."[59]

Conjectures: National Product, the Balance of Payments, and the Economic History of Early National Mexico

We began this chapter by considering estimates of Mexico's national product at the end of the colonial period. We concluded that the common source for virtually all modern estimates, José María Quirós's famous 1817 essay, is reasonably accurate. Independent estimates in the style of Raymond Goldsmith—essentially indirect estimates of national income that economic historians other than Goldsmith have also employed[60]—confirm the general size of Quirós's estimate, about 225 million pesos. The Humboldt-Aubrey estimate is less compelling and may be discarded. Virtually all the evidence we have—income, expenditure, and production—supports Quirós. Even Paul Bairoch's rule of thumb offers a close approximation to Quirós's calculation.

Quirós's estimate of the costs of the insurgency holds up less well. Historians have taken this estimate seriously.[61] It is risky for them to do so. There were sharp, localized reductions in production during the insurgency, such as the collapse of woolen production in the *obrajes* of Querétaro between 1810 and 1812, but Quirós's vision of generalized, catastrophic, sustained depression is unwarranted.

This is not to say that the insurgency had no lingering costs. We have pointed to the collapse of silver mining as one such crucial consequence. Crude calculations suggest that the fall in silver production could account for nearly all the fall in Mexican national income adduced by Coatsworth in the worst-case version of national income change between 1800 and 1845.

Yet there are other variations on the theme of Mexico's early national crisis. Our Goldsmith-style calculations—admittedly coarse—simply indicate no growth in per capita incomes between 1800 and 1840. The best-case story, which has found favor with historians in recent years, points to somewhat greater income growth around 1840 than is customarily supposed. Alamán and his circle certainly believed that there had been real per capita income growth since 1817. There must have also been large regional differences in national income. What contemporaries saw no doubt reflected where they looked. Alamán and his circle may have been more impressed by a gathering recovery around Guanajuato than by evidence of persistent stagnation elsewhere. An annual growth rate of 0.15 percent is small, even by the standards of the day. It is less than a third of the contemporary British rate and less than 40 percent of the annual growth rate of the United States.

Running throughout the period is the unifying theme of money and the balance of payments. This view of Mexico's mining economy departs a bit from the "leading sector" model of silver mining. It points instead to the monetary consequences of balance-of-payments adjustment under the silver standard. The theme underlies the work of several modern economic historians—Enrique Cárdenas, Richard Garner, Claude Morin, and Pedro Pérez Herrero all come to mind. All look to the consequences of Bourbon imperialism and to the drain of specie that Bourbon imperialism entailed. In a sense, all affirm the implicit judgment of Stanley and Barbara Stein in *The Colonial Heritage of Latin America*. The economic history of the later eighteenth century surely begins with the fiscal consequences of the Seven Years' War and Spain's "defensive modernization" of its empire.[62] Perhaps the "Independence Era" in Mexico began in 1759 and ended with the war of 1847.

The drag that the balance of payments exercised on the Mexican economy was also very much in evidence during the 1820's. Indeed, the various indicators we have for the 1820's demonstrate that the First Republic was conceived in dire fiscal straits. A net transfer of resources from Mexico during the 1820's itself worsened political conflicts, but the collapse of silver mining, poor terms of trade, and factors not discussed here—for example, the mushrooming public debt in the 1830's—must have also reduced available room for maneuver. Independence exacerbated Mexico's economic problems, but independence alone did not create them.

Finally, because Mexico did not grow in the early nineteenth century, it fell behind. Given the uncertainties of the various estimates, per capita product either fell, did not grow, or grew only very slowly. More accuracy here is better than less, but at a general level the differences are unimportant. N. F. R. Crafts estimates that product per capita grew at 0.52 percent per year in Britain in 1801–31. Roger Ransom and Richard Sutch find that real per capita income in the United States was growing at 0.39 percent yearly during the 1830s.[63] Assume that Britain, Mexico, and the United

States started from the same point in 1800. Assume further that Mexico did not grow, while Britain and the United States grew at the rates recorded. Over 40 years, Mexican income would have fallen by 15 percent against the United States and by 19 percent against Great Britain. Catastrophes mattered less than slow, steady erosion in producing widening international income differentials in the early nineteenth century. Falling behind was easy. Catching up is much harder to do.

Notes

I am grateful to the Social Science Research Council and to the National Endowment for the Humanities for support. Earlier drafts of this chapter received helpful criticism from participants in seminars at the University of California, Berkeley; the University of California, San Diego; the University of New Mexico; and the University of Texas, Austin. Discussants at the Instituto de Estudios Peruanos, and the Universidad Carlos III de Madrid, were also helpful. I am particularly grateful to Woodrow Borah, Margaret Chowning, John Coatsworth, Susan Deans-Smith, Jan de Vries, Pedro Fraile, Paul Gootenberg, Steve Haber, Dick Garner, Jean-Laurent Rosenthal, and John TePaske.

  1. Bairoch 1991: 34; Coatsworth 1978: 80–100; Fraile, Salvucci, and Salvucci 1992.
  2. Maddison 1991: 24–25; L. G. Reynolds 1985: 390–91.
  3. TePaske 1985: 119–43; Coatsworth 1978: 80–100; Quirós 1973: 231–64; Rosenzweig Hernández 1989: 23–85; Aubrey 1950: 185–98; Bairoch 1989. Also see C. W. Reynolds 1970: 311–14; Rodríguez 1986: 85–107, esp. 89n.
  4. Maddison 1983: 27–41, esp. 34.
  5. Brading 1985: 61–64. Also see Pérez Herrero 1991: 207–64.
  6. Danson 1851: 18. There are a wide range of estimates of unrecorded production, a convenient survey of which appears in Barrett 1990: 224–54.
  7. Coatsworth 1989: 27–54.
  8. Claude Morin has attacked Quirós's calculations as essentially political ("¿no trataba [Quirós] de satisfacer necesidades inmediatas de política económica?") and Rosenzweig's revisions of them as "slights of hand" ("MS Dictionary"). The source of the objection is not clear. Morin is all too correct in complaining that Quirós was not specific about his sources, informants, and assumptions, but Quirós was certainly no less forthcoming than most of his contemporaries. His methods of calculation seem, for the most part, reasonably clear. See Morin 1979: 131–32.
  9. That is, agriculture (47 percent), mining (15 percent), and manufactures (38 percent). In 1965, agriculture's share in China's GDP was 43 percent, and industry's share was 36 percent. See World Bank 1985: 150, Table A.5.
  10. Borah 1941: 386–409.
  11. Rosenzweig Hernández 1989: 45.
  12. Rosenzweig Hernández 1989: 85.

13. For other criticisms of Maddison's estimates of national product, see De Long 1992: 309n.

14. Abad y Queipo 1813: 57–58; World Bank 1985: 229.

15. *El Cosmopólita*, August 22, 1838.

16. Mora 1986, 1: 26–58. Also see Garavaglia and Grosso 1987: 11–18.

17. Alamán 1977a: 1–85.

18. Alamán 1977b: 159–242.

19. *El Siglo Diez y Nueve*, Apr. 6, 1845.

20. Sociedad Mexicana de Geografía y Estadística 1980: 25–28.

21. See Barrera Lavalle 1911: 9; Flores Talavera 1958: 26–27. I am grateful to Walter Brem of the Bancroft Library for bringing these to my attention.

22. I am grateful to Steve Haber for pointing this out.

23. Alamán 1945–47: 76, 156, 271.

24. López de Santa Anna 1952: 51–52.

25. David 1967: 151–97. Also see Douglass North 1961: 387–96. David constructed indirect estimates of changes in per capita output. Overall output per worker must equal the average output per worker in each sector of the economy, weighted by the proportion of workers in each sector. Output per capita must equal average output per worker times the fraction of the population working. An interesting discussion of David's method appears in Lee and Passell 1979: 54–61.

26. Goldsmith 1987; Goldsmith 1984: 263–88.

27. Crafts 1985: 80–81; Lévy-Leboyer and Bourguignon 1990: 96.

28. These are essentially estimates of gross domestic rather than gross national product. We are interested in the total market value of all final goods and services produced within Mexico in a given year. Calculating GNP would exclude the income of Spanish businesses (and Spaniards) employed in Mexico. In other words, Mexican GDP exceeded Mexican GNP.

29. Scardaville 1977: 67.

30. Computed from Davies 1976: 131–74.

31. Goldsmith 1984: 268. Modern low-income countries typically devote two-fifths of GDP to governmental expenditure and gross domestic investment, so an allowance of 10 percent is quite modest. See Malcolm Gillis et al. 1992: 273, 293.

Angus Maddison (1991: 7) estimates the per capita consumption (C) was probably around 85 percent of per capita GDP in 1820. In other words, $C = 0.85$ GDP, or $1.18C =$ GDP. Goldsmith's assumption is $1.1C =$ GDP. Maddison's rule of thumb yields a product of about 231 million pesos.

32. Van Young 1988: 213.

33. Cook and Borah (1971–79, 1: 58, 257) conclude that children age 15 and under were about 42 percent of the population in the early 1790's, based on an incomplete count. A tabulation of the age distribution of workers in several textile manufactories in Coyocán in 1792 indicates that child labor did not matter much. See Salvucci 1982: 220–26.

34. Nevertheless, urban market prices are probably a relevant measure of the opportunity cost of subsistence consumption.

35. Lerdo de Tejada 1967: oversized foldout, Table 14, not paginated.

36. "Translation of the Polito-Mercantile Remarks at the foot of the Balanza de Comercio of the Port of Veracruz for 25 years from the year 1796." United Kingdom 1825: 203/3, Mar. 1, 1825.

37. This estimate appears in "Moneda de Cobre," *El Siglo Diez y Nueve*, Nov. 2, 1841.

38. See *El Siglo Diez y Nueve*, Dec. 3, 1841.

39. We have no price index for the period. If the depreciation of the copper coinage measures the rate of inflation in this period, and—a big if—the purchasing power of silver was constant, we might regard our comparison as showing no real per capita growth as well.

40. Chowning 1990: 463–70; Chowning 1992: 119–59; Garavaglia and Grosso 1991: 615–71; Thomson 1989: 217–77.

41. Quirós 1973: 259.

42. Salamán (1985, 1: appen. 2) for data on *alcabala* collections.

43. Salvucci 1987: 160.

44. Quirós 1973: 221–22.

45. The *Times* directed its response to what it called the Madrid *Gazette*. I have not seen the original but surmise that the *Times* was referring to an article based on Quirós's 1817 calculations, here attributed to 1821. The giveaway is a reference to the finding that "the domestic manufactures of Mexico were reduced one third" and that "foreign manufactures, much cheaper and much better, were admitted." This is precisely what Quirós had argued. See the London *Times*, Dec. 30, 1824. Also see Griffith Dawson 1990: 69–91.

46. Velasco Avila et al. 1988: 29–54, 89–97.

47. See Charles O'Gorman's report on the gold and silver currency of Mexico in 1823 and 1824 for a lengthy discussion of the impact of the insurgency on mining output. United Kingdom 1825: 203/4, Jan. 28, 1825.

48. Coatsworth 1982: 29.

49. Garner 1982: 566, 577–88.

50. Morin 1979: 127–40, esp. 138–39.

51. Pérez Herrero 1988: 183. The translation is mine.

52. Charles O'Gorman's report on Mexican exports in United Kingdom 1825: 203/4, Mar. 1, 1825.

53. This figure assumes that re-exports from the United States were essentially British in origin.

54. Calculated from United Kingdom 1832: report by Charles O'Gorman on imports of gold and silver into Mexico in 1825, Mexico City, Jan. 5, 1831.

55. See Salvucci 1992.

56. By contrast, the net outward transfer of resources from Mexico during the so-called debt crisis reached 2.4 percent in 1988. See Gillis et al. 1992: 409.

57. [P.A.Z.], "Observaciones contra la libertad del comercio esterior, ó sea contestación al Diario del Gobierno Federal," in *El Siglo Diez y Nueve*, Nov. 21, 1841. Also see *El Siglo Diez y Nueve*, Jan. 30, 1842.

58. Campos 1844: 13.

59. United Kingdom 1825: 203/16, Charles T. O'Gorman to Admiral Lawrence Halstead, Mexico, Jan. 28, 1827.

60. O'Brien and Engerman 1991: 178–79.
61. Ladd 1976: 148–49; Walker 1986: 5.
62. Stein and Stein 1970.
63. Crafts 1985: 45; Ransom 1989: 256.

References

Abad y Queipo, Manuel, 1813. "Representación sobre la inmunidad del clero." In *Colección de los escritos más importantes que en diferentes épocas dirigió al gobierno.* Mexico City.

Alamán, Lucas. 1945–47 [1823, 1825, 1830]. *Obras de D. Lucas Alamán.* Mexico City.

———. 1977a [1843]. "Memoria sobre el estado de la agricultura e industria de la república, que la dirección general de estos ramos presenta al gobierno supremo." In Horacio Labastida, ed., *Documentos para el estudio de la industrialización en México, 1837–1845.* Mexico City.

———. 1977b [1846]. "Memoria sobre el estado de la agricultura e industria de la república en el año de 1845, que la dirección general de estos ramos presenta al gobierno supremo." In Horacio Labastida, ed., *Documentos para el estudio de la industrialización en México, 1837–1845.* Mexico City.

———. 1985 [1853]. *Historia de México desde los primeros movimientos que prepararon su independencia en el año de 1808 hasta la época presente.* 5 vols. Mexico City.

Aubrey, Henry G. 1950. "National Income of Mexico." *Estadística* 8: 185–98.

Barioch, Paul. 1989. "Wages as an Indicator of Gross National Product." In Peter Scholliers, ed., *Real Wages in 19th and 20th Century Europe: Historical and Comparative Perspectives.* New York.

———. 1991. "How and Not Why; Economic Inequalities Between 1800 and 1913: Some Background Figures." In Jean Batou, ed., *Between Development and Underdevelopment, 1800–1870.* Geneva.

Barrera Lavalle, Francisco. 1911. *Apuntes para la historia de la estadística en México, 1821 á 1910.* Mexico City.

Barrett, Ward. 1990. "World Bullion Flows, 1450–1800." In James D. Tracy, ed., *The Rise of Merchant Empires: Long-Distance Trade in the Early Modern World, 1350–1750.* New York.

Borah, Woodrow. 1941. "The Collection of Tithes in the Bishopric of Oaxaca During the Sixteenth Century." *Hispanic American Historical Review* 21, no. 3: 386–409.

Brading, D. A. 1985. "Facts and Figments in Bourbon Mexico," *Bulletin of Latin American Research* 4: 61–64.

Campos, Antonio de María. 1844. *Economía política en México. Contestación a don Carlos de Landa sobre comercio libre.* Puebla.

Chowning, Margaret. 1990. "The Management of Church Wealth in Michoacán, Mexico, 1810–1856: Economic Motives and Political Implications." *Journal of Latin American Studies* 22, no. 3: 459–96.

———. 1992. "The Contours of the Post-1810 Depression: A Reappraisal from a Regional Perspective." *Latin American Research Review* 27 (2): 119–59.

Coatsworth, John H. 1978. "Obstacles to Economic Development in Nineteenth-Century Mexico." *American Historical Review* 83, no. 1: 80–100.

———. 1982. "The Limits of Colonial Absolutism: The State in Eighteenth-Century Mexico." In Karen Spalding, ed., *Essays in the Political, Economic, and Social History of Colonial Latin America.* Newark, Del.

———. 1989. "The Decline of the Mexican Economy, 1800–1860." In Reinhard Liehr, ed., *América Latina en la época de Simón Bolívar. La formación de las economías nacionales y los intereses económicos europeos. 1800–1850.* Berlin.

Cook, Sherburne, and Woodrow Borah. 1971–79. *Essays in Population History.* 3 vols. Berkeley.

Cosmopólita, El. 1838. Mexico City.

Crafts, N. F. R. 1985. *British Economic Growth During the Industrial Revolution.* Oxford.

Danson, J. T. 1851. "Of the Quantity of Gold and Silver Supposed to Have Passed from America to Europe, from the Discovery of the Former Country to the Present Time." *Journal of the Royal Statistical Society* ser. A, 14: 11–44.

David, Paul. 1967. "The Growth of Real Product in the United States Before 1840: New Evidence and Controlled Conjectures." *The Journal of Economic History,* 27, no. 2: 151–97.

Davies, Keith A. 1976. "Tendencias demográficas urbanas durante el siglo xix en Mexico." In Woodrow Borah et al., eds., *Ensayos sobre el desarrollo urbano de México.* Mexico City.

De Long, J. Bradford. 1992. "Productivity Growth and Machinery Investment: A Long-Run Look, 1870–1980." *The Journal of Economic History* 52, no. 2: 307–24.

Flores Talavera, Rodolfo. 1958. "Historia y evolución de la estadística nacional." *Boletín de la Sociedad Mexicana de Geografía y Estadística* 86: 1–3, 13–46.

Fraile, Pedro, Richard Salvucci, and Linda Salvucci. 1992. "El caso cubano. Exportaciones e independencia." In Samuel Amaral and Leandro Prados de la Escosura, eds., *Las consecuencias de la independencia de America Latina,* pp. 80–101. Madrid.

Garavaglia, Juan Carlos, and Juan Carlos Grosso. 1987. *Las alcabalas novohispanas.* Mexico City.

———. 1991. "El comportamiento demográfico de una parroquia poblana de la colonia al México independiente: Tepeaca y su entorno agrario, 1740–1850." *Historia Mexicana* 40, no. 4: 615–71.

Garner, Richard. 1982. "Exportaciones de circulante en el siglo xviii (1750–1810)." *Historia Mexicana* 31, no. 4: 544–98.

Gillis, Malcolm, Dwight H. Perkins, Michael Roemer, and Donald R. Snodgrass. 1992. *Economics of Development,* 3d ed. New York.

Goldsmith, Raymond, 1984. "An Estimate of the Size and Structure of the National Product of the Early Roman Empire." *Review of Income and Wealth* 30, no. 3 (Sept.): 263–88.

———. 1987. *Premodern Financial Systems: A Historical Comparative Study.* New Haven, Conn.

Griffith Dawson, Frank. 1990. *The First Latin American Debt Crisis: The City of London and the 1822–25 Loan Bubble*. New Haven, Conn.

Ladd, Doris M. 1976. *The Mexican Nobility at Independence, 1780–1826*. Austin, Tex.

Lee, Susan Previant, and Peter Passell. 1979. *A New Economic History of the United States*. New York.

Lerdo de Tejada, Miguel. 1967 [1853]. *Comercio exterior de México desde la Conquista hasta hoy*. Mexico City.

Lévy-Leboyer, Maurice, and François Bourguignon. 1990 [1985]. *The French Economy in the Nineteenth Century: An Essay in Econometric Analysis*. Cambridge, Eng.

López de Santa Anna, Antonio. 1952 [1905]. *Mi historia militar y política 1810–1874. Memorias inéditas*. Mexico City.

Maddison, Angus. 1983. "A Comparison of Levels of GDP Per Capita in Developed and Developing Countries, 1700–1980." *Journal of Economic History* 43, no. 1: 27–41.

———. 1991. *Dynamic Forces in Capitalist Development: A Long-Run Comparative View*. Oxford.

Mora, José María Luis. 1986 [1836]. *México y sus revoluciones*. 3 vols. Mexico City.

Morin, Claude. 1979. *Michoacán en la Nueva España del siglo xviii. Crecimiento y desigualdad en una economía colonial*. Mexico City.

North, Douglass C. 1961. "Early National Income Estimates of the U.S." *Economic Development and Cultural Change* 9, no. 3: 387–96.

O'Brien, P. K. and S. L. Engerman. 1991. "Exports and the Growth of the British Economy from the Glorious Revolution to the Peace of Amiens." In Barbara L. Solow, ed., *Slavery and the Rise of the Atlantic System*. Cambridge, Eng.

Pérez Herrero, Pedro. 1988. *Plata y libranzas. La articulación comercial del México borbónico*. Mexico City.

———. 1991. "Los beneficiarios del reformismo borbónico: metrópolis versus élites novohispanas." *Historia Mexicana* 41, no. 2: 207–64.

Quirós, José María. 1973 [1817]. "Memoria de estatuto. Idea de la riqueza que daban a la masa circulante de Nueva España sus naturales producciones en los años de tranquilidad, y sus abatimientos en las presentes conmociones." In Enrique Florescano and Isabel Gil, comps., *Fuentes para la historia económica de México*. 3 vols. Mexico City.

Ransom, Roger L. 1989. *Conflict and Compromise: The Political Economy of Slavery, Emancipation, and the American Civil War*. New York.

Reynolds, Clark W. 1970. *The Mexican Economy: Twentieth-Century Structure and Growth*. New Haven, Conn.

Reynolds, Lloyd G. 1985. *Economic Growth in the Third World, 1850–1980*. New Haven, Conn.

Rodríguez, Jaime. 1986. "La crisis de México en el siglo XIX." *Estudios de historia moderna y contemporánea de México* 10: 85–107.

Rosenzweig Hernández, Fernando. 1989 [1963]. "La economía novohispana al comenzar el siglo XIX." In *El desarrollo económica de México, 1800–1910*. Toluca.

Salvucci, Richard J. 1982. "Enterprise and Economic Development in Eighteenth-Century Mexico. The Case of the Obrajes." Ph.D. diss., Princeton University.

———. 1987. *Textiles and Capitalism in Mexico: An Economic History of the Obrajes, 1690–1840*. Princeton.

———. 1991. "The Origins and Progress of U.S.-Mexican Trade, 1825–1884: 'Hoc opus, hic labor est.'" *Hispanic American Historical Review* 71, no. 4: 697–735.

———. 1992. "The Mexican Terms of Trade, 1825–1884: A Provisional View." Manuscript, Trinity University.

Scardaville, Michael Charles. 1977. "Crime and the Urban Poor: Mexico City in the Late Colonial Period." Ph.D. diss., University of Florida.

Siglo Diez y Nueve, El. 1841, 1842, 1845. Mexico City.

Sociedad Mexicana de Geografía y Estadística. 1980 [1839]. *Boletin de la Sociedad Mexicana de Geografía y Estadística presentado al Supremo Gobierno*. Mexico City.

Stein, Stanley J., and Barbara H. Stein. 1970. *The Colonial Heritage of Latin America: Essays on Economic Dependence in Perspective*. New York.

TePaske, John. 1985. "Economic Cycles in New Spain in the Eighteenth Century: The View from the Public Sector." In Richard L. Garner and William B. Taylor, eds., *Iberian Colonies, New World Societies: Essays in Memory of Charles Gibson*. University Park, Pa.

Thomson, Guy P. C. 1989. *Puebla de los Angeles: Industry and Society in a Mexican City, 1700–1850*. Boulder, Colo.

United Kingdom. 1825. Foreign Office. 203/3, 203/4, 203/16.

United Kingdom. 1832. Parliamentary Papers.

Velasco Avila, Cuauhtémoc, Eduardo Flores Clair, Alma Aurora Parra Campos, and Edgar Omar Gutiérrez Lopez. 1988. *Estado y minería en Mexico (1767–1910)*. Mexico City.

Van Young, Eric. 1988. "A modo de conclusión: el siglo paradójico." In Arij Ouweneel and Cristina Torales Pacheco, eds., *Empresarios, indios, y estado. Perfil de la economía mexicana (siglo xviii)*. Amsterdam.

Walker, David W. 1986. *Kinship, Business, and Politics: The Martínez del Río Family in Mexico, 1823–1867*. Austin, Tex.

World Bank. 1985. *World Development Report*. New York.

CHAPTER 9

The Economic Consequences
of Brazilian Independence

STEPHEN HABER AND

HERBERT S. KLEIN

Scholars operating in the dependency framework have long argued that Latin American political independence was not economically liberating. They have viewed the process of independence solely as a shift from a dependency on a weak core metropolitan state (Spain or Portugal) to an equal dependence on a powerful new capitalist state: Great Britain throughout most of the nineteenth century and the United States in the twentieth century. Scholars operating in this vein have assumed that Britain's "informal empire" gained it privileged access to new markets at virtually no military or political cost. Britain then flooded these new markets with its manufactures, thereby destroying local American industry in the process.[1] These scholars have further assumed that the British used their economic weight to control commercial and monetary policies in order to promote the importation of British goods at the expense of domestic manufacturing.

The argument that "economic dependence" increased as a result of political independence, and that this economic dependence dampened economic growth, is very hard to test. The process of independence and nation building in most of the major economies of Latin America involved significant destruction of physical capital, the disruption of internal trade, substantial capital flight, and long periods of political instability. Separating the effects of these factors from those related to Latin America's external economic ties is not possible.

In the case of Brazil, however, these other factors did not come into play. Brazilian independence was relatively bloodless, there was little destruction of physical capital or capital flight, and the same royal family that ruled Brazil during the colonial period continued to do so for nearly

70 years afterwards. In short, Brazil provides an excellent test case of the propositions that Latin American political independence increased its economic dependence on Great Britain and that this economic dependence resulted in economic backwardness.

The dominant tradition in Latin American economic historiography has been to assert that both of these propositions hold in the case of Brazil. In E. Bradford Burns's widely used text on Brazilian history, for example, the process of independence meant that Brazil became a virtual colony of Great Britain. "Brazil fell at once under the economic control of Great Britain from whom the Brazilians bought most of their manufactured goods, but to whom they sold only secondary amounts of their exports, a situation which would prevail for over 100 years."[2] Emilia Viotti da Costa's influential book on nineteenth-century Brazil echoes Burns's judgment. "Brazil as an independent nation would continue to have a colonial economy, but would pass from dependence on Portugal to dependence on Great Britain."[3]

It is surprising that this view has never been subjected to a systematic analysis of the relevant data. This lack of empirical research is not unexpected in light of the fact that economic data of the kind generally used by economists and economic historians are extremely scarce for most Latin American countries throughout much of the nineteenth century. While the United States, for example, began to gather population, trade, and output data in a systematic way as early as the 1790's, most Latin American countries did not initiate the compilation of similar data until the end of the nineteenth or the beginning of the twentieth century.

Our purpose here is therefore to utilize the limited data available to shed at least some light on the consequences of Brazilian independence. We test three hypotheses: that Brazil had to forego the ability to follow developmentalist commercial policies in exchange for British assistance in protecting the Portuguese crown against Napoleon; that independence had serious consequences for the direction and quantum of Brazilian trade, that is, that in the years after independence Brazil increasingly became part of Britain's informal empire, with deleterious effects on Brazilian economic growth; and that the inability to chart an independent commercial and monetary policy, coupled with the flooding of the Brazilian market with British manufactures, forestalled Brazilian industrialization. These three hypotheses clearly do not exhaust the range of questions that one could pose about the economic consequences of independence. Given the general paucity of data on the early Brazilian economy, however, these are the three for which we can provide the most complete answers. These three hypotheses also lie at the base of the set of assumptions with which most dependency theorists operate.

Our basic argument runs in the following terms. Political independence clearly did not produce structural transformation and self-sustaining growth in the Brazilian case. Brazil was an agricultural economy prior to independence and continued to be so afterwards. The transition to modern economic growth, in which agricultural productivity rose and industry began to replace traditional economic sectors, did not occur until the last decade of the nineteenth century.

We further argue that the dependency model, while explaining some features of the Brazilian economy at a superficial level, does not hold a great deal of explanatory power when one takes a detailed look at the empirical record. It is clearly the case, for example, that in the years after independence Brazilian trade was heavily biased toward Great Britain. Brazil also granted Britain a low tariff on its manufactured exports. Finally, Brazil's transition to a modern industrial economy was delayed until the last decades of the nineteenth century. But it is not clear that these developments were necessarily a consequence of independence or Brazil's trade relationship with Great Britain. In the first place, Brazil's trade prior to independence (even prior to 1808) was already biased toward Great Britain. Second, while Brazil did provide Great Britain with a favored trading relationship, it is not the case that it completely abdicated control of policy making to the British. Brazilian policy makers were not British puppets. Finally, it is highly unlikely that Brazil would have made the transition to an industrial economy during the early nineteenth century even if it had charted a more developmentalist commercial policy. Indeed, there are a whole host of reasons why Brazilian industrialization was delayed, most of which relate to internal features of Brazil's economic structure, not external economic relations. Let us take up each of these issues in detail.

Trade Policy and Britain's Informal Empire

It was Caio Prado, Jr., who first challenged traditional liberal historiography on Brazil's economic history by asserting that independence was not defined by the political decision to delink from Portugal in 1822 but rather by the declaration of free ports and the end of the Portuguese trade monopoly in 1808.[4] This was soon followed by the 1810 preferential temporary treaty with Great Britain, which initially gave a lower tariff to British imports than to those from Portugal. This was finally codified in the famous commercial treaty of 1827, which lasted until 1844.[5] The 1827 agreement was the only British commercial treaty signed with a Latin American country in the nineteenth century that defined a limit—in this case 15 percent ad valorum—on taxes on British imports.[6] It should be recalled that Great Britain offered no reciprocity, charging 180 percent ad valorum on Brazilian sugar and 300 percent on Brazilian coffee imported into England.[7] In 1828 the low tariff on British goods was extended to all of Brazil's trading partners.

Historians of Brazil have traditionally assumed that this preferential tariff system was the price the Braganza monarchy paid for its transport to America by the British, who extracted tremendous concessions in return for their help. The cost of moving the crown to Rio de Janeiro, the first step in Brazil's independence process, was the end of Portuguese trade monopolies and the granting of a privileged trading position for Great Britain. It was this crucial role for Great Britain in the long, slow process of independence that according to dependency theorists put Brazil on the path from backwardness to underdevelopment.

This interpretation has recently come under attack. To begin with, the decision to break with the Portuguese monopoly on Brazil's trade was probably taken well before 1808. While there is no question that the Braganza monarchy went to America in 1808 only under threat of a Napoleonic invasion and with tremendous British pressure, it is now recognized that much sophisticated planning and rethinking had taken place long before the actual move. Indeed, the process was far different from that portrayed in the standard model. As Fernando Novais and José Jobson de Andrade have shown, the crown, as early as the 1790's, had undertaken detailed studies of imperial trade and realized that Portugal itself was only a minor element in the total trade picture.[8] Brazil was the dominant producer of income in the empire and Portugal played a relatively minor part in its economy. Brazilian products accounted for close to 40 percent of Portugal's export and re-export trade combined and guaranteed the nation's positive balance of trade in the last decades of the eighteenth century (see Table 9.1). The idea of a monarchy and an empire centered in Brazil thus had its supporters at the royal court in Lisbon even before the formal migration.

Even more important was the fact that the colonial Brazilian economy was already integrated into the British economic sphere well before 1808. The concessions gained by Great Britain in the Methuen Treaty of 1703, and in various arrangements even earlier, guaranteed British domination of Brazilian trade. In return for a special opening of the British market for Portuguese wine, the British were granted import tariffs into Portugal and

TABLE 9.1

Brazilian and Portuguese Foreign Trade, 1796–1811

(in milréis)

Year	Imports from Brazil as % of		Exports to Brazil as % of		Total Portuguese	
	Colonial imports	Total imports	Colonial exports	Total exports	Imports	Exports
1796	86	44	93	30	26,066,037	23,541,006
1797	77	21	88	40	20,018,271	21,474,704
1798	84	39	86	39	27,531,329	27,472,616
1799	83	36	77	41	34,924,590	38,146,716
1800	84	36	70	28	34,882,283	34,205,913
1801	84	40	81	28	36,865,149	38,237,327
1802	80	33	79	30	30,908,794	34,205,662
1803	80	39	78	29	29,261,658	34,269,689
1804	82	36	76	32	31,420,910	35,966,924
1805	88	39	78	27	35,500,167	34,899,223
1806	88	43	74	24	32,544,888	34,569,819
1807	82	45	67	22	30,865,128	31,348,109
1808	89	16	89	20	3,355,457	7,505,227
1809	82	33	88	25	14,691,720	13,769,418
1810	93	18	77	18	21,001,206	16,333,180
1811	69	8	80	27	44,008,550	10,393,865
TOTAL	83	34	79	30	453,846,137	436,339,398

SOURCE: Novais 1979: appen. tables.

were allowed to establish their merchant houses in Lisbon and Oporto.[9] The Brazilian gold, diamond, and cotton trades of the eighteenth century were particularly under British domination, while the sugar and slave trades tended to be under Portuguese and Brazilian control. The patterns were established early in the eighteenth century and continued with little interruption through the nineteenth century. A study of the crucial gold trade from Brazil in the first half of the nineteenth century shows that Portuguese deficits in trade with Great Britain were made up by the shipping of legal Brazilian gold imports to Britain. Given Portugal's dependence on even basic grain imports to survive and its negative balance of trade with other European nations in the eighteenth century, legal and illegal Brazilian gold imports played a crucial role in financing Portugal's trade deficits. Much of this Brazilian gold then entered the London market, which by the middle of the eighteenth century had replaced Amsterdam as Europe's leading gold and diamond center. The overvaluation of gold by Britain also helped bring much of Brazil's gold, which initially went to other European countries, to London.[10] In fact, Portuguese exports to England accounted for 19 percent of the value of all imports into England at the height of the

Brazilian gold boom from 1736 to 1740.[11] The same pattern—Portugal serving as a mere temporary intermediary between England and Brazil—also occurred in the diamond trade.

As for Brazilian imports, already in the eighteenth century Brazilian gold guaranteed a steady supply of British manufactures to the colony. Given the weakness of the Portuguese manufacturing establishment—which could barely supply domestic needs—and the dominant and privileged role of British merchants in the Portuguese economy, a major trade link between Brazil and Great Britain as well established almost a century before independence.[12] There were, of course, short-term fluctuations in this trade connection. The Seven Years' War, declining Portuguese trade deficits at the end of the eighteenth century, and other factors may have reduced the Brazil-Portugal-Britain connection, but the basic pattern was well established and worked smoothly until 1808.

In short, it is clear that Britain had an advantageous trading relationship with Brazil relative to other countries and that the special tariff of 1827 was a crucial part of this special relationship. What is not clear, however, is that this privileged position was anything new following independence. If Brazil was indeed part of Great Britain's informal empire, then it had been so since the eighteenth century. The concessions given by the Braganza's, both before and after formal political independence, were simply the institutionalization of a trading system that had been in place for some time.

What is also not clear is the relationship between this trading relationship and Brazilian underdevelopment. In fact, the view that liberalized trade had negative consequences for economic growth both before and after independence contains a set of implicit assumptions about the net barter and income terms of trade that may or may not hold. As we discuss below, there is abundant evidence from the nineteenth century to support the view that free trade likely raised, not lowered, Brazilian national income. That is, the origins of Brazilian economic backwardness are not to be found in "immiserating trade" (that is, commerce that causes or increases misery) but are located in internal features of Brazil's economy largely unrelated to its external economic relations.

The Direction and Quantum of Trade

One might of course argue that though Britain's role in Brazil's post-independence economy was nothing new, that role might have expanded in the years after 1822. Thus Brazil's political independence might have increased its economic dependence on Great Britain. One might argue further that this pattern of trade—particularly Brazil's heavy reliance on primary-product exports—had deleterious effects on the country's long-term economic growth. Let us take up both of these issues in detail.

In contrast to the typical Spanish-American experience, Brazil's independence did not involve a major, short-run shift in the direction of trade. Brazil, at least until the 1830's, was not forced to find new buyers for traditional goods or seek new exports for new markets, except in so far as traditional supplies changed or traditional market demand shifted.

Similarly, the quantum of foreign trade over the short run did not see any major changes. As Figure 9.1 illustrates, total Brazilian imports and exports remained virtually unchanged throughout the 1820's. Moreover, in per capita terms the level of imports and exports was quite low. Total export receipts averaged less than £4 million annually throughout the decade. On a per capita basis, the figure was less than £1, roughly 5 mil-réis.[13]

Beginning in the 1830's, Brazil's foreign trade began a gradual process of growth (see Figure 9.1), but this did not mean that Brazilian export dependence increased. Indeed, it was U.S. demand for, and British disinterest in, coffee, in combination with Britain's protection of its own West Indian growers, that accounted for the major market shift in the 1830's. U.S. trade with Brazil doubled in dollar terms from the 1820's to the

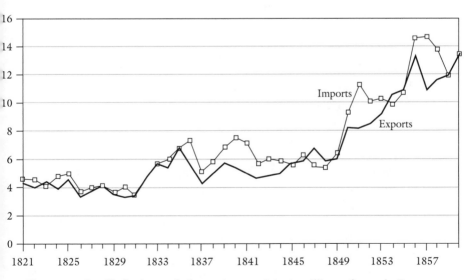

Figure 9.1. Brazil's foreign trade from 1821 to 1860, in millions of pounds. Data are taken from IBGE 1939–40: 68.

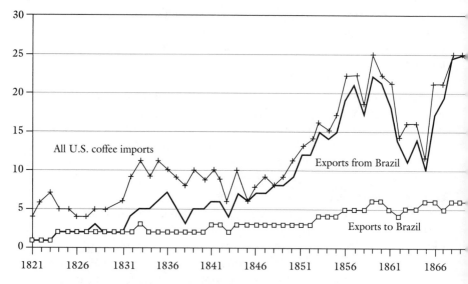

Figure 9.2. Volume of trade between the United States and Brazil from 1821 to 1870, in millions of dollars. Data are taken from U.S. Bureau of the Census 1975, vol. 2: 902, 903, 904, 907.

1830's, then took off in the 1850's, reaching six times its 1821 value by 1857 (see Figure 9.2). The result was that by the 1850's the United States was nearly as important an importer of Brazilian products as Great Britain, though it lagged behind Britain in exports to Brazil. Germany, France, and Portugal were also significant trading partners (see Table 9.2), to such an extent that British exports to Brazil had little impact on the movement of total Brazilian imports in the period 1821–49 (see Figure 9.3).[14]

One might argue that the direction of trade is less important a factor than the terms of trade. Even though Brazilian trade became more diversified after the 1830's, thereby decreasing the reliance of Brazil on a single trading partner, it may have been the case that the overall model of growth followed by Brazil was deleterious over the long term. Indeed, die-hard *dependentistas* might argue that the increase in the quantum of trade from the 1830's onwards is an indication of a deterioration in economic independence and proof positive that Brazil's political elite had been intellectually captured by free-trade ideologies propounded by its neocolonial metropolis. According to this line of reasoning, the price of Britain's role in the independence process was Brazil's abdication of developmentalist ideologies in favor of a free-trade model that over the long run would serve to underdevelop Brazil.

TABLE 9.2
Brazil's Major Trading Partners in Selected Years

	Total exports (In 000 £ sterling)	GB (%)	USA (%)	Ger (%)	France (%)	Port (%)	Total— five major partners (%)
EXPORTS TO MAJOR TRADING PARTNERS							
Year							
1842	4,584	27.9	16.6	11.8	6.0	7.5	69.7
1852	8,418	33.5	31.5	4.8	5.9	4.1	79.8
1862	13,424	37.8	12.5	4.1	12.6	6.3	73.2
1872	22,392	37.1	29.4	7.7	8.8	6.2	89.1

	Total imports (In 000 £ sterling)	GB (%)	USA (%)	Ger (%)	France (%)	Port (%)	Total— five major partners (%)
IMPORTS FROM MAJOR TRADING PARTNERS							
Year							
1842	5,656	48.4	11.8	6.1	12.0	8.0	86.3
1852	9,982	53.3	8.5	5.9	13.5	6.6	87.8
1862	10,868	51.2	6.1	5.4	18.5	6.0	87.3
1872	16,516	51.0	5.5	6.8	14.4	7.9	85.6

SOURCES: Computed from IBGE 1990: Tables 11.1, 11.3; IBGE 1939–40: 82.
NOTE: Percentages vary from percentages in the original sources. We have recomputed percentages from the absolute values listed in the sources.

Figure 9.3. Volume of exports from Great Britain to Brazil and total Brazilian imports from 1821 to 1849, in millions of pounds. Data are taken from IBGE 1939–40: 68; Porter 1851: 362–67.

This argument fails on two grounds. In the first place, it was not the case that Brazilian political elites were British puppets. Brazil may have conceded an unequal tariff structure to Britain until 1844, but it by no means abdicated control of the state to the British. The best example of this can be found in the long history of Britain's attempt to force Brazil to abolish the slave trade. Though there were international agreements to control the trade going back until the 1830's, Brazilians persisted in importing slaves until 1850, when the British navy finally enforced a naval blockade of Brazil's ports. In addition, after the 1827 trade agreement ran out in 1844, Brazilian policy makers doubled the tariff on imported goods. Though this was still too little to provide adequate protection for domestic industry (a subject we will return to in some detail later), the point still holds that the Brazilians were able to do this even though the change in policy clearly did not benefit British interests. In short, Brazilian policy makers did not lay down and die the minute they were confronted by a demand from London.[15]

In the second place, it is not clear that free trade hurt Brazil. In fact, as Nathaniel Leff has shown, the terms of trade improved for Brazil throughout the nineteenth century. Brazil's export prices increased by some 22 percent from the late 1820's to the mid-1860's, while import prices fell by roughly the same amount, producing an improvement in the barter terms of trade of 70 percent.[16] It is therefore not clear that Brazil would have been better off had it opted for a protectionist, antitrade development strategy early in the nineteenth century. Given movements in relative prices favorable to traditional Brazilian exports, it is hard to argue that the postindependence free-trade system was deleterious to national economic growth.

Forestalled Industrialization

For historians of the dependency school, the effects of independence on the growth of manufacturing were negative. The onslaught of British goods forestalled domestic industrial development.

It is clear that Brazil's postindependence experience of industrialization in no way mirrors that of the United States. In fact, one of the striking aspects of Brazil's nineteenth-century economic history was the slow transition to the factory system. As late as 1853 the entire modern sector of the cotton textile manufacture (the first industry in most countries to switch to the factory system) consisted of but eight firms employing

4,500 spindles, 178 looms, and 424 workers. This, at most, gave the modern sector of the industry a 10-percent market share of total factory-made cloth, the rest going to British imports.[17] Over the next 30 years the industry expanded but was still restricted to 43 mills employing 80,420 spindles, 2,631 looms, and 3,600 workers in 1881. By comparison, the United States in 1850 employed 92,286 workers in 1,094 mills in the modern sector of its cotton textile industry (machinery data are not available). By 1880 the U.S. cotton industry had grown to 756 mills employing nearly 11 million spindles, 227,383 looms, and 172,541 workers.[18] In short, the vision of political independence being translated into the structural transformation of the economy does not appear to hold in the Brazilian case.

It is one thing to say that Brazil did not industrialize after independence the way the United States did; it is quite another to argue that this lack of industrialization was the product of Brazil's peculiar process of independence. There are a number of reasons to think that Brazil's slow transition to an industrial economy was more the function of internal features of the Brazilian economy than it was a function of a low tariff regime imposed by the British in the years before 1844.

The argument that it was the 15 percent ad valorem tariff of 1827 that prevented the onset of industrialization in Brazil carries with it a number of implicit counterfactual assumptions. First, it assumes that Brazil could have pursued a more protectionist commercial policy. Second, it assumes that the British presence in the market meant that there was no niche in the market for domestic producers to fill. Third, it assumes that it was both technologically and financially feasible for Brazil to industrialize in the early nineteenth century. That is, this argument assumes that the internal obstacles to industrialization were negligible. An examination of the empirical record suggests that these are not reasonable assumptions.

In the first place, the assumption that Brazil could have operated under a more protectionist tariff regime does not take into account the fact that the government relied on import taxes for the largest part of its income. Truly protectionist tariffs would therefore have undermined the tax base of the state. In fact, when the 1827 agreement expired, the Brazilian Finance Minister, Manuel Alves Branco, tried to pursue a protectionist commercial policy but had to give it up because of the crisis it created for the public fisc. Indeed, the commission named to write the new tariff code recommended that the textile industry receive a 50- to 60-percent tariff in order to provide it with protection from British imports, but the Alves Branco tariff, when it was finally drafted, established only a 30-percent tariff. Alves Branco's explanation for this discrepancy was that fiscal exigencies prevented him from elevating the tariff to the level necessary to provide a reasonable amount of protection for domestic industry.[19]

The assumption that British imports prevented Brazilian manufacturers from filling a market niche also does not hold up under scrutiny. While Brazil did not have much of a modern textile industry, it had developed a large cottage textile manufacture during the eighteenth century. Surprisingly, English-made cotton goods did not wipe out this protoindustrial base. Although the history of Brazilian cottage manufacturing is still far from written, Douglas Libby's research on Minas Gerais (the most important center of cottage industry) indicates that the manufacturing base built up during the late colonial period was not eliminated by the importation of British, machine-made cloth. In fact, as late as 1827–28 the state of Minas Gerais exported some 2.3 million meters of cotton cloth and 1,964 pounds of spun cotton yarn. Home consumption, according to a contemporary observer, amounted to an additional 5.8 million meters of cloth. In the early 1830's, this industry gave employment to some 8,607 workers. Exports of cotton cloth to other parts of Brazil from Minas Gerais fell over the next decade, reaching a low of 1.2 million meters in 1839–40 under the weight of British competition in lowland areas such as Rio de Janeiro. Nevertheless, through the 1840's the industry witnessed a strong recuperation, reaching a peak of 2.6 million meters in exports in 1847–48. The survival of the spinners and weavers of Minas was likely due to the resistance and durability of the coarse *mineiro* cloth, which was favored by slave owners for clothing their bondsmen.[20]

The third assumption of the dependency argument, that Brazil had the technological and financial ability to industrialize during the early nineteenth century, is heroic at best. Brazil's lack of a domestic engineering and scientific establishment would not have been a problem at this historical juncture. Given the low technical requirements of most industrial processes during this early phase of world industrialization, and the fact that the capital goods required to establish most industries were readily purchasable on the international market (despite attempts to control their flow by the British), obtaining the required machinery and other equipment would not have been a problem for Brazil. Paying for this imported technology, however, would have been a problem. Brazilian industrialists had higher start-up costs than did industrialists in the advanced industrial economies; not only did they have to pay for the foreign-produced machinery, they also had to set aside funds to cover the cost of transport, insurance in transit, and the salaries of the technical personnel who set up their plants.[21]

At the same time that Brazilian manufacturers faced higher costs of entry, they had to operate in an economy whose ability to mobilize capital was severely constrained. Industrial firms could neither sell equity on the stock exchange in order to raise capital funds nor appeal to the banking system for loans. Between 1850 and 1885, only one cotton textile company was even listed on the Rio de Janeiro exchange, and its shares only traded hands in 3 of those 36 years.[22] The credit market was an equally primitive affair. Most credit was handled through merchant houses, not through commercial and savings banks, because formal banks were so scarce as to be almost nonexistent. As late as 1888 Brazil had but 26 banks whose combined capital totalled only 145,000 contos—roughly $48 million. Only seven of the country's states had any banks at all, while half of all deposits were held by a few banks in Rio de Janeiro.[23]

The upshot was that manufacturers could not appeal to impersonal sources of capital in order to finance their mills. The result was both a slow rate of industrial growth and a concentrated industrial structure. Significantly, when institutional innovations in the credit and capital markets took place in the last decade of the nineteenth century, Brazilian industry underwent a rapid process of growth and diversification.[24] In short, the requisite technology to industrialize was widely available, but the finance capital to purchase it was not.

In addition, there were numerous constraints on the possibilities of industrialization on the demand side as well. The fundamental problems were two. The first, as William Summerhill makes clear in his contribution to this volume (Chapter 4), was high transport costs. Until the introduction of the railroad in the last decades of the nineteenth century, the primary mode of transport was mule trains, which was an expensive alternative.[25] Indeed, the social savings provided by the railroad were quite substantial and may have accounted in 1910 for nearly 23 percent of gross national product.[26] As Nathaniel Leff explains in his chapter in this volume (chapter 2), the high cost of transport discouraged productive investment because of the low net receipts that producers received for bulky, low-value goods. This both reduced incomes in the domestic agricultural sector and lowered the returns to capital, thereby dampening technological change and the rate of growth of productivity. In short, high transport costs lowered domestic incomes by preventing the development of integrated product markets. The second problem was rural incomes; in addition to being low, they were also unevenly distributed. The existence of slavery until 1888 insured that a substantial portion of the population received less than its marginal product. In sum, the lack of industry in Brazil was largely the product of the lack of a vibrant domestic agricultural sector, the existence of slavery, high internal transport costs, and poorly developed financial intermediaries. None of these factors was the product of Brazil's relationship to external economic powers.

The dependency model of the effects of independence contains limited explanatory power when applied to the Brazilian case. The major tenets of the model do not appear to hold. Brazilian trade in the short run was not reoriented away from the colonial mother country to a new metropolis; that had already occurred in the eighteenth century. Moreover, during the course of the nineteenth century Brazilian exports became more diversified by country of destination; Brazil did not become increasingly dependent on a new, capitalist metropolis, as the dependency model suggests. Finally, Brazil's relationship with Great Britain was not the causal factor of Brazil's slow transition to an industrial economy. Factors internal to Brazil, which grew out of the country's domestic economic and social structures, were far more important.

The short answer, then, to the question of the effects of independence on the Brazilian economy is that it had virtually no effect, at least in regard to the hypotheses that we have been able to test. That Brazil had a nineteenth-century economy characterized by low rates of economic growth, free trade, and limited structural transformation is indisputable. It is difficult, however, to explain any of these features as a consequence of independence.

Notes

1. See, for example, Cardoso and Faletto 1979: 38–39.
2. Burns 1970: 102.
3. Viotti da Costa 1985: 23. Also see Frank 1967: 162–64.
4. "With the opening of Brazilian ports and the foreign competition, especially English . . . what really substantially existed of metropolitan domination was abolished in one blow. From then on, it could be considered virtually extinguished" (our translation). Prado 1967: 28.
5. The best analysis of the treaty and its background is found in Manchester 1933: chap. 8.
6. Platt 1968: 315.
7. Bethell and Murilho de Carvalho 1985: 689.
8. Novais 1979; Jobson de A. Arruda 1980.
9. See Fisher 1971; Sideri 1970.
10. Noya Pinto 1975: chap. 4.
11. Sideri 1970: 234.
12. Noya Pinto 1975: 273–74. It has recently been argued that Portuguese in-

dustry depended on Brazilian markets for survival and that Brazilian independence was crucial in destroying nascent Portuguese industrialization and in causing its economic retardation in the nineteenth century. But critics have effectively challenged these assumptions, showing the dominance of English manufactures in the Brazilian trade even in the 1790's and the orientation of much of Portugal's fragile textile industry toward Spanish markets. For the former position, see Borges de Macedo 1982; Alexandre 1986. For the critique of this work, see Noya Pinto 1975; Lains 1989; Lains 1991; Pedreira 1993.

13. Leff 1982: 80.

14. For the British data, see Porter 1851: 362–67. The correlation between exports of Great Britain to Brazil and the total volume of foreign imports into Brazil was insignificant at 0.33. Even breaking these figures down by decade shows that British influence in total Brazilian imports was only moderately significant in the 1830's and insignificant in the decades before and after that period.

15. See Bethell 1970; Eltis 1987.

16. Leff 1982: 82.

17. The market-share data are calculated from Stein 1957: appen. 1; Great Britain 1845: 355.

18. Haber 1991: Table 1.

19. Vilela Luz 1978: 24–25. It should be noted that Vilela Luz found no evidence that there was any pressure from Great Britain to keep tariffs low.

20. Libby 1991: 23–33.

21. These extra charges could increase start-up costs by as much as 60 percent. See Clark 1987: 146.

22. Levy 1977: 109–12.

23. Topik 1987: 28. By contrast, the United States in 1890 had 10,679 commercial banks controlling deposits of $3.1 billion. For a more complete discussion, see Haber, chap. 6, this volume.

24. Haber, chap. 6, this volume. Economic historians of the United States have made similar kinds of arguments about the failure of the U.S. south to industrialize, noting that the capital and credit markets of the U.S. northeast gave it a decided advantage over the south in the development of the cotton textile industry. See Davis 1957; Davis 1958.

25. Klein: 1990.

26. Summerhill, chap. 4, this volume.

References

Alexandre, Valetim. 1986. "Um momento crucial do subdesenvolvimento português: efeitos económicos da perda do império brasileiro." *Ler História* 7 (Jan.): 3–45.

Bethell, Leslie. 1970. *The Abolition of the Brazilian Slave Trade.* Cambridge, Eng.

Bethell, Leslie, and José Murilho de Carvalho. 1985. "Brazil from Independence to the Middle of the Nineteenth Century." In Leslie Bethell, ed., *Cambridge History of Latin America*, Vol. III. Cambridge, Eng.

Borges de Macedo, Jorge. 1982. *Problemas de história de indústria portuguesa no século XVIII*. Lisbon.

Burns, E. Bradford. 1970. *A History of Brazil*. Berkeley.

Cardoso, Fernando Enrique, and Enzo Faletto. 1979. *Dependency and Development in Latin America*. Berkeley.

Clark, Gregory. 1987. "Why Isn't the Whole World Developed? Lessons from the Cotton Mills." *Journal of Economic History* 47, no. 1 (Mar.): 141–74.

Davis, Lance E. 1957. "Sources of Industrial Finance: The American Textile Industry, A Case Study." *Explorations in Entrepreneurial History* 9, no. 4 (Apr.): 189–203.

———. 1958. "Stock Ownership in the Early New England Textile Industry." *Business History Review* 32, no. 2 (summer): 204–22.

Eltis, David. 1987. *Economic Growth and the Ending of the Transatlantic Slave Trade*. New York.

Fisher, H. E. S. 1971. *The Portugal Trade: A Study of Anglo-Portuguese Commerce, 1700–1770*. London.

Frank, Andre Gunder. 1967. *Capitalism and Underdevelopment in Latin America: Historical Studies of Chile and Brazil*. New York.

Great Britain, 1845. *Parliamentary Papers* xlvi. London.

Haber, Stephen H. 1991. "Industrial Concentration and the Capital Markets: A Comparative Study of Brazil, Mexico, and the United States, 1830–1930." *Journal of Economic History* 51, no. 3 (Sept.): 559–80.

IBGE [Instituto Brasileiro de Geografia e Estatísticas]. 1939–40. *Anuario Estatistico do Brasil, Ano V*. Rio de Janeiro.

IBGE. 1990. *Estatisticas Historicas do Brasil*. 2nd ed. Rio de Janeiro.

Jobson de A. Arruda, José. 1980. *O Brasil no comércio colonial*. São Paulo.

Klein, Herbert S. 1990. "The Supply of Mules in Nineteenth Century Brazil: The Sorocaba Market, 1825–1880." *Journal of Agricultural History* 64 (fall): 1–25.

Lains, Pedro. 1989. "Foi a perda do império brasileiro um momento crucial do subdesenvolvimento português?" *Penélope. Fazer e Desfazer História* 3.

———. 1991. "Foi a perda do império brasileiro um momento crucial do subdesenvolvimeno português?" *Penélope. Fazer e Desfazer História* 5.

Leff, Nathaniel. 1982. *Underdevelopment and Development in Brazil*. Vol. 1, *Economic Structure and Change, 1822–1947*. London.

Levy, Maria Bárbara. 1977. *História da bolsa de valores do Rio de Janeiro*. Rio de Janeiro.

Libby, Douglas Cole. 1991. "Proto-Industrialization in a Slave Society: The Case of Minas Gerais." *Journal of Latin American Studies* 23, no. 1 (Feb.): 1–35.

Manchester, Alan K. 1933. *British Preeminence in Brazil, Its Rise and Decline*. Chapel Hill, N.C.

Novais, Fernando A. 1979. *Portugal e Brazil na crise do antigo sistema colonial, 1777–1808*. São Paulo.

Noya Pinto, Virgílio. 1975. *O ouro brasileiro e o comércio anglo-português*. São Paulo.

Pedreira, Jorge-Miguel. 1993. "La economía portuguesa y el fin del imperio lusobrasileño." In Leandro Prados de la Escosura and Samual Amaral, eds., *La independencia americana: consecuencias económicas.* Madrid.

Platt, D. C. M. 1968. *Finance, Trade, and Politics in British Foreign Policy, 1815–1914.* Oxford.

Porter, G. R. 1851. *The Progress of the Nation.* London.

Prado, Caio, Jr. 1967. *História econômica do Brasil.* São Paulo.

Sideri, S. 1970. *Trade and Power: Informal Colonialism in Anglo-Portuguese Relations.* Rotterdam.

Stein, Stanley J. 1957. *The Brazilian Cotton Manufacture: Textile Enterprise in an Undeveloped Area, 1850–1950.* Cambridge, Mass.

Topik, Steven. 1987. *The Political Economy of the Brazilian State, 1889–1930.* Austin, Tex.

U.S. Bureau of the Census, Department of Commerce. 1975. *Historical Statistics of the United States: Colonial Times to 1970*, Vol. 2. Washington, D.C.

Vilela Luz, Nícia. 1978. *A luta pela industrializacao do Brasil.* São Paulo.

Viotta da Costa, Emilia. 1985. *The Brazilian Empire: Myths and Histories.* Chicago.

CHAPTER 10

Factor Endowments, Institutions, and Differential Paths of Growth Among New World Economies

A View from Economic Historians of the United States

STANLEY L. ENGERMAN AND

KENNETH L. SOKOLOFF

Economic historians of the United States, with their traditional reliance on Europe as the reference point, normally focus on factor endowments in accounting for the record of economic growth. They routinely attribute the country's long history of high and relatively equally distributed incomes, as well as impressive rates of advance, to an extraordinarily favorable resource endowment. This conventional framework, tracing back to Adam Smith, highlights how widespread knowledge of European technologies among a free citizenry, coupled with the relative abundance of land and other resources per capita, would be expected to, and did, yield a relatively high marginal productivity of labor or wage—and thus a relatively egalitarian society with a high standard of living and excellent prospects for realizing sustained progress. Hence, treatments of the settlement of the New World that are organized about a comparison of the thirteen colonies with the economies the settlers left behind provide a welcome fit between the evidence and the theory.[1]

Puzzles arise, however, when scholars of the United States turn to the experiences of Latin American economies. These other New World societies also began with—by European standards of the time—vast supplies of land and natural resources per person and were among the most prosperous and coveted of the colonies in the seventeenth and eighteenth centuries. Indeed, so promising were these other regions that Europeans of the time generally regarded the thirteen British colonies on the North American mainland and Canada as of relatively marginal economic interest—an opinion evidently shared by Native Americans who had concentrated disproportionately in the areas the Spanish eventually developed.[2]

Yet, despite their similar, if not less favorable, factor endowments, the United States and Canada ultimately proved to be far more successful than the other colonies in realizing sustained economic growth over time. This stark contrast in performance suggests that factor endowments alone cannot explain the diversity of outcomes. In so doing, however, it raises the question of what can.

Those seeking to account for the divergent paths of the United States and Latin America have usually made reference to differences in institutions, where the concept is interpreted broadly to encompass not only formal political and legal structures but culture as well.[3] Many specific contrasts in institutions have been proposed as being potentially significant, including the degree of democracy, the extent of rent seeking, security in property rights, the inclination to work hard or be entrepreneurial, as well as culture and religion. Where there is explicit discussion of sources of institutional differences, the norm has been to relate them to presumed exogenous differences between British, Spanish, Portuguese, and various Native American heritages. Although the possible influences of factor endowments on the path of economic and institutional development have been neither ignored nor excluded, few scholars have attempted to identify or explore systematic patterns. It is as if the deviance of the Latin American economies from the United States model has in itself been viewed as evidence of the predominance of exogenous, idiosyncratic factors. In reality, of course, it is the United States that proved to be the atypical case.

In this chapter, we explore the possibility that the role of factor endowments has been underestimated and the independence of institutional development from the factor endowments exaggerated. Our analysis is inspired by the observation that despite beginning with roughly the same legal and cultural background, as well as drawing immigrants from similar places and economic classes, the British colonies in the New World evolved quite distinct societies and sets of economic institutions. Only a few were ultimately able to realize sustained economic growth. The majority that failed shared certain salient features of their factor endowments with Latin American New World societies, and we suggest that although these conditions allowed for average standards of living that were high for that time, they were less well suited for the realization of sustained economic growth than were those prevailing in such economies as the United States and Canada.[4]

In brief, we argue that a hemispheric perspective across the range of European colonies in the New World indicates that although there were many influences, the factor endowment and attitudes toward it reflected in policy had profound and enduring impacts on the structure of respective colonial economies and ultimately on their long-term paths of institutional and economic development. While all colonies began with an abundance of land and other resources relative to labor, at least after the initial depopulation, other aspects of their factor endowments varied, which contributed to substantial differences among them in the distribution of landholdings, wealth, and political power. Some, like the colonies in the Caribbean, Brazil, or the southern colonies on the North American mainland, had climates and soil conditions well suited for growing crops, like sugar, coffee, rice, tobacco, and cotton, that were of high value on the market and much more efficiently produced on large plantations with slave labor. The substantial shares of the populations composed of slaves and the scale economies both served to generate a vastly unequal distribution of wealth and political power. The Spanish colonies in Mexico and Peru were likewise characterized early in their histories by extreme inequality, at least partially because of their factor endowments. In these cases, the extensive existing populations of indigenous peoples and the Spanish practices of awarding claims on land, native labor, and rich mineral resources to members of the elite encouraged the formation of highly concentrated landholdings and extreme inequality. In contrast, small family farms were the rule in the northern colonies of the North American mainland, where climatic conditions favored a regime of mixed farming centered on grains and livestock, which exhibited no economies of scale in production. The circumstances in these latter regions encouraged the evolution of more equal distributions of wealth, more democratic political institutions, more extensive domestic markets, and the pursuit of more growth-oriented policies than did those in the former. We suggest further that there are reasons for expecting regions with more equal circumstances and rights to be more likely to realize sustained economic growth and that the breadth of evidence provided by the experiences of New World colonies supports this view.[5]

Although we reject the simple determinism implied by the concept of "path dependence," by arguing for the long-term effects of factor endowments we are endorsing the idea that patterns of growth may be "path influenced." Given the large number of societies implicitly treated, our generalizations could well seem breathtaking, if not reckless. Such exercises in comparative history are nevertheless useful if, in specifying patterns of economic and institutional development, they help us to understand better the issues involved and how to direct our future studies of the underlying processes.[6]

A Brief Sketch of the Growth of the New World Economies

The "discovery" and exploration of the Americas by the Europeans were part of a grand and long-term effort to exploit the economic opportunities in underpopulated or underdefended territories around the world. European nations competed for claims and set about extracting material and other advantages through the pursuit of transitory enterprises, like expeditions, and the establishment of long-term settlements. At the individual level, people both elite and humble invested their energy and other resources across a range of activities and projects that were rent seeking as well as more conventionally entrepreneurial. At both the levels of national governments and private agents, formidable problems of organization were raised by what appeared to the Europeans as radically novel environments as well as by the difficulties of effecting the massive and historically unprecedented intercontinental flows of labor and capital. Surveying the histories of the New World colonies, enormous diversity in the specific types of ventures and/or institutions is evident. The explanatory factors include differences among colonies in the backgrounds of their European and African immigrants, in the backgrounds of the indigenous populations, in factor endowments narrowly defined (land, labor, climate, and other resources), as well as chance or idiosyncratic circumstances.

Common to all New World colonies was a high marginal product of labor, especially of European labor. One indication of this return to labor is the extensive and unprecedented flow of migrants who traversed the Atlantic from Europe and Africa to virtually all of the colonies (see Table 10.1) despite a high cost of transportation.[7] Moreover, the fact that over 60 percent of these immigrants were Africans brought over involuntarily as slaves is a testament to the predominance of the economic motive of capturing the gains associated with a high productivity of labor. With their prices set in competitive international markets, slaves ultimately flowed to those locations where their productivity met the international standard. There were no serious national or cultural barriers to owning or using them; slaves were welcomed in the colonies of all the major European powers, with only Spanish and British settlements drawing less than two-thirds of their pre-1760 immigrants from Africa. In contrast, nearly 90 percent of all immigrants to the French and Dutch colonies through 1760 were slaves, and the figure was over 70 percent for the Portuguese.

As the rate of movement to the New World accelerated over time, there were several salient changes in the composition and direction of the flow of immigrants. First, the fraction of migrants who were slaves grew con-

TABLE 10.1

European-Directed Transatlantic Migration, 1500–1760

(by European nation and continent of origin)

	(1) Africans arriving in New World, by region claimed		(2) Europeans leaving each nation for New World (Net)		(3) Total flow of migrants to New World (1 + 2)		(4) Flow of Africans relative to that of Europeans (1/2)
	(000)	(%)	(000)	(%)	(000)	(%)	
1500–80							
Spain	45	78.0	139	60.0	184	63.4	0.32
Portugal	13	22.0	93	40.0	106	36.6	0.14
Britain	0	—	0	—	0	0.0	0
TOTAL	58	100.0	232	100.0	290	100.0	0.25
1580–1640							
Spain	289	59.8	188	43.9	477	52.5	1.54
Portugal	181	37.5	110	25.7	291	31.9	1.65
France	1	0.2	2	0.5	3	0.3	0.50
Netherlands	8	1.7	2	0.5	10	1.1	4.00
Britain	4	0.2	126	29.4	130	14.3	0.03
TOTAL	483	100.0	428	100.0	911	100.0	1.13
1640–1700							
Spain	141	18.4	158	31.9	299	23.7	0.89
Portugal	225	29.3	50	10.1	275	21.8	4.50
France	75	9.8	27	5.4	102	8.1	2.78
Netherlands	49	6.4	13	2.6	62	4.9	3.77
Britain	277	36.1	248	50.0	525	41.6	1.12
TOTAL	767	100.0	496	100.0	1,263	100.0	1.55
1700–60							
Spain	271	10.5	193	22.2	464	13.4	1.40
Portugal	768	29.7	270	31.0	1,038	30.0	2.84
France	414	16.0	31	3.6	445	12.9	13.35
Netherlands	123	4.8	5	0.6	128	3.7	24.60
Britain	1,013	39.1	372	42.7	1,385	40.0	2.72
TOTAL	2,589	100.0	871	100.0	3,460	100.0	2.97
1500–1760							
Spain	746	19.1	678	33.4	1,424	24.0	1.10
Portugal	1,187	30.5	523	25.8	1,710	28.9	2.27
France	490	12.6	60	3.0	550	9.3	8.17
Netherlands	180	4.6	20	1.0	200	3.4	9.00
Britain	1,294	33.2	746	36.8	2,040	34.4	1.73
GRAND TOTAL	3,897	100.0	2,027	100.0	5,924	100.0	1.92

SOURCES: These data are based on unpublished estimates prepared by David Eltis. They draw on a number of primary and secondary sources, and while some of the specific numbers will no doubt be revised with further research, the basic patterns will probably not be altered. We wish to thank Eltis for permission to use these numbers in this chapter. See also Eltis forthcoming.

tinuously over the four subperiods specified in Table 10.1, from roughly 20 percent prior to 1580 to nearly 75 percent between 1700 and 1760. Second, there was a marked shift in relative numbers away from the Spanish colonies, whose share of migrants declined continuously from 63.4 percent between 1500 and 1580 to 13.4 percent between 1700 and 1760. This precipitous fall in the relative prominence of the Spanish colonies was only partially due to the extraordinary rise of British America. The rate of flow to Spanish America peaked between 1580 and 1640, when 477,000 immigrants settled in the colonies of Spain, 291,000 in those of Portugal, and 3,000 in those of France. Between 1700 and 1760, however, the numbers of new settlers in Spanish America were stagnant at 464,000, while the numbers moving to the possessions of Portugal and France had grown to 1,038,000 and 445,000 respectively. During the interval of just over a century, the flow of migrants increased dramatically to the colonies of all major nations but Spain. This steep relative decline in migration to Spanish America does not appear to have been due to an unsustainably high flow from Spain during the early phase of colonization. As implied by the population estimates for the home countries shown in Table 10.2, Spain was contributing a far smaller percentage of its citizens than Portugal, and a similar or slightly lower percentage than Britain, through 1760.[8]

Another, and not unrelated, change suggested by these figures was the growing share of immigrants settling in colonies specialized in the production of sugar, tobacco, coffee, and a few other staple crops for world markets. This is evident from the increasing proportion over time going to the colonies of Portugal, France, and the Netherlands, as well as the continued quantitative dominance—over 90 percent (see Table 10.3)—in the destinations of migrants to British America, of colonies in the West Indies and on the southern mainland. Virtually all of these colonies were heavily ori-

TABLE 10.2

Populations of European Countries During the Era of Colonization

Country	1600 (millions)	1700 (millions)	1800 (millions)	Per annum growth rate, 1600–1800
Britain	6.25	9.30	16.00	0.47
France	20.50	22.00	29.00	0.17
Netherlands	1.50	2.00	2.00	0.14
Portugal	2.00	2.00	2.75	0.16
Spain	8.50	8.00	11.50	0.15

SOURCES: McEvedy and Jones 1978: 49, 57, 65, 101, 103.

TABLE 10.3

Patterns of Net Migration to, and Wealth Holding in, Categories of British Colonies

Net migration (000)	New England		Middle Atlantic		Southern		West Indies	
	No.	Pct.	No.	Pct.	No.	Pct.	No.	Pct.
Whites								
1630–80	28	11.0	4	1.6	81	31.9	141	55.5
1680–1730	−4	−1.8	45	19.9	111	49.1	74	32.7
1730–80	−27	−10.7	101	40.1	136	54.0	42	16.7
TOTAL	−3	−0.4	150	20.5	328	44.8	257	35.1
Blacks								
1650–80	0	—	0	—	5	3.7	130	96.3
1680–1730	2	0.47	5	0.9	64	12.0	461	86.7
1730–80	−6	−0.9	−1	−0.2	150	23.4	497	77.7
TOTAL	−4	−0.3	4	0.3	219	16.8	1,088	83.2
Total								
1630–80	28	7.2	4	1.0	86	22.1	271	69.7
1680–1730	−2	−0.3	50	6.6	175	23.1	535	70.6
1730–80	−33	−3.7	100	11.2	286	32.1	539	60.4
GRAND TOTAL, 1630–1780	−7	−0.3	154	7.6	547	26.8	1,345	66.0
Wealthholding, c. 1774 (£)								
Total per capita	36.6		41.9		54.7		84.1	
Nonhuman per capita	36.4		40.2		36.4		43.0	
Total per free capita	38.2		45.8		92.7		1,200.0	
Nonhuman per free capita	38.0		44.1		61.6		754.3	

SOURCE: Galenson 1996.
NOTE: The estimates for wealthholding in the West Indies pertain to Jamaica.

ented toward the production of such crops and attracted such substantial inflows of labor (especially slaves), because their soils and climates made them extraordinarily well suited for producing these valuable commodities and because of the substantial economies in producing crops like sugar, coffee, and rice on large slave plantations. Indeed, during the era of European colonization of the New World there are few examples of significant colonies that were not so specialized: only the Spanish settlements on the mainlands of North and South America and the New England, Middle Atlantic, and Canadian settlements of Britain and France. It was not coincidental that these were also the colonies that relied least on slaves for their labor force.[9]

What stands out from the estimates presented in Table 10.4 is how small the percentages of the populations composed of those of European descent were among nearly all of the New World economies, even well into the nineteenth century. The populations of those colonies suitable for cul-

TABLE 10.4
Distribution and Composition of Population in New World Economies

Economy	Year	White (%)	Black (%)	Indian (%)	Share in New World population
		PANEL A			
Spanish America	1570	1.3	2.5	96.3	83.5
	1650	6.3	9.3	84.4	84.3
	1825	18.0	22.5	59.5	55.2
	1935	35.5	13.3	50.4	30.3
Brazil	1570	2.4	3.5	94.1	7.6
	1650	7.4	13.7	78.9	7.7
	1825	23.4	55.6	21.0	11.6
	1935	41.0	35.5	23.0	17.1
U.S. and Canada	1570	0.2	0.2	99.6	8.9
	1650	12.0	2.2	85.8	8.1
	1825	79.6	16.7	3.7	33.2
	1935	89.4	8.9	1.4	52.6
		PANEL B			
1. Barbados	1690	25.0	75.0	—	
2. Barbados	1801	19.3	80.7	—	
3. Mexico	1793	18.0	10.0	72.0	
4. Peru	1795	12.6	7.3	80.1	
5. C. Venezuela	1800–09	25.0	62.0	13.0	
6. Cuba	1792	49.0	51.0	—	
7. Brazil	1798	31.1	61.2	7.8	
8. Chile	1790	8.3	6.7	85.0	
9. U.S.–Nation	1860	84.9	14.0	1.1	
10. U.S. South	1860	61.7	37.7	0.7	
11. U.S. North	1860	96.2	2.6	1.3	
12. Canada	1881	97.0	0.5	2.5	
13. Argentina	1918	95.6	1.2	3.2	

SOURCES:
Panel A: The data for 1570, 1650, and 1825 are from Rosenblat 1954: 88 (1570); 58 (1650); 35–36 (1825). The data for 1935 are from Kuczynski 1936: 109–10.
Panel B: (1–2) Watts 1987: 311; (3–6) taken from Lockhart and Schwartz 1983: 342; (7) Merrick and Graham 1979: 29; (8) Mamalakis 1980: 7–9; (9–11) U.S. Census Bureau 1864: 598–99; (12) Leacy 1983: Series A154–184; (13) Tornquist & Co. 1919: 23.

NOTES:
Panel A: The Antilles have been included within Spanish America in all years. The 1825 category "castas," which included "mestizajes, mulattos, etc." and represented 18.17 percent of the total population in Spanish America, has been divided two-thirds Indian, one-third black, except for the Antilles, where all were considered to be blacks. In 1935, there were a number counted as "others" (generally Asian), so the distributions may not total 100 percent.

Panel B: The Argentine figure for Indians is considerably lower than that for 1825 given in Kuczynski (67.9 percent, p. 106) and by Rosenblat (31.7 percent Indian, and possibly about one-third *castas*, most being *mestizaje*), but is above that of Kuczynski (1936: 106, 110) for 1935, which is under 1 percent of the total population. As the estimate given by Lockhart and Schwartz (1983: 342) indicates, the share of Indians in the Buenos Aires population at the start of the nineteenth century was similar to that of all Argentina at the start of the twentieth century.

tivating sugar, like Barbados and Brazil, came to be quickly dominated by those of African descent who had been imported to work the large slave plantations.[10] The Spanish colonies were predominantly populated by Indians or mestizos, largely because they had generally been established and built up in those places where there had been substantial populations of Native Americans beforehand and because of the restrictive immigration policies of Spain. As a result, less than 20 percent of the population in colonies like Mexico, Peru, and Chile were composed of whites as late as the turn of the nineteenth century. The Spanish Antilles, however, did have a relatively large white population, reflecting the limited number of Indians after depopulation and the long lag between the beginnings of the settlement and the sugar boom that developed there only after the start of the nineteenth century.[11]

In contrast, because the territories that were to become the United States and Canada had only small numbers of Native Americans prior to the arrival of the Europeans, the composition of their populations soon came to be essentially determined by the groups who immigrated and their respective rates of natural increase. Because their endowments were generally more hospitable to the cultivation of grains than of sugar, these colonies absorbed relatively more Europeans than African slaves as compared to other areas of high immigration in the New World, and their populations were, accordingly, composed primarily of whites. Even with substantial numbers of slaves in the U.S. South, roughly 80 percent of the population in the United States and Canada was white in 1825, while the shares in Brazil and in the remainder of the New World economies overall were below 25 and 20 percent respectively. It would not be until later in the nineteenth century that the populations of Latin American countries like Argentina and Chile would attain the predominantly European character that they have today—through major new inflows from Europe as well as increased death rates and low fertility among native Indians. This greater prevalence of white property owners in the United States and Canada may help to explain why there was less inequality and more potential for economic growth in these economies. Both the more-equal distributions of human capital and other resources, as well as the relative abundance of the politically and economically powerful racial group, would be expected to have encouraged the evolution of legal and political institutions that were more conducive to active participation in a competitive market economy by broad segments of the population.

The estimates of the composition of population suggest that colonists of European descent could enjoy relatively elite status and rely on slaves and Indians to provide the bulk of the manual labor in most of the New World. It should not be surprising, therefore, that the principal areas of exception, the northern United States and Canada, were at first less attractive to Europeans. Reasons for their movement to the New World other than economic must have been of quite secondary importance in general. If they were not attracted primarily by the prospect of improvements in material welfare and rights to the ownership of land, it is not easy to comprehend why so many of them would have voluntarily made multiyear commitments to serve as indentured servants, braved the discomfort and not insubstantial risks of death on their voyages, and located in the adverse, disease-infested environments characteristic of the places best suited for growing sugar and tobacco. The implications of the magnitude of the intercontinental migration are made all the more compelling by the awareness that the relative, if not absolute, stagnation of the flow to Spanish colonies was to a large degree affected by the tight control of the authorities over the number and composition of migrants.[12]

Although direct information on the productivity or incomes of individuals during the colonial period is fragmentary, the overall weight of the evidence seems clear. The patterns of migration, wage rates prevailing in free labor markets, anthropometric measurements, as well as data on wealth holdings, all suggest that incomes and labor productivity for Europeans throughout the New World must have been high by Old World standards. The estimates of wealth holdings on the eve of the American Revolution for the English colonies presented in Table 10.3, for example, provide perhaps the most systematic comparative record of economic performance across colonies. The qualitative result is robust no matter which of the four alternative definitions of wealth is employed. Jamaica, representative of the many colonies in the Caribbean specializing in sugar, generated as much nonhuman wealth per capita as any group of colonies on the North American mainland, and much more per free individual. The stark contrast between the per capita and per free individual figures reflects the larger shares of the population composed of slaves, the high returns to ownership of slaves, and the much greater inequality in the sugar colonies. Among those on the mainland, the record of the southern colonies (from the Chesapeake south) fell between that of Jamaica and those of their northern neighbors (New England and the Middle Atlantic)—with roughly equivalent performance on a per capita basis but offering much more wealth to the average free individual.

Systematic estimates of the records of relative per capita income over time have not yet been constructed for many of the New World economies,

TABLE 10.5

Gross Domestic Product Per Capita in Selected New World Economies, 1700–1989

GDP PER CAPITA (1985 U.S. DOLLARS)					
Economy	1700	1800	1850	1913	1989
Argentina	—	—	$874	$2,377	$3,880
Barbados	$736	—	—	—	5,353
Brazil	—	$738	901	700	4,241
Chile	—	—	484	1,685	5,355
Mexico	450	450	317	1,104	3,521
Peru	—	—	526	985	3,142
Canada	—	—	850	3,560	17,576
United States	490	807	1,394	4,854	18,317

ANNUAL RATES OF GROWTH IN GDP PER CAPITA (%)				
Economy	1700–1800	1800–50	1850–1913	1913–89
Argentina	0.0	—	1.6	0.6
Barbados	—	—	—	—
Brazil	—	0.4	−0.4	2.4
Chile	0.4	—	2.0	1.5
Mexico	0.0	−0.7	2.0	1.5
Peru	0.1	—	1.0	1.5
Canada	—	—	2.3	2.1
United States	0.5	1.1	2.0	1.8

NOTES AND SOURCES: The main sources are Coatsworth 1993; Maddison 1991. The GDP per capita estimates for Barbados are from (for 1989) Central Intelligence Agency (1992: 30–31) and from (for 1700) Eltis 1995a. The precise estimate was computed from Eltis's estimate that GDP per capita in Barbados was 40 percent higher than in England and Wales at 1700, and by employing the relative per capita income estimates for the United States and England and Wales in 1770 prepared by A. H. Jones (1980: 68), together with the estimated rates of GDP per capita growth drawn from Coatsworth. The growth rates reported for 1700 to 1800 were assumed to apply to the period 1700 to 1770. The Canadian GDP per capita figure for 1850 was computed by using the 1870–1913 rate of growth from Maddison to extrapolate back to 1850. The Peruvian estimates of GDP per capita were computed by assuming that the ratio of it to Mexican GDP per capita in 1989 was equal to the ratio between the respective GNP per capita income estimates for that year reported in the World Bank 1991: 204–5; and that GDP per capita in Peru grew at the same rate as in Mexico between 1900 and 1913. Although Maddison has published alternative sets of estimates, which yield somewhat different growth paths (especially for Argentina) during the late nineteenth and early twentieth centuries, the qualitative implications are essentially the same for our purposes. See, for example, Maddison 1994.

but Table 10.5 conveys a sense of the current state of knowledge. The figures suggest that the advantage in per capita income enjoyed by the United States (and Canada) over Latin American economies materialized during the late eighteenth and nineteenth centuries, when the United States (as well as Canada) began to realize sustained economic growth well ahead of its neighbors in the hemisphere. Indeed, as John Coatsworth has suggested, there may have been virtual parity (given the roughness of the estimates) in terms of per capita income in 1700 between Mexico and the British colonies on the mainland that were to become the United States.

Moreover, product per capita appears to have been far greater in the sugar islands of the Caribbean, where David Eltis finds that in Barbados the level was more than 50 percent higher.[13] If the current estimates are correct, then those of European descent in Mexico and Barbados were much better off than their counterparts on the North American mainland, because they accounted for a much smaller share of the population and their incomes were far higher than those of the Native Americans or slaves (Table 10.4). Estimates of per capita income for other Latin American economies do not extend as far back, but it does seem apparent that they must have been closer to U.S. levels during this era than they have been since. Moreover, by the same logic as proposed for Mexico, incomes for populations of European descent must have been comparable or higher in South America and the Caribbean than in the northern parts of North America.

Although all of the major New World colonies may have provided high living standards for Europeans, it is clear that they evolved dissimilar economic structures and institutions early in their histories. This divergence has long been noted and explanations have often made reference to differences in the origins or backgrounds of the settlers. With the recent accumulation of evidence of wide disparities among colonies of the same European country, however, alternative sources of diversity deserve a re-examination. As economic historians of the United States, we are most impressed with the importance of factor endowments, broadly construed.

Economists traditionally emphasize the pervasive influence of factor endowments, and thus the qualitative thrust of our argument is not entirely novel. Indeed, our analysis has some antecedents in the work of Evsey Domar and W. Arthur Lewis, who were concerned with the problems that factor endowment can pose for underdeveloped economies. These scholars explored diametrically opposed cases, with Domar focusing on labor scarcity and Lewis on labor surplus.[14] We interpret factor endowment more broadly, however, and argue that the United States and Canada were relatively unusual among New World colonies, because their factor endowments (including climates, soils, and the density of native populations) predisposed them toward paths with relatively equal distributions of wealth and income and corresponding institutions that favored the participation of a broad range of the population in commercial activity. This is significant, in our view, because the patterns of early industrialization in the United States suggest that such widespread involvement in commercial activity was quite important in realizing the onset of economic growth. In contrast, the factor endowments of the other New World colonies led to highly unequal distributions of wealth, income, human capital, and political power early in their histories, along with institutions that protected the elites. Together, these conditions inhibited the spread of commercial activity among the general population, lessening, in our view, the prospects for growth.

It is convenient for both our exposition and analysis to define three types of New World colonies. The usefulness of these abstractions, drawn from the uniqueness of each society, must be judged ultimately by how meaningful and coherent our stylized types are and by the explanatory power they help provide. Our first category encompasses those colonies that possessed climates and soils that were extremely well suited for the production of sugar and other highly valued crops characterized by extensive scale economies associated with the use of slaves. Most of these sugar colonies, including Barbados, Brazil, Cuba, and Jamaica, were in the West Indies, but there were also a number in South America. They specialized in the production of such crops early in their histories, and through the persistent working of technological advantage their economies came to be dominated by large slave plantations and their populations by slaves of African descent. The greater efficiency of the very large plantations, and the overwhelming fraction of their populations that was black and slaves, made their distributions of wealth and human capital typically extremely unequal.[15] Even among the free population, there was greater inequality in such economies than in those on the North American mainland.[16]

Although the basis for the predominance of an elite class in such colonies may have been the enormous advantages in sugar production available to those able to assemble a large company of slaves, as well as the extreme disparities in human capital between blacks and whites, the long-term success and stability of the members of this elite was also undoubtedly aided by their disproportionate political influence. Together with the legally codified inequality intrinsic to slavery, the greater inequality in wealth contributed to the evolution of institutions that commonly protected the privileges of the elites and restricted opportunities for the broad mass of the population to participate fully in the commercial economy even after the abolition of slavery. Progress in these postemancipation economies was further slowed by the difficulties of adjusting to the loss of the productive technology on which they had long been based.[17]

A second category of New World colonies includes exclusively Spanish colonies like Mexico and Peru, which were characterized by relatively substantial numbers of natives surviving contact with the European colonizers and by the distribution among a privileged few (*encomenderos*) of claims to often enormous blocs of native labor, land, and mineral resources. The resulting large-scale estates, established by grant early in the histories of these colonies, were to some degree based on preconquest social organizations, whereby Indian elites extracted tribute from the general population, and endured even where the principal production activities were lacking in economies of scale. Although small-scale production was typical of grain agriculture during this era, their essentially nontradeable property rights to tribute (in the form of labor and other resources) from rather sedentary groups of natives gave large landholders the means (a major competitive advantage) and the motive to continue to operate at a large scale. For different reasons, therefore, this category of colony was rather like the first in generating an economic structure in which large-scale enterprises were predominant, as was a very unequal distribution of wealth. This second type of colony relied on the labor of natives with low levels of human capital instead of slaves; in both cases, however, the elites were racially distinct from the bulk of the population. Instead of the existence of scale economies in slavery supporting the competitive success or persistence of the largest units of production, large-scale enterprises in this second class of colonial economies were sustained by the disinclination or difficulty of the natives in evading their obligations to the estate-owning families and in obtaining positions that allowed them to participate fully in the commercial economy. These estates were not unlike feudal manors, where lords held claims on the local population that could not be easily transferred and where labor mobility was limited.[18]

To almost the same degree as in the colonial sugar economies, the economic structures that evolved in this second class of colonies were greatly influenced by the factor endowments, viewed in broad terms. Although the Spanish need not have treated the native population as a resource like land, to be allocated to a narrow elite, the abundance of low-human-capital labor was certainly a major contributor to the extremely unequal distributions of wealth and income that generally came to prevail in these economies. Moreover, without the rich supply of native labor, it is highly unlikely that Spain could have maintained its policies of restriction of European migration to its colonies and of generous awards of property and tribute to the earliest settlers. The early settlers in Spanish America endorsed having formidable requirements for obtaining permission to go to the New World— a policy that undoubtedly limited the flow of migrants and helped to preserve the political and economic advantages enjoyed by those who had earlier made the move. A larger number of Europeans vying for favors would have raised the cost of maintaining the same level of benefits to all comers, as well as increased the competition, political and otherwise, for the special privileges enjoyed by the early arrivals. Because of the differences in settlement patterns, the fights for control between creoles and *peninsulares* took a quite different form in Spanish America than did the colonial-metropolitan conflicts of British America.[19]

Paths of development similar to that observed in Mexico are repeated in virtually all of the Spanish colonies that retained substantial native populations.[20] During the initial phase of conquest and settlement, the Spanish authorities allocated *encomiendas*, often involving vast areas along with claims on labor and tribute from natives, to relatively small numbers of individuals. The value of these grants was somewhat eroded over time by reassignment or expiration, new awards, and the precipitous decline of the native population over the sixteenth century that necessarily decreased the amount of tribute to be extracted. These *encomiendas* had powerful lingering effects, however, and ultimately gave way to large-scale *estancias* or haciendas, which obtained their labor services partially through obligations from natives but increasingly through local labor markets. Although the processes of transition from *encomienda* to hacienda are not well understood, it is evident that large-scale agriculture remained dominant, especially in districts with linkages to extensive markets. It is also clear that the distribution of wealth remained highly unequal, not only at given points in time but also over time, because elite families were able to maintain their status over generations. These same families, of course, generally acted as *corregidors* and other local representatives of the Spanish government in the countryside, wielding considerable local political authority.[21]

The final category of New World colonies is best typified by the colonies on the North American mainland—chiefly those that became the United States, but inclusive of Canada as well. With the exception of the southern states of the United States, these economies were not endowed with substantial indigenous populations able to provide labor nor with climates and soils that gave them a comparative advantage in the production of crops characterized by major economies of scale or of slave labor. For these reasons, their growth and development, especially north of the Chesapeake, were based on labor of European descent who had similar and relatively high levels of human capital. Correspondingly equal distributions of wealth were also encouraged by the limited advantages to large producers in the production of grains and hays predominant in regions like the Middle Atlantic and New England. With abundant land and low capital requirements, the great majority of adult men were able to operate as independent proprietors. Conditions were somewhat different in the southern colonies, where crops like tobacco and rice did exhibit some limited scale economies, but even here, the size of the slave plantations, as well as the degree of inequality in these colonies, was quite modest by the standards of Brazil or the sugar islands.[22]

Spain had several colonies on the South American mainland that might also be placed in this category. Most notable among them is Argentina, although the Indian share of the population there remained high into the 1800's. Despite not being suited for growing sugar as a major crop, and ultimately flourishing as a producer of grains, the economy came to be characterized by substantial inequality in the distribution of land. Rooted in large grants to military leaders and favored families, this inequality may have persisted because of scale economies in raising cattle on the pampas.[23] Argentina failed to attract many immigrants until well into the nineteenth century and remained a relative backwater, partially because of Spanish restrictions on European immigration and on trade, as well as the relative absence of lures like valuable mineral resources or stocks of readily available native labor (these were concentrated in the southern part of the country). Despite such ambiguous cases, however, there appears to be no serious question that the structure of the economies in the northern colonies of the North American mainland was quite different from those of their counterparts elsewhere in the New World.

In our discussion of the first two categories of New World colonies, we raised the possibility that the relatively small fractions of their populations composed of whites, as well as their highly unequal distributions of wealth, may have contributed to the evolution of political, legal, and economic institutions that were less favorable toward full participation in the commercial economy by a broad spectrum of the population. The deviant case represented by the United States and Canada highlights this point. It seems unlikely to have been coincidental that those colonies with more homogenous populations, in terms of both human capital and other forms of wealth, evolved a set of institutions that were more oriented towards the economic aspirations of the bulk of the adult male population.

The Role of Institutions in Shaping Factor Endowment

We have suggested that various features of the factor endowments of three categories of New World economies, including soils, climates, and the size or density of the native population, may have predisposed those colonies toward paths of development associated with different degrees of inequality in wealth, human capital, and political power, as well as with different potentials for economic growth. Although these conditions might reasonably be treated as exogenous at the beginning of European colonization, it is clear that such an assumption becomes increasingly tenuous as one moves later in time after settlement. Factor endowment may influence the directions in which institutions evolve, but these institutions in turn ultimately affect the evolution of the factor endowment. It is our contention, however, that the initial conditions had long, lingering effects, both because government policies and other institutions tended generally to reproduce the sorts of factor endowments that gave rise to them and because certain fundamental characteristics of the New World economies and their factor endowments were difficult to change.[24]

Crucial legislation influencing the evolution of the factor endowment, as well as the pace and pattern of economic development in the New World colonies, were those relevant to land policy, policy regarding immigration, and the regulation of trading arrangements between colonies, the metropolis, and the outside world. During the era of colonization, most European countries followed some variant of mercantilism. Although the specifics of national policy could vary with economic and other circumstances, the aim of colonies was to benefit the metropolis. Significant changes occurred in the late eighteenth century for the British, with the successful revolution in the American colonies and the full acquisition of Canada and various Caribbean islands from the French. In the first quarter of the nineteenth century, most of the mainland North and South American colonies of Spain achieved their independence, as did Brazil from Portugal. These newly independent nations did not necessarily pursue the same sets of policies they had as colonies; at the very least, even if variants of mercantilism were still being pursued, they were now aimed at benefiting the former colonies and not the metropolis.

During the colonial period, there were significant differences throughout the New World in immigration patterns and policies. The British emigration was to a large extent of indentured labor, an extension of its domestic arrangements for agricultural labor (servants in husbandry).[25] Neither practice was to be seen among Iberian nations, where immigrants were more frequently missionaries or in the military. The distribution of Native Americans prior to European settlement meant that areas settled by the Spanish had much larger numbers than did those settled by the British, and the Spanish introduced more controls over Indians in order to better exploit this available resource and obtain labor from them. Because all New World economies were able to obtain slaves from Africa, the composition of the population in different regions reflected the numbers of whites and Native Americans only in part. More important was the nature of the crops produced and traded in international markets, a condition influenced by natural factors as well as by governmental regulations.

Lands were frequently given as grants to military men, missionaries, and other settlers, as well as made available, often through sales, to other individuals in what could be smaller holdings. The more important were governmental land grants (for example, as with the Spanish), the larger the holdings tended to be, and the more unequal the distributions of wealth and political power would become, relative to places where small holdings were made available. The size of holdings was often shaped by the nature of the crop to be produced and its technological requirements, but, as seen in the case of *encomienda* in Spanish America, the importance of renters in late nineteenth-century Argentina, and the rise of sharecropping in the postemancipation U.S. south, the distribution of land ownership need not be the same as the size and distribution of operating farms. Nevertheless, the initial policy of land distribution did have a profound influence on the distribution of wealth and political power and thus on the future course of growth. Because the postsettlement policies for allocation of land were affected by the distribution of political power determined from the policies at the time of settlement, the long-term economic and political significance of these early policies is manifest.[26]

In regard to immigration, the British, fearing overpopulation at home and responding to the perception in the colonies of an acute scarcity of labor, actively encouraged immigration to their colonies, first those in the Caribbean and then those on the mainland. Indeed, the right to migrate to British colonies remained open for people from other European countries, generating a more diverse white population and a broader base of participation in the commercial economy than was to be found elsewhere. In stark contrast, Spanish immigration was tightly controlled and even declined somewhat over time. Not only was Spain believed to be suffering from underpopulation rather than overpopulation, but the advantages that served as implicit subsidies provided to those who migrated led to a concern for limiting the flow as well. The authorities in Spain were motivated by a desire to keep costs down, while those who had already migrated sought to maintain their levels of support and privileged positions. A restrictive stance toward further immigration could not have been retained, however, if there had not already been a substantial supply of Indians to work the land and otherwise service the assets owned by the elites and the Spanish Crown; in this sense, at least, the policy must have been due to the factor endowment.[27] Overall, there were strict controls over who could settle in Spanish America, with preference shown for relatives of those already there and permission denied to citizens of other European countries as well as to those not Catholic—in the purported interest of achieving a more homogeneous white society. Grants of permission to emigrate were initially restricted to single men but were ultimately extended to married men accompanied by their families; single white women were never allowed.[28]

After the wave of independence movements early in the nineteenth century, most nations introduced or followed a relatively free immigration policy to attract new workers, mainly from Europe, with only a few restrictions on the racial or ethnic composition of the immigrants. Indeed, several countries advertised for migrants and attempted to induce, by subsidy (including land grants) or other measures, more permanent arrivals. Despite the marked easing of restrictions on immigration by Latin American countries, however, by far the dominant stream of European transatlantic migratory flows over the nineteenth century was directed to the United States, reflecting both the larger size of its economy as well as the hoped-for greater opportunities possible with the higher per capita income, the more equal distributions of wealth and political power, and the greater availability of small landholdings. It was not until late in the century that the Latin American economies received substantial new inflows of labor from Europe.[29]

African slaves were imported into some areas until the 1860's, with especially large flows into Brazil and Cuba during the 1830's and 1840's—partially due to the ending of the British and U.S. slave trades in 1808 and the emancipation of British slaves in the 1830's.[30] In the aftermath of slavery (and in the case of Cuba, while slavery still existed), extensive contract labor movements from India, China, and elsewhere in Asia took place in various parts of the Caribbean.[31] There was also some movement of contract workers from China, Japan, and, for a few years, Polynesia, to Peru for sugar production. Peru's principal export crop at midcentury, guano, was a government monopoly, using the labor of slaves, contract workers, convicts, and military deserters for production.[32] In general, however, while slaves and indentured servants dominated the eighteenth century, it was free white migration that accounted for the bulk of new immigrants to most parts of the Americas in the nineteenth century overall. There was, even here, another important difference in the nature of the immigrants to the United States, Canada, and to Latin America. The former two received migrants primarily from northwestern Europe, where economic growth was already under way and literacy was expanding. The major recipients in Latin America drew mainly from areas that had lagged, such as Argentina from Italy and Spain and Brazil principally from Italy and Portugal. Thus, even after restrictions on European migration were lifted, it is probable that those going to the United States and Canada had generally higher levels of human capital than those moving to Latin America.[33]

All the New World colonies were settled at a time of relatively low population densities in the productive sectors and thus confronted the problems of attracting sufficient labor while determining the rate at which (and by whom) new lands would be brought into production. In understanding the nature of policies toward land, it is useful to point to not only its expanse (which will also influence the ease of getting away from areas of high density), but also the soil type, climate, and disease environment, which will influence which crops can profitably be grown, as well as the desirability of settlement by different groups. Policies concerning transportation development influenced the accessibility to markets, and the willingness of the various governments to construct, operate, and subsidize such activities affected the pace of settlement and the relative production of different crops.

These considerations—which determine which crops could be produced by settlers, given appropriate trade policies and the availability of labor—thus dictate the technology to be used in profitable production and the optimum scale of production. The optimum scale will in turn affect the nature of landholdings and the form of the allocation of land, while the preferences of free workers for desired working conditions will influence the type of labor that could be used in production. It is therefore not unexpected that those British colonies in which sugar was the primary crop had a quite different racial composition of their labor force, and distribution of wealth and political power, than those in which grains were the principal crop.

Because the governments of each colony or nation were regarded as the owners of the land, they were able to set those policies that would influence the pace of settlement for effective production, as well as the distribution of wealth, by controlling its availability, setting prices, establishing minimum or maximum acreages, granting tax credits, and designing tax systems. Land policy could also be used to affect the labor force, either by encouraging immigration through making it readily available or by increasing the pool of wage labor through limiting availability. In most cases, although there were initial attempts at a slow, orderly process of settlement, this became more difficult to control over time. In the United States, where there were never major obstacles, the terms of land acquisition became easier over the course of the nineteenth century.[34] Similar changes were sought around the middle of the nineteenth century in both Argentina and Brazil as a means to encourage immigration, but these seem to have been less successful than in the United States and Canada in getting land to smallholders.[35] That the major crops produced in the expansion of the United States and Canada were grains, permitting relatively small farms given the technology of the times, may help explain why such a policy of smallholding was implemented and was effective.[36] But as the example of Argentina indicates, small-scale production of wheat was possible even with ownership of land in large units, maintaining a greater degree of overall inequality in wealth and political power.[37] Argentina, in the second half of the nineteenth century, was somewhat unusual in not having a national land policy, that being left to individual state governments. Unlike in the United States, however, where rivalry among the subfederal governments seemed to spur investment in transportation infrastructure and banks, accelerating the pace of economic growth, no such beneficial effects were manifest in Argentina. Thus, the nature of factor endowments (inclusive of soils, climates, the composition and relative sizes of populations, and existing distributions of land and political power), as well as the particular crops grown, did influence land policies, and the particular land policies pursued in different areas had significant impacts on future levels and distributions of income. While the ruling political coalitions may have gotten what they sought, that did not mean that the country would grow most rapidly.

It is rather difficult to design the counterfactual worlds necessary to demonstrate whether land policies in countries such as the United States, which generally encouraged rapid settlement, influenced economic growth relative to an alternative that would have meant slower settlement, permitting land to be sold only in larger, more expensive units. Arguments for a slower, more concentrated pattern of development in the United States were made by such contemporary observers as Henry Carey and Edward G. Wakefield, who claimed that economies of scale in production would result from higher population density and cheaper workers who would be available to labor in nascent industrial establishments if there were no "open frontier" into which potential labor could expand.[38] Whether this earlier application of the Nieboer-Domar hypothesis points to a higher national income or not, it does suggest a difference in economic structure, increasing manufacturing output relative to agriculture (or output in settled agricultural areas relative to frontier agriculture), as well as raising the returns to capital and land relative to those of labor. Greater access to land, on the other hand, promoted agriculture, led to higher rates of internal and external mobility, and was important in attaining a greater degree of equality among whites in the antebellum United States than existed elsewhere in the world at that time.[39] Together with the high per capita income, this degree of equality, in turn, led to a broad participation in commercial activity, to a large middle-class market permitting mass production of standardized goods—"the American System of Manufactures"—and to conditions conducive to a sustained increase in the commitment to inventive activity, with a corresponding acceleration of technical change.[40] In this way, the early achievement of economic growth in the United States can be related to its unusual, even for the New World, resource endowment.

The basic tripartite classification of New World colonies indicates that the United States (particularly the northern states) and Canada, with their reliance on grain agriculture and relatively small landholdings, were unique both in their rates of long-term growth and degrees of equality. The basic influence of their factor endowments was reinforced by their policies of offering small units of land for disposal and maintaining open immigration, particularly by Europeans. Elsewhere there were large landholdings, greater inequality, and, ultimately, a later achievement, if any, of modern economic growth. In much of the Caribbean, this reflected the importance of sugar plantations producing for world markets and the large number of slaves in their populations. In areas such as Mexico (where corn was the principal crop), Peru, and Argentina, land and labor policies led to large landholdings and great inequality, whether on the basis of large numbers of Native Americans (as in Mexico and Peru) or with immigrant renters (as in Argentina). The latter nations had relatively few Africans and only a small plantation sector, but their patterns of land distribution during the earlier stages of settlement meant that more substantial inequalities were generated than in the United States and Canada.

The Extent of Inequality and the Timing of Industrialization

We have argued above that, despite the high living standards all New World colonies offered Europeans, fundamental differences in their factor endowments, which were perpetuated by government policies, may have predisposed them toward different long-term growth paths. Most of these economies developed extremely unequal distributions of wealth, human capital, and political power early in their histories as colonies and maintained them after independence. The United States and Canada stand out as rather exceptional in being characterized from the beginning by high material living standards among both elites and common people, as well as by relative equality in other dimensions. It may, we suggest, not be coincidental that the economies in this latter group began to industrialize much earlier and thus realized more growth over the long run.

The idea that the degree of equality or of democracy in a society might be associated with its potential for realizing economic growth is hardly new. On the contrary, controversy over the existence and nature of the relationship can be traced back a long way.[41] Those who favor the notion that relatively unequal distributions of wealth and income have proved conducive to the onset of growth traditionally credit higher savings or investment rates by the prosperous.[42] Their focus on the capability for mobilizing large amounts of capital stems from a belief that either major capital deepening or the introduction of a radically new generation of technologies and capital equipment was necessary for sustained growth, and skepticism that labor-intensive sectors or enterprises of small scale could have generated much in terms of technological progress.[43] Proponents of the opposite view have held that greater equality in circumstances has historically stimulated growth among early industrializers through encouraging the evolution of more extensive networks of markets, including that for labor, and commercialization in general. This provided impetus to self-sustaining processes whereby expanding markets induce, and in turn are induced by, more effective or intensified use of resources, the realization of scale economies, higher rates of inventive activity, and other forms of human capital accumulation, as well as increased specialization by factors of production.[44] This perspective views the acceleration of economic growth as the cumulative impact of incremental advances made by individuals throughout the economy, rather than being driven by progress in a single industry or the actions of a narrow elite. By highlighting how the extension of markets elicits responses from broad segments of the population, this school of thought suggests a greater potential for economic growth where there are both high per capita incomes and relative equality in circumstances.[45]

Despite the complexity of the relationship between equality and the onset of growth, and the likelihood that it varies with context, we believe that recent studies on the processes of early industrialization in the United States provide support to the hypothesis that those New World economies with more equality were better positioned to realize economic growth during the eighteenth and early nineteenth centuries. The new evidence comes primarily from investigations of the sources and nature of productivity growth during that era when the United States pulled ahead. Studies of both agriculture and manufacturing have found that productivity increased substantially during the first stages of industrialization and that the

TABLE 10.6

Annual Growth Rates of Labor and Total Factor Productivity for Selected Manufacturing Industries in the American Northeast, 1820–60

Industry	Labor productivity		Total factor productivity	
	value added	gross output	value added	gross output
Boots/shoes	2.0–2.1	2.2–2.5	1.4–2.0	1.3–1.6
Coaches/harnesses	2.0–2.4	1.7–2.2	1.7–1.9	1.3–1.3
Cotton textiles	2.2–3.3	2.5–3.5	2.3–2.9	1.4–1.7
Furniture/woodwork	2.9–3.0	2.9–3.0	2.7–2.8	2.0–2.1
Glass	2.5	1.8	2.2	1.6
Hats	2.4–2.5	2.7–3.1	2.1–2.5	1.4–1.6
Iron	1.5–1.7	1.7–2.0	1.4–1.4	1.1–1.1
Liquors	1.7–1.9	1.9–2.1	1.2–1.2	1.2
Flour/grist mills	0.6–0.7	1.3–1.3	0.2–0.3	1.0–1.0
Paper	4.3–5.5	5.3–6.2	3.9–4.5	2.3–2.6
Tanning	1.2–1.7	2.0–2.6	0.7–1.1	0.9–1.1
Tobacco	2.1–2.4	1.5–2.7	1.4–2.0	0.7–1.0
Wool textiles	2.7–2.8	3.6–3.7	2.4–2.5	1.8–1.9
Capital-intensive industries	[2.0]–2.7	[2.5]–2.9	[1.8]–2.2	[1.3]–1.4
Other industries	[2.3]–2.4	2.3–[2.6]	[1.9]–2.2	[1.4]–1.6
Weighted average total— all industries	[2.2]–2.5	[2.5]–2.7	[1.8]–2.2	[1.3]–1.5

SOURCE: These estimates are drawn from Sokoloff 1986: 698, 706, 719, 722.

NOTES: The ranges of estimates reflect the different figures derived from firm data and from industry-wide data. The estimates for the capital-intensive, other, and all industries were computed as weighted averages of the relevant industry-specific figures. The capital-intensive industries include cotton textiles, wool textiles, paper, flour/grist mills, iron, liquors, and tanning. The figures in brackets pertain to averages based on fewer than the full complement of industries in the respective class.

advances were based largely on changes in organizations, methods, and designs that did not require much in the way of capital deepening or dramatically new capital equipment.[46] Reported in Table 10.6, for example, are estimates of manufacturing productivity growth between 1820 and 1860 computed from cross sections of firm data. They indicate that a wide range of manufacturing industries were able to raise productivity at nearly modern rates, despite the small firm sizes and limited diffusion of mechanization and inanimate sources of power characteristic of most industries until the 1850's. This fundamental aspect of the record, dramatized by the result that the less capital-intensive industries registered rates of total factor productivity growth roughly equivalent to those of the more capital-intensive, suggests that the sources of technological progress during the onset of growth extended across virtually all industries and were not dependent on radically new capital equipment or capital deepening. The implication that increases in the amount of capital used per worker did not play a major role in accounting for technical change during early industrialization is further reinforced by the estimates that the dominant share of labor productivity growth was due instead to advances in total factor productivity.[47]

This pattern of relatively balanced productivity growth across a broad spectrum of industries is difficult to attribute to a fundamental break-through in technology or a general increase in the capital intensity of production. On the contrary, it appears instead to be more consistent with the hypothesis that firms and individuals throughout the economy were responding to a common environmental stimulus for improvements in technology—like the dramatic expansion of markets that characterized the period. Indeed, this view, that broad advances in productivity were induced by the growth in volume and geographic extent of commerce, originating in the extension of networks of low-cost transportation and increases in income, has received strong support from recent scholarship. Studies of agriculture have found that farms with easy access to major markets became more specialized, used their labor more intensively, and were more apt to adopt new crops and products.[48] Studies of manufacturing have found that firms in proximity to broad markets maintained higher average levels of productivity and were generally distinguished by operating at a larger scale, with a more extensive division (and perhaps intensification) of labor, and with a more standardized product—but without markedly different ratios of capital to labor.[49] The conclusion that growth was stimulated by market development is consistent with both the geographic patterns of productivity as well as the incremental nature of the changes made in technique. Although their cumulative impact could have been major, it is conceivable, if not entirely natural, to think of individually marginal improvements as outcomes of efforts to respond creatively to technological problems raised by competition and opportunities in the marketplace.

Recent work with U.S. patent records has perhaps more directly demonstrated that the growth of inventive activity was strongly and positively associated with the extension of markets as economic growth began to accelerate during the first half of the nineteenth century.[50] The independent effect of expanding markets was isolated by examining how the record of patenting across geographic areas (down to the county level) varied with proximity to navigable inland waterways, the cheapest form of transportation for all but short routes prior to the railroad. Not only was patenting higher in districts with such access to broad markets, but the construction of canals or other additions to the transportation infrastructure yielded immediate and large jumps in patenting activity. Also indicative of the importance of contact with the market, and economic opportunity more gener-

TABLE 10.7

Characteristics of Inventors in the United States, 1790–1846

(Distribution of Urban Patents by Patentee Occupation)

Characteristics	1790–1804 No.	(%)	1805–1822 No.	(%)	1823–1836 No.	(%)	1836–1846 No.	(%)
General commerce & professional (merchants, doctors, gentlemen)	13	50.0	60	38.7	59	24.6	43	18.6
Artisans working with renewable materials (carpenters, shoemakers)	4	15.4	32	20.7	58	24.2	41	17.8
Precision artisans (makers of watches, jewelry, instruments)	5	19.2	16	10.3	22	9.2	26	11.3
Machinists/toolmakers	1	3.9	17	11.0	34	14.2	40	17.3
Other producers/dealers of metal products (stove manufacturers, blacksmiths)	2	7.7	17	11.0	40	16.7	49	21.2
Other occupations or none listed	1	3.9	13	8.4	27	11.3	32	13.9

Backgrounds of Great Inventors, 1790–1846

	Number	Percentage
Educational background		
None to several years of schooling	76	47.5
More than several years	22	13.8
Attended college	38	23.8
Unknown	24	15.0
Occupational class at first major invention		
Artisan	24	15.0
Farmer	8	5.0
Engineer/machinist/full-time inventor	53	33.1
Merchant/professional	36	22.5
Manufacturer	37	23.1
Other/missing	2	1.3

SOURCES: The estimates are drawn from Sokoloff and Khan 1990: 369; Khan and Sokoloff 1993: 293.
NOTES: The top panel reports the number and share of patents filed by patentees of each occupational category during four subperiods. The lower panel reports, for a group of inventors credited with responsibility for technologically significant inventions, their distribution across classes defined first by educational background and then by occupational class at the time of their first invention. Inventors whose extent of schooling is unknown seem likely to have had low levels of education.

ally, was the widening range of social classes represented among patentees in those geographic areas where patenting per capita rose. This pattern is evident in the first panel of Table 10.7, which shows how the proportion of urban patentees who were from elite occupations fell sharply as rates of patenting first began to rise rapidly from 1805 on. Even focusing on so-called great inventors credited with responsibility for significant technological discoveries, as does the second panel, one is impressed with how broad a range of the population was involved in inventive activity.

A broad spectrum of the population appears to have become engaged in looking for better ways of carrying out production, spurring the rate at which improved methods diffused as well as boosting rates of invention and innovation. Moreover, the association between patenting and access to broad markets held for ordinary patents as well as for the presumably more important patents (on average) awarded to the "great inventors." Evidence that manufacturing firms in districts with higher patenting rates, holding other factors constant, had higher total factor productivity provides further support to the interpretation that invention and technical change were genuinely induced by the expansion of markets.[51]

There are several reasons for believing that the association of markets with economic growth during the first half of the nineteenth century is relevant to the question of whether the condition of greater overall equality was an important contributor to the earlier onset of industrialization in the United States than elsewhere in the New World. First, the coincidence of high per capita incomes with equality would be expected to attract relatively more resources to the production and elaboration of standardized manufactures, because free whites of the middling sort would ultimately expend higher shares of their income on manufactures than would the poor (or than slaveholders would expend on their slaves).[52] Moreover, although the wealthy might also devote large shares of income to manufactures, they generally consumed manufactures that were nonstandard or customized. This is significant, both because markets were more likely to develop around goods or assets with uniform characteristics and because many of the most fundamental advances in technology during the nineteenth century were concerned with the production of standardized manufacturing products.

Second, greater equality in wealth, human capital, and political power likely promoted the evolution of broad, deep markets through the supply side as well. In some cases, the stimulus was associated with the existence of scale economies in activities, such as transportation or financial intermediation, with high fixed costs or capital intensity. Greater densities of potential users and beneficiaries raised the projected returns on investment in such projects and facilitated the mobilization of necessary political and financial backing. In the northeast region of the United States, for example, the great majority of banks and much of the transportation infrastructure (roads and canals) in place during the initial phase of growth were organized locally and relied on broad public participation and use.[53] Without the substantial numbers of small businesses (including farms) and households seeking better access to product and capital markets, there would have been less potential for realizing the substantial scale economies characteristic of transportation and financial intermediation—and much less investment in these crucial areas.[54]

Greater equality in economic circumstances among the U.S. population not only encouraged investment in financial intermediaries and transportation directly through the structure of demand but also through a legal framework that was conducive to private enterprise in both law and administration.[55] The right to charter corporations was reserved to state governments, and this authority was generously wielded in order to promote investments first in transportation and financial institutions but ultimately in manufacturing as well. Responding to widespread sentiment that there should be few obstacles to private initiatives, as well as to opposition to privilege, many state governments had in effect routinized the process of forming a corporation with general laws of incorporation by the middle of the nineteenth century.[56] Another example of a legal system that encouraged private enterprise is provided by the relationship between equality and rates of invention. Not only is it likely that the greater equality in human capital accounted partially for the high rates of invention in the United States overall, but the more general concern with the opportunities for extracting the returns from invention contributed to a patent system that was probably the most favorable in the world to common people at the time.[57] This pattern stands in stark contrast to that in Mexico and Brazil, where patents were restricted by costs and procedures to the wealthy or influential and where the rights to organize corporations and financial institutions were granted sparingly, largely to protect the value of rights already held by powerful interests.[58] Differences in the degree of equality in circumstances between these economies and the United States seem likely to play an important role in explaining the divergence in experience. For a variety of reasons, therefore, a large degree of inequality might be expected to hamper the evolution of markets and hence delay the realization of sustained economic growth.[59]

One might ask whether one can legitimately draw inferences about what the experiences of the New World economies in Latin America could have been like from the experience of the United States. Our implicit assumption is that there was a fundamental nature to the process of early economic growth during the eighteenth and nineteenth centuries, prior to the widespread introduction of mechanization and other heavily capital-intensive technologies, that was essentially the same across all economies.

A complex and heroic counterfactual is obviously involved, but there are reasons to be encouraged. Of central importance here is the observation that the region of the United States that was most like the other categories of New World societies—the South—had an economic structure that re-sembled those of its Latin American neighbors in some dimensions (its concentration on large-scale agriculture; its higher degree of overall in-equality) at the same time that its processes of economic growth were much like those under way in the northern United States.

The South thrived in terms of growth of output per capita but, both before and after the Civil War, lagged behind the North in the evolution of a set of political and economic institutions that were conducive to broad participation in the commercial economy and in the development of exten-sive capital and product markets.[60] The successes of the antebellum plan-tation meant that the southern population was more rural than the north-ern, with generally more production of manufactures as well as foodstuffs on the farm. Together with the greater inequality in income and human capital, this relative self-sufficiency of slave plantations reduced the extent of market development, both relative to the North and to what might oth-erwise have been in the South.[61] Moreover, the scale of labor requirements and the nature of differing seasonal patterns of production encouraged a greater degree of diversification on the part of southern slave plantations than was the case in small-scale northern agriculture, resulting in relatively few commercial cities and towns. Because manufacturing productivity was strongly associated with proximity to extensive markets, the limited extent of markets in the South likely contributed to that region's lower levels of manufacturing output per capita as well as lower productivity.[62] Inventive activity, at least as gauged by patenting, was also much lower than in the North.

The Civil War and the emancipation of the slaves led to dramatic changes in southern agriculture, with the disappearance of the plantation as a producing unit. While concentration of landholdings persisted, the dominant producing unit became the small farm, whether owner-operated or worked by tenants under various arrangements.[63] These tenants in the South, particularly blacks, generally had limited incomes and wealth rela-tive to farmers in the North, and they faced major obstacles to their accu-mulation of both physical and human capital.[64] It was several decades be-fore the South began to develop a more urbanized economy with a larger manufacturing base, and the region continued to trail the rest of the nation for nearly a century.

Despite many parallels with other New World economies that relied on slavery early in their histories, however, the South's economy was a unique case and ultimately realized a record of growth more like those of the northern United States or Canada. Within our analytical perspective, there are two features of the South that we would highlight in explaining why its economy performed better over the long run. First, its general unsuitability for sugar meant that the scale of slave plantations and the share of the population composed of slaves were never as great in the South as in the Caribbean or Brazil. Inequality in income, human capital, and political power was accordingly never as extreme. Second, much of the political and economic institutional framework in the South was determined at the federal level, or through competition between states, and therefore had many features in common with the North. These circumstances help explain why the South evolved a more commercialized and competitive economy, with a broader range of its population participating fully, than other New World economies with a legacy of slavery. Nevertheless, when one notes the similarities between the records of the South and of these others, it is hard not to be impressed with the influence of factor endowment and with the basis for employing evidence from the United States to assess, in general, how New World economies developed—or might have developed with a different factor endowment.[65]

Many scholars have long been concerned with why the United States and Canada have been so much more successful over time than other New World economies since the era of European colonization. As we and others have noted, all of the New World societies enjoyed high levels of product per capita early in their histories. The divergence in paths can be traced back to the achievement of sustained economic growth by the United States and Canada during the eighteenth and early nineteenth centuries, while the others did not manage to attain this goal until late in the nineteenth or in the twentieth century, if ever. Although many explanations have been offered, in this chapter we have highlighted the relevance of substantial differences in the degree of inequality in wealth, human capital, and political power in accounting for the divergence in the records of growth. Moreover, we have suggested that the roots of these disparities in the extent of inequality lay in differences in the initial factor endowments of the respective colonies. Of particular significance for generating extreme inequality were the suitability of some regions for the cultivation of sugar and other highly valued commodities, in which economies of production could be achieved through the use of slaves, as well as the presence in some colonies of large concentrations of Native Americans. Both of these conditions encouraged the evolution of societies where relatively small elites of European descent could hold highly disproportionate shares of the wealth, human capital, and political power—and establish economic and political dominance over the mass of the population. Conspicuously absent from the nearly all-inclusive list of New World colonies with these conditions were the British settlements in the northern part of the North American continent.

We have also called attention to the tendencies of governmental policies toward maintaining the basic thrust of the initial factor endowment or the same general degree of inequality along their respective economy's path of development. The atypical immigration policies of Spanish America have been given special emphasis in this regard; while other European nations promoted and experienced mushrooming immigration to their New World colonies, Spain restricted the flows of Europeans, leading to a stagnant or declining number of migrants to its settlements during the late seventeenth and eighteenth centuries. It was not until late in the nineteenth century that former Spanish colonies like Argentina began to recruit and attract Europeans in sufficiently large quantities to shift the composition of their populations and erode the rather elite status and positions of the small communities of old families of European descent. The New World economies that had long histories of importing slaves to exploit the advantages of their soils and climates for the production of crops like sugar also continued to be characterized by much inequality and to be dominated by small, white segments of their populations. Why extreme inequality persisted for centuries in these classes of New World economies is unclear. Certainly large deficits in wealth, human capital, and political power, such as plagued Native Americans and slaves (and free blacks, after emancipation), are difficult to overcome, especially in preindustrial societies. Elites would be expected to (and did) use their political control to restrict competition they faced over resources, and large gaps in literacy, familiarity with technology or markets, and in other forms of human capital could take generations to close in even a free and seemingly evenhanded society. Indeed, these factors undoubtedly go far in explaining the persistence of inequality over the long run in the New World cases of concern here. The close correspondences between economic standing and race, however, may also have contributed to the maintenance of substantial inequality, either through natural, unconscious processes or by increasing the efficacy of direct action by elites to retain their privileged positions and holdings.

Our discussion of why the United States and Canada led other New

World economies in the realization of sustained economic growth during the eighteenth and nineteenth centuries raises another old controversy. Past treatments of the relationship between economic growth and inequality have tended to focus either on the effect of equality on rates of capital accumulation or on the impact of growth on the extent of inequality. Our emphasis on the implications of greater equality for the evolution of markets, institutions conducive to widespread commercialization, and technological change, proposes a different direction for future research. This hypothesis is suggested by recent findings about the process of early industrialization in the United States and should be understood as pertaining to a particular era and range of inequality. It is based on the idea, consistent with the evidence examined to date, that preindustrial economies of the late eighteenth and early nineteenth centuries had a large potential for sustained productivity growth derived from an accumulation of innumerable incremental improvements discovered and implemented throughout an economy by small-scale producers with rather ordinary sets of skills. These advances in practice were induced in the United States by alterations in incentives and opportunities associated with the spread of markets, and were made possible by a broad acquaintance with basic technological knowledge as well as by broad access to full participation in the commercial economy.

Our conjecture—that other New World economies might have been able to realize growth in much the same way as the United States if not for their initial factor endowments and the governmental policies that upheld their influence—is obviously speculative and requires further study. Nevertheless, regardless of the outcome of such evaluations, the systematic patterns we have identified in the development of the New World economies should stand. Moreover, we hope that our attempt to outline a theory of how the paths of various New World economies diverged will stimulate more work on the subject and will ultimately lead to a better understanding of the interplay between factor endowments, institutions, and economic growth—in this context and in general.

Notes

The authors are grateful to David Eltis for allowing them to use some of his unpublished work, and to him, Janet Currie, Lance Davis, Seymour Drescher, Jeff Frieden, Gerald Friedman, David Galenson, Robert Gallman, Avner Greif, Stephen Haber, James Irwin, Zorina Khan, Margaret Levenstein, John Majewski, Cynthia Taft Morris, Mario Pastore, Jean-Laurent Rosenthal, Pam Starr, Federico Sturzenegger, William Summerhill, Mariano Tommasi, as well as participants in seminars at UCLA, NBER, the University of Massachusetts at Amherst, the University of Michigan, the Triangle Workshop in Economic History, Stanford University, and the University of Arizona for helpful discussions and comments. Yael Elad provided outstanding assistance at a late stage of the preparation of this chapter, and Sokoloff received valuable research support from the UCLA Institute of Industrial Relations.

1. See, for example, the discussion of colonial economic growth in McCusker and Menard 1985.

2. See the regional breakdowns provided in Denevan 1976: 289–92.

3. For general discussions of the role of institutions in worldwide economic growth, see North 1981; E. L. Jones 1988. For a recent comparison of Argentina and Canada that discusses the role of institutions and makes reference to factor endowments, see Adelman 1994.

4. For a general discussion of the diversity among British colonies in the New World, as well as of its sources, see Greene 1988. For a fascinating recent account of radical divergence even among the Puritan colonies in the New World, see Kupperman 1993, especially the discussions of the quite unusual patterns of land ownership and settlement.

5. This paragraph is based on readings in numerous primary and secondary sources. For Latin America, particularly useful secondary works were Lockhart and Schwartz 1983; McAlister 1984; Gibson 1966; Burkholder and Johnson 1994; Bethell 1984. For the British colonies, see McCusker and Menard 1985; Gallman and Wallis 1992.

6. For studies comparing records of growth in various New World economies, see Bernecker and Tobler 1993, particularly the essays by John H. Coatsworth and Daniel D. Garcia. The editors' introduction provided several of the comparisons made earlier in this section. For a useful guide to an earlier debate, see Hanke 1964; Mosk 1951.

7. Table 10.1 is based on the estimates of David Eltis. For estimates through 1830, see Eltis 1983. For recent discussions and descriptions of migration flows in the period studied, see, in particular, R. Davis 1973; Sanchez-Albornoz 1974; Curtin 1969; Emmer and Mörner 1992; Altman and Horn 1991; and the essays by Woodrow Borah, Peter Boyd-Bowman, and Magnus Mörner in Chiappelli 1976.

8. The decline in Spain's population during the early seventeenth century is generally attributed to the war between Spain and the Netherlands as well as an increased prevalence of disease throughout the Mediterranean, including outbreaks of the plague and cholera. As seen in Table 10.2, population had still not recovered by 1700. Whether the decline heightened Spanish concern about depopulation, and was a factor in accounting for the restrictive immigration policies that were implemented, is an interesting issue deserving of study. See de Vries 1976: 4–5.

9. There is now a substantial literature documenting the existence of very significant economies in the production of certain agricultural products on large slave plantations. The magnitude of these economies varied from crop to crop, but appear to have been most extensive in the cultivation of sugar, coffee, rice, and cotton; small, but present, in tobacco; and absent in grains. Overall, there are two types of

compelling evidence in support of this generalization. The first consists of comparisons of total factor productivity by size of the producing unit, as has been done for the U.S. South prior to the Civil War. The second is the consistent pattern across economies of dramatic and persistent differences in the sizes and types of farms producing different crops or in the shares of output of those crops accounted for by different classes of farms. For example, virtually all sugar in the New World was produced by large slave plantations until the wave of slave emancipations during the nineteenth century. In contrast, the great bulk of wheat and other grains were produced on small-scale farms. For further discussions of the subject and evidence, see Fogel 1989; Engerman, 1983: 635–59; Deerr 1950.

10. See, in particular, Dunn 1972 on the English colonies; Schwartz 1985 on Brazil.

11. On the Caribbean in general, and for a discussion of the patterns of Cuban settlement, see Knight 1990. For an ethnic breakdown of Caribbean populations in 1750, 1830, and 1880, see Engerman and Higman forthcoming.

12. In addition to the works cited in note 4, see also the discussions of Spanish migration in Altman 1989; Mörner 1985; Kritz 1992; as well as several old classics: Bourne 1904; Moses 1898; Haring 1947. Spanish policies also reduced the numbers of slaves being imported, through both direct limitations and decreasing demand by placing more restrictions on the use of slaves in its colonies (lessening their value to slaveholders) than other New World economies adhered to. These policies may help to account for why Spanish colonies like Mexico, Cuba, and Puerto Rico were relatively slow to turn to production of sugar on large-scale plantations. See Fogel (1989: 36–40) for discussion.

13. See Coatsworth 1993; Eltis 1995.

14. Domar 1970. The problem of growth with "unlimited supplies of labor" occupied most of W. Arthur Lewis's work on economic development. Probably the first full presentation of this model can be seen in Lewis 1955.

15. On the early Caribbean sugar plantations, see Dunn 1972; Sheridan 1974; Fraginals 1976.

16. For a detailed examination of how unequal the distribution of wealth among free heads of household on a sugar island was, see the analysis of the census of 1680 for Barbados in Dunn 1972: chap. 3.

17. See Engerman 1982.

18. See the excellent and comprehensive overview of the *encomienda*, of the evolution of large-scale estates, and of their relation to preconquest forms of social organization in different parts of Spanish America provided by Lockhart and Schwartz 1983. As they emphasize, the paths of institutional development varied somewhat in the Spanish colonies, reflecting significant differences between Indian populations in "social capabilities" and other attributes. For example, the preconquest forms of social organization for Indians in highland areas were quite different from those of populations on the plains or in the jungle. For fascinating discussion of the workings of the early *encomienda* system in Peru, including differences in the system among the colonies, of the different interests of early and late arrivals, and of the relevance of mineral resources, see Lockhart 1994.

19. For a discussion of a more traditional form of conflict between the colonies and the metropolis in respect to the empire's trade policy, however, see Walker 1979. For a discussion of a particular case—early Peru—see Lockhart 1994.

20. Indeed, there are striking similarities even in colonies that did not retain substantial native populations. In formulating policies, the Spanish authorities seem to have focused on circumstances in major colonies like Mexico and Peru, but applied them systemwide. Hence, policies like restrictions on migration from Europe and grants of large blocs of land, mineral resources, and native labor to the early settlers were generally in effect throughout Spanish America. See Lockhart and Schwartz 1983; and Lockhart 1994.

21. In addition to Lockhart and Schwartz 1983, see treatments of Mexico and Peru in Chevalier 1963; Van Young 1983; Lockhart 1994; and Jacobsen 1993: chaps. 1–4.

22. For a dissenting analysis of the Brazilian slave distributions, based on early nineteenth-century data, see Schwartz 1985: chap. 16, which is based on Schwartz 1982. For another skeptical view, see Irwin 1988.

23. On the late and never really important Argentine sugar industry, see Guy 1980. On the Argentine economy in general, see Diaz Alejandro 1970.

24. One of the reasons that government policies and other institutions tended to reproduce the sort of factor endowments that gave rise to them is that politically powerful classes sought to maintain their positions over time through limitations over who had the right to vote and who had the right to vote in secret. This could be a quite effective way of obstructing peaceful change, as seen in the classic account of how such restrictions on the franchise helped a white elite retain dominance over blacks, by Kousser 1974. Countries with greater inequality, like Mexico, Brazil, and Argentina, were characterized by much lower rates of eligibility for voting than was the United States until well into the twentieth century; higher rates of violence in effecting political change (Mexico especially); and generally less secrecy or privacy at the ballot box. Each of these conditions worked to the advantage of the politically and economically powerful. The voting situation in the United States was quite different, with very high rates of adult male suffrage throughout the nineteenth century. In the last decade of the century, many states introduced the so-called Australian ballot, which may have increased the prevalence of the "secret ballot." Nevertheless, even before this change, American politics featured much secrecy in balloting, high turnouts, party competition, close elections, and considerable peaceful political turnover, so that the system was quite different from those seen in these other countries and in Latin America overall. For a discussion of the record in the United States, see Albright 1942; Kelly, Harbison, and Belz 1983: 438–43. For discussions of the extent of suffrage and other aspects of elections in the three Latin American countries, see Perry 1978; Love 1970; Scobie 1971: 202–3.

25. See Galenson 1981; Kussmaul 1981.

26. Some of the colonies on the North American continent, such as Pennsylvania, began with proprietors—like William Penn—who were awarded very large grants of land. However, it was typically not long before these blocs began to be broken up and sold off in small plots at flexible terms. The desire to attract many

immigrants appears to have been the major impetus, and "not many of the original proprietors intended to retain their holdings intact or to manage them as large estates." See Bidwell and Falconer 1941: 60–61. For detailed discussion of the experience in Pennsylvania, see Craven 1968; and Nash 1993.

27. At first it seems somewhat puzzling, or contradictory to the idea that the factor endowment was the crucial determinant of policy, that Spanish authorities did not actively encourage immigration to colonies, like Argentina, without a substantial supply of readily available Indian labor. On reflection, however, it seems likely that Spanish policy toward immigration to places like Argentina was simply incidental, with the overall policy regarding immigration to the New World based on the factor endowments and politics in all of Spanish America. Hence, Spanish policy was probably driven by conditions in Mexico and Peru—the most populous and valued colonies. Because these centers of Spanish America had an abundance of Indian labor, the local elites and the authorities in Spain were able to maintain restrictive policies.

28. See the sources cited in note 9.

29. For the basic data on international migration during this period, see Ferenczi and Willcox 1929, 1931. Clayne Pope, David Galenson, and others have recently suggested that substantial in-migration to a sparsely settled region will generate major improvements in the position of the early arrivals as well as higher inequality overall. This may help to explain why economies like Argentina continued to be characterized by high levels of inequality. See, for example, Kearl, Pope, and Wimmer 1980; Galenson 1991.

30. See Eltis 1987.

31. For data and references on contract labor movements, see Engerman 1986.

32. See Mathew 1976.

33. For a comparison of the streams of Italian migrations to North and to South America, pointing to a different pattern for this group, see Klein 1983: 306–29, and the discussion below.

34. See the comprehensive overview of U.S. land policy in Gates 1968. There are discussions of Canadian land policy in Solberg 1987; Pomfret 1981: 111–19; Adelman 1994: chap. 2.

35. See Dean 1971; Viotti da Costa 1985: chap. 4; Solberg 1987; Solberg's essay in Platt and di Tella 1985; Adelman 1994: chap. 3.

36. On northern U.S. agriculture, see Atack and Bateman 1987; Danhof 1969. For an example of a country in Spanish America that came to be characterized by small-scale agriculture—along with a path of institutional development more like that in the U.S.—evidently for other reasons, see the discussion of Costa Rica in R. L. Woodward 1976; Perez-Brignoli 1989.

37. See Solberg 1970; Solberg 1987. In addition to grains, livestock production also increased dramatically during the late nineteenth century on the basis of large landholdings. Indeed, scale economies in the raising of livestock may have helped maintain the large estates.

38. The theme is developed by Henry Charles Carey in many of his works, such as 1858–60. The clearest statement by Wakefield is found in Wakefield 1849.

39. For systematic information on the extent of U.S. income and wealth inequality, see Williamson and Lindert 1980; Soltow 1992.

40. See the discussion in Williamson 1960. Williamson draws on Marshall 1919.

41. This point was made for the northern United States by Smith (1979, 2: 571–75) and later became the central argument in the interpretation of the history of the United States by Frederick Jackson Turner. See, for example, the collected essays in Turner 1948. James Maitland, the Eighth Earl of Lauderdale, made reference to both the United States and England in making his argument for why equality and level of income were conducive to growth. See Maitland 1962.

42. For a recent discussion of this long-debated idea, see Davis and Gallman 1994.

43. See Rostow 1960; Strassman 1956. These points were at issue during the debates among development economists during the 1950's and 1960's concerning the relative importance of theorizing about balanced growth in contrast to an emphasis on so-called leading sectors. Robert Fogel's work on the railroads represented a basic criticism of the leading-sector approach as applied to United States growth by Rostow. See Fogel 1964.

44. For a classic discussion of how the extension of markets into agricultural areas radically alters the environment in which small farmers operate, the incentives they face, and thus the decisions they make about the allocation of resources, see Schultz 1964.

45. See Strassman 1956; Sokoloff 1992.

46. See, for example, Rothenberg 1992a; Sokoloff 1986.

47. For the results of such a decomposition of the sources of labor productivity growth, and discussion, see Sokoloff 1986: 723; Sokoloff 1992. The qualitative finding of the relative insignificance of capital deepening in most industries is evident, however, from the pattern in Table 10.6 showing that when output is measured in terms of value added, the rate of total factor productivity growth is nearly as rapid as the rate of labor productivity growth.

48. See Rothenberg 1992b; Majewski, Baer, and Klein 1993.

49. See Sokoloff 1984; Sokoloff 1992.

50. The discussion below draws on Sokoloff 1988; Sokoloff and Khan 1990; Khan and Sokoloff 1993.

51. Sokoloff 1992.

52. This idea is related to the well-established relationship between per capita income and the proportion of expenditures devoted to nonagricultural products known as Engel's Law. The extension does not necessarily hold, however, because slaves were not able to choose their consumption bundles and because Engel's Law itself makes no distinction between manufactures and other nonagricultural products. We are also relying, however, on Tchakerian 1994; Bateman and Weiss 1981. These scholars find relatively little manufacturing output per capita in the South as compared to agricultural areas in the North, as well as a relative lack of firms producing standardized manufactures.

53. For an excellent overview of these developments, see Taylor 1951; Majewski 1994.

54. For discussions of the extensive scale economies in transportation and in financial intermediaries during this era, and of the importance of broad political support for investment in such enterprises, see Fishlow 1965; Goodrich 1960; Davis and Gallman 1978; Davis and Gallman 1994; Majewski 1994.

55. For similar interpretations of the role of the legal framework in promoting growth, but with different evaluations, compare Hurst 1956 with Horowitz 1977.

56. On the changing means of forming corporations in the United States, see Evans 1948. Also see Davis 1917; Livermore 1935.

57. Human capital appears to have been more broadly distributed in the United States, paralleling the greater equality in the distributions of wealth and political power. Higher rates of literacy and schooling may have contributed to the higher rates of innovation, technological diffusion, and entrepreneurship generally, which are thought to have characterized the United States. See DeBow 1854; Schultz 1964; Easterlin 1981; Olmstead and Rhode 1995. The patent system in the United States was more favorable to common people in several dimensions. First, the cost of obtaining a patent was much less, especially relative to the annual wage, than in any other country with a functioning patent system. Second, the granting of patents operated according to prescribed rules, which were independent of the social class of the applicant for the patent and appear to have been adhered to. Third, the property rights in invention entailed in a patent appear to have been well enforced by the courts, making it much easier for a person of limited wealth to secure returns to his or her inventions. No other country had such favorable conditions for inventors from modest backgrounds. For international comparisons of patent systems, as well as a discussion of the concern with enforcement in the United States, see Dutton 1984; Khan 1995; Machlup 1958.

58. See Haber 1989; Haber 1991; Beatty 1993.

59. As highly capital-intensive technologies became available, the need to involve broad segments of the population in the market economy in order to achieve sustained growth may have diminished. For a classic statement of a closely related idea, see Gerschenkron 1962: chap. 1. For a discussion of different stages in technology and in the sources of productivity growth, see Sokoloff 1992.

60. Greene 1988; Majewski 1994; V. Woodward 1971; Kousser 1974.

61. Gallman and Anderson 1977; Parker 1970; Fogel 1989; Genovese 1965.

62. Tchakerian 1994.

63. Fogel 1989; Shlomowitz 1979; Virts 1985.

64. Higgs 1977; Margo 1990.

65. For a different view, see Fogel 1989.

References

Adelman, Jeremy. 1994. *Frontier Development: Land, Labor, and Capital on the Wheatlands of Argentina and Canada, 1890–1914.* Oxford.
Albright, Spencer D. 1942. *The American Ballot.* Washington, D.C.
Altman, Ida. 1989. *Emigrants and Society: Extremadura and America in the Sixteenth Century.* Berkeley.

Altman, Ida, and James Horn, eds. 1991. *To Make America: European Migration in the Early Modern Period.* Berkeley.

——, eds. 1992. *European Expansion and Migration: Essays on the Intercontinental Migration from Africa, Asia and Europe.* Berkeley.

Atack, Jeremy, and Fred Bateman. 1987. *To Their Own Soil: Agriculture in the Antebellum North.* Ames, Iowa.

Bateman, Fred, and Thomas Weiss. 1981. *A Deplorable Scarcity: The Failure of Industrialization in a Slave Economy.* Chapel Hill, N.C.

Beatty, Ted. 1993. "Institution, Invention, and Innovation: The Evolution of a Patent System in Nineteenth-Century Mexico." Manuscript, Stanford University.

Bernecker, Walter L., and Hans Werner Tobler, eds. 1993. *Development and Underdevelopment in America: Contrasts of Economic Growth in North and Latin America in Historical Perspective.* Berlin.

Bethell, Leslie, ed. 1984. *Cambridge History of Latin America.* 5 vols. Cambridge, Eng.

Bidwell, Percy Wells, and John I. Falconer. 1941. *History of Agriculture in the Northern United States, 1620–1860.* New York.

Bourne, E. G. 1904. *Spain in America, 1450–1580.* New York.

Burkholder, Mark A., and Lyman L. Johnson. 1994. *Colonial Latin America.* New York.

Carey, Henry Charles. 1858–60. *Principles of Social Science.* Philadelphia.

Central Intelligence Agency. 1992. *The World Factbook.* Washington, D.C.

Chevalier, François. 1963. *Land and Society in Colonial Mexico: The Great Hacienda.* Berkeley.

Chiappelli, Fredi, ed. 1976. *First Images of America: The Impact of the New World on the Old.* Berkeley.

Coatsworth, John H. 1993. "Notes on the Comparative Economic History of Latin America and the United States." In Walter L. Bernecker and Hans Werner Tobler, eds., *Development and Underdevelopment in America: Contrasts of Economic Growth in North and Latin America in Historical Perspective*, pp. 10–30. Berlin.

Craven, Wesley Frank. 1968. *The Colonies in Transition, 1660–1713.* New York.

Curtin, Philip D. 1969. *The Atlantic Slave Trade: A Census.* Madison, Wisc.

Danhof, Clarence H. 1969. *Change in Agriculture: The Northern United States, 1820–1870.* Cambridge, Eng.

Davis, Joseph Stancliffe. 1917. *Essays in the Earlier History of American Corporations.* 2 vols. Cambridge, Eng.

Davis, Lance E., and Robert E. Gallman. 1978. "Capital Formation in the United States During the Nineteenth Century." In Peter Mathias and M. M. Postan, eds., *The Cambridge Economic History of Europe.* Vol. 7, *The Industrial Economies: Part 2, the United States, Japan, and Russia.* pp. 1–69. Cambridge, Eng.

——. 1994. "Savings, Investment, and Economic Growth: The United States in the Nineteenth Century." In John A. James and Mark Thomas, eds., *Capitalism in Context: Essays on Economic Development and Cultural Change in Honor of R. M. Hartwell.* Chicago.

Davis, Lance E., and Douglass C. North. 1971. *Institutional Change and American Economic Growth.* Cambridge, Eng.

Davis, Ralph. 1973. *The Rise of the Atlantic Economies.* Ithaca, N.Y.

Dean, Warren. 1971. "Latifundia and Land Policy in Nineteenth Century Brazil." *Hispanic American Historical Review* 51 (Nov.): 602–25.

DeBow, J. D. B. 1854. *Statistical View of the United States.* Washington, D.C.

Deerr, Noel. 1950. *The History of Sugar.* London.

Denevan, William M., ed. 1976. *The Native Population in the Americas in 1492.* Madison, Wisc.

De Vries, Jan. 1976. *The Economy of Europe in an Age of Crisis.* Cambridge, Eng.

Diaz Alejandro, Carlos F. 1970. *Essays on the Economic History of the Argentine Republic.* New Haven, Conn.

Domar, Evsey D. 1970. "The Causes of Slavery or Serfdom: A Hypothesis." *Journal of Economic History* 30 (Mar.): 18–32.

Dunn, Richard S. 1972. *Sugar and Slaves: The Rise of the Planter Class in the English West Indies, 1624–1713.* Chapel Hill, N.C.

Dutton, H. I. 1984. *The Patent System and Inventive Activity During the Industrial Revolution, 1750–1852.* Manchester, Eng.

Easterlin, Richard A. 1981. "Why Isn't the Whole World Developed?" *Journal of Economic History* 41 (Mar.): 1–19.

Eltis, David. 1983. "Free and Coerced Transatlantic Migrations: Some Comparisons." *American Historical Review* 88 (Apr.): 251–80.

———. 1987. *Economic Growth and the Ending of the Transatlantic Slave Trade.* New York.

———. 1995. "The Total Product of Barbados, 1664–1701." *Journal of Economic History* 55 (June): 321–38.

———. Forthcoming. "Seventeenth-Century Migration and the Slave Trade: The English Case in Comparative Perspective." In Jan Lucassen and Les Lucassen, eds., *Migrations, Migration History, History: Old Paradigms and New Perspectives.* Bern.

Emmer, P. C., ed. 1986. *Colonialism and Migration: Indentured Labor Before and After Slavery.* Dordrecht.

Emmer, P. C., and Magnus Mörner, eds. 1992. *European Expansion and Migration: Essays on the Intercontinental Migration from Africa, Asia, and Europe.* New York.

Engerman, Stanley L. 1982. "Economic Adjustments to Emancipation in the United States and the British West Indies." *Journal of Interdisciplinary History* 12 (autumn): 191–220.

———. 1983. "Contract labor, Sugar and Technology in the Nineteenth Century." *Journal of Economic History* 43 (Sept.): 635–59.

———. 1986. "Servants to Slaves to Servants: Contract Labour and European Expansion." In P. C. Emmer, ed., *Colonialism and Migration: Indentured Labor Before and After Slavery,* pp. 263–94. Dordrecht.

Engerman, Stanley L., and Robert E. Gallman, eds. 1986. *Long-Term Factors in American Economic Growth.* Chicago.

Engerman, Stanley L., and B. W. Higman. Forthcoming. "The Demographic Structure of the Caribbean Slave Societies in the Eighteenth and Nineteenth Centuries." In Franklin W. Knight, ed., *UNESCO General History of the Caribbean*, Vol. 3.

Evans, George Herberton, Jr. 1948. *Business Incorporations in the United States, 1800–1943*. New York.

Ferenczi, Imre, and Walter F. Willcox. 1929, 1931. *International Migrations*. 2 vols. New York.

Fishlow, Albert. 1965. *American Railroads and the Transformation of the Antebellum Economy*. Cambridge, Eng.

Fogel, Robert William. 1964. *Railroads and American Economic Growth: Essays in Econometric History*. Baltimore.

———. 1989. *Without Consent or Contract*. New York.

Fraginals, Manuel Moreno. 1976. *The Sugarmill: The Socioeconomic Complex of Sugar in Cuba*. New York.

Galenson, David W. 1981. *White Servitude in Colonial America: An Economic Analysis*. Cambridge, Eng.

———. 1991. "Economic Opportunity on the Urban Frontier: Nativity, Work, and Health in Early Chicago." *Journal of Economic History* 51 (Sept.): 581–603.

———. 1996. "The Settlement and Growth of the Colonies: Population, Labor, and Economic Development." In Stanley L. Engerman and Robert E. Gallman, eds., *The Cambridge Economic History of the United States*. Vol. 1, *The Colonial Period*, pp. 135–207. Cambridge, Eng.

Gallman, Robert E., and John Joseph Wallis, eds. 1992. *American Economic Growth and Standards of Living Before the Civil War*. Chicago.

Gallman, Robert E., and Ralph V. Anderson. 1977. "Slavery as Fixed Capital: Slave Labor and Southern Economic Development." *Journal of American History* 64 (June): 24–46.

Gates, Paul W. 1968. *History of Public Land Law Development*. Washington, D.C.

Genovese, Eugene D. 1965. *The Political Economy of Slavery: Studies in the Economy and Society of the Slave South*. New York.

Gerschenkron, Alexander. 1962. *Economic Backwardness in Historical Perspective: A Book of Essays*. Cambridge, Eng.

Gibson, Charles. 1966. *Spain in America*. New York.

Goodrich, Carter. 1960. *Government Promotion of American Canals and Railroads*. New York.

Greene, Jack P. 1988. *Pursuits of Happiness*. Chapel Hill, N.C.

Guy, Donna J. 1980. *Argentine Sugar Politics: Tucuman and the Generation of Eighty*. Tempe, Ariz.

Haber, Stephen H. 1989. *Industry and Underdevelopment: The Industrialization of Mexico, 1890–1940*. Stanford.

———. 1991. "Industrial Concentration and the Capital Markets: A Comparative Study of Brazil, Mexico, and the United States, 1830–1930." *Journal of Economic History* 51 (Sept.): 559–80.

Hanke, Lewis, ed. 1964. *Do the Americas Have a Common History?: A Critique of the Bolton Theory*. New York.

Haring, C. H. 1947. *The Spanish Empire in America.* New York.

Higgs, Robert. 1977. *Competition and Coercion: Blacks in the American Economy, 1865–1914.* Cambridge, Eng.

Horowitz, Morton J. 1977. *The Transformation of American Law, 1780–1860.* Cambridge, Eng.

Hurst, Willard J. 1956. *Law and the Conditions of Freedom in the Nineteenth-Century United States.* Madison, Wisc.

Irwin, James R. 1988. "Exploring the Affinity of Wheat and Slavery in the Virginia Piedmont." *Explorations in Economic History* 25 (July): 295–332.

Jacobsen, Nils. 1993. *Mirages of Transition: The Peruvian Altiplano, 1780–1930.* Berkeley.

Jones, E. L. 1988. *Growth Recurring: Economic Change in World History.* Oxford.

Jones, Alice Hanson. 1980. *Wealth of a Nation to Be.* New York.

Kearl, J. R., Clayne L. Pope, and Larry T. Wimmer. 1980. "Household Wealth in the Settlement Economy." *Journal of Economic History* 40 (Sept.): 477–96.

Kelly, Alfred H., Winifred A. Harbison, and Herman Belz. 1983. *The American Constitution: Its Origins and Development.* 6th ed. New York.

Khan, B. Zorina. 1995. "Property Rights and Patent Litigation in Early Nineteenth Century America." *Journal of Economic History* 55 (Mar.): 58–97.

Khan, B. Zorina, and Kenneth L. Sokoloff. 1993. "'Schemes of Practical Utility': Entrepreneurship and Innovation Among 'Great Inventors' in the United States, 1790–1865." *Journal of Economic History* 53 (June): 289–307.

Klein, Herbert S. 1983. "The Integration of Italian Immigrants into the United States and Argentina: A Comparative Analysis." *American Historical Review* 88 (Apr.): 306–29.

Knight, Franklin W. 1990. *The Caribbean: The Genesis of a Fragmented Nationalism.* New York.

Kousser, Morgan J. 1974. *The Shaping of Southern Politics: Suffrage Restrictions and the Establishment of the One-Party South, 1880–1910.* New Haven, Conn.

Kritz, Mary M. 1992. "The British and Spanish Migration Systems in the Colonial Era: A Policy Framework." In International Union for the Scientific Study of Population, *The Peopling of the Americas.* Vol. 1. Vera Cruz.

Kuczynski, Robert R. 1936. *Population Movements.* Oxford.

Kupperman, Karen Ordahl. 1993. *Providence Island, 1630–1641: The Other Puritan Colony.* Cambridge, Eng.

Kussmaul, Ann. 1981. *Servants in Husbandry in Early Modern England.* Cambridge, Eng.

Leacy, F. H., ed. 1983. *Historical Statistics of Canada: Second Edition.* Ottawa.

Lewis, W. Arthur. 1955. "Economic Development with Unlimited Supplies of Labor." *Manchester School of Economic and Social Studies* 23 (May): 139–91.

Livermore, Shaw. 1935. "Unlimited Liability in Early American Corporations." *Journal of Political Economy* 43 (Oct.): 674–87.

Lockhart, James. 1994. *Spanish Peru: 1532–1560, A Social History.* 2nd ed. Madison, Wisc.

Lockhart, James, and Stuart B. Schwartz. 1983. *Early Latin America: A History of Colonial Spanish America and Brazil.* Cambridge, Eng.

Love, Joseph L. 1970. "Political Participation in Brazil, 1881–1969." *Luso-Brazilian Review* 7 (Dec.): 3–24.

Machlup, Fritz. 1958. *An Economic Review of the Patent System.* Study of the Committee on the Judiciary, United States Senate. Washington, D.C.

Maddison, Angus. 1991. *Dynamic Forces in Capitalist Development.* New York.

———. 1994. "Explaining the Economic Performance of Nations, 1820–1989." In William J. Baumol, Richard R. Nelson, and Edward N. Wolff, eds., *Convergence of Productivity*, pp. 20–61. New York.

Maitland, James. 1962. *An Inquiry Into the Nature and Origin of Public Wealth.* New York.

Majewski, John. 1994. *Commerce and Community: Economic Culture and Internal Improvements in Pennsylvania and Virginia, 1790–1860.* Ph.D. diss., University of California, Los Angeles.

Majewski, John, Christopher Baer, and Daniel B. Klein. 1993. "Responding to Relative Decline: The Plank Road Boom of Antebellum New York." *Journal of Economic History* 33 (Mar.): 106–22.

Mamalakis, Markos J. 1980. *Historical Statistics of Chile: Demography and Labor Force.* Westport, Conn.

Margo, Robert A. 1990. *Race and Schooling in the South, 1880–1950.* Chicago.

Marshall, Alfred. 1919. *Industry and Trade: A Study of Industrial Techniques and Business Organization; and of Their Influences on the Conditions of Various Classes and Nations.* London.

Mathew, W. M. 1976. "A Primitive Export Sector: Guano Production in Mid-Nineteenth-Century Peru." *Journal of Latin American Studies* 8 (May): 35–57.

McAlister, Lyle N. 1984. *Spain and Portugal in the New World, 1492–1700.* Minneapolis.

McCusker, John J., and Russell R. Menard. 1985. *The Economy of British America, 1607–1789.* Chapel Hill, N.C.

McEvedy, Colin, and Richard Jones. 1978. *Atlas of World Population History.* Harmondsworth, N.Y.

Merrick, Thomas W., and Douglas H. Graham. 1979. *Population and Economic Development in Brazil: 1800 to the Present.* Baltimore.

Mörner, Magnus. 1985. *Adventurers and Proletarians: The Story of Migrants in Latin America.* Pittsburgh.

Moses, Bernard. 1898. *The Establishment of Spanish Rule in America: An Introduction to the History and Politics of Spanish America.* London.

Mosk, Sanford A. 1951. "Latin America versus the United States." *American Economic Review* 41 (May): 367–83.

Nash, Gary B. 1993. *Quakers and Politics: Pennsylvania, 1681–1726.* New ed. Boston.

North, Douglass C. 1981. *Structure and Change in Economic History.* New York.

North, Douglass C., and Robert Thomas. 1973. *The Rise of the Western World.* Cambridge, Eng.

Olmstead, Alan L., and Paul W. Rhode. 1995. "Beyond the Threshold: An Analysis of the Characteristics of Behavior of Early Reaper Adopters." *Journal of Economic History* 55 (Mar.): 27–57.

Parker, William N. 1970. "Slavery and Southern Economic Development: A Hypothesis and Some Evidence." *Agricultural History* 44: 115–25.

Perez-Brignoli, Hector. 1989. *A Brief History of Central America.* Berkeley.

Perry, Laurens Ballard. 1978. *Juarez and Diaz: Machine Politics in Mexico.* De Kalb, Ill.

Platt, D. C. M., and Guido di Tella, eds. 1985. *Argentina, Australia, and Canada: Studies in Comparative Development, 1870–1965.* London.

Pomfret, Richard. 1981. *The Economic Development of Canada.* Toronto.

Ransom, Roger L., and Richard Sutch. 1977. *One Kind of Freedom: The Economic Consequences of Emancipation.* Cambridge, Eng.

Rogers Taylor, George. 1951. *The Transportation Revolution, 1815–1860.* New York.

Rosenblat, Angel. 1954. *La Población Indígena y el Mestizaje en América.* Vol. 1, *La Población Indígena, 1492–1950.* Buenos Aires.

Rostow, W. W. 1960. *The Stages of Economic Growth.* Cambridge, Eng.

Rothenberg, Winifred B. 1992a. "The Productivity Consequences of Market Integration: Agriculture in Massachusetts, 1771–1801." In Robert E. Gallman and John Joseph Wallis, eds., *American Economic Growth and Standards of Living Before the Civil War,* pp. 311–44. Chicago.

———. 1992b. *The Transformation of Rural Massachusetts, 1750–1850.* Chicago.

Sanchez-Albornoz, Nicolas. 1974. *The Population of Latin America: A History.* Berkeley.

Schultz, Theodore W. 1964. *Transforming Traditional Agriculture.* Chicago.

Schwartz, Stuart B. 1982. "Patterns of Slaveholding in the Americas: New Evidence from Brazil." *American Historical Review* 87 (Feb.): 56–86.

———. 1985. *Sugar Plantations in the Formation of Brazilian Society: Bahia, 1550–1835.* Cambridge, Eng.

Scobie, James. 1971. *Argentina, a City and a Nation.* 2nd ed. New York.

Sheridan, Richard. 1974. *Sugar and Slavery: An Economic History of the West Indies, 1623–1775.* Aylesbury.

Shlomowitz, Ralph. 1979. "Transition from Slave to Freedom: Labor Arrangements in Southern Agriculture, 1865–1870." Ph.D. diss., University of Chicago.

Smith, Adam. 1979. *The Wealth of Nations.* Oxford.

Sokoloff, Kenneth L. 1984. "Was the Transition from the Artisanal Shop to the Nonmechanized Factory Associated with Gains in Efficiency?: Evidence from the U.S. Manufacturing Censuses of 1820 and 1850." *Explorations in Economic History* 21 (Oct): 351–82.

———. 1986. "Productivity Growth in Manufacturing During Early Industrialization: Evidence from the American Northeast, 1820 to 1860." Stanley L. Engerman and Robert E. Gallman, eds., *Long-Term Factors in American Economic Growth,* pp. 639–736. Chicago.

———. 1988. "Inventive Activity in Early Industrial America: Evidence from Patent Records, 1790–1846." *Journal of Economic History* 48 (Dec.): 813–50.

———. 1992. "Invention, Innovation, and Manufacturing Productivity Growth in the Antebellum Northeast." In Robert E. Gallman and John Joseph Wallis, eds., *American Economic Growth and Standards of Living Before the Civil War*, pp. 345–84. Chicago.

Sokoloff, Kenneth L., and B. Zorina Khan. 1990. "The Democratization of Invention During Early Industrialization: Evidence from the United States, 1790–1846." *Journal of Economic History* 50 (June): 363–78.

Solberg, Carl E. 1970. *Immigration and Nationalism: Argentina and Chile, 1890–1914*. Austin, Tex.

———. 1987. *The Prairies and the Pampas: Agrarian Policy in Canada and Argentina 1880–1913*. Stanford.

Soltow, Lee. 1992. "Inequalities in the Standard of Living in the United States." In Robert E. Gallman and John Joseph Wallis, eds., *American Economic Growth and Standards of Living Before the Civil War*, pp. 121–72. Chicago.

Strassman, W. Paul. 1956. "Economic Growth and Income Distribution." *Quarterly Journal of Economics* 70 (Aug.): 202–29.

Taylor, George Rogers. 1951. *The Transportation Revolution, 1815–1860*. New York.

Tchakerian, Viken. 1994. "Productivity, Extent of Markets, and Manufacturing in the Late Antebellum South and Midwest." *Journal of Economic History* 54 (Sept.): 497–525.

Tornquist & Co., Ernesto. 1919. *The Economic Development of the Argentine Republic in the Last Fifty Years*. Buenos Aires.

Turner, Frederick J. 1948. *A Frontier in American History*. New York.

U.S. Census Bureau. 1864. *Population of the United States in 1860*. Washington, D.C.

Van Young, Eric. 1983. "Mexican Rural History Since Chevalier: The Historiography of the Colonial Hacienda." *Latin American Research Review* 18, no. 3: 5–62.

Viotti da Costa, Emilia. 1985. *The Brazilian Empire: Myths and Histories*. Chicago.

Virts, Nancy Lynn. 1985. "Plantations, Land Tenure and Efficiency in the Postbellum South: The Effects of Emancipation on Southern Agriculture." Ph.D. diss., University of California, Los Angeles.

Wakefield, Edward G. 1849. *A View of the Art of Colonization*. London.

Walker, Geoffrey J. 1979. *Spanish Politics and Imperial Trade, 1700–1789*. Bloomington, Ind.

Watts, David. 1987. *The West Indies: Patterns of Development, Culture, and Environmental Change Since 1492*. Cambridge, Eng.

Williamson, Harold F. 1960. "Mass Production, Mass Consumption, and American Industrial Development." In First International Conference of Economic History, *Contributions and Communications*, pp. 137–48. Paris.

Williamson, Jeffrey G., and Peter N. Lindert. 1980. *American Inequality: A Macroeconomic History*. New York.

Woodward, Ralph Lee. 1976. *Central America: A Nation Divided*. New York.

Woodward, Vann. 1971. *Origins of the New South, 1877–1913*. Baton Rouge, La.

World Bank. 1991. *World Development Report*. New York.

INDEX

Index

In this index an "f" after a number indicates a separate reference on the next page, and an "ff" indicates separate references on the next two pages. A continuous discussion over two or more pages is indicated by a span of page numbers, e.g., "57–59." *Passim* is used for a cluster of references in close but not consecutive sequence.

Library of Congress Cataloging-in-Publication Data

How Latin America fell behind : essays in the economic histories of
Brazil and Mexico, 1800–1914 / edited by Stephen Haber.
    p.   cm.
Includes index.
ISBN 0-8047-2737-6 (alk. paper). —ISBN 0-8047-2738-4 (pbk. : alk. paper)
1. Brazil—Economic conditions—19th century. 2. Mexico—Economic
conditions—19th century. I. Haber, Stephen H., 1957–
HC187.H68 1997
330.972—dc20   96-12673
                                                            CIP

⊗This book is printed on acid-free,
recycled paper.

Original printing 1997
Last figure below indicates year of this printing:
06 05 04 03 02 01 00 99 98 97